CH00732970

An Introduction to
International Arbitration

Ilias Bantekas

CAMBRIDGE
UNIVERSITY PRESS

CAMBRIDGE
UNIVERSITY PRESS

University Printing House, Cambridge CB2 8BS, United Kingdom

Cambridge University Press is part of the University of Cambridge.

It furthers the University's mission by disseminating knowledge in the pursuit of education, learning and research at the highest international levels of excellence.

www.cambridge.org
Information on this title: www.cambridge.org/9781107111073

First published 2015

Printed in the United Kingdom by Clays, St Ives plc

A catalogue record for this publication is available from the British Library

Library of Congress Cataloguing in Publication data
Bantekas, Ilias, author.
An introduction to international arbitration / Ilias Bantekas.
  pages   cm
ISBN 978-1-107-11107-3
1. International commercial arbitration.   I. Title.
K2400.B36   2015
347'.09–dc23

                                        2015004542

ISBN 978-1-107-11107-3 Hardback
ISBN 978-1-107-52780-5 Paperback

Aristotle, *Rhetoric Book A*, 13:9

Καὶ το εἰς δίαιταν μᾶλλον ἢ εἰς δίκην βούλεσθαι ἰέναι. Ὁ γὰρ διαιτητὴς τὸ ἐπιεικὲς ὁρᾷ, ὁ δὲ δικαστής τὸν νόμον. Καὶ τούτου ἕνεκα διαιτητής εὑρέθη, ὅπως το ἐπιεικές ἰσχύῃ.

[It is better] to prefer arbitration from judicial determination. Because, the arbitrator takes clemency [equity] into consideration, whereas the judge [solely] the law. And it is for this reason that an arbitrator was appointed; that is, in order to apply clemency [equity].

Dimosthenes, *Against Meidias*, 94

Λέγε δὴ καὶ τὸν τῶν διαιτητῶν νόμον.
ΝΟΜΟΣ
    Ἐὰν δέ τινες περὶ συμβολαίων ἰδίων πρὸς ἀλλήλους ἀμφισβητῶσι καὶ βούλωνται διαιτητὴν ἐλέσθαι ὁντινοῦν, ἐξέστω αὐτοῖς αἱρεῖσθαι ὃν ἂν βούλωνται [διαιτητὴν ἐλέσθαι]. ἐπειδὰν δ'ἕλωνται κατὰ κοινόν, μενέτωσαν ἐν τοῖς ὑπὸ τούτου διαγνωσθεῖσι, καὶ μηκέτι μεταφερέτωσαν ἀπὸ τούτου ἐφ' ἕτερον δικαστήριον ταῦτὰ ἐγκλήματα, ἀλλ' ἔστω τὰ κριθέντα ὑπὸ τοῦ διαιτητοῦ κύρια.

Read the law on arbitrators:
LAW
    If some people argue over a private difference and wish to appoint an arbitrator, they have the right to choose whomever they desire. When, however, they reach mutual consent over the person of the arbitrator they must respect his award and must not subsequently submit the same difference to a court. Rather, the arbitrator's award is final.

Contents

Preface

A general book on arbitration faces multiple dilemmas from the outset. What should be the balance between domestic and international arbitration (despite the international outlook of the book)? How does one discuss investment arbitration without making it look peripheral and how much emphasis should one place on substantive investment law? Should the book discuss consumer and online arbitration and to what degree? This consideration is pertinent, given that the literature generally treats them as distinct from commercial arbitration. Moreover, if the book ultimately bears the title of *International Arbitration*, isn't there a danger that a considerable part of the audience will naturally wonder whether it covers inter-state arbitration as distinct, or in parallel to, private commercial arbitration? Unlike other legal disciplines whereby the law, although generally complicated is predicated on principles derived from that discipline, such as contract or tort, arbitration is hardly straightforward. Although it is largely a procedural law, no one can fully grasp it unless he or she possesses sufficient knowledge of public international law, the law of contract (certainly from a comparative perspective), comparative civil procedure, private international law (conflicts of law), commercial law and perhaps others, such as EU law. Given the positive perception of arbitration by the legal and business community in industrialised nations it is not surprising that many lawyers now specialise in discrete areas such as construction, intellectual property, maritime, public procurement and many others. All of these considerations make the task of a generalist textbook on international arbitration all that much harder.

The fundamental premise underlying this book has been to make its subject matter as accessible as possible to a wide and divergent audience which lacks expertise in one or more of the aforementioned legal disciplines. Although the author does not assume that his audience has prior familiarity with arbitration and the disciplines that feed it, there is no intention that the book should lack depth, or that its coverage should not be as extensive as its competitors. What the book intentionally lacks is volume. The aim from the outset was to produce an enjoyable, easy-to-read, methodical, yet comprehensive and in-depth book, whose size is such that it may be read and digested in a relatively short time without leaving any gaps in one's understanding. Naturally, some topics are dealt with in a more cursory manner as compared to the voluminous (and much more analytical) books on the subject, but it is the plethora of good books by experienced academics and practitioners that makes arbitration so enriching and diverse.

The author has benefited from discussions with many colleagues, but would especially like to thank the following people for reading and commenting on various draft chapters, or for extensive discussions, although naturally all responsibility lies with the author. These people are Pietro Ortolani, Tony Cole, Ikram Mahar, Ali Lazem and Richard Earle. Special thanks are also due to the publishing and editorial team at Cambridge University Press, particularly Marta Walkowiak who saw this project through from start to finish. My children Zoe and Stefanos are always a constant source of inspiration and I thank them for the countless times they disrupted my immersion into this work and made me realise a new world, which I had forgotten, through their eyes.

Athens and London, 1 January 2015

Table of cases

Australia

Austria

Belgium

Denmark

England

Finland

Estonia

France

Germany

Greece

Hong Kong

India

Ireland

Italy

Luxembourg

Turkey

United Arab Emirates

USA

Arbitral Awards (Various)

Caribbean Court of Justice

Court of Justice of the European Union

Eastern Caribbean Court of Justice

European Court of Human Rights

ICSID

International Court of Justice

International Criminal Tribunal for the former Yugoslavia

Iran-USA Claims Tribunal

Permanent Court of International Justice

UNCITRAL

Table of treaties

EU Instruments

Regulations

Table of domestic laws

Australia

Intl Arbitration Act
  s 25(1), 201/n54
  s 26, 201/n54
  s 28, 121/n65

Austria

CCP, 119
  Art 582(2), 30/n106
  Art 586(1), 114/n37
  Art 587(1), 114/n37
  Art 590, 127/n88
  Art 603, 42
  Art 617(1), 259
  Art 617(2), 260/n19

Belgium

Arbitration Law 2013, 23/n75, 148
Distribution Law 1971, 29/n98
  Art 4, 29/n98
  Art 6, 29/n98
Judicial Code
  Art 1676(8), 52/n54, 148/n41
  Art 1680(5), 214/n106
  Art 1682, 52/n55, 148/n42
  Art 1698, 52/n56, 148/n43
  Art 1705, 107/n9
  Art 1708, 52/n57, 148/n44
  Art 1715(7), 207/n73
  Art 1717(3), 207/n74
  Art 1717(3)(a)(iv), 207/n75
  Art 1717(3)(b), 208/n77
  Art 1717(3)(a)(ii), 208/n78
  Art 1717(3)(a)(v), 208/n78
  Art 1718, 23/n75

Bolivia

Ley de Arbitraje y Conciliacion
Art 10,   81/n47

Bulgaria

LICA
Art 19(2),   55
Law on Commerce
Art 292(1),   77/n35
Obligations and Contracts Act
Art 26(1)(1),   6

Channel Islands

Guernsey Trusts Law
Art 63,   80
Jersey Arbitration Law
Arts 35–40,   59/n80

Croatia

Arbitration Law
Art 6(3)(2),   74, 77/n33

Czech Republic

Arbitration Act,   50
Art 14,   114/n35
Art 30,   50/n44
Art 37(2),   42/n10
CCP 1963,   50
Electronic Signatures Act,   73/n17

Denmark

Arbitration Act,   23, 65, 137
Art 7(2),   25/n84, 260
Art 27(2),   106

England

Arbitration Act 1950
s 12(6)(b),   152
Arbitration Act 1996,   26/n86, 50, 56
s 2(1),   22/n72
s 4(1),   41/n8
s 6(1),   25
s 7,   12/n30, 28/n93

Venezuela

Institutional Rules and Soft Law

Abbreviations

AA	Arbitration Act
AAA	American Arbitration Association
AAD	*Apofaseis Anotatou Dikastiriou* (Cyprus Supreme Court reports)
AAR	arbitral appointments referee (Scotland)
ABA	American Bar Association
ABQB	Alberta Queen's Bench [Reports]
AC	Appeal Cases [Law Reports]
AD	*Annual Digest*
ADR	alternative dispute resolution
AIR	*All India Reports*
AJCL	*Australian Journal of Corporate Law*
AJIL	*American Journal of International Law*
All ER	*All England Reports*
Am Rev Int Arb	*American Review of International Arbitration*
Arab LQ	*Arab Law Quarterly*
Arb LR	*Arbitration Law Review*
Arbitration Int	*Arbitration International*
ASA Bull	*Bulletin of the Swiss Arbitration Association*
ALR	*Australian Law Reports*
B2B	business-to-business
B2C	business-to-consumer
BCLR	*British Columbia Law Reports*
Bda LR	*Bermuda Law Reports*
BGB	*Bürgerliches Gesetzbuch* (German Civil Code)
BGE	*Entscheidungen des Schweizerischen Bundesgerichts* (Swiss Supreme Court decisions)
BGH	*Bundesgerichtshof* (German Federal Court of Justice)

BIT	bilateral investment treaty
Bull Civ	*Bulletin des arrest de la Cour de Cassation* (France)
BYIL	*British Yearbook of International Law*
Cal	California
CanLII	*Canadian Legal Information Institute* (Reporter) CAS Court of Arbitration for Sports
CAT	Competitions Appeal Tribunal
CC	Civil Code
CCJ	*Caribbean Court of Justice* [Reporter]
CCP	Code of Civil Procedure
Ch D	*The Law Reports, Chancery Division*
Chinese J Int'l L	*Chinese Journal of International Law*
CIArb	Chartered Institute of Arbitrators
Cir.	Circuit (USA)
CJEU	Court of Justice of the European Union
CLC	*Commercial Law Cases* [Reporter]
CLR	*Commonwealth Law Reports* and *Cyprus Law Reports*
Comm	Commercial (division)
Conflict Resol. Q	*Conflict Resolution Quarterly*
CSOH	*Court of Session Outer House* [Reports, Scotland]
CTR	*Claims Tribunal Reports*
DIAC	Dubai International Arbitration Centre
EC	European Community
ECC	Electronic Communications in International Contracts Convention
ECHR	European Convention on Human Rights
ECR	*European Court Reports*
ECT	Energy Charter Treaty
ECtHR	European Court of Human Rights
EFTA	European Free Trade Association
EHRR	*European Human Rights Reports*
EJIL	*European Journal of International Law*
EU	European Union
EWCA	*England and Wales Court of Appeal*
EWHC	*England and Wales High Court*
F	*Federal Reporter* (USA)

FAA	Federal Arbitration Act (USA)
F App'x	*Federal Appendix* [Reporter]
Fam	Family (division)
FC	Federal Court (Canada)
FCAFC	Federal Court of Australia Full Court
FCR	*Federal Court Reports* (Australia)
FIDIC	International Federation of Consulting Engineers
Foro pad	*Foro padano* (Italy)
FRD	*Federal Rules Decisions*
F Supp	*Federal Supplement* [Reporter]
FSIA	Federal Sovereign Immunities Act (USA)
FTA	free trade agreement
HKC	*Hong Kong Cases* [Reporter]
HKCA	Hong Kong Court of Appeal
HKCFI	*Hong Kong Court of First Instance* [Reporter]
HKDC	*Hong Kong District Court* [Reporter]
HKLR	*Hong Kong Law Reports*
HRQ	*Human Rights Quarterly*
IBA	International Bar Association
ICC	International Chamber of Commerce
ICDR	International Centre for Dispute Resolution
ICJ	International Court of Justice
ICJ Rep	*International Court of Justice Reports*
ICSID	International Centre for the Settlement of Investment Disputes
ICSID Rev-FILJ	*ICSID Review-Foreign Investment Law Journal*
ICT	information and communication technology
IEHC	*High Court of Ireland Decisions*
IIA	international investment agreement
ILA	International Law Association
ILC	International Law Commission
ILM	*International Legal Materials*
ILPr	*International Litigation Procedure* [Reporter]
ILR	*International Law Reports*
INSC	*Supreme Court of India* [Reporter]
JC	Judicial Code (Belgium)
JDI	*Journal du Droit International Privé*
J Intl Disp Settlement	*Journal of International Dispute Settlement*

JOIA	Journal of International Arbitration
KB	King's Bench [Law Reports]
KKO	Korkein Oikeus (Finnish Supreme Court) [Reporter]
LCIA	London Chamber of International Arbitration
LICA	Law on International Commercial Arbitration
Lloyd's Rep	Lloyd's Law Reports
LMAA	London Maritime Arbitrators Association
Loy U Chi Int'l L Rev	Loyola University Chicago International Law Review
LT	Law Times Reports
MFN	most favoured nation
NAFTA	North American Free Trade Agreement
NCCP	New Code of Civil Procedure (Luxembourg)
NGO	non-governmental organisation
NJA	Nytt juridiskt arkiv, avdelning I (Supreme Court reports, Sweden)
NSWSC	New South Wales Supreme Court Reports (Australia)
NYS	New York Supplement
ODR	online dispute resolution
OECD	Organization for Economic Cooperation and Development
OFT	Office of Fair Trading (UK)
OGH	Oberster Gerichtshof (Austrian Supreme Court)
OHADA	Organisation for Harmonisation of African Law
Ohio St. J Disp. Resol	Ohio State Journal on Dispute Resolution
OJ	Ontario Judgments
OJ L	Official Journal of the EU (containing legislation)
OLG	Oberlandesgericht (German higher regional court)
P	Probate Division (USA)
PAL	Portuguese Arbitration Law
Pas Lux	Pasicrisie Luxembourgeoise
PCA	Permanent Court of Arbitration
PCIJ	Permanent Court of International Justice
PILA	Private International Law Act
PPP	public private partnership

QB	*Queen's Bench* [Law Reports]
QCCA	*Court of Appeal of Québec* [Reports]
QCCS	*Superior Court of Québec* [Reports]
Rev Arb	*Revue de l'Arbitrage*
Rev Crit DIP	*Revue Critique de droit international privé*
RH	*Rättsfall från hovrätterna* (Case Reports, Swedish Courts of appeal)
RICS	Royal Institution of Chartered Surveyors
S	*Southern Reporter* (USA)
SCC	Stockholm Chamber of Commerce
SCC (India)	*Supreme Court Cases* (India) [Reporter]
S Ct	*USA Supreme Court Reporter*
SchiedsVZ	*Zeitschrift für Schiedsverfahren* (German Arbitration Journal)
SGCA	*Singapore Court of Appeal* [Reporter]
SGHC	Singapore High Court
SLR	*Singapore Law Reports*
Stanford JIL	*Stanford Journal of International Law*
Texas Int'l LJ	*Texas International Law Journal*
TFEU	Treaty on the Functioning of the European Union
TILA	Truth in Lending Act (US)
Toledo LR	*Toledo Law Review*
UAA	Uniform Arbitration Act (USA)
UDPR	Uniform Domain Name Dispute Resolution Policy
UKSC	*UK Supreme Court* [Reports]
UN	United Nations
UNCITRAL	United Nations Commission on International Trade Law
UNCLOS	United Nations Convention on the Law of the Sea
UNCTAD	United Nations Conference on Trade and Development
UNGA	UN General Assembly
UNIDROIT	International Institute for the Unification of Private Law
US	*Supreme Court Reporter* (USA)
USC	United States Code
VCLT	Vienna Convention on the Law of Treaties

VSC	*Victoria Supreme Court* [Reports, Australia]
WIPO	World Intellectual Property Organisation
WLR	*Weekly Law Reports*
Wm & Mary L Rev	*William and Mary Law Review*
WTO	World Trade Organization
Yale LJ	*Yale Law Journal*
YB Com Arb	*Yearbook of International Commercial Arbitration*
ZACC	*Constitutional Court of South Africa* [Reports]
ZPO	*Zivilprozessordnung* (German Code of Civil Procedure)

An introduction to international arbitration 1

1.1 Introduction

This chapter is aimed at introducing the reader to the fundamentals of international arbitration. It will firstly cement the legal basis of the parties' autonomy to submit disputes to arbitration and subsequently trace the three phases within which international arbitration is conducted, from the drafting of the agreement all the way to the recognition and enforcement of the award in a jurisdiction other than that in which it was rendered, where pertinent. Having comprehended how arbitration works we then go on to assess other alternative dispute resolution mechanisms and their benefits (as well as disadvantages) as compared to litigation. The chapter will then examine three fundamental distinctions, namely international versus domestic arbitration, commercial versus non-commercial arbitration and institutional versus ad hoc arbitration. It concludes with two fundamental concepts, namely separability and arbitrability, whose impact the reader will encounter throughout the book. Although many other principles are fundamental to arbitration they are best reserved for other chapters.

1.2 The theoretical foundations of arbitration

Four theories are generally employed to explain the legal foundations of arbitration, namely, the jurisdictional, contractual, mixed (hybrid) and the autonomous theories. Their common underpinning is the interplay between private control and state regulation of arbitration. Adherents of the *jurisdictional theory* suggest that the role of national law, particularly that of the seat of the arbitration, is of paramount importance. While the parties are free to choose arbitration over recourse to the courts and appoint their preferred arbitrators, it is the state which permits them to do so and as a result arbitrators are perceived as exercising a public function and possess a quasi-judicial status entitling them to the immunity enjoyed by ordinary judges.[1]

The *contractual theory* is predicated on the principle of party autonomy, which is explained more fully in the following section. According to this, it is the will of the parties as expressed in their contract that dictates the choice of dispute settlement mechanism. In fact, the parties' agreement to arbitrate overrides the jurisdiction or ordinary courts, the application of conflict of law rules, as well as the vast majority of procedural rules.[2] Unlike the jurisdictional theory, proponents of the contractual theory

---

[1] See J. D. Lew, L. Mistelis and S. Kröll, *Comparative International Commercial Arbitration* (Kluwer, 2003), 74–5; E. Gaillard, *Legal Theory of International Arbitration* (Martinus Nijhoff, 2010), 15–23.

[2] Lew, Mistelis and Kröll, above note 1, at 76; Gaillard, above note 1, at 24–34.

suggest that arbitral tribunals do not exercise a public function and are instead under a mandate or contract with the parties to provide a service. It should be noted, however, that contractual theory in no way disregards the role of the state in safeguarding the arbitral process, both domestically and internationally.

The *mixed (hybrid) theory* takes the view that arbitration is neither wholly private nor wholly public. It suggests the existence of a synergy between the will of the parties and the role of the state, particularly the seat, in assisting the arbitral process. The role of the state is crucial in giving effect to the will of the parties, rather than assuming a controlling role. By way of illustration, arbitral proceedings would come to a standstill if the parties were unable to agree on the person of the chairman or if third parties refused to surrender evidence to the tribunal voluntarily; not to mention the futility of arbitration if there was no multilateral agreement to recognise and enforce arbitral awards internationally. A practical outcome from the application of the hybrid theory is that arbitral tribunals, although established by reason of contract, do exercise a public function that obliges them to adhere to fair trial guarantees. Moreover, the use of substantive and procedural rules in arbitration is no longer solely anchored to one or more legal systems. Parties are content to rely on trade usages, equitable principles and other transnational rules.[3]

The *autonomous theory*, while using the mixed theory as its platform, views arbitration as a process developed and operating solely to meet the needs of business and trade. In this light, the contractual basis of arbitration entails that national law can be bypassed by agreement of the parties and that even the law of the seat is of little, if any importance.[4] If the parties are able to communicate effectively the arbitral process need not have anything to do with domestic law or domestic institutions; it may be delocalised, as will be examined elsewhere. A particular outcome of the independence of international arbitration from domestic legal orders is the evolution of a discrete arbitral legal order, itself an expression of transnational law.[5]

In practice, all of these theories find a degree of application, although some are more prevalent than others. While reading the various chapters of this book the reader will come to realise the influence of each of these

---

[3] Gaillard, above note 1, at 35–51.   [4] Lew, Mistelis and Kröll, above note 1, at 80–1.
[5] Gaillard, above note 1, at 52–66.

theories in discrete fields of arbitration. The following section will discuss the principle of party autonomy, not as justification for the contractual theory, but as the key over-arching principle underlying the system of international arbitration.

1.2.1 Arbitration and party autonomy

Arbitration is a dispute resolution process that is consensual and private in nature and operation,[6] as opposed to ordinary litigation whereby the civil procedural rules are not generally amenable to party approval whether in whole or in part; in the majority of jurisdictions they are obligatory at all times. More specifically, the selection of judges in a particular case is determined by law and the parties cannot by agreement limit or restrict the competence or authority of the court, nor can they adapt the rules of evidence even among themselves, although it is true that this is sometimes debated in certain jurisdictions. The boundaries of party autonomy in arbitration are far wider than civil litigation and with few exceptions (especially mandatory rules concerning public interest and the parties' due process rights) the parties may choose or omit any procedural or substantive rules. This freedom is not derived from natural law, but is granted to physical and legal persons by formal law (the law of the seat of arbitration, codified in the law of contracts, civil procedure or other). Arbitration is not the only mechanism where such freedom exists. It is also encountered in other private alternative dispute resolution (ADR) mechanisms, such as mediation, conciliation, expert determination and negotiation.

Despite its otherwise private nature, arbitration would be meaningless if arbitral awards were not amenable to state-sanctioned enforcement. The losing party could unashamedly exhibit bad faith and refuse to abide with the terms of the award. As a result, it becomes obvious that unless the state sanctions, guarantees and protects the institution of arbitration, which includes the parties' agreements, arbitral process and arbitral awards, there would be no incentive to choose arbitration over litigation since it would be devoid of all legal certainty.

The fact that arbitration is based on private agreement and largely regulated by permissive rules of private law does not mean that it exists

---

[6] *Lafuno Mphaphuli & Associates (Pty) Ltd v Andrews and Another* [2009] ZACC 6, as per the RSA Constitutional Court.

wholly outside any sphere of public regulation. If this were so it would be subject to manipulation by the stronger parties and any abuses emanating from this system of dispute resolution (such as the use of arbitral awards to launder illicit proceeds) would never be resolved by reference to principles of justice and fairness. A good illustration of the public dimension of arbitration is offered in the field of consumer disputes. In European Union (EU) member states pre-dispute arbitration clauses are generally inadmissible and any post-dispute agreements must be individually nego-tiated between consumers and businesses.[7] Equally, although the parties are free to agree on the procedural rules governing arbitration they are not allowed to forego or circumvent due process guarantees ordinarily applic-able in civil proceedings.[8] As will be discussed in other sections of this chapter, states may pose further limitations to party autonomy, such as those relating to arbitrability and public policy.

It is not, however, only domestic law that has an impact on party autonomy to arbitrate. In transnational commercial transactions, multi-ple legal systems will come into operation and unless states are willing to afford arbitration agreements and arbitral awards mutual recognition and enforcement, recourse to arbitration will always entail a serious risk factor. That is the reason why several international instruments have come into place to unify and harmonise international commercial arbitration. Chief among these is the 1958 New York Convention on the Recognition and Enforcement of Foreign Arbitral Awards and the UNCITRAL Model Law on International Commercial Arbitration. The first sets out a restricted list of grounds which justify the non-recognition and enforcement of foreign awards, whereas the latter is a platform (or a standard-setting mechanism) for the unification of national arbitration laws.

Case study: The limits of party autonomy

The Bulgarian Supreme Court of Cassation was asked to determine the validity of an arbitration clause that provided only one of the parties with a unilateral right to decide whether to refer a dispute to a state

---

[7] See chapter 9.
[8] As a result, the right to fair trial applies to arbitral proceedings despite the fact that arbitral tribunals are not 'established by law' as dictated by Art 6 of the ECHR. See *Abel Xavier v UEFA* [2001] ASA Bull 566 and more generally chapter 7 section 7.6.3.2.

court or to an arbitration tribunal. It found this contractually based unilateral entitlement invalid under Article 26(1)(1) of the Bulgarian Obligations and Contracts Act. The Court's reasoning was that the unilateral right to choose the method for dispute resolution represented a potestative condition, thus rendering it unenforceable for lack of mutuality of obligation.[9]

1.3 Compulsory forms of arbitration

So far it has been demonstrated that it is solely in the discretion of the parties whether to submit a dispute to arbitration rather than the ordinary jurisdiction of regular courts. Once they have opted for arbitration, the law (of the seat, otherwise known as *lex arbitri*) will set some boundaries with the aim of ensuring the parties' equal treatment and the relative fairness of proceedings, but it will not impose arbitration on the parties. Exceptionally, states will *impose* arbitration on particular classes of private actors, typically in a limited number of disputes involving state entities or concerning some element of public interest (statute-based arbitration).[10] The exclusion of party autonomy here is allegedly justified by the speediness inherent in arbitration, the assurances of fairness provided by the state and the assumption that this is what the private actors would have chosen had they been given the option (essentially, that arbitration under the circumstances is pro-investor). By way of illustration, Greece's Public

---

[9] *Case (commercial) 193/2010*, Bulgarian Supreme Court of Cassation judgment no 71 (2 September 2011); confirmed also by the French Supreme Cassation Court judgment (26 September 2012) in *Mme X v Banque Privée Edmond de Rothschild* [2013] ILPr 12. This outcome should be distinguished from agreements whereby one of the parties will choose which among two appointing authorities would appoint the arbitrator. OLG Dresden, *case 11 Sch 01/01*, judgment (28 February 2001); see similarly *Mortini v Comune di Alidono*, Italian Constitutional Court judgment (9 May 1996), [1996] Foro pad 4, where compelling parties to submit disputes to arbitration under Italy's public procurement laws was held to be a breach of the private party's right of access to state courts.

[10] Exceptionally, compulsory arbitration has in some cases been extended to wholly private disputes. Part A of the Fourth Schedule to the Maltese Arbitration Act stipulates that condominium, traffic-related and agency disputes are subject to mandatory arbitration. Mandatory arbitration has also been introduced for any dispute in connection with building construction (to the exclusion of claims for personal injuries). Maltese Legal Notice 72 (2013).

Private Partnership (PPP) Law provides that all disputes arising from PPPs will be resolved by arbitration.[11]

Since 2001, pharmaceutical patent disputes concerning the commercialisation of generic medicines in Portugal are to be resolved through mandatory arbitration, in situations where one of the parties argues that the commercialisation of a generic medicine infringes its patent rights. In such cases a special procedure is envisaged whereby when the Portuguese national pharmaceutical agency (Infarmed) receives an application for approval of a generic pharmaceutical product, the innovator may, within thirty days, file a request for arbitration (either ad hoc or institutional), if it claims that the generic medicine is in breach of its intellectual property rights. This form of compulsory arbitration also covers interim injunctions, thus entirely excluding these disputes from the jurisdiction of ordinary courts.

Such mandatory forms of arbitration are exceptional and have rightly given rise to criticism. Given the absence of party autonomy as regards the application of substantive and procedural rules it is even questioned whether such processes have any affinity to arbitration whatsoever. In one case, the Maltese Constitutional Court held that the mandatory arbitration proceedings in question (including the appointment of arbitrators by the chairman of the Malta Arbitration Centre) did not breach the Constitution of Malta (Article 39(2)) or the right to fair trial under Article 6 of the European Convention on Human Rights (ECHR).[12] As we have already discussed, however, the Italian Constitutional Court in *Mortini v Comune di Alidono*, reached a different conclusion.[13]

1.4 Mediation and ADR

When a dispute arises between two or more persons they may choose to resolve it through several available means. If the parties are on speaking terms the natural inclination is to engage in negotiations on the basis of

---

[11] Art 31, Law No 3389/2005; Law No 3943/2011 on Tax Evasion equally provides for the settlement of relevant tax disputes in Greece through arbitration.

[12] *Untours Insurance Agency Ltd and Emanuel Gauci v Victor Micallef and Others*, App No 81/2011/1, Maltese Constitutional Court judgment (25 January 2013). It should be noted, however, that two years earlier the same court reached a different conclusion in *Vassallo & Sons Ltd v Attorney General Water Services Corp and Enemalta Corp*, App No 31/2008/1, judgment (30 September 2011).

[13] See above footnote 9.

face-to-face discussions. Negotiations are only meaningful if the parties truly desire to resolve their dispute and provided that they are prepared to make at least some concessions.[14] If they reach settlement outside an arbitral process the only way of recording their settlement is in the form of an agreement, whether a contract, a notarised deed or other. The parties may well decide to insert an arbitration clause in their agreement, in which case if a dispute were to arise in the future over the terms of the agreement they could have recourse to arbitration.

If the parties are not on speaking terms and at the same time are not bound by an agreement to arbitrate or do not otherwise wish to submit to the jurisdiction of the courts they may opt for mediation.[15] Mediation may be employed in the case of two feuding neighbours as well as in complex business disputes. The mediator listens to the parties' views and arguments and tries to come up with a proposed settlement that is acceptable to all parties. It is crucial therefore that the mediator understands what is important to each party and what are the interests and pursuits they hold as fundamental. The key to successful mediation is not the rendering of a legally accurate determination setting out which party has breached its obligations, because the breaching party will naturally reject the proposed settlement. Rather, the key is to demonstrate what went wrong, never drive any party to the corner and suggest sensible solutions for the rectification of the issue at hand. Mediators may, and usually do, have to go back and forth with amended terms before the parties reach a settlement. In many situations the most sensible solution is right before the parties' eyes but their mutual anger and resentment does not allow them to conceptualise it; divorce is the classic example!

---

[14] Controlling one's emotions and understanding the opponent's motivations and desires is key to successful negotiation. See R. Fisher, W. L. Ury and B Patton, *Getting to Yes: Negotiating Agreement without Giving In* (Penguin Books, 2011).

[15] Fromm convincingly argues that there is a human tendency to resort to authoritarianism and authoritarian institutions (such as law and the courts) in order to escape from freedom in the context of stressful situations, such as inter-personal conflicts. In such situations even rational people abandon their communicative and conflict engagement functions (or skills) and resort to the aforementioned authoritarian figures, be they mediators, judges or arbitrators. See E. Fromm, *Escape from Freedom* (Henry Holt & Co, 1986). Other scholars, such as Kuttner take Fromm's psychoanalytical analysis of authoritarianism to explain the extensive use of adjudicatory systems and proliferation of authoritarian legal institutions. See R. Kuttner, From Adversity to Relationality: A Relational View of Integrative Negotiation and Mediation (2010) 25 *Ohio St. J Disp. Resol.* 931.

Once the proposed settlement is accepted by all the parties three options are available in order to render it binding, namely: a) recording the settlement into a new contract; b) recording the settlement into an award (so-called consent awards or awards on agreed terms) in cases where the parties have already entered into an agreement to arbitrate the dispute at hand and the tribunal has already been constituted;[16] or c) recognition of the settlement by a court as having the same legal effect as a judgment, provided that this option in fact exists in the jurisdiction where the parties are situated. Article 6 of the EU Mediation Directive,[17] for example, obliges member states to ensure that the content of a written agreement resulting from mediation be made enforceable either on its own or through a court judgment, although in the latter case this does not necessarily constitute a form of judicial exequatur.

The judicial recognition of a mediated settlement differs from an arbitral award in several important respects. Firstly, the recommendations of the mediator are not binding on the parties; they are merely proposals. Secondly, an approved (by the courts) mediated settlement is binding but is enforceable internationally only under the legal regime applicable to civil judgments.[18] This means that the settlement/judgment is not enforceable as a foreign arbitral award under the terms of the 1958 New York Convention.[19] Thirdly, unlike arbitral awards, which may be subject to set aside proceedings, mediated settlements (that do not constitute consent awards) may be challenged under the law of contract, if recorded in the form of a contract, or by means of appeal or cassation if approved by a first instance court judgment. Other challenges may also be available.

1.4.1 Tiered dispute resolution

It is common for parties to complex contracts, especially in construction, to insert tiered dispute resolution clauses (also known as escalation clauses) in

---

[16] Art 30 UNCITRAL Model Law; see chapter 7 section 7.3.3.

[17] Directive 2008/52/EC of 21 May 2008 on Certain Aspects of Mediation in Civil and Commercial Matters, OJ L 136 [2008].

[18] Council Regulation (EC) No 44/2001 of 22 December 2000 on Jurisdiction and the Recognition and Enforcement of Judgments in Civil and Commercial Matters, OJ L 12 [2012].

[19] The practical significance is that membership to the 1958 New York Convention is by far higher as compared to membership in any other multilateral convention for the mutual enforcement of civil judgments.

their contracts. These provide for a series of steps in the overall dispute resolution process, whereby, subject to a definite time frame, if the dispute has not been resolved by one step (procedure) the following step is applied. By way of illustration, the first step may consist of structured negotiation, failing which the parties may turn to mediation, from there to early neutral evaluation, followed by expert determination and ultimately arbitration or adjudication. English courts have demonstrated an inclination to enforce escalation clauses, particularly where the language of the clause is mandatory, there is explicit reference to institutional rules or other defined procedure and time frames are clearly set out.[20]

The parties may well feel that traditional arbitration is unsuitable for their business needs. An enforceable award may be far lower on their agenda as compared to speedy resolution in the face of looming deadlines, especially where there exists a good deal of trust. In such cases the parties may simply desire the input of technical experts. As a result, particularly in construction disputes, it is usual for the parties to resort to expert determination whereby the dispute is submitted to an independent technical expert (chosen from a list pre-agreed by the parties) who determines purely technical issues (not matters of law) and whose decision is final and binding.[21] In large, long-term, construction projects there is usually a standing expert-determination panel because of the frequency of relevant disputes. Although expert determination is fast, technically accurate and binding, it does not constitute an arbitral award and is only enforceable as a contract.[22] The test used by Australian courts to distinguish arbitration from expert determination is whether the relevant process was in the nature of a judicial inquiry.[23]

1.4.2 Mediation and ADR as a condition precedent to arbitration

Mediation (and other forms of ADR) is usually designated as a first step in the parties' agreement to arbitrate. Where ADR procedures are stipulated as

---

[20] *Wah (aka Alan Tang) and Another v Grant Thornton Intl Ltd and Others* [2012] EWHC 3198 (Ch).
[21] *Douglas Harper v Interchange Group Ltd* [2007] EWHC 1834 (Comm); *Union Discount v Zoller* [2002] 1 WLR 1517.
[22] Under Italian law and practice, expert determination is a form of *irrituale* arbitral proceeding, which is discussed below.
[23] *Age Old Builders Pty Ltd v Swintons Pty Ltd* [2003] VSC 307.

binding in the agreement the parties must exhaust these before turning to arbitration. In this manner, ADR procedures constitute conditions precedent to arbitration. The result is that the parties cannot proceed to arbitration without first exhausting these other forms of ADR.[24] Although most condition-precedent clauses are clear and precise others require the courts to interpret the parties' intent. Where the parties have designated a particular arbitral institution in their arbitration clause, and unless otherwise specified, the institution's rules may determine whether mediation was a condition precedent. In general, courts are disinclined to ignore a condition precedent and will stay arbitral proceedings until the condition is first exhausted.[25] Exceptionally, some courts have taken the view that the voluntary nature of mediation dictates that compelling the parties to mediate defeats its very purpose if one of the parties is opposed to this process.[26]

1.5 The three phases of arbitration

The operation of international commercial arbitration can best be described as encompassing three broad phases, namely: a) the drafting and insertion of an arbitration clause in a contract, or the drafting of an agreement to arbitrate (*compromis*) in the absence of an arbitration clause; b) the commencement of arbitral proceedings by the triggering of the *compromis* or the arbitration clause by one of the parties. This phase is concluded by the issuance of a final award by the arbitral tribunal provided that it clears all relevant challenges at the seat and; c) the recognition and enforcement of the arbitral award in one or several jurisdictions, where the winning party so desires. A brief discussion of the key issues of each phase will be provided in the subsequent paragraphs.

---

[24] In *Emirates Trading Agency LLC v Prime Mineral Exports Private Ltd* [2014] EWHC 2104 (Comm), it was held that an agreement to resolve a dispute through a continuous four-week period of friendly discussion before turning to arbitration was a valid and enforceable condition precedent to arbitration.

[25] See *Kemiron Atlantic Inc v Aguakem Intl Inc*, 290 F 3d 1287 (11th Cir. 2002); but see chapter 10 section 10.5.3 for an analysis of the fork-in-the-road concept as applied to investment arbitration.

[26] *Jen-Weld Inc v Superior Court*, 146 Cal App 4th, 536 (2007), at 543.

1.5.1 Phase I: the agreement to arbitrate

The courts ordinarily possess jurisdiction over all disputes, private and otherwise,[27] and thus there is no need to insert a civil litigation clause in contracts or other agreements. Because arbitration is not an ordinary means of resolving disputes it may only be employed if the parties have expressly provided for it by mutual consent; it is therefore extraordinary. This consent may be recorded in a number of instruments, such as contracts, trust deeds, corporate articles of agreement and testamentary wills. In a limited number of countries an oral agreement equally suffices as long as it is verifiable.[28] It is now commonplace, especially in complex or transnational agreements, for the parties to insert an arbitration clause in the eventuality of a future dispute. The parties and their counsel are typically influenced by a variety of reasons in their choice of arbitration over litigation. Whatever the case, once the agreement comes into force the arbitration clause is binding throughout the duration of the agreement and if a dispute arises and one of the parties submits the dispute to a court the latter must (and will) stay the court proceedings in favour of arbitration.[29] Moreover, as will be explained shortly, even if the agreement in which the arbitration clause is contained is found to be null or void the clause itself *may* survive by virtue of the principle of separability.[30]

The arbitration clause is thus a contract within a contract. Although it is usually short, its contents are of immense significance. A typical clause will designate the seat of the arbitration, the scope and range of disputes subject to arbitral resolution, the arbitral institution (if any) under whose rules the dispute will be heard and perhaps the governing law(s) of the agreement in question. The arbitration clause will itself be governed by a discrete law, which may be different from the law governing the main agreement.[31] In practice, counsel spend the bulk of their billable hours on the intricacies of the main contract and in many cases the arbitration clause is inserted at the very end (deservedly labelled as the midnight clause), usually by adopting a standard clause recommended by a particular arbitral

---

[27] Except, of course, where jurisdiction lies with an inter-governmental court or tribunal through the operation of a treaty, as is the case with investment arbitration under bilateral investment treaties (BITs).

[28] See chapter 3 section 3.4.   [29] See s 9(1) English Arbitration Act (AA).

[30] See s 7 English AA; equally, section 1.8.1 of this chapter.

[31] See chapter 2 section 2.2.4.

institution.[32] Counsel familiar with one arbitral institution and its rules have no reason to recommend another, especially since institutions do not impose restrictions on the seat of arbitration.[33] It is important to emphasise at this point that the choice of seat for the arbitration is crucial because the procedural law of the seat determines the legality of the proceedings and the ultimate validity of the award rendered. If the parties or the arbitrator violates the law of the seat the award may be challenged and set aside or refused enforcement later on. The parties and their counsel must additionally ensure that the law of the seat, otherwise known as *lex arbitri*, and the courts of the seat are not hostile to arbitration and that they are able to guarantee the substantive and procedural rights of the parties.[34]

Where the parties to an agreement that has gone sour omitted, for whatever reason, to insert an arbitration clause when the agreement was originally drafted they may still refer their dispute to arbitration through a discrete agreement to arbitrate, known as *compromis*, or submission agreement. This is essentially a new, post-dispute, agreement and because the parties now have a good idea of the dispute the *compromis* will typically be more elaborate as compared to a short arbitration clause and may contain other information, such as the names of the arbitrator(s).

1.5.2 Phase II: the arbitral process

Once there is a valid agreement to arbitrate any of the parties to the agreement may trigger it and initiate arbitral proceedings. This phase

---

[32] See chapter 3 section 3.6 for a discussion of model and non-model arbitration clauses. The scope of the clause is important because depending on the language employed the tribunal may interpret the range of disputes (or issues) encompassed under the clause in a restrictive manner.

[33] The choice of an arbitral institution does not in any way imply that the seat of the arbitration will be in the city or country of the institution's headquarters. Rather, by choosing institutional arbitration the parties choose to be bound by particular institutional rules, select arbitrators from a list supplied by the institution (although usually optional) and be assisted throughout the process by the institution, whether in respect of clerical, legal or other support.

[34] By way of illustration, if a dispute involves a sensitive matter which may cause problems on the basis of public policy considerations, the parties may opt for a seat that is flexible on public policy issues. Under French law, for example, international awards are subject to international (as opposed to domestic) public policy restrictions, which are largely inconsequential. See chapter 7 section 7.6.3.5. Equally, parties largely interested in an expeditious arbitration may be dissuaded from choosing as their seat jurisdictions that permit appeals against arbitral awards (very rare) or appeals on points of law.

may be distinguished sequentially as follows: a) that which exists before the constitution of the tribunal and; b) that following the tribunal's constitution.

Typically, the initiating party (the plaintiff or claimant) will commence the process by transmitting a statement of claim to the parties' chosen arbitral institution,[35] or directly to the respondent or its designated agent, depending on the pertinent institutional rules. In case of ad hoc arbitration the parties may choose any other method for initiating proceedings. The statement of claim will contain a copy of the agreement and explain the claims raised by the plaintiff, in addition to the remedies sought.[36] Depending on the law of the seat the plaintiff may be compelled to communicate the statement of claim to the respondent directly, in addition to the institution.[37] In any event, the respondent will be afforded a time frame within which to respond to the claim and raise any objections.[38] If the objections concern the validity of the agreement to arbitrate the respondent will seek to prevent the constitution of the tribunal through a variety of options. If permitted by the law of the seat he or she can request the courts to rule on the alleged invalidity or non-existence of the agreement. In most cases, disputes as to the existence of arbitral jurisdiction are decided by the tribunals on the basis of their authority to decide whether they possess jurisdiction in the first place (*kompetenz-kompetenz*).[39]

In the absence of jurisdictional disputes the parties will select the persons whom they want to appoint as arbitrators. Although this will be explained in a subsequent chapter it suffices to say that where there is provision for three arbitrators each party chooses one (party-appointed arbitrators) and in the event they cannot agree on the presiding arbitrator the president may be chosen by the other arbitrators. The institutional rules ultimately

---

[35] Art 4(1) International Chamber of Commerce (ICC) Rules; Art 1.1 London Chamber of International Arbitration (LCIA) Rules.

[36] Art 4(3) ICC Rules; Art 1.1 LCIA Rules.

[37] Art 3 ICC Rules stipulates that 'all notifications or communications from the Secretariat and the arbitral tribunal shall be made to the last address of the party or its representative for whom the same are intended, as notified either by the party in question or by the other party. Such notification or communication may be made by delivery against receipt, registered post, courier, email, or any other means of telecommunication that provides a record of the sending thereof.' See also Art 4(5) ICC Rules.

[38] See Art 5(1) ICC Rules, which contemplates a period of thirty days. This period may, however, be extended by the Secretariat in accordance with Art 5(2) ICC Rules; see Art 2 LCIA Rules.

[39] For a more detailed discussion, see chapter 4 section 4.3.2.

determine the process in situations where the parties and the two arbitrators reach an impasse, failing which the matter is resolved by the courts.[40]
If the parties have not chosen any institutional rules, the procedure for
the selection of arbitrators shall be determined by the courts on the basis of
the law of the seat (*lex arbitri*). Once all arbitrators have been appointed the
tribunal is considered as having been constituted.

Following its constitution the parties may still seek to resolve issues that
are not relevant to the merits of their dispute. Examples include the
tribunal's jurisdiction (if not already resolved by the courts), the granting
of interim measures in order to safeguard sensitive evidence or assets (for
fear of dispersal and unavailability), challenges against the independence
or impartiality of the arbitrators and disputes over the applicable law.[41]

When all procedural challenges have been resolved by mutual agreement, or by the tribunal in accordance with the *lex arbitri* or the applicable
institutional rules, the discussion of the merits will take place. This is
typically undertaken through written submissions on the merits, followed
by oral hearings if the parties so desire. By this time there will be no dispute
as to the governing law of the agreement and the procedural rules of the
arbitration, which unless otherwise stated will be institutional, ad hoc
(UNCITRAL) or other, such as soft law in the form of the IBA Rules on
Taking of Evidence in International Arbitration. With the exception of
equal treatment and other due process guarantees, the parties are generally
free to choose or modify the procedural rules governing the arbitral process. For example, they may opt to forego oral hearings altogether[42] or set a
tight deadline for the delivery of the award.[43] However, such autonomy
may be limited by the operation of institutional rules to the contrary.

Although tribunals, particularly in arbitration-friendly nations, possess
broad powers there are some matters that are beyond their reach. By way of
illustration, arbitral rulings on interim measures may require enforcement

---

[40] Art 12 ICC Rules; see also chapter 4 section 4.5.

[41] For a discussion of interim measures, see chapter 5 sections 5.5.3 and 5.5.4.

[42] The Swiss Federal Supreme Court has held that the right of the parties to be heard does not
include a right to be heard orally (as long as this is consistently applied or is against the
wishes of both parties). *Re TA G v H Company*, (1997) ASA Bull 316.

[43] Art 19 ICC Rules provides that: 'the proceedings before the arbitral tribunal shall be
governed by the Rules and, where the Rules are silent, by any rules which the parties or,
failing them, the arbitral tribunal may settle on, whether or not reference is thereby made
to the rules of procedure of a national law to be applied to the arbitration.' See also s 46
English AA.

by the courts[44] and equally the authority to compel witnesses, documents and experts will not be directly bestowed upon them. In such circumstances the *lex arbitri* will allow the parties or the tribunal to request the local courts for assistance. In any event, the role of the courts is not to arbitrarily intervene in arbitral proceedings but only to assist the tribunal.

Within the deadline set by the parties and following examination of the evidence the tribunal shall deliberate and render its award. Although the tribunal may decide to issue a single (final) award dealing with all the issues raised by the parties – including even jurisdictional challenges that arose in the course of proceedings – in practice tribunals are not averse to issuing multiple awards in complex cases, each dealing with a distinct issue, such as liability and *quantum* (of compensation).[45] The *lex arbitri* will set out certain formalities which the award must satisfy, namely the signatures of the arbitrators (or just the president), the date and place rendered, a reasoned statement and perhaps others.[46] Once the award becomes final it resolves the parties' dispute and binds the parties in their mutual relations. A final award further produces *res judicata*. The principle of *res judicata* provides that a fact or right (entitlement) already determined by a competent court or tribunal in a final award on the merits cannot subsequently become the subject of litigation or arbitration as between the same parties.[47] It should be noted that an award becomes final and produces *res judicata* once it has cleared any applicable set aside challenges, or alternatively where the time limits for bringing such challenges have elapsed. A final award has exactly the same legal effect as a final court judgment.[48] Some arbitration laws require either registration or deposit of awards[49] or a writ of exequatur from the local courts, which is essentially recognition of its existence and authority for enforcement within the seat.[50] The parties and the arbitrators must be cognisant of the grounds

---

[44] Interim measures ordered by tribunals are only enforceable between the parties and hence the assistance of the courts with respect to assets, documents or evidence in the hands of third parties is necessary. See chapter 5 sections 5.5.1–5.5.3.

[45] For a discussion of the various types of awards available to tribunals under national law, see chapter 7 section 7.3.

[46] See, for example, Art 31 UNCITRAL Model Law; Art 189(2) Swiss Private International Law Act; s 52 English AA.

[47] See chapter 7 section 7.2.2.   [48] Art 824bis Italian CCP.   [49] Art 825(1) Italian CCP.

[50] Art 1212 Polish CCP. The exequatur applies in respect of domestic awards. See also chapter 7 section 7.4.3 regarding the obligatory nature, where pertinent, of depositing or registering final awards.

for setting aside – a typical example being the formalities associated with the award – lest the award be vacated (set aside) by the courts.[51]

1.5.3 Phase III: recognition and enforcement of foreign arbitral awards abroad

The objective of the award is manifold. The claimant may seek declaratory relief, compensation, restitution, recognition of a new entitlement (e.g. usucaption, otherwise known as acquisitive prescription), contract adaptation and others.[52] Where compensation is sought, the assets of the losing party may not suffice in the country where the award was rendered. Therefore, the winning party will naturally seek to enforce the award in one or more countries in which the losing party has assets. This process is by no means cheap but it is the only way to collect and may also involve a series of injunctions – during the course of arbitral proceedings or even before[53] – in the relevant states to prevent the losing party from dispersing its assets. In most cases, particularly between businesses that wish to remain creditworthy and reputable, awards are complied with voluntarily without further challenges, but situations do arise where a party challenges not only the validity of the award but also the validity of the arbitral process and even the existence of an arbitration agreement.

Had there not been an international treaty with near-global participation, such as the 1958 New York Convention, the courts of the countries where enforcement was sought would have had no obligation (or incentive) to enforce a private award rendered in a foreign country, particularly if directed against the assets of one of its nationals. The regime set up by the 1958 New York Convention and other regional treaties[54] has made international arbitration both feasible and viable. Contracting states are now obliged to recognise the existence of foreign awards and enforce them in their territory against the assets of nationals and non-nationals alike, save for assets covered by the privilege of sovereign immunity.[55] The grounds

---

[51] Art 41 ICC Rules requires that arbitrators must 'make every effort to make sure that the award is enforceable'; equally, Art 32.2 LCIA Rules.

[52] Modern arbitral statutes do not generally limit the range of remedies available to the parties in arbitral proceedings, as is the case with s 48(1) English AA. See chapter 7 section 7.5 for a discussion of available remedies.

[53] Through so-called emergency arbitration. See Art 9B LCIA Rules.

[54] See chapter 2 section 2.3.   [55] See chapter 8 section 8.6.

for refusal to enforce under the 1958 New York Convention are restricted and the general trend is to construe them narrowly with a view to avoid frustrating the enforcement of foreign awards for no good reason.

1.6 Perceived advantages of arbitration

The private nature of arbitration has given rise to several perceptions concerning its use and advantages over other traditional methods of dispute settlement. These perceptions have largely been offered without the benefit of empirical evidence because unlike the statistics available in litigation the confidential nature of arbitration necessarily means that no relevant statistics are freely available. The perceptions are generally that arbitration is: a) extensive across all industries; b) cheaper than litigation, or at least cost effective; and c) speedier. Alongside these perceptions there are several certainties that are absent in litigation, namely: a) minimisation of judicial bias by mutual appointment of arbitrators; b) confidentiality; and c) control of arbitral proceedings, including choice of seat.

Arbitration should not be viewed as a fit-all mechanism. What works for one entity on a particular occasion may not work for another under different circumstances. Moreover, the rise in the use of arbitration means that other dispute settlement mechanisms, as indeed entire jurisdictions, must become more competitive if they do not wish ultimately to become redundant. It is no accident that most countries aspire to become arbitration-friendly by adapting their arbitration laws to meet international standards and accommodate business concerns. In recent years several empirical studies have been undertaken in order to test the perceptions identified above. In a survey on corporate choices the respondents admitted that they settled 57 per cent of their disputes through negotiation or mediation and only 32 per cent of non-settled disputes were submitted to arbitration or litigation.[56] In another study by the EU it was demonstrated that despite its proven and multiple benefits, mediation in civil and commercial matters is still used in less than 1 per cent of the cases in the EU.[57] This study did not take into consideration complex (and largely transnational) commercial disputes where mediation

---

[56] Corporate Choices in International Arbitration: Industry Perspectives (2013), available at: www.arbitration.qmul.ac.uk/docs/123282.pdf.

[57] Rebooting the Mediation Directive: Assessing the Limited Impact of Its Implementation and Proposing Measures to Increase the Number of Mediations in the EU, available at:

is always the first port of call for legal counsel. The reality is that the end users of mediation will be attracted to it because of its perceived and actual benefits. When Italy introduced mandatory mediation this led to a significant decrease in the number of court cases, which in turn prompted the country's lawyers to go on strike and demand that the relevant law be declared unconstitutional. Despite the initial absence of a requirement for legal representation, 86 per cent of applicants in the first year of operation instructed a solicitor, thus demonstrating extreme caution.[58]

In a 2013 corporate perceptions study, the respondents raised concerns about the rising costs of arbitration, but neither this nor high legal fees were viewed as deterrent factors. In fact, the most important factors for deciding to engage in arbitration are the strength of the company's legal position, the weight of the available evidence and the amount of recoverable damages. It is clear, however, that business choices are conditioned by multiple factors, not just one. By way of illustration, the courts of England and Wales do not charge a daily hearing fee and hence they are the cheapest forum to settle disputes, not only as compared to other courts but also in relation to arbitration, where the fees are significant.[59] English courts are notoriously independent and produce excellently argued judgments. Even so, parties may still opt for arbitration because of the delay that may be caused by civil challenges[60] or the high legal costs in London; equally, the parties may have particular trade secrets whose exposure they would rather avoid (despite the possibility of *in camera* proceedings). Speed and confidentiality may therefore constitute factors that are more crucial to the parties in question than overall costs, in which case the choice of seat may be conditioned by the least number of challenges (both in theory and practice) against final awards. For example, one of

---

www.europarl.europa.eu/RegData/etudes/etudes/join/2014/493042/IPOL-JURI_ET(2014)
493042_EN.pdf.

[58] See G. De Berti, Mandatory Mediation: The Italian Experience Two Years On (7 June 2012), available at: www.internationallawoffice.com/newsletters/detail.aspx?g=78d73138 -a934-465a-9bca-01bc490100fd.

[59] Queen Mary University, Report on Competitiveness of Fees Charged for Commercial Court Services: An Overview of Selected Jurisdictions (17 December 2013), available at: www.law.qmul.ac.uk/news/2013/118691.html.

[60] Under s 69 of the English AA the losing party may appeal to the High Court to review the substantive points of law in the arbitral award, either by way of remitting the arbitral award to an arbitral tribunal or by setting the award aside in whole or in part (the so-called 'appeal on points of law').

the perceived advantages of New York City arbitration is that "even mistakes of fact and law do not warrant vacatur of an otherwise rational award".[61]

It is not out of the question that the courts of several states are empowered to employ expedited procedures in order to attract the resolution of commercial and civil disputes with a view to satisfying the parties' demand for speed and overall cost-effectiveness.[62] Experienced counsel will advise their clients on arbitral institutions whose rules specifically preclude delay tactics, as well as jurisdictions whose courts (and laws) have demonstrated speed and a general unwillingness to entertain protracted civil suits in relation to ongoing arbitral proceedings.

Parties to arbitral proceedings, just like in litigation, may fund their costs through third parties (e.g. banks, insurers, funds). Although third-party funding raises several ethical and public policy issues,[63] chiefly because of the incentives provided to the funder to influence proceedings in order to recover his capital and profit (e.g. the funder may not secure any profit at all from a mediated settlement), many liberal jurisdictions, such as England and Wales, are happy to accept arbitration/litigation funding, albeit subject to some limitations in the interests of justice.[64] As a result, parties with insufficient funds may be prepared to opt for arbitration in countries where third-party funding is available, even if their first choice was litigation or other means of dispute settlement.

1.7 Fundamental distinctions and principles

The remainder of this chapter will discuss three distinctions that are fundamental to one's understanding of international arbitration, namely international versus domestic arbitration, commercial versus other types of

---

[61] *Hackett v Milbank, Tweed, Hadley & McCloy*, 86 NY2d 146 (1995), at 154–5. What this means is that few, if any, stay claims will ever be successful in this jurisdiction.

[62] The US state of Delaware entertains expedited proceedings, subject to judicial control, through its court of chancery. In early 2015 Delaware adopted its Rapid Arbitration Act.

[63] *Sibthorpe v Southwark Borough Council* [2011] EWCA Civ 25, per Neuberger L.

[64] *Arkin v Borchard Lines Ltd & Ors* [2005] EWCA Civ 655; in *Harcus Sinclair v Buttonwood Legal Capital Ltd* [2013] EWHC 1193, the English High Court ruled that a third-party litigation funder was entitled to terminate the funding agreement when the likelihood of success in litigation had fallen below 60 per cent. The same principle should in theory apply to arbitration.

arbitration and ad hoc versus institutional arbitration. Moreover, it will explain two core principles that permeate arbitral proceedings, specifically, separability and arbitrability. Other concepts, such as *lis alibi pendens* (as well as stay of judicial proceedings in favour of arbitration), the role of public policy and *kompetenz-kompetenz* are examined in discrete chapters.

1.7.1 International versus domestic arbitration

The distinction between domestic and international arbitration is not crucial to all states. Whereas some national statutes apply distinct bodies of rules, most contemporary arbitration laws tend to expand the range of disputes which qualify as international and entertain the distinction for practical purposes, namely, for enforcement under the 1958 New York Convention, the inapplicability of local arbitrability and public policy limitations, and others of a similar nature.

Article 1(3) of the UNCITRAL Model Law proposes a broad definition of international arbitration, where:

(a) the parties to an arbitration agreement have, at the time of the conclusion of that agreement, their places of business in different states; or

(b) one of the following places is situated outside the state in which the parties have their places of business:

  (i) the place of arbitration if determined in, or pursuant to, the arbitration agreement;

  (ii) any place where a substantial part of the obligations of the commercial relationship is to be performed or the place with which the subject-matter of the dispute is most closely connected; or

(c) the parties have expressly agreed that the subject matter of the arbitration agreement relates to more than one country.

Paragraph 4 goes on to suggest that where a party has multiple places of business, as is the case with multinational corporations, the pertinent entity for the purposes of arbitration is that which has the closest relationship to the arbitration agreement.[65]

While most nations largely entertain the distinction they, nonetheless, extend the same regime (with minor differences) to both types of arbitration. One category of statutes focuses on the international nature of the

---

[65] But see chapter 3 section 3.9 for a discussion of third parties joining arbitral proceedings, particularly the group of companies doctrine.

dispute. An international arbitration under Article 1504 of the French Code of Civil Procedure (CCP) (a non-Model Law country) is dependent on the existence of international trade interests.[66] This is taken to mean that the arbitration is commercially linked to more than one country. The concept of 'international trade' need not involve more than one nation, so long as this is not just France.[67] Although the different nationalities of the parties or the law chosen may be relevant in distinguishing between domestic and international arbitration, neither of these is determinative in and of itself.[68] Equally, the intention of the parties as to the international nature of the arbitration is of no relevance.[69]

Elsewhere, an emphasis is placed on the parties' respective seats of business or residence,[70] as is the case with Article 176(1) of the Swiss Private International Law Act (PILA), according to which an arbitration is international if at the time when the arbitration agreement was concluded 'at least one of the parties had neither its domicile nor its habitual residence in Switzerland'. According to Article 21 of the Swiss CCP, which applies to domestic arbitrations, the domicile/seat of a legal person is that which is designated in its articles of incorporation. If no such seat is designated, this coincides with its place of effective management.[71]

Model Law nations subject all arbitrations to the same legal regime if they are seated in the country in question. This is the case, for example, with Article 46 of the Swedish Arbitration Act.[72] Even so, whereas in international arbitration the parties may choose any governing law,[73] in domestic arbitration certain restrictions as to the choice of a foreign law

---

[66] Equally, Art 49 of the 2011 Portuguese Arbitration Law.

[67] *Agence pour la Sécurité de la Navigation Aérienne en Afrique et à Madagascar [ASECNA] v M N'Doye Issakha*, French Court of Cassation judgment (17 October 2000), [2000] *Rev Arb* 648.

[68] *SARL Carthago Films v SARL Babel Productions*, Paris Court of Appeals judgment (29 March 2001), [2001] *Rev Arb* 543.

[69] *Chefaro International BV v Barrére and Others*, French Court of Cassation judgment (13 March 2007), [2007] *Rev Arb* 349.

[70] Equally, Art 1(2) of the 1993 Russian Law on International Commercial Arbitration.

[71] Even so, the parties may exclude the application of chapter 12 of the Swiss PILA (dealing with international arbitration) in writing if they have agreed to be bound by part 3 of the Swiss CCP (which deals with domestic arbitrations).

[72] The same is true also of Art 1(1) Spanish AA; Art 1154 Polish CCP; s 2(1) 2010 Scottish AA; Art 2(1) 2012 Lithuanian Commercial Arbitration Act; s 2(1) English AA; s 1025(1) German ZPO.

[73] Arts 3(1) and 9(6) of the Spanish AA.

may apply.[74] The nature of the arbitration may also impact on the right of the parties. In Belgium, for example, where none of the parties is Belgian they can agree to waive set aside proceedings before the courts, whereas if at least one of the parties is Belgian such a waiver is not possible.[75]

In Italy, prior to the 2006 Arbitration Law the CCP distinguished between domestic and international arbitrations. This distinction no longer exists. The Italian CCP has always distinguished between *rituale* and *irrituale* arbitral proceedings. This is unique to Italian law and what it essentially boils down to is that *rituale* proceedings constitute the classic form of arbitration whereby proceedings are subjected to the procedural rules of the CCP, whereas in *irrituale* proceedings the award is not enforceable but has the force of a binding contract. The Italian Supreme Court of Cassation has confirmed that *irrituale* awards have the effect of a binding contract.[76] Hence if a party subject to an *irrituale* award fails to comply the other party may commence an action for breach of contract.[77]

Overall, where statutes clearly distinguish between domestic and international arbitration, different rules will apply to each, although many will essentially be the same. Some will be radically different, as is the case with certain domestic public policy rules that are much broader than their international counterparts, such as those of France. Moreover, the seat of the arbitration is largely assessed by reference to its juridical dimension, namely as designated in the parties' agreement, or as determined by the tribunal in the absence of prior agreement. As a result, many arbitration statutes presume that the juridical seat coincides with the actual seat of the arbitral proceedings, but the parties should not stretch this presumption to its limits. Hence, according to the preparatory works of the 1972 Danish Arbitration Act, if the parties agree that the place of arbitration is Denmark

---

[74] See, for example, s 187(2) of the US Restatement (Second) of Conflict of Laws (1971); Art 34(2) of the Spanish AA refers specifically to the freedom of parties in international arbitration to choose their governing law, thus intimating that the same freedom does not exist, wholly or partially, in respect of domestic arbitrations.

[75] Art 1718 of the Belgian Judicial Code, as amended by the 2013 Arbitration Law.

[76] *Case no 527/2000*, Cassation Court judgment (13 August 2000).

[77] Even so, *irrituale* awards have several advantages, such as that they are not subject to tax, as is the case with *rituale* awards. Moreover, in certain cases where the parties' compliance is 'guaranteed' from the structure of the underlying relationship, as is the case with sports awards whose compliance is more or less automatic, there is no need for a formal award.

but the proceedings have no such connection with the country they would not fall within the scope of the Act.[78]

1.7.2 Commercial versus non-commercial arbitration

Disputes differ in many respects and it would make little sense to subject all of them to the same procedural rules. This is well recognised in arbitration. As a result, besides the distinction between domestic and international arbitration, domestic statutes and relevant treaties equally distinguish between commercial, investment, consumer (employment disputes are treated in largely the same manner in many but not all states)[79] and online disputes. Different procedures govern all of these types of disputes, albeit there are many common underlying principles. These distinctions are moreover significant because Article I(3) of the 1958 New York Convention allows member states to choose whether to subject non-commercial disputes to recognition and enforcement under the Convention, leaving the precise definition to national statutes. As a result, if a state has excluded non-commercial disputes, non-commercial awards (online awards may very well be of a commercial nature) will be refused enforcement and recognition there, although this is rare. The UNCITRAL Model Law provides a broad definition of commercial disputes, covering:

matters arising from all relationships of a commercial nature, whether contractual or not. Relationships of a commercial nature include, but are not limited to, the following transactions: any trade transaction for the supply or exchange of goods or services; distribution agreement; commercial representation or agency; factoring; leasing; construction of works; consulting; engineering; licensing; investment; financing; banking; insurance; exploitation agreement or concession; joint venture and other forms of industrial or business cooperation; carriage of goods or passengers by air, sea, rail or road.[80]

If national statutes did not view commercial disputes in broad terms the practice of arbitration would be seriously limited. In practice, arbitration-friendly states are willing to expand the list provided in the UNCITRAL Model Law. Thus Article 1504 of the French CCP is construed as also

---

[78] See O. Spiermann, National Report for Denmark (2009), in J. Paulsson (ed.), *International Handbook on Commercial Arbitration* (Kluwer, 2004, Supp no 57, 2009), 2.
[79] See Art 1(4) Spanish AA.   [80] Footnote 2, UNCITRAL Model Law.

encompassing professional activities,[81] as well as consumer activities with a transnational nature, such as the sale of stocks and other financial instruments which may otherwise fall under consumer relations. Others go even further, rendering the nature of the dispute redundant. By way of illustration, under section 1(1) of the 1999 Swedish Arbitration Act the parties may instruct the tribunal to simply ascertain a particular fact; hence the Act is not specifically limited to legal disputes as such. Likewise, section 2(1) of the Scottish Arbitration Act defines a dispute as including any refusal to accept a claim and any other difference, whether contractual or not. Some statutes make no reference to the scope of applicable disputes as is the case with section 6(1) of the English Arbitration Act, and hence provided that the dispute in question is arbitrable it is regulated under the Act.

This does not, of course, mean that all arbitration statutes take this broad view of commercial disputes. Article 177(1) of the Swiss PILA stipulates that any dispute involving property may be the subject matter of arbitration. This has been held to encompass sports sanctions where they produce economic effects on the sanctioned party[82] and this is true of all competitive sport disputes.[83]

The other three types of non-commercial disputes, namely investment (although investments are covered in footnote 2 of the UNCITRAL Model Law) and consumer (as well as employment) will be discussed in relevant chapters. It is implicit that where arbitration statutes do not specifically exclude them from their scope[84] they may otherwise be referred to arbitration under the same terms as commercial disputes. In investment arbitration, on the other hand, what is at stake is whether the dispute in question arises from an 'investment'. A particular activity, whether or not it qualifies as *commercial* in the context of international commercial arbitration, is considered an investment if designated as such under relevant bilateral or multilateral investment treaties, the parties' agreement or in a national foreign investment statute.[85]

1.7.3 Ad hoc versus institutional arbitration

The operation and administration of arbitral proceedings requires some degree of organisation and capacity. This service is provided by a multitude

---

[81] As is explicitly provided for in Art 2061 of the French CC.
[82] *Gundel v Federation Equestre Internationale*, BGE 119 II 271ff.
[83] *Re Mendy et Federation Francaise de boxe v AIBA*, CAS award (31 July 1996).
[84] Art 7(2) Danish AA.   [85] See chapter 10 section 10.3.3.

of arbitral institutions for a fee, although in their vast majority they are non-profit entities as is the case with national chambers of commerce. In addition, the majority of arbitral institutions have developed their own procedural rules[86] which are binding on the parties when they are designated as their chosen institution for the administration of arbitral proceedings. In such cases one speaks of institutional arbitration. Alternatively, the parties may decide to handle all the administrative issues themselves without the assistance of an arbitral institution and apply the procedural law of the seat (the *lex arbitri*) or the institutional rules of any other arbitral institution to the proceedings.[87] This is known as ad hoc arbitration. Both types of arbitration are recognised under the UNCITRAL Model Law and national statutes and awards rendered in both situations carry the same value.[88]

Although institutional arbitration may seem a sensible choice, there are several reasons why the parties may undertake all the administrative burdens associated with ad hoc arbitration. In small cases the institution's fee and the non-negotiable arbitrators' fees can be prohibitive. In large, complex, cases, particularly those involving state entities, the parties may wish to avoid the publicity associated with institutional arbitration. Ad hoc arbitration is no different from its institutional counterpart, given that proceedings will be subject to the law of the seat and the supervisory role of the local courts and the parties may apply any procedural rules of their choice, such as the UNCITRAL Rules.

The parties may request an entity to act as *appointing authority*, in the sense that it is granted the power to designate an arbitral institution or appoint the arbitrators once a dispute arises, although normally the designated arbitral institution is itself the appointing authority for the arbitral panel. By way of illustration, the Secretary-General of the Permanent Court of Arbitration (PCA) may be entrusted under the UNCITRAL Arbitration Rules and the Energy Charter Treaty with the task of appointing arbitrators in a particular case.[89] A unique emanation of this power is recognised in section 24 of the Scottish Arbitration Act, which introduces the concept of arbitral appointments referee (AAR). Experienced third

---

[86] Exceptionally, the London Maritime Arbitrators Association (LMAA) conducts arbitrations in London under the English AA.

[87] It is also common for ad hoc tribunals to manage all administrative aspects of a case, rather than the parties.

[88] Art 2(a) UNCITRAL Model Law.   [89] Art 27(3)(d) Energy Charter Treaty.

parties are essentially responsible for the appointment of arbitrators or umpires in situations where the parties are unable to agree among themselves. AARs, moreover, are responsible for the training and discipline of appointed arbitrators. Ordinarily, in the absence of the parties' agreement, this task would have been undertaken by the courts although it is obvious that this is not a function with which the judges are (always) familiar and it makes perfect sense to appoint experts to decide on such matters. Several professional bodies are currently registered as AARs in Scotland, including the Chartered Institute of Arbitrators (CIArb), the Royal Institution of Chartered Surveyors (RICS) and the Law Society of Scotland.[90]

1.8 Separability and arbitrability

1.8.1 Separability

Two issues are considered customary in the law of international commercial arbitration. The first is that the agreement to arbitrate is based on the parties' mutual consent, in the absence of which arbitration is not possible. The second concerns the fate of the arbitration clause in situations where the main agreement (in which it is contained) is held to be void or voidable. In such situations it is now generally recognised that the arbitration clause is separable and severable from the rest of the ill-fated agreement and survives even if the main agreement (e.g. contract, trust deed or other) does not.[91] Such an approach is vital in order to preserve the parties' entitlement to arbitration and generally trumps the rule (principally in contract law) whereby null, void or voidable agreements produce no legal effects in their entirety.[92] This is known as the principle of separability. Its practical effect is that whereas it does not, and cannot, remedy or cure the substantive fault of the agreement, separability does preserve the agreement's procedural

---

[90] H. R. Dundas, Arbitration in Scotland, in J. D. M. Lew, H Bor et al. (eds.), *Arbitration in England with chapters on Scotland and Ireland* (Kluwer, 2013), 603.

[91] Art 16(1) UNCITRAL Model Law; Art 23(1) UNCITRAL Arbitration Rules. Separability is by no means a new concept. See *Heyman v Darwins Ltd* [1942] AC 356, at 374 per Lord MacMillan.

[92] In support of separability, for example, the Estonian Supreme Court has held that an arbitration agreement that is null and void may, in certain circumstances, violate or at least ignore Estonian public policy. *Case no 3-2-1-34-04*, Supreme Court judgment (15 April 2004).

(dispute resolution) validity. As a result, the arbitral tribunal will be established under the terms of the agreement to arbitrate with the arbitrator thereafter assessing the parties' accountability and damages arising from the void or voidable nature of the contract.[93]

There are, of course, sensible limits to the separability principle. Where the tribunal or the courts determine that the arbitration clause itself is null, void or inoperable the arbitral proceedings will equally be terminated.[94] Similarly, the entire agreement, including the arbitration clause, will be considered invalid where the contract was never entered into, or where the ground for invalidity encompasses also the arbitration clause as it does the rest of the agreement.[95] It would be very difficult to sustain the argument that the arbitration clause in a contract that was forged or signed under duress was otherwise perfectly consensual and legitimate, but such a conclusion may not prevent an arbitral tribunal from assuming jurisdiction. The case law of few nations whose domestic arbitration law is not based on the UNCITRAL Model Law continues to examine the arbitration clause through a strict construction of contract law. The Luxembourg Court of Appeals, for example, has held that since the arbitration clause is an accessory contract and an integral part of a contract that is null or void, the maladies of the main contract naturally also affect the arbitration clause.[96] Such an approach is contrary to international practice and trade usages and must be viewed as exceptional.

Separability would be meaningless if any of the parties could lodge anti-arbitration suits prior to the constitution of an arbitral tribunal with a view to assessing the validity of the arbitration clause. The *lex specialis* character of arbitration agreements dictates that this befalls the jurisdiction of

---

[93] s 7 English AA. The notion of separability is not restricted to arbitration clauses in civil and commercial contracts. Art 3(d) of the 2005 Hague Convention on Choice of Court Agreements stipulates that: 'an exclusive choice of court agreement that forms part of a contract shall be treated as an agreement independent of the other terms of the contract. The validity of the exclusive choice of court agreement cannot be contested solely on the ground that the contract is not valid.'

[94] s 9(3) English AA; see *Vee Networks v Econet Wireless International Ltd* [2005] 1 Lloyd's Rep 192, per Colman J.

[95] Exceptionally, s 5(3) of the Scottish AA stipulates that a dispute about the validity of an agreement containing an arbitration agreement may be arbitrated in accordance with that arbitration agreement.

[96] Court of Appeal judgment (12 March 2003), Pas Lux 32, 399. Even so, Luxembourg courts generally recognise the principle of separability. See Court of Appeal judgment (26 July 2005), Pas Lux 33, 117.

tribunals and not the courts. Some arbitration statutes provide express recognition to this (obvious) rule. By way of illustration, Article 5(4) of the Portuguese Arbitration Law emphasises that the 'invalidity, inoperativeness or unenforceability of an arbitration agreement cannot be discussed autonomously in an action brought before a state court to that effect or in an interim measure brought before the same court, aiming at preventing the constitution or the operation of an arbitral tribunal'.

1.8.2 Arbitrability

It is not self-evident that all types of disputes may be freely submitted to arbitration by mere agreement. In fact, there are valid policy reasons why states may wish to subject certain disputes to public hearings before the courts. For one thing, most states are averse to their citizens taking the law into their own hands, as would be the case with settling criminal conduct in private.[97] The same is true of prohibited transactions, such as money laundering or drug trafficking. Financial considerations, such as tax and loss of state revenue are equally important. In every case the arbitrability of a dispute is balanced against the harm to particular public interests. In Belgium, for example, the termination of an exclusive distributorship agreement of indefinite duration governed under a foreign law is not arbitrable.[98] The public interest here is the negotiating disparity between the parties.

There is no general international rule as regards which disputes are arbitrable and which are not. The UNCITRAL Model Law does not expressly refer to arbitrability but this is somewhat implicit by its application to commercial disputes only. Even so, there are discernible trends, both regional and global. By way of illustration, EU member states in their

---

[97] There are of course exceptions even to this rule, particularly through the concept of blood money (*diya*) in the Muslim world.

[98] See Belgium's Distribution Law of 27 July 1961 (as amended in 1971), which subjects distributorship agreements performed in Belgium to the exclusive jurisdiction of Belgian courts. The requirement under Arts 4 and 6 of this Law that the parties' governing law be exclusively Belgian law was confirmed by the Cassation Court in *Sebastian International Inc v Common Market Cosmetics*, judgment (14 January 2010). The Court held that such a restriction is permissible by virtue of the fact that the 1958 New York Convention does not specify the choice of law in determining arbitrability. The Court of Cassation affirmed the lack of arbitrability in such cases. See *Air Transat AT Inc v Air Agencies Belgium SA*, Court of Cassation judgment (3 November 2011).

vast majority attach strict conditions to the arbitrability of consumer disputes whereas it is increasingly permissible to submit the private aspects (essentially contractual or tort) of anti-trust disputes to arbitration in most jurisdictions in the industrialised world.

From a legislative perspective there are several paradigms of arbitrability under domestic arbitration laws. The first allows parties to submit to arbitration any issue which they are free by law to dispose of,[99] save for matters of civil status and capacity, as is the case with Article 2059 and 2060 of the French Civil Code.[100] Other nations retain this 'free disposal' paradigm but limit it to disputes with a proprietary nature.[101] The second paradigm, which is generally similar to the first, provides that arbitration is permissible in respect of matters upon which the parties may reach a settlement.[102] Despite its seeming simplicity this paradigm provides no real clarity and hence further enquiry is required as to which disputes are beyond doubt susceptible to settlement. Many domestic laws, for example, while providing for settlement of family disputes, do not (as a matter of public interest) allow the parties to submit them to arbitration,[103] albeit there are notable exceptions to this rule.[104] The same is also true of labour disputes, which despite entailing financial (proprietary) considerations are exceptionally viewed from the lens of employment relations entailing a disparity between the parties. The third paradigm posits no general rule but imposes discrete exceptions to arbitrability in specialised laws, as is the case with the 2010 Irish Arbitration Act. Typical examples of non-arbitrability, which feature also in the context of the aforementioned paradigms, include disputes over real estate transactions[105] and residential accommodation leases[106] among others.

---

[99] Art 2(1) Spanish AA.

[100] This rule applies only in domestic arbitration. There is no equivalent rule in respect of international arbitration, thus broadening arbitrability significantly.

[101] Art 177(1) Swiss PILA; s 1030(1) German ZPO.   [102] s 1(1) 1999 Swedish AA.

[103] Art 1225 Luxembourg New Code of Civil Procedure (NCCP); Art 542(1) Romanian CCP.

[104] See chapter 3 with respect to testamentary arbitration. In a recent case the English High Court agreed to a request by the parties to refer all issues (including those relating to the financial settlements, the status of the parties' marriage and the care and parenting of their children) to arbitration under a Jewish religious court, in this case the Beth Din of New York. *A.I v M.T* [2013] EWHC 100 (Fam), paras 31–3. Exceptionally, Art 1157 of the Polish CCP allows the parties to arbitrate all civil law disputes, save for alimony claims.

[105] s 48(5)(b) of the English AA stipulates that tribunals have no power to order the specific performance of a contract relating to land; Art 1(3) Slovak AA.

[106] s 1030(2) German ZPO; Art 582(2) Austrian CCP.

In recent years, irrespective of the paradigm employed, arbitration-friendly states have significantly expanded their ambit of arbitrability to cover disputes with a significant public interest dimension that would otherwise have precluded arbitral resolution. This includes principally anti-trust (or anti-competition) and intellectual property disputes. The key to this expansion is that arbitration is permissible only with respect to the parties' (inter se) private relations, as would be the case with a cartel member selling goods at inflated prices to a third party or in cases encompassing vertical agreements between producer and supplier, or even in respect of clearance issues arising from mergers. It goes without saying that the public dimension of the infringement is not arbitrable. The pioneer in this respect has been the US Supreme Court and below we shall examine in more detail one of its key judgments, namely the *Mitsubishi* case.

This line of thinking was not immediately welcome in other parts of the world, particularly the then European Community (EC, but later EU) because of the supranational status of EC competition law and its direct effect on EC member states. The Court of Justice of the European Union (CJEU) and EU institutions have not expressly endorsed arbitrability in respect of private anti-trust claims but their silence is viewed as tacit approval.[107] EU member states, with few exceptions, adopt the *Mitsubishi* approach, albeit subject to a variety of legal justifications. In the Netherlands, anti-competition cases are arbitrable if there are assurances that the foreign tribunal will apply EU competition law.[108] In Poland, anti-trust disputes are equally arbitrable, not least because under Polish law unfair competition disputes are viewed as disputes in tort, which are arbitrable under Article 1157 CCP. The Polish Supreme Court has held that a clause providing for arbitration of 'all disputes concerning the interpretation and implementation of the terms of the agreement' covers tort claims resulting from unfair competition.[109] Exceptionally, some statutes go as far as expressly conferring the authority to arbitrate anti-trust disputes on the parties, as is the case with section 1(3) of the Swedish Arbitration Act. As the English High Court emphasised in *ET Plus SA v Welter*, the issue is not whether private enforcement in respect of anti-competitive practices is arbitrable, but 'whether they come within the

---

[107] See *Eco Swiss China Time Ltd v Benetton International NV* [1999] 2 All ER (Comm) 44, where the CJEU simply required a public policy review of pertinent awards.

[108] *A v Vertex Standard Co Ltd*, Hague Court of Appeals judgment (24 July 2013).

[109] *Case No I CSK 311/08*, Supreme Court ruling (5 February 2009).

scope of the arbitration clause, as a matter of its true construction'.[110] Even so, certain areas of EU competition law are not arbitrable, including merger control and state aid, because the EU Commission possesses exclusive competence therein.

Case study: The Mitsubishi case[111]

The parties involved were incorporated in various jurisdictions, including the USA. A sales agreement had been entered into between three companies, Soler Chrysler (Puerto Rican), Mitsubishi (Japanese) and Chrysler International (Swiss). The agreement provided for arbitration in Japan under the rules of the Japan Commercial Arbitration Association, the governing law being Swiss. Mitsubishi filed a request for arbitration against Soler claiming damages for breach of the sales agreement and Soler counterclaimed under the US Sherman Act[112] alleging anti-trust practices. The question for consideration by the US Supreme Court was whether or not the counter-claims for anti-trust breaches were arbitrable. The fact that the plaintiff argued that the matter be settled in accordance with the parties' contractual undertakings through arbitration did not entail an expectation that the arbitral tribunal examine the anti-trust violation with the purpose of punishment and the imposition of fines. These functions remained within the exclusive prerogative of the state. Neither did the plaintiff entertain the demand that the arbitral award settle the matter for the future with respect to all interested parties. The claim only concerned losses incurred as a result of one of the parties' anti-competitive behaviour. The Supreme Court, therefore, by a majority of five to three, decided that international contracts of this nature were arbitrable under the Federal Arbitration Act. It concluded that:

concerns of international comity, respect for the capacities of foreign and transnational tribunals and sensitivity to the need of the international commercial system for predictability in the resolution of disputes require that we enforce the parties' agreement, even assuming that a contrary result would be forthcoming in a domestic context.[113]

---

[110] See *ET Plus SA v Welter* [2005] EWHC 2115 (Comm), para 51.
[111] *Mitsubishi Motors Corp v Soler Chrysler Plymouth Inc*, 473 US 614 (1985).
[112] 15 USC § 1 et seq.   [113] *Mitsubishi* judgment, at 628.

1.9 The inter-disciplinary character of modern arbitration

International arbitration is not just about the law. Law is simply the context within which arbitration operates. This suggests that there are other dimensions to arbitration which are important to practitioners and which in themselves raise interesting legal issues. As this chapter has already demonstrated it was only recently that the much-praised virtues of arbitration (speed, cost, efficiency and others) were put to the test by both qualitative and quantitative studies, which largely measure perceptions from the perspective of end users. Such studies have significantly assisted the arbitration community to understand the dynamics of arbitration as opposed to litigation, but it has also shaped other market forces competing for the same prize. By way of illustration, several national courts are offering themselves as contenders to arbitration on the basis of reduced, or no, fees and by promising experienced judges and speedy results.

Even so, it is surprising that arbitration experts have not (until recently that is) explored the use of sciences that are common in the study of litigation. By way of illustration, courtroom psychology, which includes jury profiling and the limitations of eyewitness testimony, among others, have received significant attention over the span of decades, culminating in a rich bibliography.[114] The psychological realms of arbitration are still in some confusion. For example, whereas party-appointed arbitrators understandably share some sympathy for the appointing party they are expected (and bound) to be impartial and truthful. This clearly leads to incongruent results. Similarly, it is no more clear whether certain entrenched arbitral practices assist arbitrators in making sound choices or whether instead they force them to make bad ones. Obvious examples include strict time limits for rendering awards (speed versus quality decision-making) and the imposition of civil liability upon arbitrators versus the benefits of immunity. Bias, moreover, is a significant factor in international arbitration, but we are no wiser today in quantifying it and applying sensible rules to the appointment and selection (filtering) of arbitrators than we have ever been. Even so, some progress has been made. Recent research suggests that arbitrators, as authoritarian figures,[115] have the potential of steering

---

[114] See, for example, B. L. Cutler and S. D. Penrod, *Mistaken Identification: The Eyewitness, Psychology and the Law* (Cambridge University Press, 1995).

[115] In the Frommian sense described in section 1.2 of this chapter.

parties in a manner that is different to our expectations of arbitrators. Kuttner believes that this transformation may be achieved if arbitrators appreciate more fully their leadership potential through which they can assist litigants to engage with each other in creative ways and see beyond their mutual conflict.[116]

And of what relevance are the views of those employing the services of legal professionals to conduct arbitral proceedings? The answer to this question pertains to the field of psychological anthropology. There cannot be a single psychological evaluation of more than one person because of the inherently unique traits and characteristics of each personality – this of course does not prevent the exposition of theories and conditions of general application. On the other hand, it is natural that shared or common understandings between a group of people (culture) exist in all members of the group, thus rendering them collective phenomena. It is thereafter a matter of appropriate methodology as to how they will be studied.[117] When we talk about the mores and norms associated with a grouping of individuals (society or social system) what we are really investigating is the culture of the group. Culture is, therefore, a set of shared meanings communicated by language or other forms (e.g. symbols) between group members. The role of the anthropologist is twofold; on the one hand, he or she must 'discover' these shared meanings and on the other these must be translated into (same, similar, approximate or other) concepts which the observer clearly understands. First and foremost, an intimate knowledge of local culture is the best and perhaps only platform for any marketing exercise. Ultimately, if one wants to 'sell' a product or an idea (in this case, arbitration) to a community of persons that distrust the product or idea he or she must first understand the cultural underpinnings of the mistrust. Once this has been achieved, the 'seller' must promote the use

---

[116] R. Kuttner, The Conflict Specialist as Leader: Revisiting the Role of the Conflict Specialist from a Leadership Perspective, (2011) 29 *Conflict Resol Q* 103.

[117] There have been numerous approaches to collective phenomena by non-anthropologists which possess a very solid anthropological dimension, even if not wholly intended. A prominent example is the theory of interpretative communities, coined by Stanley Fish, which posits that actors within a given community (be it social, intergovernmental, industry-related) share common understandings about the culture and environment of their community and as a result interpret relevant underlying assumptions in a uniform manner. The transnational arbitration, banking and construction industries no doubt verify Fish's theory. See S. Fish, *Is There a Text in the Class? The Authority of Interpretative Communities* (Harvard University Press, 1980).

of those cognitive tools (or heuristics) which are appropriate for the circumstances, as adapted to the cognitive tools of the subject community (e.g. arbitration with tribal values for Africans, Islamic arbitration and Islamic banking for pious Muslims),[118] while at the same time recognising the distinct moral intuitions[119] of the community under consideration.

Information technology is also making significant inroads in the practice of arbitration. This is evident from the advances in online dispute resolution, the use of video in arbitral proceedings, the use of technology to reduce the costs of arbitration and the impact of new communications technologies for the exchange of information in arbitration. Whereas some of these applications concern the field of psychology (e.g. arbitrator and party attitudes in faceless online dispute resolution), others require further inquiry with regard to their ethical and regulatory dimension. By way of illustration, the use of email or social media for the purposes of notification leaves open the question of receipt of acceptance, despite the fact that it is assumed that businessmen can access their email far better (remotely) than regular post. Moreover, while the use of skype and other forms of video conferencing in order to examine witnesses and experts saves the parties from incurring unnecessary costs, it is uncertain whether such taking of testimony is permissible in accordance with the law of the country where the witness and expert are situated. As a result, set aside and enforcement problems may well arise.

---

[118] This is known as the ecological rationality of the group. See G. Gigerenzer, Heuristics, in G. Gigerenzer and C. Engel (eds.), *Heuristics and the Law* (M.I.T. Press, 2006), 17ff.

[119] See D. Kahneman and C. R. Sunstein, Indignation: Psychology, Politics, Law, in J. M. Olin, Law and Economics Working Paper (2007) 346, available at http://chicagounbound. uchicago.edo/cgi/viewcontent.cgi?article=1262&context=law_and_economics.

2 The laws and rules applicable to arbitration

2.1 Introduction

Having discussed generally the function and objectives of arbitration and after reviewing the fundamental principles that underlie it, it is now time to examine the various laws and rules that permeate the regulation and operation of international arbitration. The richness of arbitration is reflected in the nature and diversity of these rules. Some are formal laws, others are multilateral and bilateral treaties and yet others are of a private origin. Whatever their nature they are all applicable alongside each other in a web of intricate relationships. Understanding the content of these laws and rules, as well as how they operate and interact is crucial. The chapter goes on to explain the role of domestic laws, starting with the operation of substantive rules, namely the governing law of the parties' agreement, trade usages (*lex mercatoria*) and equity (*ex aequo et bono*). It then traces procedurally-oriented laws, particularly the law of the seat (*lex arbitri*), the law of the arbitration clause and the law of the country of enforcement (in respect of foreign awards). Finally, the chapter will examine the role of treaties and customary international law, pertinent soft law, particularly the role of model laws, institutional rules derived from arbitral institutions, as well as the problem of ethical standards and the application of ethical codes.

2.2 The role of domestic law(s)

Save for the recognition and enforcement of foreign arbitral awards, which is chiefly regulated by the 1958 New York Convention (a multilateral treaty), all other aspects of the arbitral process are governed by domestic law(s). Domestic law, whether general or specific to arbitration, is therefore of immense significance. No wonder the choice of seat, which in turn dictates the application of the procedural law of the seat (*lex arbitri*), is arrived at by reference to its efficiency, non-intrusiveness and other similar arbitration-friendly qualities. In the practice of international arbitration more than one domestic law typically comes into play. The parties may be of a different nationality and thus subjected to distinct personal laws (e.g. as regards their capacity) and additionally the substantive law of the main agreement may be governed by one or several domestic laws or trade usages. The same may be true of the arbitration clause, the rules governing arbitral proceedings (which may be subject to no rules at all if, for example, the tribunal is requested to decide as *amiable compositeur* or on equitable grounds). The parties may equally subject the proceedings to the rules of an arbitral institution, the discretion of the arbitrator or to one or more civil procedure codes.

It is therefore evident not only that domestic laws are the cornerstone of international arbitration but that in practice the interplay of multiple laws, self-regulation (party autonomy) and international law give rise to a regime of transnational law. Transnational law may be defined as a body of 'law' encompassing rules of both public (legislation and treaties) and private origin (trade practices, *lex mercatoria*) applicable simultaneously and harmoniously to a particular class of persons, industries or transactions. In practice, the various rules complement each other but there is a presumption in favour of party autonomy in situations of conflict. International arbitration is clearly the chief paradigm of transnational law.[1]

2.2.1 Conflict of laws rules

Every contract is subject to a particular law or legal system. This applies equally to domestic contracts, such as the purchase of fruit from the grocer, whereby the governing (or applicable) law is self-evident, as well as in cases where the actors or the subject matter of the contract is of a transnational character. The simplest way of ascertaining the applicable law to any given contract is by looking for the parties' intention because the vast majority of legal systems uphold the principle of party autonomy in the sphere of contractual relations, albeit with some (obvious) limitations.[2] The parties' intention may well be expressly recorded in the body of the contract and it usually is, in which case the contract's governing law is specified by the will of the parties. However, there are circumstances where the parties have given no thought to the governing law, whether because of poor legal advice or simply because they did not perceive it as being an important issue. In this latter case, when a dispute arises between the parties to a contract with no express governing law the court to which the dispute has been submitted must decide on the basis of which *substantive* law the facts will be determined. The judge may encounter a situation where several laws are potentially applicable, such as the parties' (distinct) personal laws, the law of the country where specific performance is to be undertaken, the law of the parties' respective seats, the law of the parties' agents and many others. In such cases the phenomenon of *conflict of* (substantive) *laws* arises. The judge has to solve this web of conflicts, but what is the legal platform (basis) from which to make his or her determination? Each country has its own set of conflict of laws rules (legislation) and a global attempt has been underway for more than a century to harmonise

---

[1] See T. Schultz, *Transnational Legality: Stateless Law and International Arbitration* (Oxford University Press, 2014).

[2] For example, most legal systems preclude the designation of a foreign governing law in a contract between two or more of their nationals when the subject matter of the contract is of a domestic character. Until the adoption of Art 38(1)(a) of the 2012 Saudi AA, which allows parties to employ any governing law, the governing law applicable to disputes between Saudi parties was always Islamic law, in accordance with *Diwan Almazalim* [Saudi supervisory authority] Decision No 143/T/4 (1992).

such rules so as to avoid inconsistencies and situations of injustice. The most extensive harmonisation has taken place in Europe, with pertinent treaties in the fields of contract,[3] enforcement of judgments,[4] matrimonial disputes[5] and others. For the purposes of this section, the revised Rome I Convention 1980 is the starting point for this discussion, being the instrument that harmonises conflicts of laws in respect of contracts in all EU member states.

When the court of a European member state receives a suit in which the contract has no express governing law, it will employ its national conflict rules in order to discover the tacit (or implied) governing law. The starting point is therefore the national conflict rules of the country where the suit was submitted, which is known as *lex forum*. The conflict rules of the *forum* (which, as explained, is in harmony with Rome I) will set out particular criteria which link the contract in question to a system of law. These criteria are known as 'connecting factors'. By way of illustration, Article 4(1) of Rome I stipulates that in the absence of a choice of law clause, the law governing the contract shall be determined as follows:

(a) a contract for the sale of goods shall be governed by the law of the country where the seller has his habitual residence;

(b) a contract for the provision of services shall be governed by the law of the country where the service provider has his habitual residence;

(c) a contract relating to a right *in rem* in immovable property or to a tenancy of immovable property shall be governed by the law of the country where the property is situated;

(d) notwithstanding point (c), a tenancy of immovable property concluded for temporary private use for a period of no more than six consecutive months shall be governed by the law of the country where the landlord has his habitual residence, provided that the tenant is a natural person and has his habitual residence in the same country;

---

[3] The 1980 Rome Convention on the Law Applicable to Contractual Obligations was consolidated several times and transformed into Regulation (EC) No 593/2008 of the European Parliament and of the Council of 17 June 2008 on the law applicable to contractual obligations (Rome I), OJ L 177. See C. M. V. Clarkson and J. Hill, *The Conflict of Laws* (Oxford University Press, 4th edition, 2011), 208–22.

[4] Council Regulation (EC) 44/2001 of 22 December 2000 on jurisdiction and the recognition and enforcement of judgments in civil and commercial matters [2001] OJ L 12.

[5] Council Regulation (EC) 2201/2003 of 27 November 2003 [2003] OJ L 338/1, concerning jurisdiction and the recognition and enforcement of judgments in matrimonial matters and matters of parental responsibility, repealing Regulation 1347/2000 [Brussels II].

    (e) a franchise contract shall be governed by the law of the country where the franchisee has his habitual residence;

    (f) a distribution contract shall be governed by the law of the country where the distributor has his habitual residence.

But even so, the situations of a contract may not be so clear as to allow for precise determinations. In such cases, paragraphs 2–4 of Article 4 of Rome I provide that:

2. Where the contract is not covered by paragraph 1 or where the elements of the contract would be covered by more than one of points (a) to (h) of paragraph 1, the contract shall be governed by the law of the country where the party required to effect the characteristic performance of the contract has his habitual residence.

3. Where it is clear from all the circumstances of the case that the contract is manifestly more closely connected with a country other than that indicated in paragraphs 1 or 2, the law of that other country shall apply.

4. Where the law applicable cannot be determined pursuant to paragraphs 1 or 2, the contract shall be governed by the law of the country with which it is most closely connected.

So far, we have examined the application of conflict rules to contracts which the parties submit to the courts in case of dispute.[6] Where a contract contains an arbitration clause and thus the parties are bound to submit pertinent disputes to arbitration, the tribunal, unlike the courts, is not obliged to assess the governing law of the contract on the basis of the conflict rules of the *lex fori*. Arbitral tribunals do not have a *lex fori* and as far as national procedural law is concerned they are only bound by the mandatory provisions of the law of their seat (the *lex arbitri*, which is examined in more detail below).[7] Although the *lex arbitri* – typically reflected in most part in the local arbitration statute – will regulate how

---

[6] Although it is inconsequential to our discussion of arbitral proceedings, the reader should at all times distinguish between the *forum* (namely the place where the dispute is to be resolved) from the applicable law (the law governing the agreement). As we shall see in several cases below, both national courts and arbitral tribunals sometimes artificially assume – where the parties have not designated a choice of law – that the applicable law should be the same as the choice of forum, as is the case with s 48(1) Swedish AA. See below note 12.

[7] Art 1(2)(e) of Rome I expressly excludes arbitration agreements from the scope of the Convention. However, as will be explained below, an *arbitration agreement* encompasses a severable arbitration clause (from the main contract) as well as a post-dispute submission agreement. The body of the main contract remains subject to conflict rules but, as will be

the tribunal is to arrive at the governing law in situations where the parties have failed to designate one, the relevant provisions in the *lex arbitri* will not ordinarily be of a mandatory nature.[8] They will be suggestive of the options available to the tribunal, as is the case with Article 28(1) and (2) of the UNCITRAL Model Law, which states that:

(1) The arbitral tribunal shall decide the dispute in accordance with such rules of law as are chosen by the parties as applicable to the substance of the dispute. Any designation of the law or legal system of a given state shall be construed, unless otherwise expressed, as directly referring to the substantive law of that state and not to its conflict of laws rules.

(2) Failing any designation by the parties, the arbitral tribunal shall apply the law determined by the conflict of laws rules which it considers applicable.

Paragraph 2 of Article 28, despite using seemingly mandatory language (*shall*) does not assimilate the seat of the arbitration with any particular *lex fori* for the purpose of ascertaining the appropriate conflict rules (i.e. that choice of forum necessarily also entails a choice of law). The tribunal may, therefore, apply any national or transnational conflict of laws rules in the absence of an express designation by the parties. The ultimate power of the tribunal in this respect lies in its competence-competence power which is explained in detail in chapter 4. The tribunal may just as well employ its own criteria (or common sense) in deciphering the law, rules, legal system, or combinations thereof that are closest to the parties' shared intention. This determination may ultimately turn out to be different to the conclusion otherwise reached by reference to the conflict rules of the seat of the arbitration. In many cases, the tribunal's power to determine the governing law of the parties' contract will stem from the institutional rules to which the parties have subjected their dispute.[9]

It is suggested, in conclusion, that there are three types of legislative approaches through which the law of the seat allows tribunals to resolve choice of law questions. The first, as exemplified in Article 28(2) of the

---

explained, the tribunal is not bound by national conflict rules. They are but an option, among many, in its armoury.

[8] By way of illustration, s 46(3) of the English AA, which is explained below, is a non-mandatory provision. This is evident from a combination of s 4(1) and Schedule 1 of the English AA.

[9] See, for example, Art 21(1) of the ICC Rules, which provides that in the absence of an express choice of substantive law 'the arbitral tribunal shall apply the rules of law which it determines to be appropriate'.

UNCITRAL Model Law and section 46(3) of the English Arbitration Act admonishes tribunals to apply conflicts of law rules, but not necessarily those of the *lex arbitri*. The tribunal is free to make use of those conflict rules 'which it considers applicable' (*voie indirecte*).[10] Under the second approach, the tribunal need not have recourse to conflict rules at all, but instead may apply the substantive law it deems 'more appropriate' to the dispute at hand or the parties' intention (*voie directe*). This is the case, for example, with section 603 of the Austrian CCP and Article 1511 of the French CCP. As we have already explained, this approach is consistent with the competence-competence power of arbitral tribunals and is usually also founded in institutional rules. The third approach is a variation of the *voie directe* and is reflected in Article 4(4) of Rome I, whereby the tribunal is required to apply the substantive law of the country with 'which it is more closely connected'. This so-called *limited voie directe* finds expression in section 1051(2) of the German *Zivilprozessordnung* (ZPO) and Article 187 of the Swiss PILA.[11] In practice, the outcome of *voie directe* and *limited voie directe* may be the same, particularly if the tribunal decides that the governing law should be that of the seat of the arbitration.[12]

After examining the (limited) applicability of national rules to arbitral proceedings,[13] we may now proceed to look at the governing law of the main contract and later the governing law of the arbitration clause.

2.2.2 The governing law of the (main) agreement

Every agreement must always be governed by some kind of law or legal system. The parties to the agreement are free to designate this law or legal system. In the previous section we examined the procedure through which

---

[10] See also Art 37(2) 1994 Czech AA; Art 1240 Luxembourg NCCP.

[11] See also Art 38(1)(b) Saudi AA; Art 39(2) Polish 2011 PILA.

[12] This is certainly a common law assumption that finds expression in English judicial practice. See particularly *Egon Oldendorff v Liberia Corp* [1995] 2 Lloyd's Rep 64 and *Parouth*, [1982] 2 Lloyd's Rep 351; Clarkson and Hill, above note 3, at 211–12.

[13] Conflict rules are relevant to Art V(1)(a) 1958 New York Convention determinations regarding the governing law of the parties' capacity to enter into an arbitration agreement. According to this provision the parties do not possess autonomy to choose the 'law applicable to them', as for natural persons this corresponds to the law of their nationality or domicile, whereas in respect of legal persons this is typically the place of their seat or incorporation. In such cases the applicable law is determined by the country of enforcement's choice of law rules. See R. Wolff, *New York Convention Commentary* (Beck-Hart, 2012), 273–4.

arbitral tribunals are directed to establish the agreement's applicable law when the parties have failed to make this determination themselves in an express and direct manner. In this section we are concerned with the character and content of the agreement's governing law, not the process by which this may be derived by the courts. It should also be noted that we are concerned with the choice of law of the main agreement or agreements, which may contain an arbitration clause, in addition to other clauses. It may have already become clear from the previous section that the governing law of a contract which is the subject matter of a dispute before an arbitral tribunal is construed differently and is subject to far fewer limitations (by law) as compared to a contract which is the subject matter of litigation. The latter is subject to conflicts of law rules, whereas the former is not.

The significance of the governing law is manifold. The agreement's governing law allows the arbitrator (or judge) to determine the parties' capacity, the existence of a breach, the possibility of renunciation, revocation, the recognition of particular trade usages and many others. The governing law of the contract may envisage more than one domestic laws, particularly where it requires specific performance in several nations or where the parties consider that a combination of laws is more favourable to their undertaking, assuming that the laws in question permit such combinations. Hence, the concept of the governing law of the contract may in fact include a variety of different laws from several nations. The scope of the governing law is limited to substantive law (e.g. law of obligations, contracts, companies), as opposed to civil procedure. Matters of civil procedure, as these relate to arbitral proceedings, are regulated by the law of the seat (*lex arbitri*) and do not pertain to the governing law of the contract.[14]

Despite the otherwise significant latitude available to the parties in arbitral proceedings to determine their governing law, this freedom is limited in the case of arbitrations of a domestic character. As we explained in chapter 1, many arbitration statutes apply in exactly the same manner to international as well as domestic arbitrations as long as they are seated in that country. Exceptionally, however, in international arbitration which

---

[14] As will be explained in chapter 6, section 6.2, the parties are free to modify or ignore those (procedural) provisions of the *lex arbitri* that are non-mandatory. The majority of the procedural provisions in arbitral statutes are non-mandatory.

involves disputes with an international dimension, the parties may choose a mutually acceptable governing law even if it is wholly unrelated to their own nationality or the law of the seat. This freedom may not always exist in domestic arbitrations, in which case the parties' agreement will be governed by the parties' common domestic law;[15] in any event, domestic arbitration laws usually have no objection to the parties applying international trade usages.[16] The obvious rationale for this limitation is that arbitration would otherwise culminate in a mechanism whereby the parties could bypass mandatory provisions of domestic law, to which they would otherwise be subjected.

Unlike the limitations posed by conflicts of law rules on the meaning of the concept of 'law' (in the sense of the governing law) which is limited in Article 1(1) of Rome I to the law of a particular legal system, such as that of France, the situation is different in respect of arbitral proceedings. Under Rome I, 'African customary law', the UNIDROIT Principles of International Commercial Contracts or 'Islamic law' are not considered national legal systems as such, the justification being that they are indeterminate and vague and hence give rise to uncertainty.[17] It is thought that trying to determine what Islamic law is in a particular case, as opposed to Saudi law which despite its sharia foundation is considered predictable, would give rise to several confusing and conflicting versions and interpretations.[18] These perceptions on the meaning of 'law' and 'legal systems' may be problematic in litigation,[19] but not for arbitration because it is not only assumed that the parties are well aware of the implications of their choice of law (and their ability to choose the law of their choice) but also because the appointment of arbitrators is based on their expertise of the parties'

---

[15] See Art 34(2) Spanish AA (by implication); s 48(1) Swedish AA (by implication).

[16] For example, Art 38(1)(c) Saudi AA.

[17] *Beximco Pharmaceuticals v Shamil Bank of Bahrain EC* [2004] 1 WLR 1784; *Musawi v RE International (UK) Ltd* [2008] Lloyd's Rep 326.

[18] This is because in strict legal terms there is no single or unified Islamic law. The four key sources of Sunni Islamic law on the basis of their hierarchy are as follows: 1) Qur'an; 2) the *sunnah* (representing the sayings and actions of the Prophet); 3) *qiyas* (human reasoning by analogy, but only if adopted by a large enough majority of Muslim scholars); and 4) *ijma*, which represents the actual consensus of the Muslim scholarly community. The four different schools of Sunni Islam, with the exception of the Qur'an, cannot always agree on the veracity of all the other sources and in any event ascribe varying interpretations to these and disputed sources. All this justifies the argument as to the non-existence of a single, coherent, verifiable Islamic law.

[19] And of course these limitations are imposed by conflict of laws rules as already explained.

chosen law. Unlike litigation, in international arbitration the parties are free to designate any 'law' as their governing law, irrespective if this is classified as a legal system or not under the Rome Convention (or other conflict of law rules). In fact, it is not uncommon for parties to designate as their governing law the *lex mercatoria*, equitable principles (*ex aequo et bono*), Islamic law, public international law and others, such as EU law,[20] that are not ordinarily considered legal systems.[21] These will be examined in more detail below.

Even so, some bias existed until recently against certain 'laws',[22] despite the clear choice made by the parties in their agreement. In the *Sheikh of Abu Dhabi* arbitration, the sole arbitrator, Lord Asquith, although finding that national law was applicable (i.e. Abu Dhabi law as grounded in Koranic law),[23] famously noted that:

> No such law can reasonably be said to exist ... [The Sheikh administers] a purely discretionary justice with the assistance of the Koran; and it would be fanciful to suggest that in this very primitive region there is any settled body of legal principles applicable to the construction of modern commercial instruments.[24]

Such an outcome would nowadays be untenable, not only because the parties' choice of law is sacrosanct, but also because the arbitrators are bound to decide the merits of a dispute based on the legal tools afforded to them by the parties. If the arbitrators dismiss the parties' choice of law, the award will almost certainly be defective and in addition they may incur some degree of liability for violating their mandate (*acta ultra vires*).

---

[20] There are several cases where the parties designated EU law as their governing law, such as ICC Award No 7319 (1992) and ICC Award No 10047 (1999).

[21] In *The Matter of the Arbitration between Raisler Corporation and New York City Housing Authority et al. and A. Rosen & Son et al.*, 32 NY2d 274, 283 (1973), the NYC Court of Appeals famously held that: 'an arbitrator may decide the issues as equity and justice require, unbound by the rigors of law'. This case may be stretching things a bit too far given that the parties had not authorised the arbitrator to act as amiable compositeur or decide the case *ex aequo et bono*.

[22] In *Kingdom of Saudi Arabia v ARAMCO* (1963) 27 ILR 117 at 169, it was claimed by the arbitrator that Islamic law could not secure the interests of private parties.

[23] *Petroleum Development (Trucial Coasts) Ltd v Sheikh of Abu Dhabi* (1951) 18 ILR 144, per Lord Asquith at 149; equally, *Ruler of Qatar v Int'l Marine Oil Co. Ltd* (1953) 20 ILR 534, per Bucknill J at 545, who stated that: 'I have no reason to suppose that Islamic law is not administered [in Qatar] strictly, but I am satisfied that the law does not contain any principles which would be sufficient to interpret this particular contract'.

[24] *Sheikh of Abu Dhabi*, above note 23.

We have already stated that the governing law may encompass a combination of different laws, each dealing with disparate parts of the contract, but occasionally the parties may subject the whole or part of their main contract to several laws *concurrently*. This has been particularly prevalent, although generally ill-advised, in contracts between states and private entities with a view to satisfying the host state's demand for respect of its domestic law while at the same time counter-balancing the risk of abuse by the host with the parallel application of a more objective law, such as international law.[25] However, because concurrent law clauses do not provide arbitrators with a clear picture of the parties' choice of law, the ultimate outcome may lead to unnecessary surprises. Consider, for example, the following clause which was inserted in three distinct contracts in the Libyan oil nationalisation cases:

This concession shall be governed by and interpreted in accordance with principles of law of Libya common to the principles of international law and, in the absence of such common principles, then by and in accordance with the general principles of law, including such principles as may have been applied by international tribunals.

There are several uncertainties associated with this clause. Firstly, is it Libyan law that should be consistent with international law or the latter with Libyan law and is this distinction even necessary? If Libyan law is incompatible with fundamental notions of international law, is it not defective under international law anyway? Secondly, had the parties really expected that Libyan law may be wholly or partially inconsistent with international law? Thirdly, how much evidence of the incompatibility between Libyan and international law must an arbitrator accept (in order to avoid accusations of bias) before turning to the default position in the choice of law clause (i.e. general principles of law)? It is no wonder that the three sole arbitrators appointed in the three nationalisation cases each reached a different interpretation of the clause. In the *BP* arbitration the default option was preferred,[26] whereas in *Texaco* it made sense to apply public international law without the need for any compatibility test with Libyan law.[27] Finally, in *Liamco* it was decided that although the governing

---

[25] Nowadays there are sound contractual techniques for extinguishing risks of this nature, such as freezing (of laws) or stabilisation (of laws and their effects) clauses.

[26] *British Petroleum Co Ltd (Libya) v Libya* (1982) 17 ILM 14.

[27] *Texas Overseas Petroleum Co and California Asiatic Oil Co (Texaco) v Libya* (1982) 62 ILR 140.

law was that of Libya, it was in conflict with international law and as a result its exclusion was warranted by the tribunal.[28]

2.2.2.1 Trade usages (*lex mercatoria*)

Article 28(1) of the UNCITRAL Model Law emphasises that the parties may choose 'rules of law' to govern their agreement rather than (domestic) laws. This means that the parties may designate non-ratified treaties, or parts thereof, equity (discussed below) as well as trade usages, none of which constitute formal law. Trade usages are a form of self-regulation and may involve rules established by the industry directly on the basis of pertinent expertise, as is the case with construction and oil and gas technical specifications, or may otherwise entail the use of standard agreements, clauses or legal instruments as is the case with insurance contracts (e.g. Bermuda form). The ultimate validation of *lex mercatoria* rests on the fact that not all legal orders are created by the nation state and accordingly that private orders of regulation can create law.[29] The employment of trade usages is extensive among parties in the same industry and in their majority they have been codified either by the industry itself,[30] or have otherwise been approved as private custom by the courts or domestic laws.[31]

It is no accident that Article 28(4) of the UNCITRAL Model Law requires that regardless of the parties' choice of law the tribunal shall in all cases take into account the usages of the trade applicable to the transaction. Although it is probably contrary to party autonomy, this injunction has been construed as an obligation on arbitral tribunals. The Swiss Federal Supreme Court refused to set aside an award in a case where the tribunal supplemented the parties' choice of law with practice arising from the UN Convention on Contracts for the International Sale of Goods and the 2004 UNIDROIT Principles of International Commercial Contracts. It argued that reference to such transnational rules was reasonable in long-standing

---

[28] *Liamco v Libya* (1982) 62 ILR 140, at 143.

[29] G. Teubner, Global Bukowina: Legal Pluralism in the World Society, in G. Teubner (ed.) *Global Law Without a State* (Dartmouth, 1997), 15.

[30] See, for example, the construction industry's FIDIC rules, which are distinguished threefold as follows: construction contracts per se (red book); plant and design-build (yellow book) and; EPC turnkey contracts (silver book).

[31] s 346 of the German Commercial Code states that 'due consideration shall be given to prevailing commercial custom and usages concerning the meaning and effect of acts and omissions among merchants'. Equally, although in a different context, s 18(1) of the 1999 Tanzanian Village Land Act recognises customary rights of occupancy.

international commercial relationships.[32] In equal measure, Article 1511(2) of the French CCP states that tribunals 'shall take into account trade usages'. The French Court of Cassation has held that an award decided on the basis of 'rules of international commerce determined by practice recognised in national case law' was compatible with 'rules of law' under Article 1511 CCP.[33]

2.2.2.2 Equity (*ex aequo et bono*)

As has already been explained, the parties must subject their agreement to 'rules of law', not necessarily a (domestic) law. Article 28(3) of the UNCITRAL Model Law stipulates that the parties may authorise[34] a tribunal to decide a case *ex aequo et bono*, which is synonymous with equity and conscience. In simple terms, the parties authorise the tribunal to dispense with all legal rules and decide the case solely on equitable grounds, essentially justice, fairness and good conscience.[35] In the seminal *Minhal* case the Paris Court of Appeals held that where the tribunal is asked to decide on the basis of equitable considerations it is presumed that the parties have waived the effects and benefits of legal rules as well as the right to expect a strict application of the law. Exceptionally, where the tribunal has been requested to decide the dispute on the basis of both equitable and formal rules French courts have advanced the view that the tribunal must first identify the chosen law and then compare it to the equitable solution, ultimately deciding the outcome (if a conflict between the law and equity exists) in accordance with its own sense of fairness.[36]

The parties may be driven in favour of equity by the fact that the relevant law is vague or indeterminate or because the dispute in question is simply a matter of fact. Has enough cement been used? Did X actually deliver the

---

[32] Swiss Federal Supreme Court judgment (16 December 2009), *case no 4A_240/2009*.

[33] *Compania Valencia de Cementos Portland SA v Primary Coal Inc*, French Court of Cassation judgment (22 October 1991) [1993] 18 *YB Com Arb* 137.

[34] Exceptionally, equity is the default position in certain arbitral institutions, unless the parties expressly agree otherwise, as is the case with s 2 of the Arbitration Rules of the tribunal of the Rosario (Argentina) Stock Exchange.

[35] See *Liberty Reinsurance Canada v QBE Insurance and Reinsurance (Europe) Ltd*, Ontario Superior Court judgment (20 September 2002), [2002] CanLII 6636 (On SC) which held as much in respect of an arbitration clause requiring the agreement to be interpreted as an 'honourable agreement'.

[36] *Halbout and Matenec HG v Hanin*, French Court of Cassation judgment (15 February 2001), [2001] *Rev Arb* 135.

goods? The Athens Appeals Court has held that where the parties request the tribunal simply to decide whether there has been consideration under the contract it is assumed that its decision will be grounded on equity.[37] Equity is only available through party consent and cannot therefore be imposed as default law by the tribunal. Requests for adjudication on the basis of equitable principles have been prominent in maritime determination disputes before the International Court of Justice (ICJ) as well as in ad hoc arbitrations on the same issue.[38] Expert determination is equally based on equitable (as well as technical) considerations, but as is explained in chapter 1 it is not a form of arbitration.[39]

The vast majority of domestic laws recognise equitable determinations by arbitrators as final awards, otherwise there would be little point in making such requests in the first place. Nonetheless, several sensible limitations are imposed. French courts have clarified that when deciding on the basis of equity tribunals are bound to observe the parties' due process rights and international public policy more generally.[40] Moreover, although the tribunal may have to moderate the effects of the parties' contractual arrangements, it may not go as far as to create a new set of relationships that were not originally intended by the parties.[41] Furthermore, if the tribunal were to render an award that includes no evident considerations of equity and instead involves a strict application of the contract on the basis of formal law this may lead to setting the award aside.[42] In line with the limitations identified above, Article 39(5) of the Portuguese Arbitration Law provides that awards rendered on the basis of equity may not be appealed to the courts (assuming the parties had agreed that appeals are possible). Finally, some Model Law jurisdictions take the view that equitable determinations must

---

[37] Athens Appeals Court judgment 4966/1975.

[38] *North Sea continental shelf cases (FRG v Netherlands, FRG v Denmark)* [1969] ICJ Rep 3, at 5; *Guinea/Guinea Bissau maritime boundary arbitration* (1986) 25 ILM 251, where it was held that delimitations must ultimately be measured against the goal of producing equitable solutions. See also Art 83(1) UNCLOS to the same effect, although unnecessarily confusing.

[39] See chapter 1 section 1.4.

[40] *CN v Minhal*, Paris Court of Appeals judgment (28 November 1996); The Swiss Federal Supreme Court has ruled that when deciding a case *ex aequo et bono* the arbitrators are only limited by public policy rules. See *Bettydo SA v Torriani*, BGE 107 Ib 63.

[41] *Société Taurus Films v Les Films du Jundi*, [2000] *Rev Arb* 280.

[42] *Leizer v Bachelier*, Paris Court of Appeals judgment (3 July 2007), [2007] *Rev Arb* 821.

always consider applicable trade usages, in accordance with Article 28(4) of the UNCITRAL Model Law.[43]

2.2.3 The law of the seat of arbitration (*lex arbitri*)

The law of the country where the arbitration is seated determines the legality of the arbitral proceedings and sets out rules and processes to assist the tribunal in its mandate. The law of the seat is known as *lex arbitri* as well as curial law. From the point of view of legislative drafting it is largely found in a distinct arbitration statute, as is the case with the English 1996 Arbitration Act, or otherwise incorporated in the code of civil procedure or a combination thereof. In the Czech Republic, for example, the 1994 Arbitration Act is supplemented (but not superseded) by the relevant provisions of the country's 1963 CCP[44] and in Greece the 1999 Law on International Commercial Arbitration (LICA)[45] is supplemented, where appropriate, by the CCP as well as specialised laws which may deviate from the LICA.[46] In the case of Czech legislation the rules for examining evidence in the CCP are more elaborate than the 1994 Act and hence arbitrators may have recourse to these if the parties so wish. The Czech Supreme Court has consistently held that the CCP should be applied only to the extent that it does not violate the fundamental principles of arbitral law recognised by the Czech Republic.[47]

In federal nations, such as the USA, there is a single federal statute and as many state statutes as there are states. The US Federal Arbitration Act (FAA) was originally enacted in 1925 and covers both domestic arbitrations as well as international arbitrations[48] under the New York and Panama conventions (discussed below). Whereas state statutes typically regulate arbitration within state borders, several states have also adopted distinct statutes covering international arbitration. However, in order to

---

[43] *Food Services of America Inc (Amerifresh) v Pan Pacific Specialties Ltd*, [1997] 32 BCLR (3d) 225.

[44] See Art 30, Act No 216/1994 on Arbitral Proceedings and Enforcement of Arbitral Awards [1994 Arbitration Act].

[45] Law No 2735/1999.

[46] Art 31, Law No 3389/2005 on PPPs provides that any disputes arising from relevant partnership and ancillary agreements will be resolved by arbitration.

[47] Czech Supreme Court, *case No 32, 1528/2005*.

[48] s 2 FAA. See *Citizens Bank v Alafabco Inc*, 539 US 52 (2003) at 58, according to which the FAA covers any international transaction within the ambit of federal law.

avoid conflicts with the FAA they usually subjugate themselves to the FAA, unless the parties choose otherwise.

The *lex arbitri* refers to both substantive and procedural law and operates as a type of platform or safety net for arbitration, even if the parties never make any use of it whatsoever. Its utility for the arbitral process lies in the fact that both the parties and the arbitrator may seek some assistance (or intervention) from the local courts in situations where neither the parties nor the arbitrator are empowered to undertake a particular action, as is the case with compelling the attendance of witnesses, enforcement of interim measures, attachment of assets and others. Equally, the mandatory rules relating to the conduct of arbitral proceedings (such as due process and party equality) or the legal requirements for the validity of awards are subject to the prescriptions laid down by the law of the seat. As a result, both the parties and the arbitrator must ensure that they have fully complied with this law otherwise the award risks being set aside. Moreover, an award will most probably be refused recognition and enforcement in a third state if it has been made in violation of the *lex arbitri* (assuming it has not already been set aside in the seat).[49]

How can the local courts assist the parties? We have already alluded to the fact that arbitral proceedings may require testimony from particular witnesses, the production of evidence not in the possession of the parties (third-party disclosure) or the need to ensure that critical assets are not liquidated or dissipated before an award is rendered. Arbitral tribunals do not as a rule possess powers to compel third parties to testify or issue subpoenas for the production of material evidence. In equal measure they have no authority to issue freezing or other orders against the parties' assets, let alone against the assets of third parties. Such orders and processes can only be undertaken by, and through, the courts.[50] Furthermore, the parties may petition the local courts to remove an arbitrator or replace him or her

---

[49] Art V(1)(d) 1958 New York Convention. Exceptionally, under French law awards set aside at the seat of the arbitration may still be recognised and enforced in France. See *Société Hilmarton Ltd v Société OTV*, French Court of Cassation judgment (23 March 1994), [1995] 10 *YB Com Arb* 663 and *Société Polish Ocean Line v Société Jolasry*, French Court of Cassation judgment (10 March 1993), [1993] *Rev Arb* 255. This is not out of disrespect for the *lex arbitri*, but, as already explained, it is predicated on the French doctrine whereby the validity of an international award must be assessed by the rules of the country where recognition and enforcement is sought.

[50] See, for example, Art 27 UNCITRAL Model Law concerning the taking of evidence and the discussion in chapter 6.

with someone else where the arbitrator is challenged for alleged illegal conduct (e.g. corruption) or is unable to fulfil his or her mandate.[51] Moreover, as has already been identified, the *lex arbitri* may constitute the default law in situations where the parties have failed to reach agreement on a particular issue, such as their choice of law.

It should be observed that, unlike the consensual (*lex voluntatis*) nature of choice of law clauses, the *lex arbitri* is automatic and obligatory, although domestic arbitration statutes typically distinguish between mandatory and permissive provisions in the *lex arbitri*. By way of illustration, the parties cannot exclude the application of French procedural law to arbitral proceedings taking place in France because the local courts continue to possess jurisdiction over the proceedings and can intervene if local law so demands, or if requested by the arbitrators.

Delocalised Arbitration

The idea that arbitral proceedings may somehow be 'floating' or 'delocalised' by reason of the parties' consent, namely that there will exist no particular seat and therefore no *lex arbitri*, is probably best reserved for the realms of imagination;[52] or is it? Exceptionally, for the sake of stretching party autonomy the law of the seat may find no compelling reason to force the parties to use local procedural rules provided that the proceedings do not violate due process rights. The Greek Areios Pagos has held that an arbitration conducted in Greece under foreign procedural laws was valid so long as the parties' right to equal treatment was respected.[53] Moreover, there is an ever-increasing trend for arbitration-friendly nations to assist arbitral proceedings seated abroad. Belgian courts, for example, are authorised to assess the validity of arbitration agreements,[54] adopt provisional or conservatory measures,[55] take evidence,[56] as well as recognise and enforce provisional or conservatory measures ordered by a tribunal seated abroad.[57]

---

[51] Art 13(3) UNCITRAL Model Law.

[52] Although see chapter 9 section 9.6.1, dealing with online arbitration, concerning the debates about the arbitrator and the parties being situated in different locations.

[53] Areios Pagos judgment 830/1972.

[54] Art 1676(8) Judicial Code (JC) (as incorporated in the JC by a 2013 Arbitration Law).

[55] Art 1682 JC.   [56] Art 1698 JC.   [57] Art 1708 JC.

2.2.3.1 The law of the European Union

This is a complex issue and in order to avoid confusion it should be pointed out that its treatment in this section encompasses only substantive EU law as this applies in a seat of arbitral proceedings that is also a member state to the EU.[58] This is because EU law, as a supranational legal system, binds EU member states and certain instruments, such as regulations, produce direct effect without the need for any implementing legislation. What this means is that EU law is an integral part of the *lex arbitri* of EU member states and by implication any violation of EU law will entail a breach of the law of the seat, thereby culminating in possible set aside proceedings. As was already discussed earlier in the chapter, a significant part of EU law is either inapplicable to arbitral proceedings (e.g. conflict rules) or is permissive in nature or at least compatible with arbitral proceedings, as is the case with the arbitrability of anti-trust (competition) disputes.

Even so, there are areas of EU law from which the parties cannot opt out contractually or otherwise. By way of illustration, awards may be set aside by EU member state courts if they are in conflict with Articles 101 (anti-competitive practices) and 102 (abuse of dominant position) of the Treaty on the Functioning of the European Union (TFEU). A violation of these provisions is a breach of EU public policy according to the CJEU.[59] Furthermore, the parties to an arbitration agreement are not allowed to circumvent particular (mandatory) EU legislation, as is the case with the EU Commercial Agents Directive.[60] In *Accentuate Ltd v Asigra Inc*,[61] the English High Court held that the parties could not circumvent the indemnity and compensation provisions of the Directive and any award that was in breach of these mandatory provisions would be refused on grounds of public policy. Even so, it is wholly unclear what parts of EU law possess a mandatory nature such that the parties may not opt out without breaching EU public policy. The two mentioned in this section are obvious contenders but this is not so with every piece of EU legislation and the parties to

---

[58] Hence, this section will not deal with issues such as conflict of laws, or the governing law of the parties' contract; but see, chapter 10 section 10.2.2 for a brief discussion of EU foreign investment law.

[59] Joined cases C-29504 to C-29804, *Vincenzo Manfredi v Lloyd Adriatico Assicurazioni SpA, Antonio Cannito v Fondiaria Sai SpA and Nicoló Tricarico, Pasqualina Murgolo v Assitalia SpA*, [2006] ECR-I 06619.

[60] Council Directive 86/653/EEC on the coordination of the laws of the member states relating to self-employed commercial agents.

[61] *Accentuate Ltd v Asigra Inc* [2009] EWHC 2655 (QB).

arbitration agreements must usually tread carefully, and one should not rule out the prospect of a unique referral by arbitral tribunals to the CJEU with respect to matters involving EU public policy.[62]

2.2.4 The law of the arbitration clause

The arbitration clause is an integral part of the parties' main agreement and ordinarily there should not be any dispute as to the law governing the arbitration clause. Nonetheless, because of the separability principle the arbitration clause may have a life that is distinct from the main agreement. If the main agreement (trust, contract or other) is found to be inoperable, null or void, the arbitral tribunal to which a dispute is referred must determine whether the arbitration clause itself is valid and operable. Such a determination as to the validity of the arbitration clause must be assessed in accordance with the law applicable to the clause itself. The same is true of the parties' capacity to enter into an arbitral agreement in the first place.

It is questioned, in the absence of any designation by the parties, whether the proper law of the arbitration clause is that of the seat or that which coincides with the governing law of the main contract. There are two disparate schools of thought on this matter. English courts have generally taken the view that the default law should be the law of the seat,[63] whereas US courts are inclined to accept that in the absence of an express choice the governing law of the main agreement should be deemed as encompassing all clauses, including the arbitration clause. The latter option seems to conform more closely to the parties' wishes.[64]

---

[62] See chapter 4 section 4.2 and chapter 5 section 5.4. At present, this is only undertaken indirectly through references by national courts on behalf of arbitral tribunals (where national law so permits). See, for example, *Bulk Oil Ltd v Sun International Ltd* [1984] 1 All ER 386. The appeal was made in accordance with s 69 English AA which allows appeals against awards on points of law. In the case at hand, the disputed point of law concerned EU law.

[63] *C v D* [2008] 1 Lloyd's Rep 239 (CA), per Longmore LJ, para 16; for a contrary result, see *Peterson Farms Inc v C & M Farming Ltd* [2004] All ER (D) 50, effectively overturning *Roussel-Uclaf v GD Searle & Co* [1978] 1 Lloyd's Rep 225; equally, *case (Civil) no 184/2004*, Bulgarian Supreme Court of Cassation, judgment no 630 (28 July 2004). This is also the position taken by Art V(1)(a) of the 1958 New York Convention.

[64] For a general discussion, see I. Bantekas, The Proper Law of the Arbitration Clause: A Challenge to the Prevailing Orthodoxy (2010) 27 *JOIA* 1.

The law of the arbitration clause is significant for a number of reasons. If the parties choose to incorporate the clause in an instrument that prohibits the inclusion of such clauses under the law governing the clause, such as a will or trust, it will not be considered as a valid arbitration agreement. Equally, the law governing the arbitration clause will determine whether it is defective, particularly null and void or inoperable. Several jurisdictions have shown themselves willing to remedy the violation of mandatory rules by retrospectively approving the parties' chosen governing law for their arbitration clause, despite its breach of the forum's mandatory rules. An illustration is pertinent. Article 19(2) of the Bulgarian LICA stipulates that arbitration between Bulgarian parties must always be conducted in Bulgaria under Bulgarian law. In one case the parties ignored this rule by subjecting their contract to English law and arbitrated their dispute in London, ultimately seeking to enforce the award in Bulgaria. The country's Supreme Court of Cassation has ruled on other occasions that awards granted to Bulgarian parties in foreign jurisdictions must be enforced in Bulgaria.[65] The rationale is to ensure respect for the 1958 New York Convention in the event of a clash with Bulgarian law. In the case at hand, the Court held that the Bulgarian restriction regarding the choice of seat and governing law (for Bulgarian nationals) is not of a public policy nature, otherwise it would conflict with the 1958 New York Convention. Instead, it emphasised that the validity of the arbitration clause must be assessed in accordance with the law governing it (English law in the case at hand).[66] It is not certain whether this outcome is exceptional or part of a growing trend with a view to salvaging arbitral awards.

Case study: Disputes over the law of the arbitration clause

In the case of *C v D*[67] the parties had entered into a standard Bermuda form, entailing in the case at hand an insurance contract governed by New York law, with London designated as the seat of arbitration. The Bermuda form came about as a result of excessive monetary judgments in US courts, which litigants wished to avoid, albeit New York law in the field of insurance is generally perceived as more flexible

---

[65] *Case no 183/2004*, Supreme Cassation Court judgment no 717 (27 July 2005).
[66] See A. Ganev, Bulgaria, in *World Arbitration Reporter* (Juris, 2nd edition, 2010), 17.
[67] *C v D*, above note 63.

and best suited to the exigencies of insurance disputes.[68] During the course of the arbitral proceedings the insurer (respondent) argued that the arbitrator had acted in violation of his mandate by paying insufficient regard to the proper choice of law of the contract and that therefore the award should be vacated. While this defence would have been available under the procedural laws of New York[69] this was not the case with the 1996 English Arbitration Act. Understandably, it was crucial for the respondent to convince the Court of Appeal that the proper law of the contract (i.e. New York law) should also follow the arbitration clause. Longmore LJ dismissed this argument on what seem to be policy grounds, stating that:

> No doubt New York law has its own judicial remedies for want of jurisdiction and serious irregularity but it could scarcely be supposed that a party aggrieved by one part of an award could proceed in one jurisdiction and a party aggrieved by another part of an award could proceed in another jurisdiction. Similarly, in the case of a single complaint about an award, it could not be supposed that the aggrieved party could complain in one jurisdiction and the satisfied party be entitled to ask the other jurisdiction to declare its satisfaction with the award. There would be a serious risk of parties rushing to get the first judgment or of conflicting decisions which the parties cannot have contemplated.[70]

2.2.5 The law of the country of enforcement

The ultimate aim of the winning party is to enforce the award in a country where the losing party has sufficient assets. The losing party's assets may

---

[68] See R. Jacobs et al., *Liability Insurance in Commercial Arbitration: The Bermuda Form* (Hart, 2nd edition, 2009).

[69] The defence was 'manifest disregard of the law', which is not, however, among the four statutory grounds for vacating (setting aside) awards under s 10 of the US FAA, 9 U.S.C. § 1. In *Hall Street Associates LLC v Mattel Inc*, 128 S. Ct. 1396 (2008), the US Supreme Court intimated that although the courts cannot invent new grounds for vacating awards, manifest disregard of the law could fall within existing grounds under s 10. While some circuit courts have rejected the 'manifest disregard' defence as an independent ground, such as *Citigroup Global Markets Inc v Bacon* 562 F 3d 349 (5th Cir. 2009) and *Ramos-Santiago v United Parcel Serv.* 524 F 120 (1st Cir. 2008), others have argued the opposite. See *Dewan v Walia* 544 F App'x 240 (4th Cir. 2013) and *Stolt-Nielsen SA v AnimalFeeds Int'l Corp.* 548 F 3d 85 (2nd Cir. 2008). See also chapter 7 section 7.6.4 which deals with challenges against awards on points of law.

[70] *C v D*, above note 63, para 16.

be spread across several jurisdictions and hence enforcement may be sought in more than one country. Although the enforcement of foreign arbitral awards is regulated chiefly by a multilateral treaty, the 1958 New York Convention (as well as other regional conventions), this treaty allows member states to construe concepts such as public policy and arbitrability on the basis of their domestic law.[71] This should not be misunderstood as providing general authority to member states to restrict or otherwise inhibit the recognition and enforcement of foreign awards, particularly since it is undisputed that the 1958 New York Convention must be interpreted in accordance with international law as opposed to the law of the country of enforcement.[72]

However, the 1958 New York Convention does not define public policy, arbitrability or the requirements for the validity of the arbitration clause, thus leaving pertinent determinations to domestic law. Besides the general application of Article 31(1) of the Vienna Convention on the Law of Treaties 1969 (VCLT) the *travaux* of the 1958 New York Convention do not suggest that arbitrability and public policy must be construed from a dimension other than that prescribed under the *lex fori*.[73] Chapter 8 deals with the issue of public policy, but it suffices to mention here the French approach, which is exceptional, whereby international arbitral awards are treated as being unrelated to any particular legal order and therefore their validity is determined in accordance with the law of the country where recognition or enforcement is sought (i.e. French law).[74] In every case, it is important that arbitrators ensure the award's compatibility with the law of the countries where enforcement is sought, although admittedly this will depend on the nature of the dispute and the parties' prior contractual conduct.

In practice, arbitration-friendly nations and their courts construe the relevant concepts through a transnational lens with a view to eliminating procedural hurdles. We have already discussed how the Bulgarian Supreme Cassation Court dealt with a 'foreign award' rendered in England between

---

[71] Art V(2) 1958 New York Convention.

[72] See, for example, *Hebei Import and Export Corp v Polytek Engineering Co Ltd* [1999] 2 HKC 205. Such an interpretation is consistent with Art 31(1) of the 1969 VCLT, according to which a treaty shall be interpreted in good faith and in accordance with the ordinary meaning of its terms 'in their context and in light of its object and purpose'.

[73] See J. D. Fry, Désordre Public International under the New York Convention: Whither Truly International Public Policy, (2009) 8 *Chinese J Int'l L* 81; Wolff, above note 13, 380ff.

[74] *Société PT Putrabali Adyamulia v Société Rena Holding et Société Moguntia Est Spices*, French Court of Cassation judgment (29 June 2007), [2007] *Rev Arb* 517.

two Bulgarian nationals. In French law, domestic public policy rules are much broader than their international counterparts. As a result, violation of domestic public policy does not necessarily entail a violation of international public policy,[75] which in turn reduces many of the obstacles for the enforcement of foreign awards in the French legal order.

In recent years it has been queried whether the country of enforcement may impose conflicts of law requirements as these would ordinarily apply to the parties' agreement, despite the fact that these are not listed in the 1958 New York Convention. The opinion of this author is that this is not permissible. The US Court of Appeals for the Second Circuit has taken an antithetical position, relying on the *forum non conveniens* principle to dismiss a petition for enforcement of a Peruvian award because of its fundamentally Peruvian nature and public interest factors entrenched in the country's domestic law.[76] This is in line with what commentators describe as a deferential, albeit selective, stance to the decisions of seat courts setting aside arbitral awards on dubious grounds.[77] This deferential stance is also evident in the sphere of public policy. In *Honeywell v Meydan Group* the High Court in London upheld a Dubai International Arbitration Centre (DIAC) award against the owner of a racecourse in Dubai rejecting allegations that the underlying contract was procured through bribery and despite the fact that bribery proceedings were ongoing in Dubai.[78]

2.3 Treaties and customary international law

Multilateral treaties regulating international commercial arbitration deal primarily, if not exclusively, with the enforcement of foreign awards as well as the validity of arbitration agreements. The most significant and global (in terms of ratification) treaty of this nature is the 1958 New York Convention on the Recognition and Enforcement of Foreign Arbitral

---

[75] *SA Intrafor Cofor et Subtec Middle East Co v Cagnat*, Paris Court of Appeals judgment (12 March 1985), [1985] *Rev Arb* 299.

[76] *Figueiredo Ferraz e Engenharia de Projeto Ltda v Peru*, 635 F 3d 384 (2d Cir. 2011).

[77] See *TermoRio SA Esp & LeaseCo Group v Electranta SP et al*, 487 F 3d 928, which again applied the *forum non conveniens* argument; see contra, *Corporación Mexicana de Mantenimiento Integral v Pemex-Exploración y Producción* (SDNY 27 August 2013).

[78] *Honeywell v Meydan Group LLC* [2014] EWHC 1344 (TCC).

Awards.[79] Its aim is twofold: on the one hand member states are bound to recognise and enforce foreign awards (subject to a finite number of exceptions) while on the other they must also respect the validity of arbitration agreements, both pre-dispute and post-dispute. While this may seem self-evident, one must consider that because arbitration clauses look towards the future the laws of several countries regarded them until recently as speculative and as such prohibited them.[80] Several countries in South America and the Muslim world regarded speculative clauses or agreements as either offensive to their public policy or as otherwise void.[81]

The paradigm of the 1958 New York Convention was later followed by a number of regional treaties, such as the 1975 Inter-American Convention on International Commercial Arbitration (Panama Convention),[82] which went on to remove yet more barriers such as nationality requirements for arbitrators.[83] The Panama Convention complements the 1958 New York Convention in several ways. In one case it was employed by a US District Court in order to recognise and enforce an award set aside at the seat (Mexico) on the ground that the Convention provided US courts with discretion to confirm an award when the nullifying judgment violated the United States' basic notions of justice.[84] Other regional conventions, such as the 1983 Riyadh Convention on Judicial Cooperation between States of the Arab League have failed to make a significant impact

---

[79] Its predecessor was the 1927 Geneva Convention on the Execution of Foreign Arbitral Awards, which is still binding upon existing parties that have not yet ratified the 1958 New York Convention.

[80] In fact, the 1923 Geneva Protocol on Arbitration Clauses was meant to address this issue. This is still in force in several nations in their relations with countries that have not yet ratified the 1958 New York Convention. See Arts 35–40 of the 1998 Jersey (Channel Islands) Arbitration Law.

[81] Speculative contracts, known as *gharar fahish* (which may encompass arbitration clauses although in practice they are subject to a tacit exception) and interest-based foreign arbitral awards (as well as loan agreements to this effect) are specifically prohibited under Islamic law, but are not prohibited in all sharia-based nations. See Federal Supreme Court of Abu Dhabi, *case No 245/2000*, judgment (7 May 2000), which noted that the pressing international business environment necessitates the imposition of interest.

[82] The 1979 Inter-American Convention on Extra-territorial Validity of Foreign Judgments and Awards reinforces the Panama Convention by stipulating that it extends to awards dealing with civil, commercial and labour disputes.

[83] Art 2(1) Panama Convention.   [84] *Pemex* judgment, above note 77.

because of their obsession with particular rules (sharia-inspired) and their concomitant public policy attributes.[85] Even so, Gulf nations have either adopted the UNCITRAL Model Law (e.g. Bahrain) or have expressly removed many of the obstacles dictated by classical Islamic law, as is the case with the UAE progressive arbitral law and jurisprudence.

The Council of Europe, in addition to enforcement, has been concerned since the early 1960s with harmonising the arbitration laws of its member states in the same manner as this has been achieved in the field of civil jurisdiction. In 1961 it opened for signature the European Convention on International Commercial Arbitration and in 1966 the European Convention providing a Uniform Law on Arbitration. While the first of these was significant, the subject matter of both has largely been taken over by the UNCITRAL Model Law, which reflects global, as opposed to regional, consensus.[86] The Model Law will be discussed in more detail in the following section.

Unlike international commercial arbitration, which is only partly regulated by treaties, the very existence of investment arbitration is predicated on customary international law as well as treaty law. More specifically, multilateral treaties such as the 1965 Convention on the Settlement of Investment Disputes between States and Nationals of Other States (ICSID Convention), chapter 11 of the North American Free Trade Agreement (NAFTA) and the 1998 Energy Charter Treaty (ECT)[87] expressly provide for investment arbitration, as do also several free trade agreements (FTAs). In addition, the legal basis for investment arbitration (namely, arbitration between a state and a foreign private investor) has been found to exist in BITs despite the fact that the investor is not a party to the BIT. This is a significant departure from classical arbitration law, which otherwise requires an agreement between the parties to a dispute in order for arbitration to take place. Controversies have arisen with respect to the interpretation of Article 42(1) of the ICSID Convention, which stipulates that in the absence of a choice of law clause an investment tribunal 'shall apply the

---

[85] Art 37(e) of the Convention stipulates that arbitral awards are not to be recognised and enforced among signatory nations where any part of the award contradicts 'the provisions of the Islamic *sharia*, the public order or the rules of conduct of the requested party'.

[86] There exist other notable efforts to duplicate the work of the UNCITRAL Model Law at regional level, principally the Organisation for Harmonisation of African Law (OHADA) 1999 Uniform Act on Arbitration, which is widely ratified.

[87] Particularly Arts 26 and 27 ECT.

law of the contracting state party to the dispute ... and such rules of international law as may be applicable'. Where there is a conflict between a treaty (BIT or international investment agreement (IIA)) and the parties' contract, the tribunal will distinguish between disputes/violations arising from the treaty (and accordingly apply the governing law prescribed in that treaty) from disputes/violations arising from the contract (and accordingly apply the governing law prescribed there). Where there is an overlap between domestic and international law, it is suggested that investment tribunals may resolve the conflict on the basis of their competence-competence power and in the majority of cases general international law is preferred.[88]

Customary law consists of the fusion of sufficient and consistent state practice of several nations with the belief that such practice conforms to a legal obligation (*opinio juris*). Customary international law, although central in construing key investment concepts such as expropriation and the various types of treatment afforded to foreign investors, is also crucial in the arena of commercial arbitration. For one thing, customary law dictates that where states and state instrumentalities engage in commercial activities (*jure gestionis*) with foreign private actors they do not enjoy immunity from suit before foreign courts or arbitral tribunals.[89] As a result, default awards will still be validly rendered even if states fail to appear under claims of immunity. States are only entitled to immunity where the transaction in question was undertaken in a public, official, capacity (*jure imperii*). It has generally been recognised that states enjoy immunity from attachment proceedings irrespective of the commercial or public nature of the act.[90]

Moreover, when states are engaged in arbitral proceedings they may not invoke their internal law as justification for violating a rule of

---

[88] H. E. Kjos, *Applicable Law in Investor-State Arbitration: The Interplay between National and International Law* (Oxford University Press, 2013), 213ff. See, for example, *Compãnia del Desarrollo de Santa Elena SA v Costa Rica*, ICSID Award (17 February 2000), para 64; *Enron Corp and Ponderosa Assets LP v Argentina*, ICSID Decision on Jurisdiction (14 January 2004), paras 206–9.

[89] Arts 10(1) and 17, UN Convention on Jurisdictional Immunities of States and their Property.

[90] Arts 18 and 19, UN Convention on Jurisdictional Immunities of States and their Property; but see *Republic of Argentina v NML Capital Ltd*, 695 F 3d 201 *affirmed*, where the US Supreme Court rejected the argument that worldwide post-judgment (or award) discovery orders violate the US Federal Sovereign Immunities Act (FSIA) and by extension customary international law; see also chapter 8 section 8.6.

international law, including a contractual obligation with a private entity.[91] National courts and arbitral tribunals have held, for example, that such non-reliance on internal law applies even with respect to peremptory rules of public policy such as the prohibition of usury[92] or the sovereign authority to impose taxes.[93]

2.4 General principles of law

General principles, which may on occasion overlap with customary international law, encompass legal rules and principles that are common to the majority of domestic legal orders and which operate in the same or similar manner. In this sense, general principles are among the primary sources of international law in accordance with Article 38(1)(c) of the ICJ Statute. For the purposes of arbitration they include, among others, the principles of estoppel, that of loyalty between the parties, prohibition of abuse of procedure and the maxim *nemo commodum capere potest de sua propria injuria*.[94] In the practice of commercial arbitration, arbitral tribunals are compelled to derive general principles where the parties have provided them with relevant authority and it is commonplace for the courts to refer to foreign jurisprudence or scholarly writings affirming these principles in order to confirm the universal nature of a particular principle.[95] In an earlier section dealing with the governing law of contracts the reader will recall that in the context of the Libyan nationalisation cases the default option in the parties' choice of law clause was general

---

[91] Art 27 VCLT; Art 2(2) Spanish AA; see also *Metalclad Corp v Mexico*, Award (30 August 2000), para 70 (although this is an investment award).

[92] In *Anaconda-Iran Inc v Iran*, Award No ITL 65–167-3 (10 December 1986), para 145, Iran's claim that the payment of interest on the award would be tantamount to usury and hence contrary to Islamic law was rejected as being irrelevant. The tribunal held that international law was the applicable law.

[93] *Ecuador v Occidental Exploration & Production Co.* (*OEPC*) [2006] EWHC 345 (Comm), where an English court (not an investment tribunal) looked to the tax exclusion stipulations of Art X of the 1993 US–Ecuador BIT rather than Ecuadorian claims that tax was not arbitrable under its laws.

[94] See A. Zimmermann et al., *The Statute of the International Court of Justice* (Oxford University Press, 2nd edition, 2013), 903–8.

[95] In *Barnmore Demolition and Civil Engineering Ltd v Alandale Logistics Ltd and Others*, case no 2010/5910P, judgment (11 November 2010), the Irish High Court, in determining the appropriate standard of review as to the existence of an arbitration agreement made use of well-known international academic literature.

principles of international law.[96] One of the chief aims of model laws is to codify these general principles in their particular spheres of interest.

2.5 Model laws

Throughout this book significant reference is made to the UNCITRAL Model Law on International Commercial Arbitration, initially adopted in 1985 and subsequently amended in 2006. Model laws are not treaties, hence not binding or amenable to ratification by states.[97] Nonetheless, they are adopted by inter-governmental organisations with input from state representatives and their adoption is accompanied by official *travaux*. Their objective is to harmonise domestic law and practice in a particular area of importance to transnational commerce. They are typically drafted in the format of a statute in order that states may adapt them in their domestic legal order with as few modifications as possible. In fact, a number of countries have incorporated the Model Law verbatim, without any changes. The Model Law forms an integral part of the 2010 Irish Arbitration Act. In accordance with section 6 of the Act, the Model Law has the force of law in Ireland, and under section 8(1) and (2) when applying the Act and the Model Law Irish courts should base their interpretation on the *travaux* of the Model Law. Unlike other treaties, particularly those prepared over the course of several decades by the UN International Law Commission, model laws reflect best practices and do not exhibit any radical departures. It is no wonder, therefore, that non-Model Law jurisdictions share most of the features of the Model Law. The key benefit underlying the adoption of the Model Law as a domestic arbitration statute is that it renders the country in question arbitration-friendly and allows for greater reciprocity.

2.6 Institutional rules

Where the parties choose an arbitral institution, as opposed to ad hoc arbitration, such as the International Chamber of Commerce (ICC) or the

---

[96] See section 2.2 of this chapter.
[97] Another prominent example is the Organization for Economic Cooperation and Development (OECD) Model Tax Convention on Income and on Capital; in the USA, the Uniform Arbitration Act (UAA), a model law addressed to states, has been adopted by over twenty states.

Stockholm Chamber of Commerce (SCC), they are doing much more than simply agreeing on a venue for the arbitration. Rather, they are consenting to be bound by the arbitral institution's rules, which are equivalent to the rules laid down in civil procedure codes for the conduct of civil proceedings. Although exceptional, the parties may agree that the arbitration be administered by one institution but governed by the rules of another institution.[98] These institutional rules regulate in detail the arbitral process from the moment the arbitration clause is triggered through the submission of a notice of claim up to the issuance of the award. Naturally, they do not supersede the mandatory provisions of the *lex arbitri*, as is the case for example with due process guarantees or the right of the parties to challenge awards.[99]

Although institutional rules do not constitute formal law they are binding by their incorporation in the parties' arbitration agreement. As a result, no party can unilaterally waive the application of the rules once chosen and the courts of the seat are bound to enforce them as a reflection of party autonomy.[100] It is not surprising, therefore, that arbitral institutions regularly revise these rules in accordance with the suggestions put forward by scholars and practitioners. Revisions also often occur because the institutions realise gaps in their rules which affect the parties in arbitral proceedings.

Moreover, practitioners fluent in one particular set of institutional rules tend to prefer settling disputes under the rules of that institution as opposed to those of another. This of course makes sense because one needs time to be acquainted with a new set of rules and diversity is not particularly welcomed in the fast pace work of international counsel. As a result, given that most cases are handled by particular arbitral institutions, which in turn attract the top arbitrators, the relevant institutional rules have assumed an authoritative role that resonates (and is otherwise reflected) in the work of other arbitral tribunals.

UNCITRAL has adopted its own set of arbitral rules. These follow the pattern of other institutional rules, but since UNCITRAL is not an arbitral institution the intention was that they be adopted by the parties to

---

[98] As was the case in *Insigma Technology Co Ltd v Alstom Technology Ltd*, Singapore Court of Appeals judgment (2 June 2009), [2009] SGCA 24.

[99] See also chapter 1 section 1.7.3.

[100] *Tecnimont SPA v JP & Avax*, French Court of Cassation judgment (25 June 2014). The case at hand concerned the 30-day rule for challenging arbitrators under the ICC Rules.

regulate ad hoc arbitrations (as in the case of the Iran–USA claims tribunal) or otherwise be employed to substitute the rules of other institutions.[101] Where the parties and their counsel are not experienced in any particular institutional rules it is not uncommon to stipulate that a future dispute will be subject to UNCITRAL arbitration, which is merely a reference to the UNCITRAL Arbitration Rules and not institutional arbitration.

Practical need for revision of institutional rules

In one case, the parties had chosen the Danish Institute of Arbitration for their institutional arbitration but its rules were silent on evidentiary procedures. Equally silent was the 2005 Danish Arbitration Act, which grants a broad flexibility to arbitrators regarding the admissibility, relevance and weight of evidence. Given the lack of clarity one of the parties requested the courts for guidance as a preliminary issue even before the arbitration commenced. The Danish Supreme Court upheld the validity of the petition (lack of legal certainty)[102] and the Danish Institute subsequently revised its rules and incorporated a section on evidence. It does not, therefore, come as a surprise that some courts rely on the rulings of arbitral institutions by which they interpret their rules in order to construe gaps or ambiguities in the formal law.

2.7 Soft law instruments in international arbitration

The institutional rules examined in the previous section are all soft law instruments, as is also the UNCITRAL Model Law. The difference with other soft law is that institutional rules are binding on the parties because of their incorporation by reference in their arbitration clause or

---

[101] See also UNCITRAL Notes on Organising Arbitral Proceedings.

[102] *Vestas Wind Systems A/S v ABB A/S, Danish Supreme Court judgment* (13 January 2012). Had the party's request been found to violate the primacy afforded to arbitration as a result of the arbitration clause it would have stayed the request and the issue in question would have been settled by the tribunal once constituted.

submission agreement. Soft law instruments that are not incorporated by reference are not therefore contractually binding and hence it is queried whether their application in arbitral proceedings is justified as a form of trade usage, custom or best practice. Much like general international law, soft law instruments are an important component in the field of international arbitration.[103] However, unlike international law whereby soft law originates from inter-governmental bodies, such as the UN, their counterparts in arbitration, save for the Model Law, are largely the products of private initiatives, such as those from the International Bar Association (IBA). This demonstrates that the stakeholders of international arbitration (counsel, arbitrators, arbitral institutions and trade or industrial actors) have achieved a considerable degree of self-regulation which rivals that of the banking and construction industries. This is all the more so given that the available soft law is extensively applied by the parties in arbitral proceedings. The vast majority is procedural in character and qualifies as *lex mercatoria* in the same manner as other substantive soft law or trade usages, as is the case with the International Federation of Consulting Engineers (FIDIC) rules.

Among its many rules and guidelines on arbitration, the IBA developed in 2010 a set of Rules on the Taking of Evidence in International Arbitration with the aim that they be used in situations where no other evidence rules exist (e.g. ad hoc arbitrations under UNCITRAL rules) or in order to supplement existing laws and regulations and indeed to harmonise the taking of evidence in international arbitration.[104] It is not surprising that national courts routinely refer to the IBA Rules in order to assess best practices and decide matters not covered by local statutes.

Local courts have started to examine soft law even if the issue in question is otherwise covered by the *lex arbitri*. The Austrian Supreme Court (*Oberster Gerichtshof*) was asked to set aside an award because it subsequently came to the attention of the claimant that one of the arbitrators was a member of the supervisory board of the respondent's

---

[103] The term soft law refers to instruments that are not meant to be binding agreements subject to any signature or ratification. Although positivists generally reject the idea of soft law by arguing that there is either hard law or no law at all, the majority of scholars contend that soft law serves to accommodate the complexities arising from the binary conception of law. See J. D'Aspremont, Softness in International Law: A Self-Serving Quest for New Legal Materials, (2008) 19 *EJIL* 1075.

[104] For a detailed analysis of the IBA Rules, see chapter 6.

grandparent company. The Court decided the matter as to whether the arbitrator's conflicts of interest were so severe as to outweigh legal certainty on the basis of the IBA Guidelines on Conflicts of Interest in International Arbitration, ultimately dismissing the claim.[105]

---

[105] Austrian Supreme Court (OGH), *case no 20b112/12b*, judgment (17 June 2013).

3 The agreement to arbitrate

3.1 Introduction

An agreement to arbitrate is the fundamental premise for any arbitration and it is no wonder that the early treaties on arbitration, particularly the 1923 Geneva Protocol, focused on ensuring the validity of arbitral clauses worldwide in addition to the enforceability of subsequent awards.[1] In order

---

[1] See also Art II(1) 1958 New York Convention.

for a dispute to be validly submitted to arbitration an agreement is required between the disputing parties; not a contract, merely a binding *agreement*.[2] The concept of *agreement* is broader than the form or instrument within which it is recorded, which, other than contracts, may (if the pertinent domestic law allows) include trust deeds, corporate articles of agreement, bills of lading and even oral agreements. In the majority of legal systems agreements are usually synonymous with contracts and most of the afore-mentioned instruments share many of the characteristics of contracts. What is required in every case is clear and unequivocal consent to submit existing or future disputes to arbitration. With the exception perhaps of consumer disputes, the majority of nations now recognise the validity of pre-dispute arbitration clauses in main contracts or other agreements, in addition to post-dispute arbitration agreements.

The chapter will set out the various parameters and peculiarities of arbitration agreements and will then provide an overview of the instru-ments in which they are contained, including in what manner an agree-ment to arbitrate may be derived implicitly through contract interpretation or conduct. We shall then examine the scope of arbitration agreements, their validity and their application to third parties. We will round up the discussion with a brief assessment of multi-party arbitrations and the principle of confidentiality.

3.2 Pre-dispute and post-dispute agreements

Two types of agreements exist in law and practice by which two or more disputing parties submit their difference to arbitration, namely, pre-dispute arbitration clauses and post-dispute arbitration agreements, other-wise known as *compromis* or submission agreements.[3] An arbitration clause is simply a clause, among many, in an agreement stipulating that in the event of a future dispute the parties *shall* have recourse to arbitra-tion. Given that the eventuality of a future dispute is merely a speculation at the time when the arbitration clause is inserted, it is considered a speculative agreement in its own right. As has already been mentioned in the previous chapter, several countries have traditionally viewed – and a few still do – speculative contracts as being null or void and have

---

[2] Art 7 [both options] UNCITRAL Model Law.   [3] Art 7(1) [option I] UNCITRAL Model Law.

accordingly encompassed arbitration clauses within this regime of nullity. A very small number of US states, such as West Virginia, continue to forbid pre-dispute arbitration clauses that are akin to adhesion contracts, on the basis that the FAA allows the use of contractual defences under State law,[4] which in such circumstances finds the pre-dispute clauses in question unconscionable.[5] US State practice seems sensible,[6] but the (admittedly dying) practice of considering all pre-dispute clauses as void on the ground that they are speculative is problematic and it is not surprising that the 1958 New York Convention clearly obliges contracting states to abandon this practice as does also the Panama Convention. It is obvious that if states could unilaterally prohibit or nullify pre-dispute arbitration clauses by reference to their domestic legal order, the system of international arbitration would come to a halt. It is for this reason that the doctrine of separability should be viewed as a rule of customary international law (in the case at hand applicable to the relations of private parties), whereby even if the main agreement is considered null and void under one or more applicable legal systems (i.e. the law of the seat or the governing law of the contract) the arbitration clause survives and, assuming it is not itself null or void, it may validly trigger arbitral proceedings.[7] From a practical perspective, pre-dispute arbitration clauses are by far the most prevalent form of arbitration agreement.

Where a dispute arises and the parties have not incorporated an arbitration clause in their existing agreement they can still have recourse to arbitration provided they enter into a (new) agreement to arbitrate their difference. This new, post-dispute, agreement will be distinct from their original agreement and will in all likelihood be far more elaborate as compared to a short arbitration clause because the parties are now well aware of the dispute and must agree on the details of the arbitration. Thus,

---

[4] As sustained by the US Supreme Court in *AT & T Mobility LLC v Concepcion* (2011) 131 S Ct 1740.

[5] See, for example, *Brown v Genesis HealthCare Corp et al.*, 724 S E 2d 250 (2011).

[6] It is instructive that the State of Alabama, which applies the same unconscionability defences to pre-dispute arbitration clauses, has recently adopted an arbitration statute which makes it clear such clauses are generally allowed. Section 1(4) of the Alabama 2014 Arbitration Act, reads that the 'term "enforceable agreement to arbitrate" means an agreement, or a contractual term, to submit to arbitration one or more existing or subsequent controversies between or among the parties to the agreement or contract that is valid and enforceable under the laws of this state or the United States of America'.

[7] Art 16(1) UNCITRAL Model Law.

whereas an arbitration clause typically stipulates the parties' chosen seat and arbitral institution, a submission agreement may well specify: a) the exact nature of the dispute and the procedural rules available to the arbitrators; b) the governing law, which may have changed since the original agreement was drafted; c) the names of other willing parties that have subsequently become parties to the original agreement (such as contractors, subcontractors, insurers through subrogation, etc.); d) detailed rules or guidelines on ethics; e) distinct institutional rules and soft law, such as rules on the taking of evidence.

3.3 An agreement in writing

Article 7(2) of the UNCITRAL Model Law points out that an arbitration agreement must be in writing (the so-called *formal validity* of the agreement to arbitrate).[8] In practice, this formal validity requirement is now generally understood to encompass any express recording of the parties' intention to submit their dispute to arbitration in such a way that leaves no room for doubt. It is not merely a matter of proof (*ad probationem*) but at least in principle a condition for the validity of the arbitration agreement (*ad validitatem*).[9] It should be noted that despite the clarity inherent in the requirement of a written agreement the practice of nations is nothing but uniform, although there are several areas of convergence. A ten-year study by UNCITRAL on the application of the formal validity requirement under Article II(2) of the 1958 New York Convention revealed several divergences.[10] It was discovered, among others, that some states enforce awards only when the parties have signed the contract containing the arbitration clause or the *compromis*,[11] whereas others exclude oral agreements even if

---

[8] As does also Art II(2) 1958 New York Convention.

[9] Art 1226 of the Luxembourg NCCP provides three alternative (written) forms for the submission agreement, namely: as minutes before the arbitrators, in the form of a notarised document, or as a private agreement.

[10] UNCITRAL Working Group II (Arbitration), Compilation of Comments by Governments, Note by the Secretariat, UN Doc A/CN.9/661 (6 May 2008). See S. I. Strong, What Constitutes an Agreement in Writing in International Commercial Arbitration? Conflicts between the New York Convention and the Federal Arbitration Act, (2012) 48 *Stanford JIL* 47.

[11] UNCITRAL Working Group II (Arbitration), Preparation of Uniform Provisions on Written Form for Arbitration Agreements, Note by the Secretariat, UN Doc A/CN.9/WG.II/WP.139 (14 Dec 2005), para 12.

subsequently ratified by the parties, as well as submission agreements based on trade usages.[12] Articles 7(3) and (4) of the UNCITRAL Model Law go on to specify that:

(3) An arbitration agreement is in writing if its content is recorded in any form, whether or not the arbitration agreement or contract has been concluded orally, by conduct, or by other means.

(4) The requirement that an arbitration agreement be in writing is met by an electronic communication if the information contained therein is accessible so as to be useable for subsequent reference; "electronic communication" means any communication that the parties make by means of data messages; "data message" means information generated, sent, received or stored by electronic, magnetic, optical or similar means, including, but not limited to, electronic data interchange (EDI), electronic mail, telegram, telex or telecopy.

This extensive definition of an arbitration agreement in writing was intended to bring it into line with the 1996 UNCITRAL Model Law on Electronic Commerce and the 2005 United Nations Convention on the Use of Electronic Communications in International Contracts.[13] Electronic signatures must be distinguished from digital signatures. An electronic signature is anything in electronic form which may serve as indisputable evidence that the signing entity intended its signature as producing legal effect. An electronic signature is generated by a computer or a computer-like device, a particular form of which is a digital signature.[14] It is now accepted by the majority of nations that an agreement recorded by electronic means of communication is valid.[15] Arbitral legislation based on the UNCITRAL Model Law either explicitly recognises electronic signatures or at least

---

[12] Ibid., para 13; for a discussion of trade usages (otherwise known as *lex mercatoria*) in arbitration, see chapter 2 section 2.2.2.1.

[13] UN GAOR 51st session, Supp No 17, UN Doc A/51/17 (1996), annex I; UNGA Res 60/21 (23 November 2005).

[14] A digital signature comprises 'data appended to, or a cryptographic transformation of, a data unit that allows a recipient of the data to prove the source and integrity of the data unit'. See S. Mason, *Electronic Signatures in Law* (Cambridge University Press, 3rd edition, 2012), 189.

[15] *Chloe Z. Fishing Co v Odyssey Re (London) Ltd*, 109 F Supp 2d 1236, 1250 (S.D. Cal. 2000); *Great Offshore Ltd v Iranian Offshore Engineering & Construction Company*, Indian Supreme Court judgment (25 August 2008) [2008]14 SCC (India) 240; *Oonc Lines Limited v Sino-American Trade Advancement Co Ltd*, Hong Kong Court of First Instance judgment (2 February 1994), [1994] HKCFI 193.

recommends them where the parties' agreement is recorded by electronic means.[16] Under Czech law it is recommended that parties entering into an arbitration agreement by email sign the communication by electronic signatures, lest the clause be declared null and void.[17]

We shall see in the following sections that the requirement of an agreement in writing must be understood broadly and should not be subject to formalistic interpretations. The fundamental criterion is a clear record of the parties' intention to arbitrate. The parties must ensure that the form of their agreement to arbitrate be consistent with the general law applicable to the instrument of their choice (e.g. contract, trust or other). The Swiss Federal Supreme Court, although generally inclined towards substance rather than form, has emphasised that arbitration agreements must be interpreted in accordance with general principles of contract interpretation.[18]

3.3.1 Oral agreements

The difficulty with oral agreements to arbitrate is that they provide a limited degree of legal certainty, particularly in the absence of any verifiable record of the agreement. In such cases, how does one prove or disprove the existence of an agreement to arbitrate? In the case of written agreements the signature of the parties suffices, whereas as regards oral agreements the existence of the agreement would need to be confirmed by reference to witnesses and other circumstantial evidence, although this is also true of written agreements lacking signatures. Many legal systems that strictly adhere to form are not willing to accept oral agreements,[19] whereas others give little credence to oral agreements, particularly as concerns important legal relationships and transactions.

---

[16] s 126(a) of the German Civil Code (BGB) which concerns electronic signatures and is thus integral to the construction of the 'written' requirement under Art 1031(1) Code of Civil Procedure (ZPO) states that: (1) if the statutory written form is to be substituted by electronic form, the author of the statement must add his name to the statement and append a qualified electronic signature; (2) in the case of a contract, the parties must each electronically sign a document identical in wording in the manner prescribed in subsection 1.

[17] This is in accordance with Act No 227/2000 on Electronic Signatures.

[18] *Case 4A_438/2013*, judgment (27 February 2014).

[19] Art 9(2) of the 2012 Saudi Arbitration Law expressly states that anything other than a written agreement to arbitrate is void.

Even so, Article 7(3) of the UNCITRAL Model Law recognises the possibility of oral agreements to arbitrate, in addition to the strict written form. In such cases, the verification of the agreement is subject to the civil evidence rules of the contract's governing law or the law of the arbitration agreement (if different from the governing law). Those national legal systems that accept oral arbitration agreements do so in three alternative ways. The first, exemplified by Danish law, implicitly allows oral arbitration agreements as long as the parties' intentions can be established with sufficient certainty.[20] The second expressly allows oral agreements, provided there is some sort of written record, such as an exchange of emails or a subsequent agreement between the parties.[21] The third concerns oral agreements confirmed by conduct and usage. Article 6(3)(2) of the Croatian Arbitration Law, for example, states that where a party 'communicates to the other a written communication referring to an arbitration agreement concluded earlier orally and the other party fails to object in time, such failure may be considered an acceptance of the offer according to acceptable usages in relevant transactions'. The oral character of the agreement, where permitted, need not only concern the existence of the agreement itself, but also other related conditions of a written agreement, such as the parties' agreement on time limits, the person of the arbitrators and others, as is the case in Swedish law.[22]

3.3.2 Incorporation by conduct or common usage

Article 7(3) of the Model Law expressly refers to arbitration agreements concluded 'by conduct' without, however, any further elaboration. By way of illustration, it is standard practice in the harbour towing industry for the towing boat to haul its clients without drawing up a contract as this would be wholly impractical, particularly since towing operates on a rolling basis and one does not know who their next client will be. It may be implicit in such conduct/transaction (assuming it is recognised under the laws of the

---

[20] O. Spiermann, National Report for Denmark (2009), in J. Paulsson (ed.), *International Handbook on Commercial Arbitration* (Kluwer, 1984, Supp no 57, 2009), 7.

[21] Art 7(4) of the 1999 Greek Law on International Commercial Arbitration; equally s 2(1) of the 2010 Irish Arbitration Act (by reference to the Model Law); Art 9(3) of the 2003 Spanish Arbitration Act (by implication).

[22] K Hobér, *International Commercial Arbitration in Sweden* (Oxford University Press, 2011), 95.

coastal state) that any dispute arising between the parties will be submitted to arbitration as a result of common usage. In this case, it is the conduct (towing) that implicitly gives rise to the arbitration agreement. Alternatively, one may claim that the existence of an arbitration agreement in the parties' conduct is the result of common usage inherent in the conduct at hand. Section 1031(2) of the German ZPO provides that an agreement in writing is deemed to exist if in accordance with 'common usage' the arbitration clause is considered to be part of that document.

3.3.3 Incorporation by conduct-based estoppel

Before examining this heading in more detail, it should be explained that estoppel is a procedural rule (and an evidentiary one at that) whereby a person is precluded from denying or relying on a fact, either because it has been proved elsewhere or because the person has accepted or denied the fact by his very conduct (e.g. through a promise or consistent practice). A species of *conduct* is the parties' participation in arbitral proceedings without having complained at the first possible instance (*limine litis*) that no written agreement exists. Such conduct-based estoppel makes a dispute over a written agreement redundant where the party disputing its existence has freely participated in the arbitration without raising a defence.[23] Article 7(5) of the UNCITRAL Model Law expressly states that 'an arbitration agreement is in writing if it is contained in an exchange of statements of claim and defence in which the existence of an agreement is alleged by one party and not denied by another'.[24] From a legal point of view conduct-based estoppel is also treated as a waiver of litigation in favour of arbitration.[25] Alternatively, the parties may record their agreement in the minutes of the tribunal at its first hearing.[26]

French courts have also admitted an alternative form of conduct-based estoppel. They generally assume a 'common intent to arbitrate' where one

---

[23] *Slaney v International Amateur Athletics Association*, 244 F 3d 580, 591 (7th Cir. 2001); *Golshani v Iran*, French Court of Cassation judgment (6 July 2005), [2005] 302 *Bull Civ* 252.

[24] See also Art 5(4) of the 1994 Hungarian Arbitration Act.

[25] Luxembourg District Court judgment no 1115/2007 (24 April 2007); *Case no 3-2-1-38-02*, Estonian Supreme Court judgment (28 March 2002).

[26] Art 2(2) of the 2002 Slovak Arbitration Act.

of the parties has by its silence accepted arbitration, particularly where there is a history of consistent and repeated practice by the parties to arbitration in successive contracts, even if the disputed contract in question contains no arbitration clause.[27] Such conduct-based estoppel has been confirmed by the courts of Hong Kong,[28] but rejected by Canadian courts on the basis that tacit assent cannot be arbitrarily presumed through other proof of positive action.[29] Equally, in English law, silence is not considered an acceptance of offer.[30]

3.3.4 Incorporation by reference

Article 7(6) of the UNCITRAL Model Law stipulates that 'the reference in a contract to any document containing an arbitration clause constitutes an arbitration agreement in writing, provided that the reference is such as to make that clause part of the contract'. A and B (a bank) enter into a loan agreement that does not contain an arbitration clause but specifically refers to the bank's standard terms of business as being binding upon the parties. Party A should have read the standard terms carefully because they oblige the parties to submit future disputes arising from their loan contract to arbitration, despite the fact that A has not specifically signed the bank's standard terms. In *Kastrup Trae-Aluvinduet A/S (Denmark) v Aluwood Concepts Ltd (Ireland)*, the Irish High Court held that an arbitration agreement had been validly incorporated into the contract between the parties by reference to standard conditions and that it was irrelevant that the other party did not have a copy of the conditions to which the contract referred.[31] It is generally accepted that the instrument incorporated by reference need not be an agreement

---

[27] *Van Dijk* case, Paris Court of Appeals judgment (18 March 1983).

[28] *Hissan Trading Co Ltd v Orkin Shipping Corporation*, Hong Kong Court of First Instance judgment (8 September 1992), [1992] HKCFI 286.

[29] *Achilles(USA) v Plastics Dura Plastics (1977) ltée/Ltd*, [2006] QCCA 1523; but see a contrary approach in *Ferguson Bros of St Thomas v Manyan Inc*, Ontario Superior Court of Justice judgment (27 May 1999), [1999] OJ No 1887, where it was held that a cheque referring to an invoice amounted to a record of the issuer's consent to arbitration, given that this was inserted in a contractual offer to which the issuer had heretofore not replied in writing.

[30] *Felthouse v Bindley*, [1862] 6 LT 85.

[31] *Kastrup Trae-Aluvinduet A/S (Denmark) v Aluwood Concepts Ltd (Ireland)*, case no 129 MCA, High Court judgment (13 November 2009), citing *Credit Suisse Financial Products v Societe General d' Enterprises*, [1997] CLC 168.

previously concluded by the parties. It may just as well be one of the parties' standard terms or an instrument to which none of the parties has any other relationship.[32]

A bill of lading, which may include an arbitration clause, is a significant paradigm for understanding incorporation by reference. A bill of lading is typically signed by the master of the vessel and according to Article 3(3) of the Hague-Visby Rules the bill is signed by either the carrier or the master of the vessel or the agent of the carrier. As a result, the arbitration clause, because of the doctrine of incorporation, binds the holder of the bill of lading, even though the bill of lading does not bear his or her signature. Article 7(6) of the Greek LICA subjects disputes arising from the bill of lading to the arbitration clause contained in the carriage of goods contract if there is express reference in the bill of lading to the charter party.[33] However, this principle does not apply to all contracts, particularly those with a loose connection even if entered by the same parties. Where there are multiple agreements between the same parties incorporation by reference should be viewed as applicable only where the agreements in question form part of a single economic transaction. Accordingly, the Coimbra Court of Appeal ordered a dispute over three related contracts to be heard by state courts when only one of the contracts included an arbitration agreement.[34] In the case at hand, the Court of Appeals could not be certain that the parties intended to submit disputes arising from all three agreements to arbitration; clearly a matter of poor drafting.

Not all UNCITRAL Model Law-based statutes accept incorporation by reference, although this is exceptional. Under Bulgarian law, a merchant is deemed tacitly to have accepted an offer by another party with which the merchant is in a long-term relationship if the offer is not rejected immediately.[35] However, such a tacit acceptance is not deemed to encompass the arbitration clause included in the offer, as the written form is not considered to have been complied with.[36] In most cases there is a

---

[32] See *Thyssen Canada Ltd v Mariana (The)*, Canadian Court of Appeal judgment (22 March 2000), [2000] 3 FC 398; *Fai Tak Engineering Co Ltd v Sui Chong Construction & Engineering Co Ltd*, Hong Kong District Court judgment (22 June 2009), [2009] HKDC 141.

[33] Equally, Art 6(3)(2) of the 2001 Croatian Arbitration Law; Art 10(5) of the 2008 Slovenian Arbitration Law.

[34] *S, LDA and MJ v A, SA and R SA*, case no 477/11.8TBACN.C1, Coimbra Court of Appeal judgment (19 December 2012).

[35] Art 292(1), Law on Commerce.

[36] A. Alexiev, National Report for Bulgaria, in J. Paulsson (ed.), *International Handbook on Commercial Arbitration* (Kluwer Law International 1984, Supplement No 61, September

presumption that mere reference to the general conditions also encompasses the arbitration clause therein, even if not explicitly stipulated by the parties.[37] Exceptionally, the Singapore High Court has taken the view that the parties must expressly refer to the arbitration clause in the incorporated instrument.[38]

Arbitration in flow-through clauses

In the construction industry it is common for the main contractor to agree with his subcontractor that the latter shall be liable to the owner of the project with respect to the specific work of the subcontractor as stipulated in the design documents (plans and specifications). However, some flow-through (of liability) clauses are drafted in a manner that extends the subcontractor's liability to works not undertaken by him and which are described in the main contractor's agreement with the owner. In such unfortunate cases the subcontractor succeeds the general contractor in the agreement's arbitration clause. In *Maxum Foundations Inc v Salus Corp* the subcontract provided that:

To the extent applicable to, or arising in connection with, the Work, the subcontractor shall be bound by, and expressly assumes for the benefit of the contractor, all obligations and liabilities which the contract documents impose upon the contractor.

The court could only conclude that the subcontract had effectively incorporated the arbitration clause of the main contract.[39]

2010), 8; equally, Ruling of the Supreme Court of Slovakia, file No 2, 245/2010 (30 November 2011), although this ruling has been severely criticised by Slovak commentators.

[37] Athens Court of Appeal judgment 7195/2007; *Skandia International Insurance Company and Mercantile & General Reinsurance Company and others*, Bermuda Supreme Court judgment (21 January 1994), [1994] Bda LR 30; *Lief Investments Pty Limited v Conagra International Fertiliser Company* [1998] NSWSC 481; *Pueblo Film Distribution Hungary K.F.T. (Hungary) v Laurenfilm S.A.*, Spanish Supreme Court judgment (31 May 2005), *rec. 743/2003*.

[38] See *Concordia Agritrading Pte. Ltd v Cornelder Hoogewerff*, Singapore High Court judgment (13 October 1999), [1999] 3 SLR 618, although it is not unlikely that this decision may be reversed if a test case were to come along.

[39] *Maxum Foundations Inc v Salus Corp* 779 F 2d 974 (4th Cir. 1985).

3.4 Types of instruments containing arbitration clauses

Two entities that wish to resolve future disputes by means of arbitration are free to choose from a range of legal instruments in order to declare their intent to arbitrate, provided that the law governing the arbitration agreement allows them to employ such instrument. In the following sections we shall examine the inclusion of arbitration clauses in contracts (although, as already stated, the agreement to arbitrate is in most cases itself a contract), trusts, corporate articles of agreement (or corporate by-laws) and testamentary wills.

3.4.1 Contracts

Contracts constitute the most common form of legal instrument containing the parties' agreement to arbitrate. In practice, post-dispute agreements are unlikely to be recorded in any form other than contracts. Contracts share many common features among all nations and there are now many common principles[40] or standardised contracts in diverse fields such as construction and procurement. Even so, there may well exist several differences in substance or form across nations despite the best of harmonisation efforts. Polish civil law, for example, does not view mere agreements lacking the qualities of contracts as binding and enforceable. This is also the case in English law. However, English contract law distinguishes between three types of contractual clauses, namely conditions, warranties and innominate terms. A *condition*, unlike a *warranty*, is fundamental to a contract and hence if breached the innocent party may repudiate the contract and claim damages.[41] *Innominate* terms concern the effect of the breach, whereby if found to have substantially deprived the innocent party of the benefits of the contract as a whole the contract is deemed terminated.[42]

Ultimately, the arbitration clause and the post-dispute submission agreement must conform to their appropriate contract law, in which case

---

[40] See, for example, the so-called principles of European contract law (PECL) and the UN Convention on Contracts for the International Sale of Goods.

[41] See, for example, *Kuwait Rock Co v AMN Bulkcarriers Inc* [2013] EWHC 865 (Comm), where clauses allowing ship owners to withdraw their vessels upon late payment of hire were described as conditions.

[42] *Hong Kong Fir Shipping v Kawasaki Kisen Kaisha* [1962] 2 QB 26.

form may play a crucial role. By way of illustration, Article 548(2) of the Romanian CCP stipulates that if a contract concerns a dispute connected with the transfer of a property right and/or the creation of another right *in rem* related to immovable assets, the arbitration agreement must be authenticated by a notary public under the sanction of absolute nullity. Hence, even if the parties record their agreement to arbitrate in a standardised contract there is no assurance that this will be valid under the law governing the contract or the arbitration clause therein. Other nations take a less formalistic approach to the arbitration agreement. Swiss courts have held that the signatures of all parties are not required provided that the agreement was actually concluded.[43]

3.4.2 Trusts

Trusts typically involve an agreement between the owner of property (the settlor) transferring said property to a trustee for the benefit of present or future beneficiaries. In the common law this triangular relationship is typically governed by a trust deed (although there can be trusts without a written agreement), which, however, only encompasses the settlor and the trustee, even if as a result of the deed the trustee (who now holds legal title over the property) owes fiduciary and other duties to the beneficiaries. The beneficiaries are clearly third parties to the deed and ordinarily (if contract rules were applicable) would be excluded from the ambit of an arbitration clause incorporated therein.[44] Civil law nations, on the other hand, view the formation of trust vehicles from the point of view of contract (as is the case with the *treuhand*)[45] and hence find few legal obstacles to accepting arbitration clauses in trust instruments, viewing them as contracts for the benefit of third parties. In any event, jurisdictions whose economies are driven by trusts (but also others), view beneficiaries as parties to arbitration clauses in trust instruments. Thus, section 63 of the 2007 Guernsey Trusts

---

[43] *Compagnie de Navigation et Transports SA v MSC Mediterranean Shipping Co SA*, BGE 121 II 38; equally *Case no 2-05-23561*, Estonian Court of Appeals judgment (9 March 2007), which held that an unsigned agreement is valid even through an exchange of letters and faxes, assuming there is both offer and consideration.

[44] By way of illustration, in *Schoneberger v Oelze*, 96 P 3d 1078 (Ariz., 2004), at 1084, the Arizona Court of Appeals held that a mandatory arbitration clause in a trust deprived the beneficiaries, absent a mutual agreement, of their right of access to court and was thus unenforceable against them.

[45] See P. LaPaule, Civil Law Substitutes for Trusts, (1927) 36 *Yale LJ* 1126.

Law and Article 41 of the 1984 Panama Trusts Law, as is the case with the majority of similar statutes in South and Central America,[46] recognise the validity of arbitration clauses in trust instruments, albeit with some limitations in certain jurisdictions.[47]

3.4.3 Corporate articles of agreement

An agreement to arbitrate may also be found in a company's articles of establishment (or incorporation) or its by-laws, which otherwise sets out the identities of the initial shareholders and directors and the functions and other characteristics of the legal person.[48] The obvious complication is that as the company's shares are continuously bought and sold a range of new shareholders are subject to the arbitration clause of the original articles of incorporation or by-laws. Although few arbitration statutes specifically refer to corporate arbitration (whether in respect of internal or external disputes), the tendency among those that do is to provide for strict conditions as regards the incorporation of arbitration clauses in corporate statutes. Under Article 11(bis)(3) of the Spanish Arbitration Act the insertion of an arbitration agreement in a corporate statute requires the vote in favour of, at least, two thirds of the votes attached to the shares into which the capital is divided. Moreover, challenges against corporate resolutions should be submitted to the decision of a panel of one or more arbitrators under the auspices of an arbitral institution.

Most jurisdictions, as is the case of India, treat corporate articles as contracts that bind everyone encompassed therein,[49] including, of course, relevant arbitration clauses.[50] Whether or not a particular corporate

---

[46] For example, Art 44 of Paraguay's Ley No 921 de Negocios Fiduciarios.

[47] This is true particularly in respect of testamentary arbitration. See Art 10 of the 1997 Bolivian Ley de Arbitraje y Conciliación No 1770.

[48] Art 3 of the 1992 Finnish Arbitration Act states that arbitration clauses in the bylaws of an association, a foundation, a limited liability company or another company or corporate entity and by which the parties or the person against whom a claim is made are bound shall have the same effects as arbitration agreements; equally, Art 1163 of the Polish CCP.

[49] Indian Companies Act (1956), s 36; confirmed by the Indian Supreme Court in *Dale & Carrington Investment Ltd v P K Prathapan*, [2005] 1 SCC (India) 217.

[50] By implication, agreements that are initially extraneous to a company's Articles, when they themselves are incorporated, attached or expressly related to the Articles, become susceptible to the arbitration clause contained in the initial Articles. *Rangaraj v Gopalakrishnan*, AIR 1992 SCC (India) 453.

matter falls within an arbitration clause depends on the phrasing of the clause and the arbitrable nature of the issue under consideration. Under the terms of the 2003 Italian Corporate Arbitration Law arbitration clauses incorporated in a non-listed company's articles of incorporation or its by-laws (the latter represents the rule in Italy) bind all members of the company. Similar clauses in the by-laws of listed companies are regulated by the relevant provisions of the 2006 Arbitration Law as incorporated in the Italian CCP. Disputes arising out of non-listed companies' by-laws must be filed at the Registry of Enterprises and be available to all members. The law allows third-party intervention in the arbitral proceedings, either voluntarily or following a party's request or an order by the tribunal, but only as regards the company's members.

The concerns over the rights of shareholders, where these are third parties to agreements concluded by some shareholders or by the board of directors with other entities, may be resolved by permitting arbitration in order to enforce a shareholder's derivative action. In the USA, if the shareholder can demonstrate a violation of either a duty of care or a duty of loyalty, then he or she can successfully challenge the actions of the board in the form of a derivative suit. Such derivate suits involve a complex two-tier process through which the shareholder first sues the corporation, which thereafter proceeds to sue the entity at fault. Where the corporation is successful in its own suit the shareholder can then satisfy his or her own claim. There is little uniformity regarding such derivative suits as they are regulated by state, rather than federal, law. In the state of New York, for example, they are permitted as long as the aim is to secure a judgment in the corporation's favour.[51] The California Court of Appeals has held that a derivative suit brought by a shareholder whose claim was based on an arbitration agreement between the corporation and a third entity is susceptible to arbitration, even though no such agreement existed between the suing shareholder and the third entity. The Court held that the suing shareholder was required to arbitrate because the causes of action sued upon belong to the corporation and not the plaintiff.[52]

[51] *Eisenberg v Flying Tiger Line, Inc*, 451 F 2d 267 (2nd Cir. 1971).
[52] *Frederick v First Union Securities*, 122 Cal. Rptr. 2d 774 (Ct. App. 2002), at 779.

> **Case study: Corporate arbitration clauses**
>
> In *Claimant v Defendant*, the articles of incorporation of a company that was subsequently dissolved provided that any dispute arising in connection with the articles and out of the corporate relationship would be finally settled by an arbitral tribunal. The defendant argued that the arbitration clause was no longer valid since the company had been dissolved and hence the operation of its articles had been terminated. In parting with its established precedent, whereby the validity of an arbitration clause depends on the existence of the agreement in which it is contained, the Austrian Supreme Court held that a company's articles of association remain applicable even after its dissolution where the dispute in question arose from the corporate relationship.[53]

3.4.4 Testamentary wills

A will is ordinarily a unilateral act *mortis causa* drawn up by the testator for the benefit of his or her legatees.[54] As a result, although it is usually in writing, most legal systems accept other evidence in the absence of a written will. Whatever the case, a testamentary will is not an agreement as such. It assumes many of the qualities associated with agreements when the terms of the will are 'accepted' (for lack of a better generalisation) by the intended beneficiaries and assuming there are available assets free from other claims. Most countries refuse to recognise and enforce arbitration clauses in wills as a matter of arbitrability or because they view them as contrary to public policy.[55] Exceptionally, however, several nations see no inherent tension between arbitration and inheritance laws. Article 3 of the 1992 Finnish Arbitration Act and Article 10 of the 2003 Spanish Arbitration Act specifically permit arbitration clauses in wills. Equally acceptable are submission agreements between the heirs to resolve disputes arising from the will.

---

[53] *Claimant v Defendant*, Austrian Supreme Court (OGH) judgment (8 May 2013).
[54] Art 1712 Greek Civil Code.
[55] *In re Will of Jacobovitz*, 295 NYS 2d 527 (1968), at 529, it was ruled that arbitration in probate proceedings was against public policy.

The obvious limitation with arbitration clauses in wills is that where they encompass real estate or assets in more than one country the disputes in question may not be arbitrable everywhere. Moreover, third parties to the will, such as creditors or those claiming rights to the deceased's estate, will fall outside the ambit of the arbitration clause. Equally, the will as an instrument of recording the parties' intention to arbitrate may not be acceptable by the law of the seat or that of the country of enforcement.

3.5 The parties' capacity to enter into arbitration agreements

For good reason, Article 34(2)(a)(i) of the UNCITRAL Model Law stipulates that an award will be set aside[56] if anyone of the parties did not have the capacity to enter into an arbitral agreement. Capacity is (or should be) assessed by reference to one's personal law,[57] which may coincide with the law of one's nationality (or most effective nationality in case a person has multiple), the law of one's habitual (or otherwise effective) residence, or one's religious law (if any), such as Islamic law for Muslims (but only in relation to a small group of matters).[58] As these may conflict with each other it is important that the parties ensure that at each stage of the arbitral process they have eliminated the possibility of the award being set aside or refused enforcement by reason of legal incapacity.[59]

At the most basic level, domestic laws generally provide that a minor or a person with impaired mental faculties lacks the capacity to enter into contracts (to avoid manipulation), including arbitration clauses. A diminished contractual capacity may also pertain to particular classes of individuals, such as women in certain Muslim nations,[60] beneficiaries in respect

---

[56] Or refused recognition and enforcement under Art 36(1)(a)(i) UNCITRAL Model Law.

[57] s 103(2)(a) of the English AA stipulates that a person's capacity is assessed by 'the law applicable to him'.

[58] Art 46(1) and (2) of the English Family Law Act 1986, for example, regulates the recognition of overseas divorce, annulment and legal separation taking effect in England. The position is simple enough. A Muslim divorce (*talaq*) obtained outside England is enforceable in England – and hence the parties may further seek ancillary relief or resolve other financial matters – if the *talaq* is effective under the laws of the country in which it was obtained (*lex matrimonii*).

[59] This is particularly so given that Art V(1)(a) of the 1958 New York Convention requires that capacity, for the purposes of enforcement of foreign awards, is determined by reference to the parties' applicable law.

[60] See M. Zahraa, The Legal Capacity of Women in Islamic Law, (1996) 11 *Arab LQ* 245.

of the trust's assets, shareholders (as opposed to directors) in respect of a company and others. In all these cases the subject matter determines the most appropriate law for the assessment of capacity; for example, the country of incorporation or effective seat will determine who possesses the authority to sign a contract, or arbitration clause, on behalf of a company. In yet other jurisdictions it may well be the case that all, or certain, legal persons do not have the capacity to enter into arbitration agreements absent authorisation from a state instrumentality, in which case the legal person's capacity is perceived of as being conditional (or limited).[61] Going a step further, for the purposes of investment arbitration, state entities entering into arbitration clauses/submission agreements may require express authorisation by their government.[62] In exceptional cases some countries demand such authorisation even in respect of commercial arbitration.[63]

A species of capacity is the possession of authority to enter into an arbitration agreement on behalf of another person, in such a way that the agreement entered into by the *agent* binds the *principal*. If the purported agent does not possess the necessary authority, which in most cases requires a written agreement,[64] then the principal is not bound. If the authority exists, however, the principal, although seemingly a third party to the agreement, is bound by the arbitration agreement signed by the agent. Article 1167 of the Polish CCP stipulates that unless otherwise stated by the principal, the agent is presumed to possess authority to bind the principal through the adoption of agreements to arbitrate.[65] In light of the doctrine of separability it is often argued in jurisdictions hostile to arbitration that the agent requires two distinct authorisations

---

[61] Prior to the adoption of the 2012 Law (Art 10(2) thereof), Art 5 of the 1983 Saudi Arbitration Act obliged the parties to submit arbitration agreements for approval to a competent authority responsible for the subject matter of the dispute. See A. Baamir and I. Bantekas, Saudi Law as Lex Arbitri: Evaluation of Saudi Arbitration Law and Judicial Practice, (2009) 25 *Arbitration Int* 239, at 243–4.

[62] Art 25(3) ICSID Convention. See chapter 10 section 10.3.5.1.

[63] Art 10(2) of the 2012 Saudi Arbitration Law.

[64] For example, Greek Supreme Cassation Court [Areios Pagos] judgment *88/1977* [1979] IV Yb Com Arb 269, although this is not necessary with respect to a company's board of directors.

[65] Even so, the Polish Supreme Court, *case no III CZ/02* ruling (8 March 2002) held that in respect of arbitration clauses the agent's power of attorney must specifically mention his authority to enter into an arbitration agreement. This decision has been severely criticised and perhaps may no longer apply under Polish law.

by the principal; one for the main contract and another in respect of the arbitration clause. While lower Russian courts have at times sustained this argument it has been rejected by the country's Supreme Arbitrazh Court.[66]

The law may exceptionally deny capacity only in respect of specific transactions, as is the case in the majority of European nations with pre-dispute arbitration clauses in consumer agreements.[67] No doubt, one may view such restrictions through the lens of public policy or as limitations to contractual freedom rather than as a curtailment of capacity.

3.6 The scope of agreements to arbitrate

Article 7(1) of the Model Law makes it clear that the parties cannot validly agree to refer *any* future dispute arising between them to arbitration. An arbitration clause must concern 'all or certain disputes that have arisen or which may arise between them in respect of a *defined legal relationship*'. The 2011 Portuguese Arbitration Law goes a step further, stipulating that the arbitration agreement may not only refer contentious disputes to arbitration, but also the power to the tribunal to 'complete and adapt contracts with long-lasting obligations to new circumstances'.[68]

Neither international treaties nor domestic laws prescribe the manner or scope of an agreement to arbitrate as this is quintessentially within the realm of party autonomy. Nonetheless, the parties should be cognisant of the fact that the tribunal's mandate depends on declaring as precisely as possible what disputes and pertinent legal relationships are referred to it. It is by no means self-evident that all possible disputes and relationships arising from the parties' agreement fall within the scope of such reference; for even if the tribunal were to unilaterally expand its scope of reference one of the parties (typically the losing one) may at a later stage claim that the tribunal acted *ultra vires* and rightly so. As a result, the parties are generally advised by arbitral institutions to draft broad (assuming that this is what they wish), but not necessarily detailed, submission clauses in order to avoid future interpretative problems.

French courts, for example, assume that only broadly worded clauses will be deemed as covering both contractual and tort claims arising from

---

[66] *Case no 12311/10*, Presidium of the Supreme Arbitrazh Court judgment (12 April 2011).
[67] See chapter 9 section 9.4.1.   [68] Art 1(4).

the contract.[69] The most often cited narrow clause concerns disputes *'arising from* the contract', suggesting consent to submit to arbitration only those disputes encompassed by the particular contractual relationship. In practice, in the course of a contractual relationship the parties' disputes may well arise as a result of conduct unrelated to their contract as such. By way of illustration, criminal behaviour by one of the parties will give rise to an independent claim in tort or perhaps unjust enrichment. In order to ensure that all related matters are referred to arbitration, standardised (or model) clauses with appropriate phrasing have been developed by arbitral institutions.

Model arbitration clauses

'all disputes arising out of or in connection with the present contract';[70]
    'any dispute arising out of or in connection with this contract, including any question regarding its existence, validity or termination'.[71]

Civil law jurisdictions have generally been inclined to afford a broader scope to otherwise narrowly drafted arbitration agreements in situations where this clearly reflected the parties' shared intention. Article 808-quater of the Italian CCP introduces a presumption whereby if there is doubt as to the boundaries of the arbitration agreement, the tribunal or court interpreting it must do so in the broadest manner possible as 'extending to all disputes arising from the contract or from the relationship to which the agreement refers'.[72] Such statutory provisions eliminate the need for carefully drafted model clauses the objective of which is to make it absolutely certain that the agreement to arbitrate extends to all disputes arising from the parties' relationship, whether contractual or other.

The interpretative approach regarding the scope of arbitration clauses was until recently rather different in England and the USA.[73] In *Fili*

---

[69] *Sucres et Denrées (SUCDEN) v Multitrade Cairo*, Paris Court of Appeals judgment (19 May 2005), [2006] *Rev Arb* 455.
[70] ICC standard clause.   [71] LCIA standard clause.
[72] Equally, Art 15(2) of the 1996 Maltese Arbitration Act; Art 550(3) Romanian CCP.
[73] In the USA no presumption similar to that in the *Fili Shipping* case exists uniformly across federal courts. See *Cape Flattery Ltd v Titan Maritime LLC*, 647 F 3d 914 (9th Cir. 2011), whereas the 2nd Circuit has adopted the liberal approach in cases such *as Threlked & Co Inc v Metallgesellshaft Ltd (London)* 923 F 2d 245 (2nd Cir. 1991).

Shipping, which involved several charter-party agreements whose arbitration clause extended to 'any dispute arising under this charter' one of the claimants argued that bribery had taken place. Such conduct would ordinarily have rested outside the arbitration clause because it did not arise under the charter. The House of Lords, however, held, following largely continental precedent and language, that the courts must assume that businessmen entering into an arbitration clause are rational actors and as such are more likely to have intended to subsume within the clause all relevant disputes, unless they have explicitly stated otherwise.[74] As a result, the tort of bribery was held to be encompassed under the parties' arbitration agreement.

3.7 Legal effects of agreements to arbitrate

The legal effect of an arbitration agreement is that it may not be withdrawn or in any other way unilaterally revoked by any of the parties even if no longer perceived as favourable to their interests. The parties' agreement to arbitrate binds them throughout the life cycle of their relationship (whether contractual, trust-based or other). Exceptionally, the parties may validly apply to the courts for interim measures (or an emergency arbitrator if the institutional rules so permit) before or following the constitution of the tribunal in order to preserve crucial evidence or other assets, but this is not a violation of the agreement to arbitrate.[75]

3.8 Problematic arbitration agreements

3.8.1 Null and void arbitration agreements

The UNCITRAL Model Law does not explain under what circumstances an arbitration agreement is null, void, inoperable or incapable of being enforced. Therefore, given the absence of a uniform or customary

---

[74] *Premium Nafta Products Limited and others v Fili Shipping Company Ltd,* [2007] 4 All ER 951; equally, *Fiona Trust & Holding Corp v Privalov and Ors* [2007] EWCA Civ 20; see also for a similar liberal approach by Australian courts, *Commandate Marin Corp v Pan Australia Shipping Pty Ltd* (2006) 157 FCR 45.

[75] Art 9 UNCITRAL Model Law. See chapter 5 sections 5.5 and 5.5.3.

definition the law applicable to the arbitration agreement dictates when an arbitration agreement is considered defective. There are several reasons rendering a contract null or void, such as the absence of offer or consideration (or its equivalent in civil law nations), the lapse of a deadline specified by the parties or statute, the occurrence of an unlawful act which caused one of the parties to sign the contract (misrepresentation, duress or fraud), the absence of capacity, the non-arbitrability of the subject matter, violation of public policy (e.g. an agreement to pay a bribe) or even the occurrence of a significant mistake. Moreover, contracts may be null and void by reason of an error in form, such as the absence of the parties' signature. There could, of course, be other reasons. In one case, the Portuguese Supreme Court held that an arbitration agreement was manifestly null and void where it was clear that the appointment of one or more arbitrators would not guarantee independence and impartiality and that such an agreement would impinge on the parties' right to a fair trial.[76]

Whether the defect in the arbitration agreement gives rise to absolute nullity (non-remediable) or qualified nullity (remediable) is a matter of domestic law and party autonomy. The UNCITRAL Model Law may be read as exhorting states not to subject arbitration agreements to the same strict technical rules applicable to ordinary contracts but to salvage them where possible, particularly where they do not offend public policy or other peremptory domestic norms. A few examples will be provided to illustrate the tendencies of national institutions and the flexibility they are willing to afford.

Under Luxembourg law if the arbitrators have failed to meet the deadlines set by the parties and one party does not agree to an extension, the arbitration clause is dissolved as a result of the party's bad faith. Equally, if the parties have set a deadline for the delivery of an award and this is not delivered in time the obligation of the parties to arbitrate expires.[77] Luxembourg courts insist that the issue of time limits and extensions are intrinsic to the arbitration clause, which can only be altered by an alteration of the clause itself. Hence, it is within the contractual remit of each party to refuse any extension.[78]

---

[76] *X v Z*, case no 170751/08.7YIPRT.L1.S1, Portuguese Supreme Court judgment (12 July 2011).

[77] District Court judgment, no 11376 (15 January 2009).

[78] Court of Appeal judgment (5 July 2006), Pas Lux no 33, 263.

In equal manner, Article 1168(1) of the Polish CCP stipulates that: 'if a person appointed in an arbitration agreement as an arbitrator or as a chairman of an arbitral tribunal refuses to perform this function, or if the performance of this function by that person turns out to be impossible for other reasons, the arbitration agreement loses its force unless the parties have agreed otherwise.' Moreover, failing a different agreement of the parties, an arbitration agreement loses its force if the arbitral tribunal indicated in that agreement has not accepted the case for resolution, or if the resolution of the case turned out to be impossible for other reasons.[79] This is a harsh outcome because the impossibility of performance by the arbitrators should not eliminate the parties' expressed desire to settle their dispute through arbitration, unless their intention was to settle their disputes only with the specific arbitrators and no others.

3.8.2 Inoperable and ineffective arbitration agreements

An agreement is inoperable or ineffective where the information provided therein makes it impossible to understand what the parties had in mind. This is the case where the parties' chosen arbitral institution does not exist, there is no dispute to speak of, or the agreement to arbitrate envisages both arbitration and litigation without granting clear primacy to arbitration.[80] These defects are the result of poor drafting but the arbitrator cannot be left to guess such matters without risking the infliction of harm on one of the parties. It is evident that in most cases the defect is remediable if both parties are genuinely desirous of the arbitration to go ahead. For example, the parties can designate a new, mutually acceptable, arbitral institution and declare their unequivocal preference for arbitration. In practice, one of the parties may by that stage be negatively inclined and employs the defect to render the arbitration agreement inoperable or ineffective. A few indicative examples are provided below.

---

[79] Art 1168(2) CCP.

[80] This last circumstance, known as *bilateral option clause* is not always viewed as inoperable in arbitration-friendly jurisdictions and the courts seek to find a solution on the basis of conflict of laws rules. See *Nedspice Sourcing BV, Tybex Warehousing BV and others* ('*Xin An Jiang*'), Hague Appeals Court judgment (22 May 2012). There is no uniform approach to this issue, however.

The approach of German courts is to salvage the arbitration agreement where possible and not be held back by technicalities if the parties' intention was to submit future disputes to arbitration. The *Oberlandesgericht* (OLG) Berlin has held that in case the arbitration institution designated in an arbitration agreement does not exist, the arbitration agreement has to be interpreted using established principles of contract interpretation, such as the history of the negotiations and the intent of the parties in order to determine the competent arbitration institution. The designation of an inexistent arbitration institution does not, per se, impact the validity of the arbitration agreement.[81] This is also the position of the Estonian Appeals Court, which has held that the failure of the parties to indicate their preferred arbitral institution does not serve to invalidate the arbitration agreement.[82]

However, not all courts are prepared to take this (sensible) approach. The Danish Supreme Court held that an arbitration clause was void because the designated arbitral institution did not exist, namely the Copenhagen Maritime Arbitrators' Association.[83] Similarly, the Federal Arbitrazh Court of the Moscow Circuit dismissed an arbitration clause under the UNCITRAL Arbitration Rules which authorised the ICC as appointing authority, deeming it to be inoperable.[84] In both cases the intent of the parties was clear and in respect of the Moscow court ruling there is evidently no appreciation of the concept of appointing authority which is consistent with Russian arbitration legislation, which itself is premised on the UNCITRAL Model Law.

Case study: Dual option clauses

In one case, the parties' dispute resolution clause made reference to the possibility of both litigation and arbitration in case of future disputes. Two questions arise, namely, whether the clause is valid, and if so, which of the two options prevails. The French Court of

---

[81] OLG Berlin, judgment (3 September 2012); equally held by the BGH (Federal Supreme Court of Justice) in *F v G*, judgment (14 July 2011), *SchiedsVZ* (2011) 284.

[82] *Case no 2–06-39773*, Court of Appeals judgment (28 May 2007). Even so, commentators stress another case by the same court where the same failure of the parties was found to have invalidated their arbitration agreement. See *case no 2–05-984*, Appeals Court judgment (6 March 2009).

[83] *Dregg EHF v Jensen Shipping A/S*, Danish Supreme Court, judgment (12 June 2012).

[84] *Case no KG-A40/9109/09*, Moscow Federal Arbitrazh Court ruling (21 September 2009).

> Cassation held that the clause was valid and that unless the parties decide otherwise litigation prevails. The reference in the clause to a particular arbitral institution was viewed by the Court as a mere indication of the chosen institutional rules should the dispute be submitted to arbitration.[85]

3.9 Third parties to arbitration agreements

An arbitration agreement, whether concluded by contract, trust deed or other valid means, binds only those persons that are parties to the instrument wherein it is contained or which have otherwise accepted it (as in the case of the trustee or heirs to a testamentary will).[86] This privity is fundamental to the operation of agreements, particularly contracts. States are generally disinclined towards opening up the legal effects of agreements to third parties not only because this violates party autonomy but also because the designation of who is or is not a party (including attendant rights and obligations) ultimately risks becoming a random exercise with unforeseen consequences in the sphere of private relations. Nonetheless, there do exist exceptional situations where an otherwise third party claims rights or duties or has otherwise benefited from a contract (and an arbitration clause) to which it is not a party through the operation of rules of private law.[87] It is assumed that where an agreement confers a direct benefit on a third party that does not subsequently object to the benefit, such person is estopped from contesting the applicability of the arbitration clause within that agreement.[88] Section 8 of the English Contracts (Rights of Third Parties) Act clearly stipulates that where a third party seeks to rely on an existing arbitration clause it is bound by it. Moreover, existing

---

[85] *M-Real Alizay v Thermodyn*, Cassation Court judgment (12 June 2013), [2013] I *Bull Civ* 121.

[86] See *Oxford Shipping Co Ltd v NYK (The Eastern Saga)*, [1984] 2 Lloyd's Rep 373, confirming the general rule under English law that third parties are generally excluded from arbitral proceedings.

[87] *GmbH v S Aktiengesellschaft*, case no 7Ob266/08f, [OGH] Austrian Supreme Court judgment (30 March 2009); *A v Assuranceforeningen Gard*, Finnish Supreme Court decision, (KKO) 2007:39.

[88] *American Bureau of Shipping v Société Jet Flint SA*, 170 F 3d 349 (2nd Cir. 1999), at 353.

parties to an arbitration clause may agree that a third party be treated as a party to the clause.[89]

By way of illustration, an insurer has a direct interest in arbitral proceedings between two persons claiming insurance (one of which is its insured client) over an accident. In fact, the insurer may either subrogate (substitute) the assignee (the entity it has insured) in the arbitral proceedings, or join the assignee as an additional party. Besides assignment, third parties usually include agents and principals as well as successors, whether by reason of a testamentary will, contract or other private relationship, such as transfer or conveyance of claim to a non-signatory to the original contract.[90] A particular form of succession concerns corporate shares. It is reasonable that successive shareholders are bound by the arbitration clause in the company's original by-laws or articles of agreement.[91] However, the extension of the arbitration clause to (a third party) assignee does not find acceptance in all jurisdictions. In Bulgaria, for example, the assignment of rights under a subcontract does not automatically imply the assignment of the rights encompassed under the arbitration clause of the original contract (upon which the subcontract is naturally premised).[92]

The application of the so-called *group of companies* doctrine is yet another instance whereby third parties have been held to be bound by an arbitration agreement to which they are not original parties. It is applied by very few countries and its underlying rationale is that a non-signatory company may be bound or benefit from an arbitration agreement signed by another company within the same group if it was involved in the particular transaction or undertaking.[93] The Lisbon Appeals Court has dismissed this doctrine on the ground that simply because the defendants are in a group relationship is not enough to extend the arbitration agreement to the

---

[89] In *Fortress Value Recovery Fund I LLC & Ors v Blue Skye Special Opportunities Fund LP & Ors* [2013] EWCA Civ 367, para 36, the English Court of Appeals held that in the case at hand the limited partnership deed did not explicitly encompass third parties.

[90] *Case no 2–06-39773*, Estonian Court of Appeals judgment (28 May 2007).

[91] Areios Pagos judgment 842/2008.

[92] Bulgarian Supreme Cassation Court *Decision No 70* (15 June 2011) and *Decision No 46* (8 May 2011).

[93] The leading case is *Dow Chemical France v Isover Saint Gobain*, ICC Case No 4131, interim award (23 September 1982). In *Peterson Farms Inc v C & M Farming Ltd* [2004] Arb LR 50, the English Commercial Court found the doctrine detestable.

companies that were not parties to it.[94] The Swiss equivalent to the group of companies doctrine is known as intervention theory, whereby the intervention must be justified by demonstrating a clear intention to be bound by the arbitration agreement.[95] Given the uncertainty surrounding this 'doctrine' it is unclear whether seemingly similar pronouncements by national courts should be viewed as granting it recognition. The answer is probably not. The Athens Appeals Court, for example, has ruled that an arbitration agreement entered into by a company binds its shareholders,[96] but it is not suggested that the group of companies doctrine generally applies in Greek law.

Where a third party validly claims a right or obligation under an arbitration clause the outcome is both substantive (reaping of benefits) as well as procedural. The procedural dimension means that the third party enjoys the right to participate in the arbitral proceedings, whether as an additional party or by means of subrogation. There may well exist sound policy reasons to restrict the *locus standi* of otherwise entitled third parties from arbitral proceedings. In Germany, the *Bundesgerichtshof* (BGH) has held that standard-form arbitration clauses (in the case at hand an agency agreement with a stock broker) conferring the right to initiate or participate in arbitration to third parties must be interpreted restrictively.[97] The same rule may have to apply to third-party funders of arbitration because although their substantive rights from the parties' agreement is not in doubt (i.e. their share of the winning party's compensation) their direct involvement in the arbitral proceedings (as a party) may jeopardise the right to a fair trial.

As will become evident below, French courts have pushed the boundaries for third parties to be bound by arbitration agreements more than any other national courts. They have done so by adopting an 'objective' approach which does not require the third (non-signatory to the arbitration agreement) party to express its willingness to participate in the arbitration.[98] This objective approach has been applied subject to a 'subjective'

---

[94] *C SA v V, AS and Others*, case no 3539/08.6TVLSB.L1-7, Lisbon Court of Appeals judgment (11 January 2011).

[95] *X v Y Banka and Z*, Swiss Federal Court judgment (20 September 2005).

[96] Athens Appeals Court Judgment *6815/1994*.

[97] Case no *XI ZR 168/08*, judgment (8 February 2011).

[98] *Constructions mecaniques de Normandie (CMN) v Fagerdala Marine Systems (FMS) and Patroun Korrosionsschutz Consuult und Consulting (PKC)*, French Supreme Cassation Court judgment (26 October 2011).

criterion, whereby it must be demonstrated that the non-signatory was fully aware of the existence of the arbitration agreement. This subjective criterion is applied under the so-called 'double-predictability' doctrine, which assumes that the expectations of both the original party to a contract and a non-signatory are protected. From the perspective of the non-signatory this assumption requires evidence of a legitimate expectation that any disputes with the signatories would be resolved by recourse to arbitration. This is consistent with the more recent jurisprudence of the French Cassation Court which requires the direct involvement of the third party in the performance of the contract in order for it to be bound by the agreement to arbitrate.[99]

Case study: Group of companies doctrine

In the *Dow Chemical* case a claim for arbitration was brought by two companies associated with the plaintiff, but which were not parties to the original agreement with the respondent, namely Dow Chemical France and Dow Chemical USA. The latter was the parent company and was found to 'exercise absolute control over its subsidiaries having either signed the relevant contracts or, like Dow Chemical France, effectively and individually participated in their conclusion, their performance and their termination'. The tribunal, also relying on trade usages, opined that the aforementioned group of companies constituted 'one and the same economic reality' and that as a result were encompassed in the arbitration agreement entered by the subsidiary even though they were not parties. This outcome was subsequently endorsed by the Paris Appeals Court, which refused to set the award aside.[100]

---

[99] *Amplitude v Iakovoglou*, Supreme Cassation Court judgment (7 November 2012); in *Dubai UAE et al v Mr Khaled Ali*, Paris Appeals Court judgment (26 February 2013), it was held that: 'the arbitration clause stipulated within an international agreement has a validity and efficacy of its own, which accordingly commands extending its application to parties directly involved in the performance of the contract and all related disputes if it is shown that their contractual relation and their activities can trigger the presumption that all parties accepted the arbitration clause, the existence and scope of which were known to the parties.'

[100] *Société Isover-Saint Gobain v Société Dow Chemical France*, Paris Appeals Court judgment (22 October 1983), [1984] *Rev Arb* 98.

3.10 Multi-party arbitrations

In the previous sections we analysed under what circumstances a third party to an arbitration agreement may be bound by the agreement and ultimately by the award rendered. In this section we shall proceed to examine the implications arising from the existence of several parties to a contract containing an arbitration clause, in addition to circumstances where there are several contracts with different parties and one or more of these desire to enjoin the various arbitrations in a single, unified, proceeding.

It is common in complex international projects, such as sovereign financing and insurance, as well as in construction, for the principal parties to carry out many of the agreed terms through subcontractors. Although this may be achieved through subsequent (to the main contract) sub-contracting agreements, in practice the parties usually (but not exclusively) enter into joint ventures or other forms of consortia which exist for the duration of their agreed business relationship. All of the partners in the joint venture have their distinctive role and the obligations of each are well documented. The joint venture typically assumes liability for the failure of one of its partners to perform, but each retains its corporate identity. Where the arbitration clause of such a multi-party contract is triggered against its contractual counterpart, these disparate parties to the same contract are forced to agree on a variety of common interests, such as choice of arbitrators, legal representation and others. Agreement is not always guaranteed, as the *Dutco* case aptly demonstrated. Dutco had entered into an agreement with a consortium of two German companies and when a dispute arose initiated arbitral proceedings against them under the ICC Rules in France. As this was meant to be a tribunal composed of three arbitrators, the ICC requested the consortium to designate its preferred arbitrator so that the two party-appointed arbitrators could go on to choose the president. Alas, each of the parties to the consortium wanted to appoint their own arbitrator but reluctantly agreed to appoint one jointly, reserving their right to subsequently challenge the ICC's decision on the basis that it deprived them of the right to choose an arbitrator of their choice. The argument certainly makes sense from a strictly legal perspective, given that unlawful arbitral composition is a ground for setting aside and non-enforcement of awards, but at the same time it is clearly impractical. In the case at hand, the French Court of Cassation approached the issue from a public policy perspective and held that the absence of equality in the appointment of arbitrators sufficed to set the award aside.[101] As a direct result of the *Dutco* judgment the ICC swiftly amended its rules in order to dispel any uncertainty for future litigants. Article 12(6)–(8) of the ICC Rules stipulates that:

(6) Where there are multiple claimants or multiple respondents, and where the dispute is to be referred to three arbitrators, the multiple claimants, jointly, and the multiple respondents, jointly, shall nominate an arbitrator for confirmation pursuant to Article 13.

(7) Where an additional party has been joined, and where the dispute is to be referred to three arbitrators, the additional party may, jointly with the claimant(s) or with the respondent(s), nominate an arbitrator for confirmation pursuant to Article 13.

(8) In the absence of a joint nomination pursuant to Articles 12(6) or 12(7) and where all parties are unable to agree to a method for the constitution of the arbitral tribunal, the Court may appoint each member of the arbitral tribunal and shall designate one of them to act as president. In such case, the Court shall be at liberty to choose any person it regards as suitable to act as arbitrator, applying Article 13 when it considers this appropriate.

In this manner it is now clear that several parties to a single arbitration agreement, whether as claimants or respondents, must nominate and appoint a single (joint) arbitrator. Although some commentators suggest, albeit faintly, that this 'restriction' may lead to enforcement failure in some countries, allegedly because of the deprivation of the right to appoint one's preferred arbitrator (unlawful composition),[102] this is highly unlikely. By designating the ICC or other institutional rules[103] in their arbitration agreement the parties expressly accept that their choice of arbitrator will be undertaken by joint, mutual, consent and that in case of disagreement the arbitral institution will make the appointment on their behalf.[104] Even

---

[101] *BKMI and Siemens v Dutco*, French Cassation Court judgment (7 January 1992), [1993] 18 Yb Com Arb 140.

[102] Art V(1)(d) 1958 New York Convention.

[103] See Art 13(4) Stockholm Chamber of Commerce (SCC) Rules.

[104] Art 816-quater (1) of the Italian CCP clearly states that should more than two parties be bound by the same arbitration agreement, each party may request that all or some of them be summoned in the same arbitral proceedings and may by common agreement appoint an equal amount of arbitrators. If the parties fail to reach a common agreement as to the joinder of their cases there will be as many arbitrators as there are individual respondents

so, if the courts accept that such a procedure is indeed unfair, they will refuse enforcement despite the parties' consent to this procedure.

Where, on the other hand, there are several contracts with different parties, each of which is linked to one another, logic dictates that joining all the disputes into a single arbitral process would not only save the parties time and money but it would also avoid conflicting awards. The situation may well arise in complex funding arrangements or even construction projects where the various contractors and subcontractors are each tied to one another by means of distinct agreements – as opposed to a consortium or a joint venture. Were such a scenario to emerge in the context of litigation, local civil procedure codes empower judges to join all the discrete suits if there is sufficient unity in the subject matter and among the parties.[105] In the sphere of arbitration, however, the principle of party autonomy dictates that only the will of the parties to each arbitration agreement can empower the tribunal to join cases together.[106] Even so, Article 10 of the ICC Rules makes the point that in order for the ICC Court to approve such joinder/consolidation the arbitration agreements must, in addition, to the parties' consent and unity in persons and subject matter, be *compatible*. This is logical, given that despite their otherwise common subject matter the governing law of the various agreements may be diverse, all of which may be in conflict with one another on several issues of importance. In such circumstances, if the parties wish to continue with the consolidation they may have to agree that the tribunal apply a single governing law.

Court-ordered consolidation is exceptional and perhaps a deterrent (as a choice of seat) to those involved in projects encompassing the same parties and subject matter, otherwise they would have made express reference to the possibility of consolidation in their contract. In the vast majority of cases where court-ordered consolidation is stipulated in statute, the

---

(paragraph 2). Where, however, a joinder of the cases is necessitated by law and the parties do not reach mutual agreement on a joinder the arbitration cannot proceed (paragraph 3).

[105] See, for example, Rule 19, Title IV, US Federal Rules of Civil Procedure.

[106] See Art 10 ICC Rules. In *Abu Dhabi Gas Liquefaction Co Ltd v Eastern Bechtel Corp* [1982] 2 Lloyd's Rep 425, the English Court of Appeal, while highlighting the efficiency of consolidated proceedings emphasised that the courts cannot enforce consolidations without the consent of the parties. In the case at hand, the court was empowered, however, to appoint the sole arbitrator in both cases and hence decided to appoint the same arbitrator with a view to avoid conflicting awards. This method of appointing the same arbitrator to multiple proceedings is known as *concurrent* (proceedings).

consent of the parties will also be sought, as is the case, for example, with section 1297.272 of the California CCP, which states:

Where the parties to two or more arbitration agreements have agreed, in their respective arbitration agreements or otherwise, to consolidate the arbitrations arising out of those arbitration agreements, the superior court may, on application by one party with the consent of all the other parties to those arbitration agreements, do one or more of the following:

(a) Order the arbitrations to be consolidated on terms the court considers just and necessary.
(b) Where all the parties cannot agree on an arbitral tribunal for the consolidated arbitration, appoint an arbitral tribunal in accordance with Section 1297.118.
(c) Where all the parties cannot agree on any other matter necessary to conduct the consolidated arbitration, make any other order it considers necessary.

A peculiar form of consent-based consolidation is the so-called method of *string arbitration*, which is prevalent in many of the commodities markets. There, the initial seller sells the product to a buyer who then goes on to sell it to subsequent buyers down a string of sales. If the product is found to be defective at the end of the string it would make sense for the entire string of purchases (and the initial seller) to be consolidated in arbitral proceedings, but this is hardly self-evident. Each buyer must consent to the consolidation as per the principle of party autonomy and it is for this reason that several commodities markets (and increasingly others such as the shipping industry) have devised string clauses which bind each buyer and seller in the string to arbitral proceedings. It goes without saying that unless all contracts are identical (in terms of law and substance) except for the parties and the price, it would be impossible for string arbitration to function properly.[107]

3.11 Confidentiality

In chapter 1 we highlighted the fact that the confidential nature of arbitration is one of its greatest attributes to its end users. However, unlike other aspects of arbitration which are uniformly regulated across most jurisdictions, confidentiality remains vexed, disputed and subject to many

---

[107] For representative clauses from the cocoa trade, see R. Dand, *The International Cocoa Trade* (Woodhead Publishing, 2010), 402.

exceptions. Confidentiality is a broad legal concept which encompasses the element of privacy. In international commercial arbitration *privacy* pertains to the proceedings as such and the documentation (including the evidence and other material) between the parties and the tribunal. Article 25(4) of the UNCITRAL Arbitration Rules stipulates that:

Hearings shall be held *in camera* unless the parties agree otherwise. The arbitral tribunal may require the retirement of any witness or witnesses during the testimony of other witnesses. The arbitral tribunal is free to determine the manner in which witnesses are examined.

The confidentiality of the hearings process is guaranteed in the vast majority of institutional rules. However, privacy is not always automatic but is dependent on a request or prior agreement of the parties. Article 22(3) of the ICC Rules states:

Upon the request of any party, the arbitral tribunal may make orders concerning the confidentiality of the arbitration proceedings or of any other matters in connection with the arbitration and may take measures for protecting trade secrets and confidential information.[108]

This suggests that confidentiality, at the very least, requires prior agreement between the parties, in the absence of which the tribunal is under no obligation to observe the privacy of the hearings or other proceedings. It is no accident therefore that parties to arbitration agreements insert confidentiality clauses therein.

The next question is whether there exists an implicit confidentiality in arbitral proceedings. The answer to this question varies across jurisdictions. The classical position as expounded by English common law takes the view that there does indeed exist an 'implied term in every agreement to arbitrate that the hearing shall be held in private', which extends to all pertinent documents.[109] Even so, English courts have recognised that this implied duty is not unlimited.[110] In one case it was held that the 'content of

---

[108] See also Art 26(3) ICC Rules regarding the privacy of hearings.

[109] *Hassneh Insurance Co of Israel v Mew* [1993] 2 Lloyd's Rep 243, at 247 per Colman J; see also *Dolling-Baker v Merret* [1991] 2 All ER 890; equally in *Ali Shipping Corporation v Shipyard Trogir* [1998] 1 Lloyd's Rep 643. Historically, this implied duty under the common law stems from the purely private nature of arbitration. *Russell v Russell* (1880) 14 Ch D 471, at 474.

[110] It has been suggested that there is no breach of duty in disclosing the mere fact that arbitration is taking place, provided that there is a legitimate reason to do so. Needless to

the obligation may depend on the context in which it arises and on the nature of the information or documents at issue'.[111] Equally, in *Associated Electric and Gas Insurance Services Ltd v European Reinsurance Co of Zurich*, the Privy Council had no hesitation to bypass the parties' confidentiality agreement in order to allow the award rendered in a prior arbitration between the same parties to be used as 'precedent' in a subsequent arbitration.[112] It should be noted that the English Arbitration Act makes no reference to confidentiality and hence the default position is that found in the Civil Procedure Rules (CPR rule 62.10). It is instructive that the reason given for omitting confidentiality from the Act by the drafting committee was 'grave difficulties over the myriad exceptions', which made it next to impossible to formulate a statutory rule.

The English approach to broad and implicit confidentiality of arbitral hearings and related documents is not universally shared. The chief reason underlying implicit confidentiality is the concept of legitimate public interest, which is constitutional in nature. The argument is that if an international arbitration concerns matters which touch upon genuine public interest, such as access to potable water or environmental degradation, there is a legitimate interest for the public to be aware of such issues. This rationale is definitely sound but in the absence of any hard rules it is difficult to know where the line should be drawn. There are two extremes to this issue. In the first scenario, authoritarian states and their instrumentalities enter into an agreement with a foreign investor – typically production sharing agreements for the extraction of natural resources – which is not, however, grounded on the public law of the host state but the private law of a third nation. The investor naturally suggests a confidentiality clause, which the host state 'accepts' and hence is justified in later asserting that it would violate its duty of confidentiality if it were to divulge to the public information about its contractual or arbitral dealings with the investor. The mechanics of such confidentiality violate, among others, the internal dimension of (economic) self-determination, which encompasses a collective right over a country's natural resources.

---

say that the actual proceedings should remain confidential at all times. *The City of Moscow v Bankers Trust* [2004] EWCA Civ 314 per Cooke J.

[111] *Emmot v Wilson & Partners Ltd* [2008] EWCA Civ 184.

[112] *Associated Electric and Gas Insurance Services Ltd v European Reinsurance Co of Zurich* [2003] 1 WLR 1041.

On the other extreme, several liberal democracies, such as Australia, take the view that although the privacy of the hearings should be respected, as well as the contractual confidentiality agreed to between the parties and arbitrators, confidentiality itself is not an absolute right. In *Esso Australia Resources Ltd v The Honourable Sidney James Plowman*, it was held that the 'public's legitimate interest in obtaining information about the affairs of public authorities' prevailed over the parties' confidentiality agreement.[113] In the USA, in the absence of a confidentiality rule it is not surprising that Article 34 of the AAA's International Arbitration Rules obliges members of the tribunal to keep all matters relating to the arbitration confidential, unless otherwise agreed by the parties. Although US courts have not entertained the notion that a legitimate public interest prevails over arbitral confidentiality, they have nonetheless rejected the idea of an implicit obligation of confidentiality.[114]

In passing, it should be noted that in international investment arbitration a rather interesting trend has arisen which represents a watershed for the otherwise complex confidentiality debate. There, where sensitive human rights and environmental issues appear, tribunals have allowed interested (third) parties, typically non-governmental organisations (NGOs), to appear as *amici* and submit briefs,[115] although they are not granted access to the parties' documents. Such an outcome is probably untenable in the sphere of international commercial arbitration as there is no legal basis in institutional rules or arbitral statutes. The public international law character of investment arbitration justifies further inroads into confidentiality, particularly the requirement for transparency inserted in most contemporary BITs[116] and the ongoing efforts by UNCITRAL through its Convention on Transparency in Treaty-based Investor-State Arbitration, adopted in July 2014.

---

[113] *Esso Australia Resources Ltd v The Honourable Sidney James Plowman*, (1995) 193 CLR 10. One should, however, note that in *Mobil Cerro Negro Ltd v Petroleos de Venezuela SA* ([2008] EWHC 532), the English High Court made a more general point that, although in ordinary circumstances an arbitration application is subject to the confidentiality provisions of the CPR of the English courts, in matters of public interest the court is entitled to make public its judgment in respect of an arbitration application. But, care must be taken to preserve confidentiality in relation to matters to which confidentiality properly attaches.

[114] *United States v Panhandle Eastern Corp*, (D Del, 1988) 118 FRD 346.

[115] See specifically the legal basis for this in Art 37(2) of the revised (in 2006) ICSID Arbitration Rules. See chapter 10 section 10.8.3

[116] See Art 11 US Model BIT (2012).

If the parties to (commercial) arbitral proceedings desire to achieve confidentiality they should make an express provision of this in their submission agreement and choose an arbitral institution whose rules provide for strict confidentiality. If they cannot avoid choosing a seat that has a history of lifting confidentiality agreements they should be prepared to make an argument about why their particular dispute and documents have no public interest dimension.

4 The arbitral tribunal

4.1 Introduction

The first three chapters concerned fundamental issues underpinning international commercial arbitration, both substantive and procedural. The following chapters will discuss the operation of actual proceedings, from the constitution of the arbitral tribunal until the issuance of an award and the range of challenges that may be levelled against it. The present chapter examines the institution of the tribunal by reference to its distinctiveness from the courts, its discrete powers, as well as from the perspective of the legal nature of the office of arbitrator. Unlike the courts which are permanent institutions each tribunal must be constituted afresh, although as we shall see the commencement of proceedings does not coincide with the constitution of the tribunal. In the course of this chapter we shall be looking at various general and specific powers of arbitral tribunals, although the focus is on those that do not require any court assistance. Powers requiring judicial assistance for their enforcement, as is the case with interim measures, will be analysed in chapter 5 which deals with the relationship between tribunals and the courts.

One of the key features of arbitral tribunals is the relationship between the parties and the arbitrators and between them and their chosen arbitral institution. This is generally of a contractual nature and determines the nature of appointments, including selection, challenges and liability of arbitrators, all of which will be examined in detail. The chapter rounds off with an analysis of substitute arbitrators and the types, range and methods of fee assessments applicable in arbitral proceedings.

4.2 Are arbitral tribunals courts?

Before responding to this question one should distinguish between the administration of law and justice on behalf of a state or states from the mere exercise of a judicial function in a particular instance. The first can only be undertaken by courts constituted under public laws. A mere ad hoc judicial or quasi-judicial function, however, may be undertaken by anyone enjoying sufficient capacity if the law so permits. On the basis of this distinction it may be argued that arbitral tribunals do not qualify as courts because, unlike ordinary courts, their constitution is predicated on private agreement (usually a contract between them and the parties), their procedural (evidence, discovery etc.) and substantive rules (governing laws) are set out by the parties, the arbitrators' salaries are equally paid by the parties and awards are not enforceable internationally under the same regime as judgments.[1] Moreover, some of the functions of tribunals, including their awards, are subject to judicial review (set aside proceedings) or further assistance by the courts of the seat. Although states support arbitration they generally distance themselves from arbitral proceedings, principally to avoid accusations of intervention and to disassociate themselves from any liability incurred by tribunals. The Czech Constitutional Court, for example,

---

[1] In Italian law the parties may agree that the award will have the force of a regular award (*rituale*) or simply that of a contract (*irrituale*). See *Itelco SpA in liquidazione v Marpe Construcoes, Instalacoes Tecnicas SA and Others*, case No 21585, Italian Cassation Court judgment (12 October 2009). For a brief analysis regarding the enforcement of foreign judgments, see chapter 8 section 8.4.

has held that although arbitrators substitute the state in its judicial function they do not enjoy the status of judges and hence any violations attributable to arbitral tribunals and arbitrators are not attributable to the state.[2] Even so, the guarantees afforded to the arbitral process and arbitral awards under public laws (arbitration statutes) and multilateral treaties demonstrates that although arbitral tribunals are not assimilated to regular courts they possess several powers and attributes associated solely with courts.

In the context of EU law, the CJEU does not consider that arbitral tribunals qualify as 'courts' because in its opinion they lack establishment by law, permanence and compulsory jurisdiction. Hence, arbitral tribunals are prevented from requesting preliminary rulings for the clarification and interpretation of issues relating to EU law.[3] As a result, in the exceptional case that a tribunal requires relevant clarification it must direct its request to the courts of the seat, as is the case, for example, with Article 27(2) of the 2005 Danish Arbitration Act.[4] Such a characterisation by the CJEU, however, has no bearing on the fact that awards issued by arbitral tribunals produce *res judicata* in exactly the same manner as court judgments.[5]

It should be noted that despite the liberal construction of arbitration and party autonomy it would be wrong to assume that every dispute resolution process that outwardly resembles arbitration should be viewed as such. This consideration applies to 'arbitration' conducted under the auspices of trade associations with limited membership. The New York Diamond Dealers Club (DDC), for example, operates an arbitration process that is recognised by the courts of the state of New York, at least, but is largely outside the framework of conventional arbitration.[6] The principal

---

[2] Czech Constitutional Court, *case no IV US174/02*, judgment (15 July 2002).

[3] Case 102/81 *Nordsee Deutsche Hochseefischerei GmbH v Reederei Mond Hochseefischerei Nordstern AG and others* [1982] ECR 1095; Case C-394/11 *Belov v CHEZ Elektro Balgaria and Others*, CJEU judgment (31 January 2013), para 38; Case C-125/04 *Denuit and Cordenier v Transorient- Mosaique Voyages et Culture SA*, [2005] ECR I-00923, para 13; C-555/13 *Merck Canada v Accord Healthcare Ltd and Others*, CJEU judgment (13 February 2014), para 17.

[4] This is also the case with ss 5–10 of the Norwegian Arbitration Act in respect of preliminary rulings to the EFTA Court; the same result may also be achieved indirectly by petitioning a competent national court to refer a legal issue to the CJEU. See, for example, *Bulk Oil Ltd v Sun International Ltd* [1984] 1 All ER 386. The appeal was made in accordance with s 69 English AA, which allows appeals against awards on disputed points of law.

[5] For an analysis of *res judicata*, see chapter 7 section 7.2.2.

[6] L. Bernstein, Opting Out of the Legal System: Extralegal Contractual Relations in the Diamond Industry, (1992) 11 *Journal of Legal Studies* 115.

criticisms against trade association-related arbitration is that it may operate liberal (even ad hoc or informal) discovery or hearing rules whose legality may be challenged by the parties. Equally, they may be open to claims of ethnic or religious bias in a way that violates domestic legislation against non-discrimination, although in principle party autonomy dictates that some discrimination (which does not, however, violate due process and party equality) is an entrenched (and lawful) dimension in the parties' choice of arbitrators.[7]

4.3 Powers of arbitral tribunals

4.3.1 General powers of arbitral tribunals

Depending on its mandate and constitution, an entity may possess *powers*, *functions* or both. A power refers to an authority, express or implied, involving a binding decision-making capacity upon its intended addressees. A power may be granted by law or private agreement (between the power-holder and the assignee) as is the case with the mandate of tribunals to decide a dispute. A function, on the other hand, does not confer decision-making authority to the assignee, but merely the ability to carry out a specific action. Although this dichotomy is usually employed to describe non-judicial (or quasi-judicial) entities, such as UN subsidiary organs, it is useful also in the context of arbitral tribunals. Administration of oaths and registration of awards constitute functions. On the other hand, the determination of jurisdiction and the issuance of interim orders are powers bestowed upon arbitral tribunals.

In general, arbitral tribunals possess only those powers or functions conferred upon them by the parties[8] and their chosen institutional rules. Moreover, the laws of the seat usually confer additional powers upon tribunals.[9] Certain powers that would otherwise pertain to arbitral tribunals are conferred by the *lex arbitri* on its courts. By way of illustration,

---

[7] See below the case study in section 4.5.

[8] By way of illustration, tribunals have no authority to order consolidation of proceedings or concurrent hearings under s 35(2) of the English AA.

[9] Art 1700(5) of the Belgian JC, for example, confers the power to decide claims concerning the verification of writings and the alleged forgery of documents; equally Art 1470(1) French CCP.

tribunals are generally powerless to enforce an order to subpoena witnesses, preserve evidence or attach the parties' assets.[10] A tribunal may obviously issue a relevant order which is binding on the parties, but if the party against which it is issued refuses to comply the order is not enforceable in the seat.

Although in theory tribunals must conform to their mandate as reflected in the arbitration agreement, there are many instances whereby national courts have accepted that tribunals can go beyond their mandate in order to reach a just outcome. This is by no means a universal rule and should be approached with caution but it is certainly worth noting as a trend that departs from established arbitral wisdom. In chapter 2 we referred to a case where the tribunal supplemented the parties' choice of law with practice arising from the UN Convention on Contracts for the International Sale of Goods and the 2004 UNIDROIT Principles of International Commercial Contracts. The Swiss Federal Supreme Court in that case refused to set the award aside on the basis that such transnational rules were reasonable in long-standing international commercial relationships as was the one at hand.[11]

Occasionally, the power of the tribunal to circumvent its express mandate under the arbitration agreement stems from the parties' governing law or the law of the seat. This is true, for example, as regards their authority to *adapt* contracts or *fill gaps* in the parties' agreements. As to the former, it is recognised by most civil codes that arbitrators (just like the courts) may adapt a contract to fundamentally changed circumstances, such as price adjustments in long-term contracts.[12] This power is equally applicable where the change of circumstance renders performance exceptionally difficult or results in the terms of the contract being grossly damaging to one of the parties.[13] It is also assumed, although with a degree of caution, that arbitrators are entitled to fill certain gaps in the course of interpreting a contract, by implying terms which are necessary but which have not been expressed therein. By way of illustration, reasonableness may be inferred from the contract, but even if it is not and the parties have not expressly agreed how the tribunal is to decide the price of a product or a service, this

---

[10] English Arbitration Act, ss 42–5.

[11] *Chemical Products case, no 4A_240/2009*, Swiss Federal Supreme Court judgment (16 December 2009).

[12] Arts 288 and 388 of the Greek Civil Code; see *Werfen Austria GmbH v Polar Electro Europe BV, Zug Branch*, Finnish Supreme Court decision (2 July 2008), (KKO) 2008: 77.

[13] Art 3571 Polish CC.

determination must be premised on a test of reasonableness. The law of the seat may also confer power on the tribunal to disregard a particular entitlement of the parties with a view to expediting proceedings and minimising the risk of unnecessary delays. Section 25(2) and (3) of the Swedish Arbitration Act, for example, allows the arbitrators to reject evidence that is manifestly irrelevant or untimely at the point when its admission is sought. Equally, the *lex arbitri* may authorise the tribunal to withhold the award until its fees are paid.[14]

4.3.2 *Kompetenz-kompetenz* power of arbitral tribunals

Article 16(1) of the UNCITRAL Model Law states that the tribunal: 'may rule on its own jurisdiction, including any objections with respect to the existence or validity of the arbitration agreement'. Courts and entities exercising a judicial function, as is the case with arbitral tribunals, possess an inherent power to determine whether or not they possess authority to examine their authority as well as the breadth and scope of such authority in any given case. This power is derived from peremptory rules of constitutional or customary international law.[15] The fact that this power may be subject to judicial review, as stipulated under paragraph 3 of Article 16 of the UNCITRAL Model Law, or exist in parallel with the authority of regular courts does not diminish the rationale for which it is conferred on arbitral tribunals.

The principle of separability, discussed in chapter 1, essentially dictates that the power of arbitral tribunals to determine their jurisdiction (otherwise *kompetenz-kompetenz* power or competence-competence) is not limited to the existence, validity or scope of the arbitral agreement, as clearly suggested by the word 'including' in Article 16(1) of the UNCITRAL Model Law. Several courts around the world have expanded the scope of arbitral jurisdiction, encompassing within it questions involving the choice of arbitral institution and institutional rules,[16] the choice of seat (or location)[17] as well as questions regarding the tribunal's proper

---

[14] s 7(1), Schedule 2 and s 56 English AA.

[15] Advisory Opinion on the *Effect of Awards of Compensation made by the UN Administrative Tribunal*, (1954) ICJ Rep 47, at 51; *ICTY Prosecutor v Tadić*, Decision on the defence motion for interlocutory appeal on jurisdiction, 105 ILR 453, para 21.

[16] *Ace Bermuda Insurance Ltd v Allianz Insurance Company of Canada*, [2005] ABQB 975.

[17] *Insigma Technology Co Ltd v Alstom Technology Ltd*, [2009] SGCA 24.

constitution.[18] The Swiss Federal Supreme Court has emphasised that any interpretation of an arbitration agreement must assume that the parties intended to provide the tribunal with broad jurisdiction. A combination of comprehensively worded clauses and the principle of separability dictate that the entirety of claims resulting from an agreement (conclusion, validity and termination) fall within the jurisdiction of the tribunal.[19]

In practice, where a contract is the result of deceit, forgery, corruption or other illegality it would be wholly exceptional for the arbitration clause therein not to suffer from the same defect. Yet, as already explained in chapter 1 the autonomy of the arbitration clause dictates that the tribunal declare its jurisdiction over the dispute, even if the defect is examined simultaneously by the criminal courts or is otherwise subject to other judicial or administrative proceedings. The separability principle was meant to preserve arbitral jurisdiction under such circumstances so as to make civil redress possible; hence, the scope or seriousness of the defect does not affect arbitral jurisdiction if the parties had agreed to arbitral resolution in the first place. Even so, some national courts have demonstrated an acute antipathy to the autonomy of arbitration clauses despite the customary nature of this principle. In parting with well-established case law from the Brazilian Supreme Court, the Rio Grande do Sul Appeals Court held that the existence of a police investigation report suggesting forgery of the agreement in which the arbitration clause was contained was sufficient to annul the legal effects of the clause.[20] Although lawyers practicing in jurisdictions that produce such judgments must exercise caution, others should not attach any importance to these for the reasons identified above.

Challenges alleging lack of jurisdiction typically arise once the plaintiff submits his statement of claim and it is natural that Article 16(2) of the UNCITRAL Model Law requires that such challenges must be raised no later than the submission of one's statement of defence. However, if it later becomes apparent that the tribunal is breaching its mandate by considering matters not submitted to it under the arbitration agreement, the parties may raise jurisdictional challenges at any stage during the arbitral proceedings. Although the Model Law does not specifically address whether or

---

[18] *M/S Anuptech Equipments Private v M/S Ganpati Co-Op Housing*, [1999] AIR 219 (Bombay).
[19] *Ferrotitanium case 4A_452/2007*, judgment (29 February 2008), [2008] 2 ASA Bull 376 and *case 4A_438/2013*, judgment (27 February 2013).
[20] *Companhia de Geração Térmica de Energia Elétrica (CGTEE) v Kreditanstalt für Wiederaufbau Bankengruppe*, Appeals judgment (12 June 2013).

not the tribunal has the power to examine its jurisdiction on its own motion, this is emphasised in the affirmative in the *travaux*.[21]

Under France's most recent arbitral enactment, Decree No 2011–4 (adopted in 2011), the principle of competence-competence is specifically set out,[22] particularly as to its negative dimension. Besides the traditional positive dimension of the competence-competence principle, which empowers the tribunal to determine the boundaries of the jurisdiction conferred upon it by contract and law, it has also been found by the French courts to possess a negative quality. This negative quality stipulates the existence of a chronological priority rule, whereby national courts are precluded from deciding on the arbitral tribunal's jurisdiction,[23] save in situations where the tribunal has yet to be constituted or seized,[24] as well as in circumstances where the agreement to arbitrate is manifestly null and void.[25]

There may well be situations where the parties' agreement does not specifically grant authority to the tribunal to determine threshold jurisdictional issues. Such a situation arose in *BG v Argentina* before the US Supreme Court. In the absence of explicit tribunal powers (in the case at hand no reference was made in the parties' agreement to institutional or other rules), the Supreme Court held that the courts of the seat possess authority to decide issues such as whether there exists a valid arbitration agreement as well as the scope of that agreement. Conversely, in similar circumstances, tribunals, rather than the courts, are entitled to determine procedural issues such as 'waiver, delay … time limits, notice, laches, estoppel and other conditions precedent to an obligation to arbitrate'.[26]

If the tribunal dispenses with challenges against its jurisdiction in the form of a preliminary order any of the parties may request that the matter be heard by the courts of the seat.[27] In such situations there is no recourse to

---

[21] UNGA Official Records, 40th session, Supp 17, UN Doc A/40/17 (1985), Annex I, para 150.

[22] Art 1465 CCP, which emphasises the 'exclusive' nature of arbitral competence-competence.

[23] *Etablissement Raymond Gosset v Carapelli*, Supreme Cassation Court judgment (7 May 1963), [1964] *JDI* 82; reaffirmed in *American Bureau of Shipping (ABS) v Copropriété Maritimes Jules Verne*, Supreme Cassation Court judgment (26 June 2001), [2001] 3 *Rev Arb* 529.

[24] A tribunal is considered seized under French law when constituted and the arbitrators have accepted their mandate (Art 1456(1) CCP), unless agreed otherwise by the parties (Art 1461 CCP).

[25] *Quarto Children's Books v Editions du Seuil*, French Supreme Cassation Court judgment (16 October 2001), [2002] *Rev Arb* 919.

[26] *BG Group Plc v Argentina*, 134 S Ct 1198 (2014), at 2007.

[27] Art 16(3) UNCITRAL Model Law.

a further appeal if the court dismisses the challenge,[28] save for exceptional circumstances where, as under section 32(6) of the English Arbitration Act: 'the question involves a point of law which is one of general importance or is one which for some other special reason should be considered by the court of appeal'. Where the tribunal delivers its decision in the form of an award it may only be susceptible to set aside proceedings rather than the proceedings under Article 16(3) of the UNCITRAL Model Law. Even so, several senior courts have taken the view that the form of the decision (award or order) is subordinate to the determination of the relevant issue as a preliminary (rather than as a final) matter.[29]

Arbitral tribunals may ultimately decide that they possess no jurisdiction. There is some authority to the effect that such negative jurisdictional decisions are not subject to judicial review under Article 16(3) of the UNCITRAL Model Law because it would be inappropriate to compel arbitrators reaching a negative ruling to continue the proceedings.[30] Conversely, it has been held that even if negative rulings or awards are not reviewable under Article 16(3) they are certainly amenable to set aside proceedings under Article 34 of the Model Law, albeit the exhaustive grounds listed therein do not encompass challenges against erroneous jurisdictional decisions.[31] Hence, the matter is open to debate!

Case study: The power to determine set-off claims

A set-off claim is essentially a counter-demand by A against a claim for payment made by B against A. By means of the set-off claim, A demands that B's claim against him be consolidated (or set-off) against B's original obligation. Although the rationale underlying set-off claims is reasonable and without significant hurdles in the context of litigation, it may be problematic in arbitral proceedings

---

[28] Art 16(3) UNCITRAL Model Law; s 31 English AA.

[29] *Incorporated Owners of Tak Tai Building v Leung Yau Building*, Hong Kong Appeals Court judgment (9 March 2005), [2005] HKCA 87; *PT Asuransi Jasa Indonesia (Persero) v Dexia Bank SA*, [2006] SGCA 41.

[30] UNGA Official Records, 40th session, Supp 17, UN Doc A/40/17 (1985), Annex I, para 163. The Swiss Federal Supreme Court in *case 4A_669/2012* judgment (17 April 2013) rejected the argument that the disinclination of an arbitral tribunal to acknowledge its own jurisdiction (due to a finding that the parties shared a common intent to terminate the arbitration agreement) violated their right to be heard.

[31] See BGH *case III ZB 44/01*, judgment (6 June 2002), [2003] *SchiedsVZ* 39.

where the set-off claim is not encompassed in the agreement to arbitrate. If the *lex arbitri* (or the agreement to arbitrate) does not grant tribunals authority to consolidate set-off claims in the proceedings there is a clear danger that the award may be set aside as *ultra vires* (i.e. that the tribunal has exceeded its authority). Article 817 *bis* of the Italian Code of Civil Procedure grants the arbitrator authority to decide set-off claims, irrespective of whether the set-off arises from the parties' arbitration agreement. This provision is innovative,[32] as it preserves the arbitral tribunal's jurisdiction even beyond the original scope of application of the parties' agreement. However, the jurisdiction of the arbitral tribunal on set-off counter-claims is subject to an important qualification. Whenever the objection relates to the obligation to pay a sum of money which is higher than the sum of money originally requested by the claimant, the arbitral tribunal can only decide on the objection within the limits of value of the original claim.

4.4 Organisation of the tribunal

Even in institutional arbitration, whose modalities and processes are catered for by the parties' chosen institution, the parties and the tribunal must make a series of practical arrangements. Firstly, there is the crucial issue of deadlines and time limits (and decisions for extension thereof), followed by the place where the arbitrators shall meet, the fixing of oral hearings, the language of the proceedings (as well as the use of interpreters) and other matters of an organisational nature.[33] Although these are issues befalling party autonomy they may ultimately be decided (as dictated by the pertinent institutional rules) by the presiding arbitrator in case of disagreement between the parties.

In addition, the arbitrators themselves will have to devise a mechanism by which to meet, converse and ultimately decide on the merits or other procedural matters. The arbitrators' character and experience are crucial in

---

[32] See also Art 377 Swiss CCP, applicable to domestic arbitration, but there is no reason why it cannot be extended to international arbitration. Equally, s 29 Swedish AA implicitly suggests that set-off claims are admissible. Specifically, it provides that a claim invoked as a defence by way of set off shall be adjudicated in the same award as the main claim.

[33] See chapter 6 section 6.4.

this regard. By way of illustration, the parties' lawyers may well linger on endlessly with no end in sight, further producing waves of evidence with little, or no, value. It is within the remit of the arbitrators' duty of acting expeditiously and effectively to restrict counsel to the presentation of relevant evidence and within the strict time limits set out in advance.[34] The same principles apply *mutatis mutandis*, where the rules so permit, in all other matters of an organisational nature.

4.5 Constitution of tribunal and appointment of arbitrators

One must distinguish between the commencement of arbitral proceedings as such from the date of the tribunal's constitution. Proceedings generally commence when the respondent receives the plaintiff's submission of claim for arbitration,[35] whereas a tribunal is constituted upon appointment of the arbitrator(s). Although the parties need not wait until the tribunal is constituted in order to address certain urgent matters,[36] most substantive and procedural matters cannot be dealt with before the appointment of the arbitrator(s). Unlike regular courts where the person of the judge is indistinguishable from the institution of the court, an arbitral tribunal is meaningless without the particular arbitrators chosen by the parties. Given that the parties to a civil dispute possess no authority to select, let alone, appoint judges it follows that the person (identity) of the judge is immaterial for the conduct of regular judicial proceedings. Party autonomy in relation to arbitration, on the other hand, dictates that an arbitral tribunal is lawfully constituted only when the person of the arbitrators has been approved by the parties. This general freedom to appoint arbitrators, irrespective of qualifications or experience, is an inherent and indispensable dimension of the principle of personal autonomy.[37]

The selection of arbitrators is not straightforward because there is always the fear of bias and the parties are well aware that unlike litigation

---

[34] See chapter 6 section 6.7.

[35] Art 21 UNCITRAL Model Law; a distinct aberration to this rule is Art 14 of the 1994 Czech Arbitration Law whereby proceedings commence when the statement of claim is received by the arbitral institution or the arbitrator (in ad hoc arbitrations).

[36] Art 9 UNCITRAL Model Law on pre-constitution interim measures.

[37] English AA, ss 15(1) and 16(1); equally, if not almost verbatim, Arts 586(1) and 587(1) of the Austrian CCP; *Electra Air Conditioning BV v Seeley International Pty Ltd* [2008] FCAFC 169.

there is no appeal against an arbitral award. The *lex arbitri*, first of all, determines the number of arbitrators and in the vast majority of cases domestic statutes require an odd number (one or three).[38] The rationale behind this rule is to avoid unnecessary impasses in situations of disagreement between arbitrators. Exceptionally, some statutes, such as section 15(2) of the English Arbitration Act are content with an even number[39] because they assume that the party-appointed arbitrators will ultimately agree among themselves the outcome of the dispute or that in any event one of them will effectively exercise the role of chairman possessing the deciding vote in case of disagreement.[40] Some legal systems are prepared to stretch the limits of party autonomy in this respect even further by permitting the appointment of legal persons as arbitrators.[41] A legal person acting as arbitrator is not without problems due to the absence of transparency and lack of personal and ethical accountability among others.

In practice, parties select an odd number of arbitrators and in addition, although they may choose a tailor-made procedure for their selection, they rely on the appointment rules of their chosen arbitral institution. They may, of course, condition their appointments to specific criteria, such as expertise, nationality, or other. In situations of three-member panels the parties select an arbitrator each (party-appointed arbitrators) and assuming no agreement exists regarding the person of the third arbitrator, who necessarily casts the deciding vote, this task befalls the two party-appointed arbitrators.[42] It should be pointed out that although party-appointed arbitrators may be selected by the parties with some degree of self-interest it is expected that they perform their duties independently and impartially.[43] Lack of impartiality or independence makes the award susceptible to set aside challenges, in addition to any contractual (or tort)

---

[38] Art 1451(1) French CCP. Para 2 of Art 1451 orders that where the parties' agreement provides for an even number, an additional arbitrator shall be appointed.

[39] This extension of party autonomy has been shared by the Indian Supreme Court in *MMTC v Sterlite Industries Ltd*, AIR (1997) SCC (India) 605.

[40] s 20 English AA. The function of chairman should be distinguished from that of umpire. Umpires do not as a rule take part in proceedings, but only have a role to play where one or more arbitrators are challenged and removed, in accordance with s 21 English AA. There is no provision for the function of chairman in the UNCITRAL Model Law.

[41] *Sogecable SA v Auna Telecommunicaciones SA*, Madrid Audencia Provincial judgment (29 July 2005).

[42] Art 11(3)(a) UNCITRAL Model Law.

[43] This is mandatory and not subject to agreement by the parties. See Art 12(1) UNCITRAL Model Law.

liability of the arbitrator.[44] In situations of a sole arbitrator, or in respect of panels of three or more arbitrators, where the party-appointed arbitrators cannot agree on the person of the president he or she shall be chosen either by the courts of the seat or an *appointing authority*, if the parties have already designated such an authority.[45] In order to avoid recourse to the courts, institutional rules typically stipulate that the executive body of the institution will perform the functions of appointing authority and hence the tribunal will be constituted without judicial interference.

In practice, the parties' counsels propose several candidates among a *list* of arbitrators with a note on their particular expertise as it relates to the dispute at hand. Where the names of those proposed in the two lists do not overlap then each party chooses its own candidates (i.e. where the number is odd) and these in turn appoint a president if the parties are unable to agree. Alternatively, arbitral institutions maintain lists of candidates which they suggest to the parties, chiefly on the basis of expertise (including language) with the subject matter of the dispute. Most arbitral institutions maintain *open lists*, in the sense that although they select the persons registered therein the parties are free to ignore these and choose anyone they desire.[46] Those institutions operating *closed lists* limit the parties only to those persons in their register. Several criticisms have been levelled against the closed list system on the ground that it resembles an exclusive club that inhibits diversity and breeds an elitist culture.

Where, however, the parties or their chosen institutional rules make no providence for a binding determination by an appointing authority, any party may request the courts to decide the matter.[47] If the courts were not ultimately authorised to provide a definitive resolution to appointment impasses then the party with the weaker argument would do anything in its power to frustrate the arbitration agreement by objecting to the appointment of the presiding arbitrator. Unlike the parties, which may not have demanded any particular expertise or set out further criteria, the court

---

[44] As a result, legal systems that recognise the institution of *arbitrator advocate*, namely that party-appointed arbitrators are expected to defend the claims of their appointee, thus leaving independent determinations to the umpire, may become problematic at the phase of enforcement. See M. L. Smith, Impartiality of the Party-Appointed Arbitrator, (1990) 6 *Arbitration Int* 320.

[45] For a discussion of the role of appointing authority, see chapter 1 section 1.7.3.

[46] Art 19 WIPO Arbitration Rules.

[47] s 18 English AA; Art 11(4) and (5) UNCITRAL Model Law.

cannot simply appoint anyone by plucking them from the street. No wonder paragraph 5 of Article 11 of the UNCITRAL Model Law stipulates that the court 'shall have due regard to any qualifications required of the arbitrator by the agreement of the parties and to such considerations as are likely to secure the appointment of an impartial arbitrator ... and shall take into account as well the advisability of appointing an arbitrator of a nationality other than those of the parties'. In practice, the courts encourage the parties to suggest suitable candidates, as the judges are unlikely to be familiar (and why should they be?) with relevant lists or appropriate candidates. Even so, the courts may well decide that the facts of a dispute require disregarding the parties' original choice as to the arbitrator's nationality. In a dispute between a US and a Quebecoise party the agreement stipulated the arbitral proceedings would be governed by the Quebec CCP. The Superior Court of Quebec had no doubt that the best suited arbitrator would have to be Quebecoise despite the fact that the parties had originally excluded their compatriots.[48] The principle enunciated in Article 11(5) of the UNCITRAL Model Law is meant to ensure the constitution of the tribunal in a manner that is as close as possible to the intentions of the parties as expressed in their arbitration agreement. Hence, it has been accepted that if there is no real contention the courts should not intervene.[49] Nonetheless, it is equally accepted that the courts may disregard the intention of the parties in exceptional circumstances, including where their intransigence leads to unnecessary delays and inhibits the expeditiousness of arbitral proceedings.[50]

Finally, it should be stressed that given the delays incurred until the courts make a determination under Article 11(5) of the UNCITRAL Model Law it would have been absurd if any further appeals were available to the parties. Paragraph 5 and consistent state practice make this rule rather clear.

Non-discrimination laws and party autonomy in arbitrator appointments

In *Jivraj v Hashwani* it was initially held by the English Court of Appeals that the practice of appointing Ismaili arbitrators in commercial disputes between members of this religious community was

---

[48] *I-D Foods Corp v Hain-Celestial Group Inc* [2006] QCCS 3889.
[49] *Montpellier Reinsurance Ltd v Manufacturers Property & Casualty Ltd*, Bermuda Supreme Court judgment (24 April 2008) [2008] Bda LR 24.
[50] *Union of India v M/S Singh Builders Syndicate* (2009) 4 SCC (India) 523.

contrary to English employment legislation.[51] This decision was overturned by the Supreme Court on the ground that since arbitrators were
not subordinate to their appointees and thus not under contract to
provide a service they were not subject to equality or employment
laws.[52] Of course, this is hardly the same as affirming the paramount
nature of party autonomy in the choice of arbitrators, which the
Supreme Court failed to stress.

4.5.1 Duties of arbitrators

Before venturing into the legal relationship between the parties and arbitrators, as well as the potential liability and challenges against arbitrators, it
is wise to briefly set out their duties. One should discern between duties
imposed by law and those imposed by the parties – although some commentators identify ethical duties as a distinct category. Party-imposed duties
are contained in the instrument of appointment, institutional rules and
relevant *lex mercatoria*. Besides the duty to be independent and impartial
and respect due process rights (including treating the parties with equality)
the UNCITRAL Model Law imposes no other duties on arbitrators, largely
because additional duties would constitute grounds for challenges and hence
justification for further delays. There is, of course, no prohibition against
introducing other duties. Some commentators recognise the existence of the
following duties: to act with care, to act promptly and to act judicially.[53]

4.6 Relationship of arbitrators to parties

We have already determined that arbitral tribunals are not courts but do
nonetheless exercise a judicial function. This determination, however,
refers to the institution of the tribunal not the status of arbitrators as per
their relationship to the parties. Unlike the courts, the institution of the
tribunal is distinct from the person of the arbitrators. The arbitrators,

---

[51] *Jivraj v Hashwani* [2010] EWCA Civ 712, paras 28–30.
[52] *Jivraj v Hashwani* [2011] UKSC 40.
[53] N. Blackaby and C. Partasides, *Redfern and Hunter on International Arbitration* (Oxford University Press, 2009, 5th edition), 327–36.

although contractually linked to an arbitral institution, are equally distinct from it and each one of them may incur liability for damages or tort against any of the parties or against the arbitral institution. It is thus of crucial importance to ascertain the legal nature of the arbitrator's appointment, which encompasses his legal relationship to the parties.

This relationship is not susceptible to any general rule under the various sources of international law, including general principles. Domestic laws while generally averse to recognising arbitrators as public officials or as persons exercising a public function,[54] (but see the Austrian position below) are nonetheless receptive to the idea that the conduct of arbitrators may generate liability in contract (or exceptionally also in tort) vis-à-vis the parties (e.g. for gross negligence, corruption, unnecessary delays, failure to disclose, etc.).[55] Even so, in order to protect the institution of arbitration and ensure that awards produce the same effects as judgments, all functions concerned with the rendering of the award as such are immune from liability. By way of example, no liability arises as a result of the reasoning adopted by the arbitrators to justify their award.

Although there exists a clear contractual arrangement with the parties and arbitral institutions, the precise nature and scope of such agreements differ in both theory and practice. It is suggested that this might take the form of a mandate (in which case arbitrators are considered agents of the parties),[56] an agreement for the provision of services (of an intellectual nature on the part of arbitrators), a trusteeship agreement[57] or other complex combinations thereof. The Austrian Supreme Court, for example, has confirmed that although the arbitrators' appointment is governed by public law the relationship between the parties is contractual and is itself governed by the services contracts provisions of the Civil Code.[58] The practical significance of the Austrian public law nature of the arbitrators' appointment is that their liability must be assessed on the same grounds as that of judges.

---

[54] Art 813(2) Italian CCP.   [55] Art 813(1)ter Italian CCP.

[56] Under the Dutch Civil Code, where an arbitration is governed by Dutch law an agreement of instruction is established between the parties and the arbitral tribunal. See B. van der Bend et al., *A Guide to the NAI Arbitration Rules* (Kluwer, 2009), 13.

[57] This seems to be the dominant position in Sweden, although no references to arbitrator liability are made in the country's Arbitration Act and there is no available case law. See K. Hobér, *International Commercial Arbitration in Sweden* (Oxford University Press, 2011), 160.

[58] Austrian Supreme Court, *case 6 Ob 207/06v*, judgment (30 November 2006).

4.7 Liability of arbitrators

Having determined the contractual nature of the arbitrators' relationship with the parties and arbitral institutions, the next question to be addressed is whether such relationship should render them vulnerable to the full gamut of contractual liability in dispensing their judicial functions. Although the question seems self-evident one should be mindful of the risks to the arbitrators' judicial integrity as a result of a liability based solely on the law of contract. Moreover, whereas contractual liability typically requires a breach as well as evidence of harm and sufficient attribution, the parties may have varying expectations of the arbitrator (many times unrealistic) and it is also likely that the arbitrator's conduct, although somewhat negligent, may not cause them any identifiable harm. As a result, it is not always clear whether the *sui generis* liability of arbitrators is best described as contractual, tort-based or alternatively as a combination of the two.[59] By way of illustration, although most national courts are prepared to accept that arbitrators may be liable for any harm caused for their failure to make a full disclosure about circumstances jeopardising their independence and impartiality,[60] there are no judgments discussing liability absent claims of harm. This tension is amply exemplified in the law and practice of many jurisdictions. In accordance with Article 37(2) of the Spanish Arbitration Act arbitrators may incur liability for their failure to deliver an award within the specified time limits set out by the parties. Despite the express wording of the Act the Spanish Supreme Court has found this threshold far too high. Instead, it has held that what is required is clear, manifest and grossly negligent conduct by the arbitrator before liability could be imposed, emphasising that any other approach would be damaging to the institution of arbitration.[61]

Two theories, both expressed in statute, dominate the landscape. The *contractual school* maintains that arbitrators enjoy little or no immunity

---

[59] Given the above considerations it is certainly not a *strict liability* obligation. It seems closer to a standard of performance requiring the exercise of *reasonable care* without guaranteeing any particular end result. Common law jurisdictions have accepted an additional *sui generis* fault-based liability in respect of services contracts for professionals such as lawyers or doctors, which gives rise to a concurrent (in addition to the contractual) duty in tort to take reasonable care. See *Thake v Maurice* [1986] QB 644, at 677, 684–7.

[60] *Société Annahold BV v L'Oréal*, Paris Court of Appeals judgment (9 April 1992), [1996] *Rev Arb* 486.

[61] *Case no 429/2009*, Spanish Supreme Court judgment (22 June 2009).

(unlike regular judges)[62] when acting in gross negligence or bad faith because they violate the contractual duties incumbent upon them. Adherents of the *status school*, encompassing most common law nations, suggest that the assumption of judicial functions by arbitrators entitles them to a status equivalent to that enjoyed by judges.[63] Both verge towards a standard of qualified immunity for conduct other than gross negligence and bad faith. There are several arguments in favour and against the positions held by both schools, principally that if arbitrators faced the threat of civil, criminal or disciplinary liability they would be unable to discharge their judicial duties effectively,[64] whereas the opposite argument stresses that negligent arbitrators have little incentive to conclude the case as diligently as possible. By way of example, if an arbitrator were to breach confidentiality or refuse to offer an award, the parties would not only be saddled with significant legal fees and a waste of valuable time but they would suffer a non-outcome (an artificial *non liquet*) for which they are not to blame. With the exception of the USA, several common law jurisdictions such as the UK have introduced a limited, or qualified, immunity for arbitrators. Section 29(1) of the English Arbitration Act provides that arbitrators are only liable for acts or omissions done in the discharge of their duties where they are 'shown to have been in bad faith'.[65]

Besides their contractual liability to the parties, arbitrators may be liable towards third parties (with whom they have no contractual relationship) by means of an unlawful act in the course of their arbitral duties, such as experts and witnesses. This is liability in tort and may arise, among other reasons, because of insults to the expert's personality or as a result of unauthorised disclosure. Injured parties are increasingly provided with a direct action against arbitral institutions regardless of any complementary actions against arbitrators.[66] In turn, many institutions have incorporated liability limitation provisions in their rules, albeit these cannot always override the application of mandatory norms of contract and tort law. The general trend seems to be heading towards a limitation of immunities for arbitrators, particularly since arbitral institutions are becoming

---

[62] Regular judges face disciplinary liability from their peers, which could even result in dismissal from the service if the conduct is of a gross nature.

[63] See *Bremer Schiffban v South India Shipping Corp Ltd*, [1981] AC 909, per Donaldson J.

[64] *Cort v AAA*, 795, F Supp. 970 (ND Cal. 1992), at 973.

[65] This is limited to fraud under s 28 of the 1992 Australian International AA.

[66] Art 21(a) Spanish AA.

increasingly frustrated with the prospect of losing business to competing institutions on account of arbitrators that fail to discharge their duties diligently. This trend may well be assessed by reference to the increase in insurance coverage sought by arbitrators.[67]

Contractual liability of arbitrator in an UNCITRAL jurisdiction

Like all arbitration statutes modelled under the UNCITRAL Model Law the Finnish Arbitration Act does not contain a provision on the liability of arbitrators. A landmark judgment by the Finnish Supreme Court in 2005 changed the landscape and gave potential arbitrators in Finland something to think about.[68] In the case at hand, in the course of construction arbitration one of the parties realised that the arbitrator appointed by the other party had previously acted as its legal counsel. As a result, proceedings against this person (X) commenced before the civil courts for damages related to his failure to make a full disclosure, and the question which arose was whether the liability of the arbitrator to the parties was contractual, tort-based or both. The case ultimately reached the Supreme Court which held that the liability of an arbitrator was predicated solely on his contractual obligations to the parties, thus requiring a causal link between the alleged act or omission (failure to disclose) and the harm caused (in this case the other party's legal and other expenses). No liability could arise under tort, namely the 1974 Finnish Tort Liability Act, and even the contractual character of arbitrator liability was deemed to be exceptional.[69]

4.8 Ethical rules for arbitrators

Ethical issues have always been a thorny issue in international arbitration, particularly as regards the impartiality and independence of arbitrators, although the shift has also turned to the parties' representatives. As a result,

---

[67] Unlike Art 21(1) of the Spanish AA where such insurance is mandatory, most arbitral institutions are not covered. See M. Jolivet, La Responsabilité des Centres d'Arbitrage et leur Assurance, (2012) 1 *Revue Générale du Droit des Assurances* 7.

[68] See G. Möller, The Finnish Supreme Court and the Liability of Arbitrators, (2006) 23 *JOIA* 95.

[69] *Ruola Family v X*, Supreme Court decision (31 January 2005), (KKO) 2005: 14.

most institutional rules encompass relevant ethics provisions, in addition to more detailed ethical codes, such as the American Arbitration Association (AAA) Code of Ethics for Arbitrators and the IBA Rules of Ethics for International Arbitrators.[70] Although it is expected that arbitrators must be impartial and independent, lest the award be set aside under the *lex arbitri* or refused enforcement at a later stage, there is no single internationally accepted standard of impartiality.[71] As a result, while ethical issues are largely driven by institutional codes of conduct which prescribe, among others, the extent of disclosure and possible conflicts of interest, the ultimate arbiter of such issues are the courts of the seat. These in turn are not averse to relying on the standards adopted in institutional rules.[72] As has already been demonstrated in this chapter the ethics of arbitral proceedings coincide in practice with contractual or tort liability for failure to disclose or failure to act impartially and independently. It has been suggested that arbitrators have consented to these ethical rules through the acceptance of their appointment and mandate.[73]

The parties' representatives are an integral part of the arbitral process, despite the fact that their role is often underplayed in the academic literature. An assessment of their duties, ethical and legal, is offered in chapter 6.[74]

4.9 Impartiality and independence of arbitrators

Parties with different nationalities choose international arbitration, among other reasons, with a view to avoiding the bias of domestic courts. It is natural,

---

[70] Mini codes of ethics may also be found in some multilateral treaties, such as Annex 14(c) of the EU–Korea FTA and the code of conduct prescribed for persons sitting on dispute settlement panels under chapters 19 and 20 of NAFTA.

[71] English courts are generally in agreement that the appropriate test for impartiality is that of 'real possibility of bias', as per the judgment in *AT&T Corp. v Saudi Cable Co* [2000] 2 Lloyd's Rep 127; the IBA Rules of Ethics, on the other hand, provide that prospective arbitrators should disclose all facts or circumstances that may give rise to 'justifiable doubts' as to their impartiality; Art 3(1) of the Portuguese Chamber of Commerce Code of Ethics introduces an 'absolute' impartiality test.

[72] US courts rely heavily, for example, on the AAA/ABA Code of Ethics for Arbitrators in Commercial Disputes in order to decide issues of independence and impartiality. See *Merit Insurance Company v Leatherby Insurance Company*, 714 F 2d 673 (7th Cir. 1983); *Brandeis Instel Limited v Calabrian Chemicals Corporation*, 656 F Supp. 160 (SDNY 1987); *Reeves Brothers, Inc v Capital-Mercury Shirt Corp*, 962 F Supp. 408 (SDNY 1997).

[73] See S. Brekoulakis, Systemic Bias and the Institution of International Arbitration: A New Approach to Arbitral Decision Making, (2013) 4 *J Intl Disp Settlement* 553.

[74] See chapter 6 section 6.8.

therefore, that they expect the highest standards of impartiality and independence from arbitrators. Unlike conventional judges, however, who may sit in judgment of the same party or hear the same counsel numerous times during their tenure without any particular conflict, the fact that arbitrators are appointed by the parties (sometimes on more than one occasion), and are usually engaged as professional advocates as their principal profession, gives rise to questions of partiality and independence. As a result, the relevant standards have to accommodate the particularities of international arbitration, especially the desire of parties to appoint the best possible arbitrators while at the same time eliminating any avenues for bias and conflict.

There are four broad grounds upon which an arbitrator(s) may be challenged, namely: a) lack of impartiality and independence; b) lack of agreed qualifications;[75] c) absence of physical or mental capacity to conduct proceedings[76] and; d) otherwise refusal or failure to conduct proceedings and render an award.[77] As to the first of these, the standard set out in Article 12(1) of the UNCITRAL Model Law is by now a general principle of the law of nations but as will be demonstrated its interpretation has given rise to controversies. It posits that arbitrators have a duty to disclose 'any circumstances likely to give rise to justifiable doubts as to [their] impartiality or independence'. This standard clearly requires an avoidance of a perception or appearance of bias. The fact that an arbitrator has met, conversed, taught or even collaborated with one of the parties in the past is not necessarily sufficient for a finding of impartiality. This gives rise to challenges based on an *appearance of bias*. Here, there exists no evidence (and the arbitrator has disclosed none) of a direct conflict of interest, but on the basis of particular relationships or considerations of a personal nature the likelihood of impartiality may be logically deducted. There is no single standard internationally and differing views abound.[78]

Most courts in arbitration-friendly nations are inclined to assume a relatively narrow disclosure duty given that the UNCITRAL Model Law

---

[75] Art 12(2) UNCITRAL Model Law.   [76] Art 14(1) UNCITRAL Model Law.

[77] s 24(1)(c) and (d) English AA; Art 14(1) UNCITRAL Model Law. This ground may also arise where the arbitrator failed to render a timely award. See *Ting Kang Chung John v Teo Hee Lai Building Constructions Ltd and Ors* [2010] SGHC 20; *NBCC Ltd v JG Engineering Pvt Ltd*, Indian Supreme Court judgment (5 January 2010), [2010] INSC 5.

[78] *Metropolitan Properties Co Ltd v Lannon* [1969] QB 577, per Denning LJ at 599, which upheld the challenge; see contra *Peoples Security Life Insurance Co v Monumental Life Insurance Co*, 991 F 2d 141 (4th Cir. 1993), at 146.

does not require full or open-ended disclosure, albeit this duty starts from the moment of appointment until the close of arbitral proceedings.[79] The duty to disclose extends to those facts which may objectively raise doubts about one's impartiality and independence. As a result, it has been held that an arbitrator had not breached his duty by failing to disclose that he was a limited partner in a company established by one of the parties' managing directors[80] and the same was equally true in respect of a law-yer/arbitrator who had in the past once represented (in an unrelated dis-pute) one of the parties.[81] In a re-insurance case decided by the US Second Circuit Appeals Court the respondent argued that the award should be vacated (set aside) because two arbitrators failed to disclose their service as arbitrators in a concurrent arbitration which involved common wit-nesses, similar legal issues and a related party. The court rejected the claim by reference to established case law whereby *evident partiality* exists only 'where a reasonable person would have to conclude that an arbitrator was partial to one party'. Such partiality may be assessed by reference to the extent of the alleged personal interest, the directness of the relationship and its connection to the impugned arbitrator as well as its proximity in time.[82] The court acknowledged that prior interactions are not reflective of bias, emphasising that 'in specialized fields such as re-insurance, where there are a limited number of experienced arbitrators, it is common for the same arbitrators to end up serving together frequently'.[83] What this case law clearly suggests is that where a person is appointed as arbitrator repetitively by the same party in similar disputes justifiable doubts may

---

[79] Art 12(1) UNCITRAL Model Law; *J&P Avax SA v Société Tecnimont*, Paris Court of Appeals judgment (12 February 2009), [2009] *Rev Arb* 186.

[80] OLG Naumburg, *case 10 SchH 03/01*, judgment (19 December 2001); but see Art 815(1) Italian CCP, where one of the grounds for challenging an arbitrator is: 'if he or she is linked to one of the parties, to a company controlled by that party, to its controlling entity or to a company subject to common control by a subordinate labour relationship or by a con-tinuous consulting relationship or by a relationship for the performance of remunerated activity or by other relationships of a patrimonial or associative nature which might affect his or her independence'.

[81] OLG Hamburg, *case 9 SchH 01/015*, judgment (12 July 2005).

[82] *Applied Indus Mats Corp v Ovalar makine Ticaret Ve Sanayi AS*, 492 F 3d 132 (2d Cir. 2007), at 137; *Three S Del Inc v DataQuick Info Sys Inc*, 492 F 3d 21 520 (4th Cir. 2007), at 530; in the Cypriot case of *Stavrou v Tylli*, (2007) 1B CLR 1172, partiality was defined as 'any form of behaviour which tends to compromise and destroy the confidence that parties must have in their arbitrators, that the latter would render a just award'.

[83] *Scandinavian Reins Co v St Paul Fire & Marine Ins Co*, 668 F 3d 60 (2nd Cir. 2012).

in fact be assumed.[84] Scholarship and case law has consistently found that the following grounds give rise to an appearance of bias which would render an arbitrator susceptible to disqualification:

1) a significant financial interest in the relevant project or dispute, or in a party or its counsel;
2) a close family relationship with a party or its counsel;
3) non-financial involvement in the relevant project, dispute or the subject matter of the dispute;
4) a public position taken on the specific matter in dispute;
5) involvement in the settlement discussions of the parties; and
6) an adversary relationship with a party.[85]

Sometimes an *appearance of bias* may arise not by the parties' association or prior relationship with an arbitrator, but by reason of the particular attitude, stance or utterances of the arbitrator. In a case decided by a Cypriot court, following conclusion of the hearing the arbitrators discussed the case with one of the parties and were quoted as saying that it was 'a waste of time'. It was held that such behaviour constituted impermissible misconduct which destroyed the trust placed in the arbitrator.[86] In another case, however, the Danish Supreme Court stipulated that where a practitioner has taken a position with regard to an issue that is subject to arbitral proceedings (legal or factual) in the abstract, he or she is not considered as having lost his or her impartiality or independence.[87] In the case at hand, the practitioner had consulted one of the parties during negotiations and his position had not been considered by the party.

4.10 Challenges against arbitrators and their removal

When one of the four grounds listed in the previous section arises any of the parties may challenge the arbitrators and request their removal. It goes

---

[84] *Chomat v A*, Paris Commercial Tribunal judgment (6 July 2004), [2005] *Rev Arb* 709.

[85] D. Bishop and L. Reed, Practical Guidelines for Interviewing, Selecting and Challenging Party-Appointed Arbitrators in International Commercial Arbitration, (1998) 14 *Arbitration Int 395*, at 406–8.

[86] *Bank of Cyprus Ltd v Dynacon Ltd and Another* (1990) 1B AAD 717.

[87] *JMK Transport ApS v Danish Crown AMPA*, Danish Supreme Court, judgment (19 December 2009).

without saying that the parties may by mutual consent, given the contractual nature of appointment, terminate an arbitrator's tenure at any time irrespective of fault,[88] subject to the payment of adequate compensation. The challenge procedure befalls the sphere of party autonomy and in respect of institutional arbitration this matter is principally regulated by the chosen institutional rules, or exceptionally by a procedure devised by the parties themselves.[89] In the absence of such an agreement, any of the parties, after becoming aware of relevant circumstances, may challenge the arbitrator by means of a reasoned statement. Unless the challenged arbitrator withdraws or the other party agrees to the challenge the arbitral tribunal itself shall decide on the challenge,[90] as part of its wider *kompetenz-kompetenz* powers. If the outcome is not to the liking of the challenging party it may further, albeit without the possibility of subsequent appeal, challenge the arbitrator before the local courts. Nonetheless, such an action does not have the effect of suspending arbitral proceedings.[91] It should be pointed out that parties are not prevented from challenging arbitrators appointed by them if the relevant ground is discovered following appointment or constitution of the tribunal.[92] Given the urgency of the request, it is not surprising that time limits for challenges at the various stages of proceedings are short. Where the parties choose not to request judicial determination or otherwise ignore the defect, even though it was clearly known to them, they are prevented from subsequently raising pertinent set aside proceedings. This outcome is based on conduct-based estoppel or is otherwise viewed as a waiver of the challenge entitlement.

4.11 Substitute arbitrators and truncated tribunals

When an arbitrator resigns or his mandate is revoked by the parties or the court to which a challenge request has been submitted, the tribunal is one or more arbitrators short of its original composition. Although Article 15 of the UNCITRAL Model Law stipulates that a substitute arbitrator may be appointed, several important issues require a concrete answer. For one thing, if the agreement to arbitrate specifically named the parties' chosen

---

[88] s 23 English AA; Art 590 Austrian CCP.   [89] Art 13(1) UNCITRAL Model Law.
[90] Art 13(2), UNCITRAL Model Law.   [91] Art 13(3), UNCITRAL Model Law.
[92] Art 12(2), UNCITRAL Model Law.

arbitrators or their number thereof, a breach of the agreement might occur where the parties opt to continue the proceedings solely with the remaining arbitrators (truncated tribunal) or without one or more of the originally named arbitrators.[93] Increasingly, more and more institutional rules cater for truncated proceedings and unless there is disagreement between the parties there is little reason why truncated awards should be viewed as suffering from a defect that renders them unenforceable.[94] Even so, the tribunal and the parties must tread with caution because a string of cases suggests that where the operation of a truncated tribunal is deemed to be contrary to the (constitutional) principle of equal treatment the award may be set aside.[95]

Exceptionally, if the arbitration agreement (especially in the form of a submission agreement) leaves no doubt that the parties envisaged only particular persons as arbitrators the removal of any one of these renders the agreement inoperable. In cases of reconstituted tribunals with a substitute arbitrator the tribunal is usually granted authority under the applicable institutional rules to determine if and to what extent prior proceedings should be repeated.[96] The situation is less straightforward as regards authority to continue proceedings through a truncated tribunal. Article 15(5) of the ICC Rules, for example, stipulates that such determination is to be made by the Court (the ICC's executive organ) after taking 'into account the views of the remaining arbitrators and of the parties and such other matters that it considers appropriate in the circumstances'.

In every case, the original law (chiefly institutional rules) applicable to the appointment and challenges of arbitrators ordinarily governs all post-challenge and substitution procedures,[97] albeit many rules beg to differ on this point, as is the case with Article 15(4) of the ICC Rules. The issue is particularly important especially in situations where the party-appointed arbitrator resigns and the appointing party appoints a substitute without

---

[93] Arts 15 UNCITRAL Model Law and 56 ICSID Convention do not explicitly reject the proposition that a truncated tribunal might render an award but envisage that the truncated period will be short, the vacancy filled as soon as possible by a substitute arbitrator.

[94] *Himpurna California Energy Ltd v Indonesia*, final award (16 October 1999), [2000] XXV YB Com Arb 186, at 194, where the tribunal emphasised that it was not only entitled but obliged to continue.

[95] *ATC-CFCO v Compagnie Minière de l'Ogooue – Comilog S.A.*, Paris Appeals Court judgment (1 July 1997), [1998] *Rev Arb* 131; *First Inv Corp of the Marshall Islands v Fujian Mawei Shipbuilding, Ltd*, 858 F Supp. 2d 658 (E.D. La. 2012).

[96] Art 15(4) ICC Rules.   [97] Art 15 UNCITRAL Model Law.

consulting its opponent. It is clear that if the parties were not originally obliged to consult each other on the appointment of party-nominated arbitrators no such obligation exists with respect to substitutes either.[98]

4.12 Fees and expenses of arbitration

One should distinguish between the fees of the arbitrators and those of the arbitral institution. The latter, even if a non-profit organisation must pay for its administrative costs and will charge a fee for its services. The fee for arbitrators and the arbitral institution must be further distinguished from the expenses incurred by both. Expenses and fees are payable in full by the parties. The formula for calculating these is set out in institutional rules and in order to avoid suing the parties for non-payment, said rules typically oblige the parties to deposit in advance part or all of the anticipated fees and expenses,[99] or exceptionally some laws stipulate that the arbitrators may withhold the final award until such time as the parties make full payment.[100] Although the latter outcome may be consistent with the parties' (including the arbitrators') contractual arrangements it does give rise to concerns over the right of access to justice.[101] As a result, it is not recognised in many national statutes and is not set out in the UNCITRAL Model Law.

Three methods are typically employed to assess arbitrator fees in international commercial arbitration, namely the *ad valorem*, the 'time spent' and the 'fixed fee' methods. The *ad valorem* method contemplates fees as a percentage of the total amount of the dispute, including any counterclaims.[102] Another method is to assess fees on the basis of a rate, hourly

---

[98] *Gordian Runoff Ltd v The Underwriting Members of Lloyd's Syndicates* [2002] NSWSC 1260.

[99] Art 36 ICC Rules; the Austrian Supreme Court has affirmed that tribunals may issue enforceable awards against a party for the non-payment of a due deposit on costs and fees. OGH, *case no 3 Ob 89/85*, judgment (30 October 1985); see further OGH, *case no 7 Ob 252/05t*, judgment (8 March 2006), cited in F. T. Schwartz and C. W. Conrad, The Revised Vienna Rules: An Overview of Some Significant Changes (and a Preview of the New Austrian Arbitration Law 2014), (2013) 31 *ASA Bull* 797, at 810–11.

[100] s 7(1), Schedule 2 and s 56 English AA.   [101] See s 40 Swedish AA.

[102] ICC Rules, Appendix III, Art 2(1). The final sum, however, under paragraph 2 may be adjusted by reference to the 'diligence and efficiency of the arbitrator, the time spent, the rapidity of the proceedings, the complexity of the dispute and the timeliness of the submission of the draft award'.

or daily, which the arbitrators spend on the case, including at hearings as well as reading the evidence. This method, which is the more prevalent, is in tune with the assessment of fees for lawyers and, besides, good record-keeping requires a good deal of trust and integrity on the part of arbitrators. In order to avoid excessive charging there are typically several caps on daily, or overall, chargeable hours. Finally, especially in large and complex cases in which the parties have selected prominent arbitrators, the latter's fees are fixed from the outset irrespective of how many hours they spend on the case and how long the proceedings last.

In both ad hoc and institutional arbitration (but primarily the former) the parties may consider the fees to be excessive, especially if the time ultimately spent on the case is much smaller than originally envisaged (e.g. because the parties decide to settle half way through). Arbitration statutes or general civil law typically entitle the parties to challenge excessive fees before the courts, and in Portugal, in particular, two judgments to this effect by the Lisbon Appeals Court have definitely turned the tide (in domestic arbitral proceedings) in favour of institutional arbitration.[103]

In practice, the winning party is entitled to all reasonable costs and if only partially successful is entitled to a partial reimbursement of its costs,[104] albeit arbitration statutes and institutional rules may vary somewhat. Some statutes, such as section 60 of the English Arbitration Act place a mandatory ban on pre-dispute agreements concerning liability for arbitration expenses, whereas others do not.

---

[103] Lisbon Court of Appeals judgment on arbitrators' fees (11 July 2013) [*Arbitrators' Fee* case I]; Lisbon Court of Appeals judgment on arbitrators' fees (2 May 2013) [*Arbitrators' Fee* case II].

[104] s 42 of the Swedish AA, for example, stipulates that unless otherwise agreed by the parties, the arbitrators may, upon request by a party, order the other party to pay compensation for the opposing party's costs, and determine the manner in which the compensation to the arbitrators shall be finally allocated between the parties; equally, Art 595 Romanian CCP.

5.1 Introduction

This chapter is a seeming misfit in a book dealing with a private method of dispute resolution. Surely, the very rationale of arbitration is aimed at leaving the courts outside the parties' dispute. In the course of this chapter the reader will discover that arbitration needs the courts but the courts do not need arbitration – only insofar as this is desired to reduce their work loads. Without an effective judicial system and domestic arbitration laws that cater for a synergy between tribunals and the courts, arbitration may ultimately run into a dead end. The courts are there to make sure that unless there are serious legal impediments for arbitration to continue, that no one or anything can effectively delay or terminate arbitral proceedings or in any other way frustrate the parties' agreement to arbitrate.

This chapter will examine the relationship between arbitral tribunals and the courts of the seat, as well as their relationship with the courts of third nations and transnational courts. It will go on to examine the role of the courts prior to and after the constitution of the tribunal as well as once arbitral proceedings have been terminated.

5.2 The relationship between tribunals and the courts

It should have become clear so far that although it is possible for an arbitral process to commence and terminate without any recourse to the local courts, the tribunal does not operate outside the *lex arbitri* and in addition if it runs into trouble (e.g. the parties cannot agree on the person of the chairman) the local courts assume a critical role. Hence, tribunals are dependent on the local courts in order to resolve certain procedural disputes over which they have no discretionary powers or authority. However, one should not go as far as to argue that tribunals are subservient to the courts. The authority of the courts extends only to those issues of the arbitral process that are either outside the scope of the parties' agreement (e.g. third-party disclosure) or which are covered by a public policy rule (e.g. absence of equal treatment). This conclusion is further justified by the prohibition of appeals against arbitral awards.[1]

There are two (key) reasons for this compulsory relationship between tribunals and the courts. The first ensures for all persons the right to a fair trial and the maintenance of public policy rules. If the courts were unable to appoint a chairman, impose interim measures or assess procedural irregularities the arbitral process may never culminate in an award or worst still the stronger party has every incentive to manipulate its weaker counterpart. The second reason is that because the authority of the tribunal is contractual in nature it extends only upon those persons that have granted

---

[1] Set aside proceedings do not constitute an appeal (on the merits) but an application for annulment in respect of procedural defects.

it relevant authority under contract.[2] As a result, third parties, such as experts, witnesses, persons in possession of assets or evidence of relevance to the arbitral proceedings, are under no contractual obligation to adhere to an order of the tribunal, even if their participation in the proceedings is deemed crucial. Moreover, such persons may have no incentive to cooperate with the tribunal. If the *lex arbitri* did not empower the courts to assist the tribunal by addressing binding orders to third parties (where appropriate), the right to fair trial of the original parties would be severely jeopardised. Furthermore, an order of the tribunal on the parties themselves (e.g. to produce evidence) is only binding as a matter of contract (based on their agreement to adhere to institutional rules which permit the tribunal to issue an order). Given that only final awards are binding (by law) on the parties, orders issued by tribunals are not binding unless they are enforced by the courts. Of course, parties rarely disobey tribunal orders because their case will ultimately be heard and decided by the same arbitrators. Disobeying, challenging and displeasing one's arbitrators is not the best way forward!

What is at issue in practice is the degree and nature of court assistance to the arbitral process. Foreign investors and traders subject to the *lex arbitri* of developing (or arbitration-hostile) nations may well fear that the courts, rather than assist, will 'intervene' arbitrarily in favour of the local party. Conversely, in arbitration-friendly nations the parties may be apprehensive of the various levels of available recourse (which add to delays and cost) or even the disinclination of the local courts to intervene, save in exceptional circumstances, for fear of being branded as interventionist. One will recall from the previous chapters that industrialised nations have realised that attracting arbitrations is lucrative and hence are keen to avoid their courts and laws from being labelled as interventionist. However, the best approach cannot surely lie in any of the two extremes. Local courts that assist arbitral proceedings by acting expeditiously and effectively are a blessing for the parties and it is no wonder that experienced counsel choose their seat by reference (to a large measure) to the efficiency of the

---

[2] Exceptionally, the Luxembourg Court of Appeals has gone as far as to hold that if the arbitration clause stipulated that all disputes arising from the contract are to be resolved by arbitration, then the parties may not order interim measures from the courts as this is beyond what the parties agreed. Court of Appeals judgment (21 October 2009), [2010] *Journal des Tribunaux Luxembourg* 72.

local courts, especially in complex disputes.[3] This approach is reflected in the UNCITRAL Model Law. Whereas Article 5 emphasises that 'in matters governed by this Law, no court shall intervene except where so provided', there are numerous provisions in the Model Law whereby the 'competent' local court is empowered to assist the tribunal by issuing a binding judgment or order.[4]

The remainder of the chapter will discuss those situations where the local courts are empowered to make binding determinations in assistance of arbitral proceedings, by reference to the stage of the proceedings, namely pre-constitution, main proceedings and post-award.

5.2.1 *Locus standi*

Locus standi refers to the capacity of a person (natural or legal) to be a party to judicial or arbitral proceedings, whether as a plaintiff or respondent. It should be stressed that despite the contractual character of arbitral proceedings, which ordinarily dictates that only the parties can pray to the courts for interim or other interlocutory relief, some arbitration statutes also confer this right to other entities. Section 72(1) of the English Arbitration Act stipulates that 'a person alleged to be a party to arbitral proceedings but who takes no part in the proceedings' may apply for a declaration, injunction or other appropriate relief in order to discern the existence of a valid arbitration agreement, the tribunal's proper constitution and the propriety of the issues submitted for resolution. One might argue that section 72(1) reflects common sense, so, to go a step further, is it possible for a non-party (to the arbitration agreement) to apply for stay of arbitral proceedings? The clear answer is no, but under circumstances it may be possible for a party to parallel civil proceedings to request a stay of such proceedings until an arbitration (to which the claimant is not a party) in a related matter is concluded.

In *Reichhold Norway v Goldman Sachs*, Reichhold purchased from Jotun, a Norwegian company, shares in Jotun Polymer, a subsidiary of Jotun. In

---

[3] In order to attract arbitral business, in addition to making arbitration more efficient, several countries have set up special chambers in their judicial system to deal exclusively with issues arising from arbitral proceedings. This is true of New York, Miami and Madrid. In 2010 a specialised First Instance Court focusing on arbitration was created in Madrid (First Instance Court no. 101 of Madrid), with exclusive jurisdiction for judicial supervision of and assistance to arbitrations seated in the judicial district of Madrid. However, the Court does not possess jurisdiction in respect of set aside proceedings.

[4] See, for example, Arts 6, 8, 10, 11, 13, 16, 27, 34–36 of the UNCITRAL Model Law.

making the purchase Reichold had relied on financial advice from Goldman Sachs. It later transpired that Jotun Polymer's profits were much lower than reported which led Reichhold to initiate arbitration in Norway against Jotun pursuant to the arbitration clause in the sale agreement for damages and breach of warranty. At the same time it triggered court proceedings against Goldman Sachs for negligent misstatement in London. Goldman Sachs applied for a stay of the civil action against itself, pending the outcome of the arbitration case. The legal twist, of course, lay in the fact that Goldman Sachs was not a party to the arbitration agreement between Reichold and Jotun. The Court of Appeal focused on the commercial reality of the case and held that it possesses an inherent right to stay proceedings, ultimately sustaining the stay application.[5]

5.3 The authority of courts prior to the tribunal's constitution

Prior to the constitution of the tribunal there are at least three situations where the assistance of the courts may be necessary to the parties or the arbitral institution. These concern the enforcement of the arbitration agreement through anti-suit applications; the constitution of the tribunal in situations where the parties are unable to agree on the persons of one or more arbitrators and; challenges against the jurisdiction of the tribunal, which typically entail an argument denying the existence of an arbitration agreement altogether. We have already discussed the role of the courts in the appointment of arbitrators[6] as well as their complementary function in the tribunals' *kompetenz-kompetenz* power.[7] In this chapter we shall confine ourselves to anti-suit applications and injunctions.

5.3.1 Anti-suit applications

The existence of a valid agreement to arbitrate necessitates that any disputes falling within the scope of said agreement may not be submitted to the courts without the consent of all parties. If this were not so the

---

[5] *Reichhold Norway v Goldman Sachs* [2000] 2 All ER 679. In *Wealands v CLC* [1999] 2 Lloyd's Rep 739, it was held that a stay may be granted even if the party making the application is a third party to an existing claim.
[6] See chapter 4 sections 4.5 and 4.10.   [7] See chapter 4 section 4.3.2.

arbitration agreement would be devoid of any legal significance. Article II of the 1958 New York Convention states:

1. Each contracting party shall recognise an agreement in writing under which the parties undertake to submit to arbitration all or any differences which have arisen or which may arise between them in respect of a defined legal relationship, whether contractual or not, concerning a subject matter capable of settlement by arbitration . . .

3. The court of a contracting state, when seized of an action in a matter in respect of which the parties have made an agreement within the meaning of this article, at the request of one of the parties, shall refer the parties to arbitration, unless it finds that the said agreement is null and void, inoperative or incapable of being performed.

Consequently, where a dispute subject to an arbitration agreement is submitted to the courts, any of the parties may file an anti-suit (anti-litigation essentially) application by which the courts must suspend or terminate judicial proceedings and refer the parties to arbitration under the terms of their agreement. This is because under international law (the 1958 New York Convention, regional arbitration treaties and state practice in the form of national arbitral statutes) an agreement to arbitrate is an exception to (and consequently supersedes) the otherwise exclusive jurisdiction of civil courts in respect of commercial (international and domestic) disputes. Article 8 of the UNCITRAL Model Law aptly provides that:

(1) A court before which an action is brought in a matter which is the subject of an arbitration agreement shall, if a party so requests not later than when submitting his first statement on the substance of the dispute, refer the parties to arbitration unless it finds that the agreement is null and void, inoperative or incapable of being performed.
(2) Where an action referred to in paragraph (1) of this article has been brought, arbitral proceedings may nevertheless be commenced or continued, and an award may be made, while the issue is pending before the court.

The rule enunciated in Article 8 of the UNCITRAL Model Law applies to the substance of the dispute and not to any emergency interim measures requested from the courts prior to the constitution of the tribunal.[8] It is contested whether the parties to an arbitration agreement may approach the courts in order to clarify preliminary matters rather than wait for the tribunal to decide such matters once constituted. Besides the obvious

---

[8] Art 9 UNCITRAL Model Law.

delays to subsequent arbitral proceedings there is also the risk that certain preliminary questions may well pertain to the substance of the dispute.[9] In a Danish case, the absence of specific rules or guidance in respect of evidentiary matters led one of the parties to petition the courts for a preliminary ruling prior to the commencement of arbitral proceedings. Although such a petition seemingly violates the authority of the arbitration agreement, the Danish Supreme Court ultimately held that in the absence of any guidance in the pertinent rules of the designated institution (the Danish Institute of Arbitration) or indeed in the country's Arbitration Act, the request to the courts was valid and did not constitute a violation of the arbitration clause.[10]

Anti-suit injunctions issued by the courts of the seat against civil actions abroad possess a qualitative dimension that is different to injunctions addressed to other domestic courts. In *Angelic Grace*, Millett LJ emphasised that where 'an injunction is sought to restrain a party from proceeding in a foreign court in breach of an arbitration agreement governed by English law, the English court need feel no diffidence in granting the injunction, provided that it is sought promptly and before the foreign proceedings are too far advanced'.[11] The rationale of this judgment is predicated on four grounds, namely: a) that the other party should not be burdened with the expense of appearing in those proceedings; b) that injunctions are actions *in personam* and hence are not directed against foreign courts; c) injunctions must be made as early as possible and; d) the aim of the injunction was to enforce a contract subject to English substantive law, not to attack the foreign court's decision. By way of example, a delay of six months from the time of a failed jurisdictional challenge in Brazil was not prohibitive to the granting of an injunction,[12] whereas an injunction application submitted seven years after proceedings had been brought in Italy was duly rejected.[13] The following section on *lis alibi pendens* will provide the reader with a fuller picture of the situation.

---

[9] See below for a discussion of this very issue by the House of Lords in *Channel Tunnel Group v Balfour Beatty Ltd* [1993] AC 334.
[10] *Vestas Wind Systems A/S v ABB A/S*, Danish Supreme Court judgment (13 January 2012).
[11] *Angelic Grace, The* [1995] 1 Lloyd's Rep 87; but see contra *Toepfer v Société Cargill* [1998] 1 Lloyd's Rep 379.
[12] *DVA v Voest (Jay Bola)* [1997] 2 Lloyd's Rep 279.
[13] *Toepfer International v Molino Boschi* [1996] 1 Lloyd's Rep 510.

Before we proceed to the next section it is useful to mention in passing that there is some debate in the literature and judicial practice regarding the appropriate standard of review regarding challenges directed against the existence of an arbitration agreement, namely whether this should be the subject of a *prima facie* review or the object of a fuller judicial consideration. The dominant opinion is in favour of a fuller review but only a few national courts have even pondered at this issue.[14]

5.3.2 *Lis pendens*: parallel proceedings before tribunals and courts

It is not unusual for recalcitrant parties to a dispute to commence parallel proceedings before the courts of several nations. There may be a variety of reasons for situations of this nature, particularly if the parties' agreement does not contain a choice of forum clause. Whatever the case, in the event of parallel judicial proceedings (otherwise known as *lis alibi pendens*) it is imperative that the most appropriate forum be definitively identified in order to avoid conflicting judgments and unnecessary costs. This is usually achieved through regional jurisdictional conflict rules, such as the Brussels I Regulation[15] which was discussed in chapter 2 (as well as below in this section), as well as by the jurisdictional conflict rules of each nation. However, it is clear that unless domestic jurisdictional conflict rules are harmonised the risk of conflicting outcomes cannot be ruled out.

In general, civil law courts and their laws apply a first-in-time rule in situations where proceedings are pending before another competent court involving the same subject matter (cause of action) between the same parties. This means that the first seized court will be the one to determine the issue of jurisdiction and in the absence of a choice of forum clause it will also likely declare that it possesses jurisdiction over the dispute. This first-in-time rule is equally reflected in the Brussels

---

[14] See *Barnmore Demolition and Civil Engineering Ltd v Alandale Logistics Ltd and Others*, Irish High Court judgment (11 November 2010), [2010] IEHC 544 whose judgment was, however, inconclusive although commentators suggest that it was in favour of a fuller review.

[15] Council Regulation 44/2001 of 22 December 2000 on jurisdiction and the recognition and enforcement of judgments in civil and commercial matters [2001] OJ L 12. This Regulation is conveniently known as Brussels I.

I Regulation.[16] In fact, the CJEU has gone as far as to argue that the first-in-time rule in the Brussels I Regulation applies even where the first proceedings commenced in breach of an exclusive jurisdiction clause (but not arbitration clause) in the parties' agreement,[17] in which case an anti-suit injunction by the court legitimately seized against the court not so seized constitutes an unacceptable interference with that court's jurisdiction. Common law nations, on the other hand, have traditionally found themselves to possess an inherent jurisdiction to stay their own proceedings in the interest of justice, even where the parallel proceedings in another nation are not between the same parties or do not concern the same subject matter or cause of action.[18]

In cases of parallel proceedings between the same parties and the same cause of action before a court[19] and an arbitral tribunal the situation is markedly different. Neither the first-in-time rule nor the discretionary power of the courts constitute convincing arguments because the 1958 New York Convention, as already demonstrated (among other instruments), makes it clear that in jurisdictional conflicts between a court and an arbitral tribunal, the court must stay its proceedings in favour of arbitration, unless it finds that the agreement is null and void, inoperative or incapable of being performed.[20] The only discretion available to the *lex fori* (or the law of the seat) is whether the authority to decide on the existence of a valid arbitration clause belongs to the tribunal (in accordance with its *kompetenz-kompetenz* powers) or whether it belongs also to

---

[16]   Brussels I, Art 9(1) and (2).

[17]   *Erich Gasser GmbH v MISAT Srl*, case C-116/02, [2003] ECR I-14693, as well as *Gregory Paul Turner v Felix Fareed Ismail Grovit, Harada Ltd & Changepoint Ltd*, case C-159/02, [2004] ECR I-3565.

[18]   See C. M. V. Clarkson and J. Hill, *The Conflict of Laws* (Oxford University Press, 2011), 102 and 114–22. It is under this light that common law courts developed the doctrine of *forum non conveniens*, which does not of course apply to arbitral proceedings. Exceptionally, the US Court of Appeals for the Second Circuit has relied on *forum non conveniens* to dismiss a petition for enforcement of a Peruvian award because of its allegedly fundamentally Peruvian nature and public interest factors entrenched in the country's domestic law. *Figueiredo Ferraz e Engenharia de Projeto Ltda v Peru*, 635 F 3d 384 (2d Cir. 2011).

[19]   Parallel proceedings can also co-exist between an arbitral tribunal and a specialised commission that may or may not qualify as a judicial or quasi-judicial entity, such as national competition commissions. In *ET Plus SA v Welter* [2005] EWHC 2115 (Comm), the English High Court stayed competition proceedings in favour of arbitration, even though the issue in question would have fallen within the jurisdiction of the Office of Fair Trading (OFT) and the Competition Appeals Tribunal (CAT).

[20]   See s 9 English AA.

the courts. In English law, tribunals possess authority to determine the existence of a valid arbitration agreement (s 30(1)(a) English Arbitration Act) but at the same time any of the parties may pray to the courts for a stay of litigation (s 9(1) English Arbitration Act). It is also of no legal significance to argue that arbitral proceedings should be stayed because a court has issued a judgment in violation of the parties' arbitration agreement. Such a judgment should be annulled and the dispute referred anew to arbitral proceedings in accordance with the arbitration agreement.[21] Common sense finally dictates that national courts will be inclined to stay arbitral proceedings in favour of litigation where the arbitration agreement provides for a choice of law and a seat that ultimately circumvents mandatory rules.[22]

5.3.2.1 *West Tankers* and jurisdictional conflicts under EU law

This state of affairs was never in doubt until a ruling of the CJEU in the *West Tankers* case created unnecessary confusion and turmoil in the arbitration community. Article 1(2)(d) of Brussels I Regulation, which deals with the jurisdiction of national courts in respect of civil and commercial disputes, excludes arbitration from the relevant jurisdictional provisions.[23] Article 27 of the Brussels I Regulation then makes it clear that the *lis pendens* rule determines which national court has priority in entertaining a civil dispute (namely the courts of the country first seized of a suit). So far there is no conflict between arbitration and litigation. However, in the *West Tankers* case,[24] the CJEU upset this state of affairs

---

[21] A decision to this effect was issued by the Swiss Federal Supreme Court, thus sustaining the judgment by the court first seised in Panama. See *Fomento de Construccuones Contratas SA v Colon Container Terminal SA*, [2001] ASA Bull 544. The underlying rationale has been heavily criticised and it is doubtful that it will be repeated. See C. Oetker, The Principle of Lis Pendens in International Arbitration: The Swiss Decision in Fomento v Colon, (2002) 17 *Arbitration Int* 137.

[22] See *Accentuate Ltd v Asigra Inc* [2009] EWHC 2655 (QB), which concerned an attempt to circumvent mandatory provisions of the 1986 Commercial Agents Directive 86/653.

[23] Even so, the CJEU had ruled in *Marc Rich & Co AG v Societá Italiana Impianti PA*, case C-190/89, [1991] ECR I-3855, that Brussels I was applicable to parallel civil and arbitral proceedings in situations where the validity of an arbitration clause was affirmed by an arbitral tribunal but rejected by the courts of a member state. In *Van Uden v Deco Line*, case C-391/95, [1998] ECR I-7091, the CJEU went even further by arguing that interim measures are not covered by the arbitration exclusion in Brussels I, because they are not ancillary but, rather, parallel to arbitral proceedings.

[24] *Allianz Spa (formerly Riunione Adriatica Di Sicurita SpA) and Others v West Tankers Inc* [2009] 1 AC 1138.

by arguing that the existence of an arbitration clause did not automatically exclude the jurisdiction of national courts on the same matter and that in any event national courts seized of a dispute (which was already the subject of an arbitration agreement) possessed the necessary authority to determine whether they indeed enjoyed jurisdiction. As a result, the exclusivity of arbitration agreements could not be sustained by anti-suit injunctions.

The facts of the case are as follows. Erg Petroli SpA chartered a vessel, the Front Comor, from West Tankers Inc. The charter-party agreement was governed by English law and contained an arbitration clause designating London as the seat. In the course of the performance, the Front Comor collided with a pier in Syracuse that was owned by Erg Petroli. The latter naturally triggered its insurance policy but at the same time went on to commence arbitral proceedings against West Tankers in London with the aim of recovering the uninsured portion of its loss. In the meantime, Erg Petroli's insurers, Allianz SpA and Assicurazioni Generali SpA, exercised their subrogation rights against West Tankers, in accordance with their standard agreement with Erg Petroli and brought a claim against West Tankers in Italian courts to recover the sum paid out as a matter of tort liability under Article 5(3) of Brussels I Regulation. West Tankers, on their part, prayed to an English court for an anti-suit injunction against the pending litigation in Italy. The English court granted their application (including declaratory relief) on the basis that the Italian proceedings were clearly in breach of the arbitration clause between Erg Petroli and West Tankers. The insurers appealed the English court's judgment to the (then) House of Lords, which in turn referred the matter to the CJEU on the question of whether an anti-suit injunction could be granted to restrain proceedings in another EU member state or whether such an order was precluded by Brussels I Regulation.

The CJEU proceeded to examine the jurisdictional conflicts from the perspective of Brussels I Regulation, not through the lens of the exceptional regime governing arbitration under international law. As a result, it found that the insurers' claim for damages was clearly encompassed under Brussels I Regulation and that the existence or not of a valid arbitration agreement was a preliminary issue within the scope of the claim for damages. It was not a far leap for the CJEU to conclude that this preliminary issue fell within the jurisdiction of the Italian court and that 'to prevent a court of a member state (which normally has jurisdiction to resolve a dispute from ruling) on the applicability of [Brussels I] to the dispute brought before it, necessarily amounted to stripping that court of the power to rule on its own jurisdiction under [Brussels I]'. Consequently, and under this particular prism, the CJEU held that restraining a national court from ruling on its own jurisdiction was contrary to the core rationale of Brussels I Regulation, as well as against fundamental principles of justice, because the Italian court in the case at hand would be prevented from assessing the existence and validity of the arbitration agreement, upon which the applicant's anti-suit application rested, thus allegedly depriving the claimant of judicial protection. As a result, and wholly contrary to the *lex specialis* regime of international arbitration, the CJEU concluded that such an anti-suit injunction was incompatible with Brussels I.

The *West Tankers* judgment provoked widespread dismay from the arbitration community because it ignored the long-standing principle whereby consent to arbitration prevented the jurisdiction of ordinary courts on the same matter. In *West Tankers* the English Court of Appeals was prevented from granting an anti-suit injunction against an Italian court (so as to allow arbitration proceedings),[25] which in turn prompted the same court in *National Navigation* to rule that a Spanish judgment upholding the non-existence of an English arbitration clause had to be recognised in England under section 33 of Brussels I Regulation.[26] In effect the Court of Appeals was forced to concede, contrary to established case law, that a civil judgment in breach of an arbitration agreement did not constitute a manifest breach of a fundamental principle of English law and as a result did not amount to a breach of public policy within the meaning of Brussels I Regulation.

In the course of the CJEU judgment West Tankers had continued parallel arbitration proceedings against the insurers to claim compensation for the damages suffered, consisting of legal fees and expenses for the ordinary proceedings and indemnification against any liability. In 2011 the arbitral tribunal declared its lack of jurisdiction on the basis that the right to bring proceedings in courts having jurisdiction under Brussels I Regulation must prevail over the right to be sued exclusively before an arbitral tribunal in the presence of an arbitration agreement. West Tankers appealed the

---

[25] Although this was pretty much standard practice for the Court. See, for example, *Through Mutual Assurance Association (Eurasia) Ltd v New India Insurance Co Ltd (The Hari Bhum) (No 1)* [2005] 1 Lloyd's Rep 67.

[26] *National Navigation Co v Endensa Generacion SA* [2010] 1 Lloyd's Rep 193 (CA); see equally, *DHL GBS (UK) Ltd v Fallimento Finmatica SpA* [2009] 1 Lloyd's Rep 430.

tribunal's ruling under Section 69 of the English Arbitration Act and in 2012 the English High Court rejected the arbitral decision and found that the tribunal was not deprived by reason of EU law of the jurisdiction to award damages for breach of the obligation to arbitrate.[27]

The outcomes from the *West Tankers* saga do not sit well with the EU Commission or indeed the global arbitration industry and it is not surprising that several EU national courts have found exceptions to the *West Tankers* ruling. Contrary to the practice of the CJEU, the Paris Court of Appeal in the *Fincantieri* case excluded the application of Brussels I Regulation to a judgment by a court in Geneva on the basis of the existence of an arbitration agreement between the parties.[28] The Paris Court of Appeals went on to refuse enforcement of a judgment by an Italian court on the ground that said judgment violated the negative dimension of the *kompetenz-kompetenz* principle recognised under French arbitration law; namely, that arbitral tribunals possess the right to determine their own jurisdiction prior to any similar determination by a civil court (hence, refuting the application of the first-in-time principle in situations of conflict between parallel arbitral and judicial proceedings). Equally, English courts have gone on to issue anti-suit injunctions in favour of arbitration against courts seated outside the EU.[29]

5.3.2.2 The Recast Brussels I Regulation

Following the aforementioned confusing situation, the EU Commission engaged several scholars and organised expert meetings with a view to making appropriate amendments to Brussels I, in such a way as to leave no doubt about the need to honour and uphold arbitration agreements.[30] The

---

[27] *West Tankers Inc v Allianz Spa and Generali Assicurazioni Generali Spa* (2012) EWHC 854 (Comm).

[28] *Legal Department of the Ministry of Justice of Iraq v Fincantieri Cantieri Navali Italiani*, Paris Appeals Court judgment (15 June 2006), [2007] *Rev Arb* 87.

[29] See *Shashoua v Sharma* [2009] EWHC 957 (Comm), which concerned an anti-suit injunction against an Indian court; *Midgulf International Ltd v Groupe Chimique Tunisien* [2010] EWCA Civ 66, which equally involved an anti-suit injunction against a court in Tunisia.

[30] Commission, 'Green Paper on the Review of Council Regulation (EC) No 44/2001 on Jurisdiction and the Recognition and Enforcement of Judgments in Civil and Commercial Matters' COM (2009) 175 final; Commission, 'Proposal for a Regulation of the European Parliament and of the Council on jurisdiction and the recognition and enforcement of judgments in civil and commercial matters' COM (2010) 748 final.

amended (Recast) Brussels I Regulation which came into effect in early 2015[31] clarifies in paragraph 1 of recital 12 that:

This Regulation should not apply to arbitration. Nothing in this Regulation should prevent the courts of a member state, when seized of an action in a matter in respect of which the parties have entered into an arbitration agreement, from referring the parties to arbitration, from staying or dismissing the proceedings, or from examining whether the arbitration agreement is null and void, inoperative or incapable of being performed, in accordance with their national law.

Article 73(2) and paragraph 3 of recital 12 of the Recast Brussels I Regulation further make it clear that the 1958 New York Convention supersedes the Regulation. However, there is a minor twist. The third paragraph of recital 12 affirms that:

where a court of a member state, exercising jurisdiction under this Regulation or under national law, has determined that an arbitration agreement is null and void, inoperative or incapable of being performed, this should not preclude that court's judgment on the substance of the matter from being recognised or, as the case may be, enforced in accordance with this Regulation. This should be without prejudice to the competence of the courts of the member states to decide on the recognition and enforcement of arbitral awards in accordance with the [1958 New York Convention] which takes precedence over this Regulation.

The existence of an arbitration agreement, therefore, does not prevent the circulation of judgments on the merits within the EU. Such circulation notwithstanding, the courts of EU member states may validly recognise and enforce an award under the 1958 New York Convention even if this award is in conflict with a judgment on the merits issued by a national court. Therefore, the rationale of recital 12(3) is twofold: on the one hand it aims at ensuring the functionality of Brussels I Regulation even when a defence of lack of jurisdiction due to the existence of an arbitration agreement has been raised, but on the other hand it makes it clear that recognising and enforcing a conflicting arbitral award would never be tantamount to a

---

[31] Regulation (EU) No 1215/2012 of the European Parliament and of the Council of 12 December 2012 on jurisdiction and the recognition and enforcement of judgments in civil and commercial matters (recast) [2012] OJ L351/1.

violation of EU law, since the 1958 New York Convention takes precedence over the Recast Regulation.[32]

5.3.2.3 Anti-arbitration injunctions ordered by third states

A particularly vexatious category of anti-arbitration injunctions are those issued by the courts of the state other than that of the seat of arbitration. This concerns disputes involving a state or state instrumentality and contracts containing an arbitration clause from which the state wants to escape. The national courts of the state party typically go on to declare either that its compatriot entities do not have the capacity to enter into arbitration agreements or that the subject matter of the dispute (or the existence of corruption therein) render the dispute non-arbitrable.[33] Although such actions are now rare and usually lead to a settlement, they give rise to conflicting proceedings between several national courts and lawfully established tribunals. In practice, national courts other than the one issuing the anti-arbitration injunction accept such judgments on the basis of comity but arbitral tribunals exercising their *kompetenz-kompetenz* powers may, and usually do, reach a different conclusion.

The Pertamina case

The Indonesian state-operated company Pertamina and the Swiss KBC entered into a partnership to develop a geothermal power station in Indonesia. When the Indonesian government suspended the project KBC initiated arbitral proceedings in Switzerland and was granted an award in its favour, ordering Pertamina to pay damages in the amount of US\$ 260 million. Pertamina filed a request before Indonesian courts to annul the Swiss award (which was successful on grounds of public policy!) but in the meantime KBC had already enforced the award in the USA. Pertamina requested the Indonesian court to issue an injunction to prevent KBC from seeking to enforce its award in the USA and elsewhere, which was equally successful. KBC, in turn, prayed to the US courts to restrain Pertamina from enforcing the

---

[32] See European Parliament, Legal Instruments and Practice of Arbitration in the EU (2015), available at: www.europarl.europa.eu/RegData/etudes/STUD/2015/509988/IPOL_STU% 282015%29509988EN.pdf, at 195–8. But see the problematic symbiosis between arbitral tribunals and national courts as a result. Ibid., at 195ff.

[33] See E. Gaillard, *Legal Theory of International Arbitration* (Martinus Nijhoff, 2010), 70–5.

Indonesian injunction in the USA, which was duly granted by the US District Court for the Southern District of Texas, which later found Pertamina in contempt for disregarding its temporary restraining order. The case eventually reached the Fifth Circuit Court of Appeals which took the view that 'legal action in Indonesia, regardless of its legitimacy, does not interfere with the ability of US courts, or courts of any other enforcement jurisdictions for that matter, to enforce a foreign arbitral award'.[34]

5.4 Arbitral tribunals and transnational courts

In chapter 4 section 4.2 we examined the relationship between arbitral tribunals and the CJEU, particularly whether tribunals are entitled to request preliminary rulings in matters relating to an interpretation of EU law. The CJEU has consistently held that unlike the courts, most arbitral tribunals cannot be deemed as established by law and that moreover they lack permanence and compulsory jurisdiction (on account of their creation by contract) and hence are not entitled to make relevant requests.[35] The exception to this rule concerns arbitral tribunals with compulsory jurisdiction, such as Portugal's tax tribunals which are not established by the parties' mutual agreement but rather by statute.[36]

It should be emphasised, if it is not already clear, that the CJEU is not a 'competent' court of the nature envisaged under the UNCITRAL Model Law and has no authority over arbitral proceedings in EU member states.[37] Moreover, arbitral tribunals do not have access to other international courts without the intervention of the authorities of the seat. The authority of international courts and tribunals, such as the ICJ, to accept referrals from other entities depends on their statute. The ICJ, for example, only entertains contentious disputes between states and requests for advisory opinions from inter-governmental organisations. As a result, while

---

[34] *Karaha Bodas Co (KBC) LLC v Perusahaan Pertambangan Minyak Dan Gas Bumi Negara [Pertamina]*, 335 F 3d (2003) 357.

[35] Case C-377/13, *Ascendi Beiras Litoral e Alta, Auto Estradas das Beiras Litoral e Alta SA v Autoridade Tributária e Aduaneira*, CJEU judgment (12 June 2014), paras 22–9.

[36] Portuguese Decree-Law No 10/2011.

[37] For a brief analysis of the relationship of EU law to arbitration (besides the previous section), see chapter 2 section 2.2.3.1.

referrals from commercial tribunals are excluded, because Article 96(2) of the UN Charter permits requests for advisory opinions from UN specialised agencies on matters within the scope of their activities, the World Bank, as a specialised agency, may submit such requests on behalf of an ICSID tribunal. This conclusion is born from the special relationship between ICSID and the World Bank (Group) as specified in Articles 1–17 of the ICSID Convention.

Finally, it should be noted that there is no general rule of international law resolving claims of jurisdiction between inter-governmental tribunals *inter se* or between inter-governmental tribunals and arbitral tribunals. In practice, inter-governmental tribunals have intimated that they possess an inherent power to suspend their own proceedings, whether in the 'interest of international judicial order' or as 'a matter of comity'.[38] Hence, in situations where an investment tribunal under the auspices of an inter-governmental organisation such as ICSID or NAFTA is seized of a case that qualifies for both investment and commercial arbitration, the investment tribunal may relinquish its jurisdiction if it deems that despite the investment nature of the dispute the parties' agreement had explicitly referred future disputes to commercial arbitration.

5.5 The role of courts during arbitral proceedings

Once the tribunal has been constituted the role of the courts is to ensure against the eventuality of *non liquet* (i.e. that a dispute may not be conclusively resolved because of the absence of a sufficient body of substantive rules), eliminate dead ends which effectively terminate proceedings (e.g. disagreement over a substitute arbitrator), as well as safeguard vital interests of the parties (through interim measures) so that these may be available during and at the end of proceedings. It is instructive, although by no means effective or practical, that certain legal systems aspiring to be arbitration-friendly prohibit recourse to the courts once the tribunal has been constituted. The Slovak Supreme Court, for example, has affirmed that upon commencement of arbitral proceedings the courts have no authority to issue interim measures (as opposed to

---

[38] See *Southern Pacific Properties Ltd v Egypt*, Preliminary Objections to Jurisdiction I (27 November 1985), para 84.

enforcing an interim measure ordered by a tribunal).[39] Equally, in accordance with Article 1506(1) of the French CCP, which provides that the parties may seek interim measures from the courts in international arbitration prior to the constitution of the tribunal, it is implicit that once the tribunal has been constituted any interim remedies can only be sought by the tribunal itself.[40]

It should be noted that local courts may be empowered to assist arbitral proceedings seated abroad by ordering that certain actions be undertaken within their jurisdiction. By way of illustration, Belgian courts enjoy authority under the country's 2013 Arbitration Law in respect of certain suits and actions linked to arbitrations seated abroad, namely with respect to the validity of arbitration agreements;[41] adoption of provisional or conservatory measures;[42] taking of evidence[43] and recognition and enforcement of provisional or conservatory measures ordered by a tribunal (seated abroad).[44] It is equally possible for the courts of the seat to be requested to issue certain worldwide orders, such as *mareva* injunctions (essentially interim freezing orders),[45] but their success will depend on the existence of bilateral or multilateral agreements for the enforcement of civil judgments.

In the following sections we shall examine measures relating to the attendance of witnesses and evidence-taking, measures relating to documentary disclosure, as well as interim measures relating to the preservation of evidence, relevant assets and the parties' status quo.

5.5.1 Attendance of witnesses and evidence-taking

Article 27 of the UNCITRAL Model Law, which deals with court assistance in taking evidence, is not encompassed within the ambit of interim measures. No doubt this is largely artificial given that there may well be an urgency in compelling a witness to testify before the tribunal or otherwise making a deposition under oath. Article 27 goes on to say that:

---

[39] Ruling of the Slovak Supreme Court, *file no 5, 24/2013* (12 June 2013).
[40] See also, *Sociétés Elf Aquitaine and Total v MX and others*, Supreme Cassation Court judgment (12 October 2011), [2012] 1 *Rev Crit DIP* 121.
[41] Art 1676(8) Belgian Judicial Code (JC).   [42] Art 1682 JC.   [43] Art 1698 JC.
[44] Art 1708 JC.
[45] The Supreme Court of Cyprus, for example, has shown a distinct inclination in the use of such orders in order to assist arbitrations seated there. See *Seamark Consultancy Services Ltd v Joseph Lasala and Others* (2007) 1A AAD 162.

The arbitral tribunal or a party with the approval of the arbitral tribunal may request from a competent court of this state assistance in taking evidence. The court may execute the request within its competence and according to its rules on taking evidence.

This provision may be read as entailing two distinct requests, namely one relating to the attendance of witnesses and another concerning the actual taking of evidence. The principal difference between the two is that the latter requires the courts to assume the role of evidence taker, typically in the course of civil proceedings. It is usual in such proceedings for the *lex arbitri* to entitle arbitrators not only to be present but moreover to pose questions to the witnesses.[46] Although the relevant process is under the control of the courts, the ultimate end users of the evidence obtained will be the tribunal and hence it is natural that the arbitrators participate actively. The formalities of the *lex arbitri* in the taking of evidence should not be under-estimated, although such restrictions are exceptional because of the paramount role of party autonomy in the conduct of arbitral proceedings (including evidence-taking).[47]

It is instructive to note some of these exceptional departures from party autonomy in the sphere of evidence-taking. Section 26(1) of the Swedish Arbitration Act does not allow tribunals to administer oaths and truth affirmations to witnesses and experts. Hence, even where a witness is willing to testify before the tribunal, if an oath is required under law (that of the *lex arbitri* or the intended country of enforcement), the discharge of the oath must be referred to the courts, lest the award may be deemed procedurally defective. That is why the second sentence of Article 27 is vitally important and as a rule when a court is asked to take evidence it is not restricted by the evidence rules imposed on the tribunal by the parties.[48] In a notable case, the Dubai Court of Cassation refused to enforce a foreign arbitral award rendered in favour of the claimant on the ground that the arbitrator had failed to swear witnesses in the proceedings in the manner prescribed for court hearings by UAE law.[49]

---

[46] s 1050 German ZPO; s 26(2) Swedish AA.   [47] See chapter 6 section 6.2.

[48] Art 184(2) Swiss PILA; see also chapter 6 section 6.6ff.

[49] *International Bechtel Co Ltd v Department of Civil Aviation of the Government of Dubai*, Dubai Court of Cassation, case No 503/2003, judgment (15 May 2004).

Compelling witnesses to attend and testify in arbitral proceedings is intrinsic to the proper functioning of arbitration. Section 43 of the English Arbitration Act provides that:

(1) A party to arbitral proceedings may use the same court procedures as are available in relation to legal proceedings to secure the attendance before the tribunal of a witness in order to give oral testimony or to produce documents or other material evidence.
(2) This may only be done with the permission of the tribunal or the agreement of the other parties.
(3) The court procedures may only be used if:
   a) the witness is in the United Kingdom, and
   b) the arbitral proceedings are being conducted in England and Wales or, as the case may be, Northern Ireland.
(4) A person shall not be compelled by virtue of this section to produce any document or other material evidence which he could not be compelled to produce in legal proceedings.

In order to avoid abuse, it is clear that the assistance of the courts in the taking of evidence or in compelling witness attendance must be undertaken only at the request of the tribunal (or a majority thereof),[50] or on the basis of party consent.[51] The courts do not possess the authority to undertake such actions at their own initiative.

In the USA, where the seat of the tribunal is in that country, section 7 of the FAA empowers tribunals to subpoena witnesses in order to appear or disclose evidence in their possession. It goes on to say that:

If any person or persons so summoned to testify shall refuse or neglect to obey said summons, upon petition the United States district court for the district in which such arbitrators, or a majority of them are sitting may compel the attendance of such person or persons before said arbitrator or arbitrators, or punish said person or persons for contempt in the same manner provided by law for securing the attendance of witnesses or their punishment for neglect or refusal to attend in the courts of the United States.

Given the strict character of section 7 subpoenas it is no wonder that several district courts have argued that they can only be imposed against

---

[50] s 7 US FAA.
[51] *Soh Beng Tee & Co Pte Ltd v Fairmount Development Pte Ltd*, [2007] 3 SLR (4) 86; *ALC v ALF*, [2010] SGHC 231.

witnesses under the control of the parties to the arbitration in question.[52] This limitation, however, is not apparent in section 7 FAA and is not stipulated in the context of Article 27 of the UNCITRAL Model Law. As a result, other courts have justifiably held that section 7 applies to material evidence in the possession of third parties to arbitral proceedings.[53] In general, a request to the courts for witness appearance or the surrender of evidence by non-parties should satisfy the delicate balance between the right to a fair trial (which is at risk where key documents are not made available) and respect for party autonomy, which assumes that the parties were aware of the potential difficulties of securing evidence in the hands of their adversaries or that of third parties when opting for arbitration over litigation. In the majority of cases party autonomy will prevail and the courts will not perceive document production refusals as impeding the parties' fair trial guarantees.

5.5.2 Documentary disclosure in the hands of third parties

In the previous section we examined requests for assistance in respect of evidence in the hands of parties to the dispute or persons under their control. At the very end we also discussed a few cases involving third parties. In general, there is no rule in the UNCITRAL Model Law or elsewhere that prohibits or otherwise endorses third-party disclosure by an order of the courts. This matter will be determined by the pertinent disclosure rules of the *lex arbitri*. One should distinguish between disclosure applications when the tribunal makes a request to the courts of the seat and situations where the request is made by a foreign tribunal.

In English law the courts may compel a third party to disclose evidence in arbitral proceedings in two distinct circumstances. Where the requesting party defines the requested documents with specificity or a certain degree of recognition the court may order disclosure by means of a witness summons.[54] Conversely, where the requesting party is unable to describe

---

[52] *Integrity Insurance Co v American Centennial Insurance Co*, 885 F Supp 69 (SDNY, 1995).

[53] See *Meadows Indemnity Co Ltd v Nutmeg Insurance Co*, 157 FRD 42 (MD Tenn. 1994); *National Broadcasting Co Inc v Bear Sterns Co Inc*, 165 F 3d 184 (2nd Cir. 1999), at 188, regarding pre-hearing depositions and document discovery in respect of third-party witnesses.

[54] s 43 English AA, in conjunction with rule 34.2 of the 1998 Civil Procedure Rules. See *Tajik Aluminium Plant v Hydro Aluminium AS and Ors* [2005] EWCA Civ 1218, paras 24–5.

or define the requested documents with precision (as is usually the case) the courts are unable to order a witness summons[55] and the only remedy is that of (third-party) disclosure. Not surprisingly, this is an exceptional measure and the requested party is merely obliged to supply a broad range of documents.[56] Unlike section 12(6)(b) of the 1950 English Arbitration Act, which empowered English courts to make disclosure orders in respect of arbitral proceedings seated there, sections 43 and 44 of the 1996 Arbitration Act do not confer such power on the courts. Such a power belongs to the discretion of the tribunal which may either admit the evidence without disclosure or otherwise order disclosure from third parties.[57]

Where the request for disclosure comes from a tribunal seated abroad it seems that tribunals do not satisfy the status of 'judicial authority' so as to be able to make independent requests under the terms of Article 1 of the 1970 Hague Convention on the Taking of Evidence Abroad in Civil or Commercial Matters. Section 1(a) of the English 1975 Evidence Act has been construed as excluding requests made by arbitral tribunals seated abroad.[58] As a result, arbitral tribunals must first apply to the courts of the seat, which in turn may address a letter of request to the courts of England and Wales (although there is no guarantee that it will be entertained). In US law, on the other hand, the situation is different. Under section 1782(a) of the Federal Rules of Civil Procedure, district courts may order a person who 'resides or is found' in the district to produce documents 'for use in a foreign or international tribunal . . . upon the application of any interested person'. Much like the CJEU, as examined above and the Hague Convention, US courts had until recently assumed the view that section 1782(a) did not encompass private arbitral tribunals. This state of affairs changed in respect of arbitral tribunals with *In re Roz Trading*,[59] although it was the US Supreme Court in *Intel Corp v Advanced Micro Devices Inc* which extended the application of section 1782(a) to the directorate-general of competition of the EU Commission.[60] Roz had triggered an application clause in its contract with a subsidiary of Coca Cola and

---

[55] *BNP Paribas & Ors v Deloitte & Touche LLP* (2003) EWHC 2874 [Comm].

[56] Ibid., para 16.   [57] Ibid., paras 7–16.

[58] *First American Corporation and Others v Zayed and Others* [1999] 1 WLR 1154; *Commerce and Industry Insurance Co of Canada and another v Certain Underwriters at Lloyd's of London and another* [2002] 1 WLR 1323.

[59] *In re Roz Trading*, 469 F Supp 2d 1221 (ND Ga. 2006).

[60] *Intel Corp v Advanced Micro Devices Inc*, 542 US 214.

commenced arbitral proceedings in Vienna. Roz applied to the district court in Georgia for the disclosure of important documents alleged to be found in Coca Cola's headquarters. The court relied on the *Intel* reasoning, finding the tribunal to fall within the scope of section 1782. It was thereafter a matter of being persuaded to use its discretion, which the Georgia court was inclined to grant, noting that under the circumstances any other means of discovery would lead to uncertain results.[61]

5.5.3 The nature of interim measures and the interplay between courts and tribunals

An interim measure is a temporary measure whose purpose is to address an urgent[62] situation prior to the issuance of an award whereby, in accordance with Article 17(2) of the UNCITRAL Model Law, one of the parties requests the tribunal to:

(a) maintain or restore the status quo pending determination of the dispute;

(b) take action that would prevent, or refrain from taking action that is likely to cause, current or imminent harm or prejudice to the arbitral process itself;

(c) provide a means of preserving assets out of which a subsequent award may be satisfied; or

(d) preserve evidence that may be relevant and material to the resolution of the dispute.[63]

The words 'preserve' and 'maintain' clearly suggest that interim measures are not meant to alter the proprietary nature of their object. For example, an asset may be frozen without, however, altering its ownership; the owner simply loses the ability to use or convey the object for a limited time. Consequently, attachment orders, which require the seizing of property in order to ensure satisfaction of a judgment, are antithetical to the rationale and pursuit of interim measures. An interim measure issued by the courts

---

[61] *In re Roz Trading*, above note 59, at 1229; see also *In re Hallmark Capital Corp*, 534 F Supp 2d 951 (D Minn. 2007).

[62] Although, exceptionally, s 44(ii) of the English AA caters (also) for situations lacking the element of urgency.

[63] See A. Yesilirmak, *Provisional Measures in International Commercial Arbitration* (Kluwer, 2005).

must necessarily conform to an action that already exists under the *lex arbitri*. Advanced legal systems will provide for a range of possible actions established under statute or judge-made law. Some national statutes stipulate that if a particular action does not exist the courts may adapt existing actions to the parties' request if by doing so they do not violate the *lex arbitri*.

One of the obvious problems with requesting interim measures from the tribunal is that the request itself offers an opportunity to the other party to dissipate its assets or otherwise dispose of the evidence in its possession. In order to mitigate against this eventuality, Article 17B of the UNCITRAL Model Law provides for the possibility of preliminary orders, whereby the tribunal is authorised to grant interim measures without notice to the other party. Preliminary orders are tantamount to *ex parte* applications before national courts and, given the limited authority of arbitral tribunals in respect of interim measures, it is natural that the parties will prefer to apply *ex parte* to the courts rather than rely on tribunals' preliminary orders. This conclusion is further justified by the fact that interim measures imposed by tribunals affect only the parties to arbitration and hence have no legal consequences in respect of third parties.

Interim measures granted by arbitral tribunals entail significant enforcement limitations, chiefly because their orders are not binding upon third parties, whereas the requesting party may desire an enforceable (*erga omnes*) instrument for use in the seat as well as abroad. Several domestic laws, such as Article 11(3) of the Spanish Arbitration Act, allow the parties to seek interim measures from the courts either before or during arbitral proceedings.[64] Another option is to empower tribunals to render interim measures in the form of awards, although this is certainly unusual in developed arbitral jurisdictions.[65] In this manner the requesting party need not seek court assistance given that the award (on interim measures) is enforceable as such. The OLG Frankfurt has held that interim relief is in exceptional circumstances possible even when an award has been rendered

---

[64] Under Art 23 of the Spanish AA interim measures granted by the arbitral tribunal shall be subject to set aside and enforcement proceedings regardless of the form of those measures.

[65] In French law, for example, decisions on interlocutory issues and generally all those that do not terminate the procedure are not afforded the status of awards. See *Société Crédirente v Compagnie Générale de Garantie*, Paris Court of Appeals judgment (29 November 2007), [2009] *Rev Arb* 741.

(assuming that the challenging party is lawfully pursuing set aside proceedings), but the claim for relief cannot be tantamount to suspending the application of the terms of the award.[66]

So far we have examined the nature, scope and qualities of interim measures available in the course of arbitral proceedings. It should also have become clear that whereas authority for granting interim measures lies with both arbitral tribunals and the courts only the latter possess authority to issue binding and enforceable measures.[67] Is there, however, any priority or hierarchy between the two? Prior to the constitution of the tribunal it is self-evident that the parties may have recourse to the courts, unless the pertinent institutional rules direct them to make use of emergency arbitrators first.[68] Following the constitution of the tribunal the parties are generally afforded the possibility of either approaching the courts directly,[69] or after having pursued a similar request with the arbitral tribunal. National laws are flexible on this issue, as is also Article 9 of the UNCITRAL Model Law, and hence the appropriate outcome in each case will be determined by the parties' agreement and the applicable institutional rules. Article 9 of the UNCITRAL Model Law makes it clear that it is not incompatible with the arbitration agreement for the parties to request from the courts an interim measure of protection.[70] If this were not so recourse to the courts for urgent measures of protection would always give rise to a violation of the parties' arbitration agreement. Finally, it should be emphasised that although interim measures facilitate a just outcome, they are subservient to party autonomy and are not part of the mandatory body of rules of the seat, in the sense that the parties may freely waive recourse to interim measures.[71]

Channel tunnel case and the appropriateness of court injunctions

The contract for the construction of the Channel Tunnel involved an operator (Eurotunnel) and a consortium of Franco-British construction

---

[66] OLG Frankfurt, *case SchH 6/13*, judgment (13 June 2013).
[67] Exceptionally, under Art 818 of the Italian CCP, arbitral interim relief is expressly forbidden. This provides that: 'arbitrators cannot grant sequestrations or other interim measures, unless otherwise provided by law'.
[68] For example, Art 29 ICC Rules.   [69] s 4(3) Swedish AA.
[70] Equally, Art 26(3) UNCITRAL Arbitration Rules; Art 25.3 LCIA Rules; Art 23(2) ICC Rules.
[71] Art 17(1) UNCITRAL Model Law.

companies (TML). It provided that in case of disputes the parties would first resort to expert determination and in case of disagreement with the experts' outcome the dispute could be referred to arbitration in Brussels under the ICC Rules. A dispute arose over payment for the tunnel's cooling system because it was not envisaged in the original plan and was later added through a variation order. After several failed attempts to collect the amounts claimed TML threatened to suspend work, which would have had a domino effect on the project as a whole. In response, Eurotunnel sought an interim injunction from English courts with a view to preventing TML from carrying out its threat. TML naturally argued that because the nature and scope of the intended injunction was in fact similar (if not the same) with the substance of the dispute at hand, the court should dismiss the application and refer the parties to arbitration in accordance with their contract. The case was entertained by three different layers of courts, from first instance all the way to the House of Lords, all of which produced different outcomes. The House of Lords ultimately decided not to grant the relief sought, without, however, relying on a solid rule but rather by reference to the particular circumstances of the cases. Lord Mustill emphasised this by stating:

> It is true that mandatory interlocutory relief may be granted even where it substantially overlaps with the final relief claimed in the action: and I also accept that it is possible for the court at the pre-trial stage of the dispute arising under a construction contract to order the defendant to continue with a performance of the works. But the court should approach the making of such an order with the utmost caution and should be prepared to act only when the balance of advantage plainly favours the grant of relief. In the combination of circumstances which we find in the present case, I would have hesitated long before proposing that such an order should be made.[72]

5.5.4 Measures for the preservation of evidence, assets and the parties' status quo

We have already discussed the nature of interim measures under Article 17(2) of the UNCITRAL Model Law and the four key measures therein. National legal systems may of course encompass further categories of

---

[72] *Channel Tunnel Group v Balfour Beatty Ltd* [1993] AC 334, at 367.

measures to which the parties may have recourse, provided of course that the decisions of the courts of the seat are enforceable abroad, where pertinent. In practice, most applications for interim measures concern the preservation of assets and valuable evidence. It should be borne in mind that if a national legal system empowers the parties to seek an injunction in the context of litigation this should also be available to arbitral proceedings. In respect of asset preservation the following case is instructive. In *Black Swan Investment v Harvest View Ltd*,[73] a British Virgin Islands (BVI) case, the plaintiff commenced proceedings against a South African national in his home country in respect of a personal claim; it also transpired that the defendant owned two BVI companies. Black Swan sought a freezing injunction against these companies in support of its South African proceedings, despite the fact they were unrelated to the litigation and no direct claim against them was possible. Bannister J held that whenever a BVI court is capable of exercising *in personam* jurisdiction over a defendant, the statutory power to grant an interlocutory injunction 'in all cases in which it appears to the court or judge to be just and convenient' gave the court 'strict jurisdiction' to grant an order. Clearly, this outcome is available to arbitral proceedings. The EU is acutely aware of the need for some uniformity in this field and in 2014 adopted Regulation 655, which establishes a European account preservation order with the aim of preserving assets while legal proceedings are in process.[74]

An application for the preservation of evidence may require a disclosure or a summons order as described in a previous section, but it may also concern situations where the evidence sought to be protected is not merely of a documentary nature. In construction disputes it may be important to preserve the structure in such a way so that an expert or the arbitrators may later assess whether appropriate materials or techniques were employed by the contractors. Equally, in cases concerning the quality of goods the plaintiff will naturally demand that the goods bought be stored in a safe place for subsequent inspection.[75]

Applications for the preservation or restoration of the status quo are in fact easier to quantify in most circumstances. In the *Channel tunnel* case,

---

[73] *Black Swan Investment v Harvest View Ltd*, claim no. BVI HCV (Com) 2009/399, Eastern Caribbean Court of Justice judgment (23 March 2010).

[74] EU Regulation 655/2014, establishing a European Account Preservation Order procedure to facilitate cross-border debt recovery in civil and commercial matters, OJ L 189.

[75] See also chapter 6 section 6.6.6, concerning the inspection of evidence.

discussed in detail in a previous section, the operators of the tunnel were eager that overall work did not halt because it would have created a string of delays causing them to default against their obligations to contractors, subcontractors, financiers and others. As a result, while they continued to dispute the other party's claim they were keen for the project to continue unabated. Despite the fact that the House of Lords was hesitant to offer relief in that case – on the ground that the relief sought was similar to the substantive arbitral claim – there are no doubt other situations where the interim relief is clearly distinguishable from the main claim under the parties' arbitration agreement. A typical example arises where a manufacturer halts distribution of a good to his distributor, arguing a breach of their distribution agreement. Until the matter is resolved, the distributor will be in breach of his obligation to his network of agents, will be unable to pay salaries or refund his lenders and will no doubt suffer a reputational damage. Therefore, he has every interest to demand that the mutual obligations arising from the distribution agreement with the manufacturer remain intact until the issuance of the award.

5.6 The role of courts after an award is rendered

Once an award is rendered the parties will be under a strict deadline to submit an application to the courts for setting the award aside. The determination of such applications are final and not subject to further layers of appeal or cassation. In certain circumstances when an award has not been subject to set aside proceedings and is considered final, several legal systems may require some form of exequatur (confirmation). Article 1516 of the French CCP, for example, goes on to say that 'an arbitral award may only be enforced by virtue of an enforcement order (exequatur) issued by the Tribunal de grande instance of the place where the award was made or by the Tribunal de grande instance of Paris if the award was made abroad'. Paragraph 2 of Article 1516 makes it clear that exequatur proceedings shall not be adversarial, whereas paragraph 3 stipulates that the relevant application may be submitted by the 'most diligent party', which is typically one of the parties; even so, French courts have construed this to also encompass individual arbitrators themselves.

Exceptionally, the courts of the seat may deem it appropriate to issue worldwide orders once an award has become final in order to assist the winning party's subsequent efforts to enforce the award. In *Republic of Argentina v NML Capital Ltd*, which was not however related to arbitral proceedings, the US Supreme Court affirmed in 2014 a US District Court's worldwide post-judgment discovery order directed to two banks with presence in the US, thereby rejecting Argentina's argument that the order was barred under the US FSIA.[76] The Supreme Court found no basis in the FSIA for restrictions on post-judgment discovery efforts, as distinct from immunity from jurisdiction or immunity from execution. It held that the FSIA focuses only on two types of immunity, namely from jurisdiction and execution and hence it is silent on discovery in aid of execution of a judgment against a foreign-sovereign debtor's assets.[77] There is no reason why such an order may not be applied to aid post-award discovery efforts.

Finally, although this will be discussed in more detail in a subsequent chapter, it is worth noting that the courts of the country where enforcement of a foreign award is sought possess authority to determine whether the award should be recognised or enforced in accordance with the 1958 New York Convention or other instrument.[78] The role of the enforcement court is not akin to the functions examined in this chapter, chiefly because the award under consideration has not been delivered by a tribunal seated there and hence the nature of supervision and assistance is qualitatively different.

---

[76] See chapter 8 section 8.6 on the status of immunity in international law and arbitral proceedings.

[77] *Republic of Argentina v NML Capital Ltd*, 695 F 3d 201 *affirmed*.

[78] Exceptionally, French law treats international awards as unrelated to any particular legal order and therefore their validity is determined in accordance with the law of the country where recognition or enforcement is sought (i.e. French law). See *Société PT Putrabali Adyamulia v Société Rena Holding et Société Mnogutia Est Epices*, Court of Cassation judgment (29 June 2007), [2007] *Rev Arb* 507.

6 The conduct of arbitral proceedings

6.1 Introduction

This chapter examines the applicable rules and processes in the conduct of international arbitral proceedings. As the reader will come to realise there are very few elaborate rules as to how arbitral proceedings should be conducted, in contrast to the detailed regulation in respect of ordinary civil proceedings. Given the differences between the major legal systems and the goals of speed, cost-effectiveness and flexibility which arbitration promises to its end users, it is natural that no single model of civil procedure is promoted; whatever the particular attributes of such national models they are generally inflexible and slow. That international arbitration operates successfully in the absence of such predetermined rules (as far as written and oral pleadings are concerned) demonstrates perhaps that the over-regulation of litigation may come at the expense of speed and flexibility, not to mention cost.

Here, we shall examine the foundations of conduct rules, as well as the limitations to party autonomy in designing and enforcing such rules by the parties or arbitral institutions. In this respect, we shall be guided by a variety of soft law instruments that have had a significant impact in addressing gaps and queries often raised by arbitrators and parties. The bulk of the chapter is devoted to understanding current practice in both written pleadings as well as the procedure relevant to oral hearings.

6.2 The function of the party autonomy rule

We have already discussed the over-arching significance of party autonomy in relation to the design of the agreement to arbitrate and the use of substantive law chosen by the parties in order to construe their main agreement and their arbitration clause. The voluntary character of arbitration would be seriously undermined if the parties were unable to dictate how arbitral proceedings are to be held and conducted, particularly if deprived of their desire to achieve flexibility and speed. The control of the process is hardly an end to itself. Its purpose is to mitigate the adverse qualities of litigation or ADR and hence ultimately to satisfy the parties' business demands in a particular case. By way of illustration, if the dispute concerns a sensitive or pressing issue, the parties may well urge the tribunal to resolve the dispute as timely as possible, perhaps through fast-track proceedings. Equally, if the parties feel that a hearing would spiral costs and provide little clarity to the dispute, they can decide to dispense with an oral hearing altogether, agreeing solely to a documents-based process.

The prevalence of party autonomy in the conduct of arbitral proceedings is manifest in both the 1958 New York Convention and the UNCITRAL Model Law, as well as customary international law; the latter as evidenced by the consistent laws and judicial practice of states, as well as the proliferation of institutional rules to this effect. Article 19(1) of the UNCITRAL Model Law provides that the 'parties are free to agree on the procedure to be followed by the arbitral tribunal in conducting the proceedings', whereas Article V(1)(d) of the 1958 New York Convention stipulates that a foreign

award may be refused enforcement and recognition if 'the arbitral procedure was not in accordance with the agreement of the parties'. It is precisely
because of such party autonomy considerations that neither institutional
rules nor domestic laws impose a civil procedure process in the same
detailed manner as that which regulates ordinary litigation. The parties
are free to choose any model they desire or no model whatsoever, or
alternatively leave this task to the tribunal.[1]

6.2.1 Limitations to party autonomy: fair trial guarantees

Given the extensive use of institutional arbitration, or at least well-
established arbitration rules, such as those of UNCITRAL, all of which
provide a set of private procedural rules to the parties based on their
prior consent,[2] it is evident that states understand the need for business
parties to control arbitral proceedings. However, the parties' control of
arbitral proceedings is not without limits. Arbitral proceedings are legal
proceedings, even if arbitral tribunals are not always perceived as 'established by law'[3] and as a result the proceedings are subject to sensible fair
trial guarantees. We emphasise the word *sensible*, because although Article
6(1) of the ECHR requires that proceedings be public or that (implicitly)
national authorities must promote access to justice, at least in favour of the
weaker party, such obligations are in conflict with the rationale underlying
arbitration. It has already been observed that the parties may agree that
arbitral proceedings are confidential and in general it is inconceivable that
the stronger party or the state (other than perhaps in consumer arbitration)
should finance the expenses, legal or other, of the weaker party as a means
of legal aid or in order to rectify the parties' financial disparity.[4]

---

[1] See, for example, Art 22.1(vi) LCIA Rules.

[2] On the nature of institutional rules, see chapter 2 section 2.6.

[3] In chapter 4 section 4.2 we discussed why the CJEU does not generally view arbitral
tribunals as established by law, but this largely concerns the capacity of arbitral tribunals
to request preliminary rulings.

[4] Exceptionally, the Portuguese Supreme Court in *Wall Street Institute de Portugal – Centro
des Ingles SA WSI – Consultadoria e Marketing and others v Centro des Ingles Santa Barbara
LDA*, judgment no 311/2008 (30 May 2008), held that where a party to arbitral proceedings
had become indigent it was entitled to legal aid and hence recourse to litigation, whereby
legal aid is available. The Court's rationale was based on the argument that the interest
sacrificed by the rejection of the arbitration clause was purely procedural as opposed to the
substantive interest in the case of the right to a fair trial; see, however, Art 380 of the Swiss
CCP, which excludes the possibility of legal aid from domestic arbitral proceedings. The

It is therefore imperative to circumscribe the fair trial exceptions inherent in the party autonomy principle, as this applies to the regulation of arbitral proceedings on the basis of consent. The agreement to arbitrate should be our starting point. It is now well settled that exclusion clauses in commercial contracts by which the parties freely dispose (or waive) their right to litigation before ordinary courts do not prejudice fair trial guarantees in and by themselves.[5] Free and open consent is paramount because mandatory arbitration has not always been perceived as being compliant with the right to fair trial.[6] As regards actual arbitral proceedings, two principles are universally accepted as being applicable, namely: due process and fair hearing, and tribunal independence and impartiality. The latter has already been discussed in chapter 4.9 and hence will not be iterated here. Due process is a broad principle encompassing many different aspects of proceedings. Its most salient manifestation for our purposes is party equality, which is guaranteed under Article 8 of the ECHR. According to this, the tribunal, even if the parties' agreement indicates otherwise, must treat all litigants in the same manner without any distinction or discrimination; essentially, what it allows for one party it should equally allow to the other. Fair treatment in the context of arbitration is in no way dependent on or related to the parties' resources. It simply concerns access to and availability of the same procedural remedies and entitlements to all parties.[7]

If some human rights considerations are binding on arbitral (commercial) tribunals, is it also the case that arbitral proceedings must take into

---

Swiss Federal Supreme Court in *case no 4A_178/2014*, judgment (29 July 2014) confirmed that the same exclusion also applies to international arbitrations.

[5] In *Sumukan Limited v Commonwealth Secretariat* [2007] EWCA Civ 243, the English Court of Appeal held that an agreement in an arbitration clause to exclude an appeal to a court on a point of law under s 69 of the Arbitration Act 1996 (the exclusion agreement) did not breach the right to a fair trial as guaranteed under Art 6 of the ECHR. Equally, as far back as the early 1960s, in *Osmo Suovaniemi and Others v Finland,* Application No 31737/1996, Decision (23 February 1999) and *X v Germany,* Application No 1197/1961, Decision (5 March 1962), the ECtHR and the Commission stressed that waivers in favour of exclusive arbitration are consistent with the right to a fair trial.

[6] *Bramelid and Malstrom v Sweden,* (1983) 5 EHRR 249. Conversely, the Maltese Constitutional Court has held that mandatory arbitration proceedings under Maltese law (including the appointment of arbitrators by the chairman of the Malta Arbitration Centre) did not breach either the Constitution of Malta (Art 39(2)) or the right to fair trial under Art 6(1) of the ECHR. *Untours Insurance Agency Ltd and Emanuel Gauci v Victor Micallef and Others,* App No 81/2011/1, Maltese Constitutional Court judgment (25 January 2013).

[7] See s 46 Hong Kong Arbitration Ordinance (2011).

consideration the human rights obligations of the seat (and perhaps the country of enforcement) in the conduct of proceedings? Although there is some confusion on this matter, the simple answer must be an affirmative one.[8] The seat's human rights obligations are part of its *lex arbitri* and the tribunal would fail in its duty to produce an enforceable award were it to ignore the human rights obligations of the seat and the intended country of enforcement. In practice, although one cannot require arbitrators to be appraised of the expanding jurisprudence of the European Court of Human Rights (ECtHR) and that of other tribunals, arbitral institutions and counsel must ensure, and typically do, that the parties' procedures are compliant with fundamental fair trial guarantees.[9]

Case study: the Pirelli case

The insolvency of one of the parties to arbitration does not imply the discontinuance of arbitral proceedings under French law. In the *Pirelli* case, the French Court of Cassation confirmed the right for the insolvent party to rely on arbitration.[10] Generally, the French courts have taken the view that the refusal to hear the insolvent party's counter-claims by an arbitral tribunal amounts to a violation of the right to access to justice and equality of the parties, unless the counter-claims can be dissociated from the requests for relief. The Court of Cassation in the *Pirelli* case confirmed that the right of access to arbitration is consistent with the same principles found in Article 6 of the ECHR, which concern the right of access to justice and judicial remedies. However, in the *Pirelli* case, the Court of Cassation added that in order to rely on this principle in arbitration proceedings the counter-claims must be inseparably inter-linked with the request for relief.

---

[8] *Transado-Transportes Fluviais do Sado v Portugal*, App No 35943/02, ECtHR judgment (16 December 2003); see equally *Nordsee Deutsche Hochseefischerei GmbH v Reederei Mond Hochseefischerei Nordstern AG and others*, case 102/81 [1982] ECR 1095, where the CJEU held that the application of EU law cannot be limited by contractual exceptions or carve outs; equally, *Société Licensing Projets and others v Société Pirelli & C SpA and others*, Paris Appeals Court judgment (17 November 2011). See also Art 396(2) of the Swiss CCP, which allows a limited review of domestic arbitral awards where the claimant alleges a violation of the ECHR.

[9] See Art 22(1) ICC Rules, which provides that both the parties and the tribunal must ensure that the proceedings are conducted in a cost-effective and expeditious manner.

[10] *Société Pirelli & C SpA v Société Licensing Projets and others*, judgment (28 March 2013).

6.2.2 Limitations to party autonomy: *lex arbitri* and public policy

There are yet other limitations on the parties' autonomy to set out the procedural rules of their choice. The most important among these is the mandatory provisions of the *lex arbitri*, including its public policy.[11] One form of limitation may implicate the conferral of a power upon the tribunal that is not stipulated by the parties' agreement. Section 56 of the Hong Kong Arbitration Ordinance confers on arbitral tribunals authority to issue orders concerning the discovery of documents or the delivery of interrogatories. On the other extreme, countries adhering to a particular belief or value system may, while generally respecting party autonomy, qualify all relevant actions through a cultural relativist lens.[12] Article 25(1) of the 2012 Saudi Arbitration Law, for example, provides that:

The two parties to arbitration may agree on procedures to be followed by the arbitration tribunal in conducting the proceedings, including their right to subject such proceedings to effective rules of any organization, agency or arbitration center within the Kingdom or abroad, provided said rules are not in conflict with the provisions of *Sharia*.

This limitation (conformity with the sharia) is ambiguous and indeterminate because it cannot be traced back to the Arbitration Law, but is subject to an indeterminate body of sharia principles that are not necessarily embedded in statute. This ambiguity has manifested itself in relation to proceedings which implicated the law or legal system of Muslim nations requiring general conformity with the sharia. In *International Bechtel Co Ltd v Department of Civil Aviation of the Government of Dubai*, the Dubai Court of Cassation refused to enforce a foreign arbitral award rendered in favour of the claimant on the ground that the arbitrator had failed to swear witnesses in the proceedings in the manner prescribed by UAE law for court hearings.[13]

---

[11] See chapter 8 section 8.4.2.7

[12] Relativism is a construct that is invoked in the field of human rights. There, it is taken to mean that culture ultimately validates the legitimacy and application of particular rights, thereby rejecting the notion that human rights apply to all without distinction; i.e. that human rights are universal. In the field of commerce and arbitration it may be (arbitrarily) invoked, as in the *Bechtel* case, to deny the application of longstanding arbitral principles because of their alleged incompatibility with cultural norms. See J. Donnelly, Cultural Relativism and Universal Human Rights, (1984) 6 *HRQ* 400.

[13] Dubai Court of Cassation, *case No 503/2003*, judgment (15 May 2004). This same result was later reaffirmed by the Dubai Cassation Court in *case No 322/2004*, judgment (11 April 2005).

Apart from fair trial concerns, the *lex arbitri* in industrialised nations is generally rather relaxed regarding the permissibility of procedural rules dictated by the parties. Sometimes, however, the line is unclear. It is accepted, for example, that, whether explicitly or implicitly, applications by the parties for expedited or fast-track arbitral procedures are consistent with the right to fair trial. In contrast, where a tribunal proceeds on the basis of a *summary judgment*, in which case it chooses not to hear the parties or assess their evidence by weeding out what it perceives as superfluous (even as per the parties' agreement) it fails to discharge its duty of due process.[14]

6.2.3 Limitations through institutional rules

Although it is usually stipulated that institutional rules constitute limitations upon party autonomy, this is not entirely true. The parties have a choice as to whether to subscribe to particular rules (or other soft law) and even so they are generally permitted to exclude or modify such rules in order to meet their business or other needs. As a result, the limitations imposed by institutional rules are best viewed as self-limitations. Some institutional rules provide that where the parties have failed to agree on a particular procedural matter, the tribunal shall exercise broad powers. Article 22.1 of the LCIA Rules provides a list of some of these powers, as follows:

The arbitral tribunal shall have the power, upon the application of any party or (save for sub-paragraphs (viii), (ix) and (x) below) upon its own initiative, but in either case only after giving the parties a reasonable opportunity to state their views and upon such terms (as to costs and otherwise) as the arbitral tribunal may decide:

(i) to allow a party to supplement, modify or amend any claim, defence, cross-claim, defence to cross-claim and reply, including a request, response and any other written statement, submitted by such party;

(ii) to abridge or extend (even where the period of time has expired) any period of time prescribed under the arbitration agreement, any other agreement of the parties or any order made by the arbitral tribunal;

---

[14] T. T. Landau, Claims for further Particulars or for Summary Dismissal: Are they an Acceptable Practice? In S. R. Bond et al. (eds.), *Arbitral Procedure in the Dawn of the New Millennium* (Bruylant, 2005), 47–55.

(iii) to conduct such enquiries as may appear to the arbitral tribunal to be necessary or expedient, including whether and to what extent the arbitral tribunal should itself take the initiative in identifying relevant issues and ascertaining relevant facts and the law(s) or rules of law applicable to the arbitration agreement, the arbitration and the merits of the parties' dispute;

(iv) to order any party to make any documents, goods, samples, property, site or thing under its control available for inspection by the arbitral tribunal, any other party, any expert to such party and any expert to the tribunal;

(v) to order any party to produce to the arbitral tribunal and to other parties documents or copies of documents in their possession, custody or power which the arbitral tribunal decides to be relevant;

(vi) to decide whether or not to apply any strict rules of evidence (or any other rules) as to the admissibility, relevance or weight of any material tendered by a party on any issue of fact or expert opinion; and to decide the time, manner and form in which such material should be exchanged between the parties and presented to the arbitral tribunal.

As we shall discuss in a subsequent section, institutional rules may differ as to the power of the tribunal to request the production of documents. Some may, in fact, refer specifically to electronic disclosure,[15] whereas others are silent on the matter. The International Centre for Dispute Resolution (ICDR) Guidelines on Information Exchanges, for example, require that the parties make available to each other documents in their possession.

6.3 The phases of arbitral proceedings

Recourse to arbitration commences upon the claimant's request (or notice) of arbitration, which must be served to the respondent and notified to the arbitral institution, if any. The notice sets out the details of the dispute, the legal basis of arbitration (arbitration clause or submission agreement), as well as the remedies sought, and invites the respondent to participate in the proceedings.[16] The respondent is given a deadline by which to respond to the claimant's notice of arbitration. In this the respondent may challenge the claim on jurisdictional or other grounds, or in the event that there is no contention he may designate his choice of arbitrator and set out his

[15] See, for example, Art 3(a) of the ICDR Guidelines on Information Exchanges in International Arbitration.
[16] Art 3 UNCITRAL Rules.

arguments against the case put forward by the claimant.[17] This process ultimately leads to the formation and constitution of the tribunal, which may then dispense with any jurisdictional claim put forward by the parties before entering into its examination of the merits.

Upon dispensing with jurisdictional matters the tribunal will issue what is known as its procedural order No 1, which will set out the procedure (oral hearings, witness hearings, post-hearing briefs etc.) to be followed, the pertinent deadlines, the documents to be submitted, fees, its examination of liability and quantum as distinct issues and others. Before a tribunal issues its preliminary order No 1 it usually hears the parties in the course of a preliminary (unofficial) meeting with a view to better comprehending their concerns and to ensure a common understanding so as to avoid future challenges and delays.[18]

Institutional rules use varying terminology to describe the same action and hence many terms are used interchangeably, although they are effectively describing the same thing. It is common for arbitral institutions to require arbitrators to draw up *terms of reference* for each dispute before proceeding to an examination of the merits,[19] which is largely equivalent but not identical to a procedural order No 1. This is a document that essentially contains a summary (or list) of the parties' claims and counter-claims, the applicable law and rules (if modified by the parties) and the issues referred to arbitration. The purpose of the terms of reference is to ensure that the parties are clear as to what is being determined and that there is no space for subsequent challenges concerning the arbitrators' authority, the rules to be followed, or the scope of arbitration. In ICC arbitration, the arbitral process commences once the arbitrator and the parties sign the terms of reference.[20] If a party refuses to participate in drawing up the terms or refuses to sign them the tribunal submits them to the Court (the ICC's highest executive organ) for approval.[21] No further claims are possible once the terms have been signed, unless authorised to do so by the tribunal under circumstances determined by it,[22] especially if their existence was not originally known to the claimant.

---

[17] Art 4 UNCITRAL Rules.
[18] Preliminary meetings are envisaged in para 9 of the UNCITRAL Notes on Organizing Arbitral Proceedings.
[19] Art 23(1) ICC Rules.   [20] Art 23(2) ICC Rules.   [21] Art 23(3) ICC Rules.
[22] Art 23(4) ICC Rules.

The procedural order No 1 or the terms of reference[23] will set out the roadmap of the proceedings until the issuance of the award and will require the parties at the first instance to produce their initial written submissions. This is essentially a *statement of claim* by the claimant,[24] followed by a *statement of defence* by the respondent.[25] These will contain the necessary material and evidence relied upon by the parties in order to satisfy the tribunal of their arguments. Depending on the institutional rules, any subsequent agreement by the parties, or the tribunal's order, there could still be further written submissions in the form of requests for the production of additional documents, whether as rejoinder, counter-rejoinder or other, the aim of which is to supplement one's claim or counterclaim or respond to a new claim or counterclaim.

Once the written submissions phase has elapsed the tribunal may convene a pre-hearing conference by telephone or video conferencing in order to ensure smooth transition to the oral hearing, if the parties have agreed to an oral hearing. Following the end of the oral process, the parties may be allowed to submit post-hearing briefs in one or two rounds, after which the tribunal terminates the proceedings and convenes to issue its award.

6.4 Language and seat of proceedings

It may seem self-evident that the language and seat of the proceedings will have been determined by the parties from the outset. This is not, however, always the case. In the absence of prior agreement the tribunal is generally empowered to deal with such matters at the preliminary stages of the proceedings. The choice of an appropriate language may be dictated by several factors, such as the language of the pertinent evidence, that of the parties and the costs of translation, among others. The choice of language will also determine the appropriateness of the arbitrators, because it makes little sense for the parties to translate all their documents solely for the benefit of the arbitrators; for they may just as well appoint native speakers.[26]

---

[23] Arts 22(2) and 24(1) of the ICC Rules require the tribunal to convene a case management conference in order to consult the parties on the procedure to be followed and the deadlines it is setting out.

[24] Art 20 UNCITRAL Rules.   [25] Art 21 UNCITRAL Rules.

[26] See paras 17–20 UNCITRAL Notes on Organizing Arbitral Proceedings.

The seat of the arbitration is usually set out by the parties, whether directly or indirectly. Even so, the tribunal may decide that in the interests of expedience and cost-effectiveness some parts of the proceedings should be held in locations other than the designated seat; albeit this does not alter the juridical seat of the proceedings. The tribunal may be driven to such a decision because several important inspections need to be undertaken in a particular location, or because many of the witnesses reside in a city other than the seat.[27] Where the parties have failed to specify a seat, this task befalls the tribunal. We have already stated the importance of choosing a seat, chiefly because of the paramount role of the law of the seat in arbitral proceedings. Paragraph 22 of the UNCITRAL Notes on Organizing Arbitral Proceedings spell out some of the factual and legal factors that influence the choice of seat:

(a) suitability of the law on arbitral procedure of the place of arbitration;
(b) whether there is a multilateral or bilateral treaty on enforcement of arbitral awards between the state where the arbitration takes place and the state or states where the award may have to be enforced;
(c) convenience of the parties and the arbitrators, including the travel distances;
(d) availability and cost of support services needed; and
(e) location of the subject-matter in dispute and proximity of evidence.

6.5 Written submissions

The parties' written submissions usually constitute the most significant component of the proceedings in terms of probative evidentiary value. Official or undisputed documents that demonstrate or reflect the veracity of a particular claim or fact carry, or should carry, greater evidential weight than uncorroborated oral testimony. The tribunal's terms of reference or procedural order No 1 will set out the claims and counter-claims of the parties as well as the precise nature of the dispute to be decided and on the basis of this the parties will be driven to produce appropriate documentary evidence. Although rare, the claimant may supply all its documentary evidence through its notice of arbitration, given that there is no apparent limitation as to the volume of

---

[27] Ibid., para 23.

evidence that the claimant may submit with its notice.[28] In practice, documentary evidence is submitted following the court's first procedural order. Article 20(2) and (4) of the UNCITRAL Rules provides that the claimant's statement of claim shall include the following particulars:

2. a) the names and contact details of the parties;
   b) a statement of the facts supporting the claim;
   c) the points at issue;
   d) the relief or remedy sought;
   e) the legal grounds or argument supporting the claim. . . .

4. The statement of claim should, as far as possible, be accompanied by all documents and other evidence relied upon by the claimant, or contain references to them.[29]

If there is to be no oral hearing, it is evident that the claimant's written pleadings must be as comprehensive as possible as the tribunal will determine the merits of the dispute on this body of evidence. Equally, the respondent must respond to the claims and arguments raised by the claimant and submit evidence supporting such counter-claims.[30] No doubt, the arguments and claims raised by the parties and the remedies they seek must be consistent and within the scope of their agreement to arbitrate and, moreover, they must comply with the governing law of their contract. The parties may of course subsequently decide to forego the limitations of the governing law (where permissible), but if they do not it is up to the tribunal to dismiss claims that are outside the ambit of the law or the parties' agreement. Article 22 of the UNCITRAL Rules states that:

During the course of the arbitral proceedings, a party may amend or supplement its claim or defence, including a counterclaim or a claim for the purpose of a set-off, unless the arbitral tribunal considers it inappropriate to allow such amendment or supplement having regard to the delay in making it or prejudice to other parties or any other circumstances. However, a claim or defence, including a counterclaim or a claim for the purpose of a set-off, may not be amended or supplemented in such a manner that the amended or supplemented claim or defence falls outside the jurisdiction of the arbitral tribunal.

It is clear from this provision that neither party may set forth a set-off defence, whether as a claim or counterclaim, if such a defence is not considered as falling within the scope of their arbitration agreement.

---

[28] See Art 20(1) UNCITRAL Rules. [29] See also Art 23 UNCITRAL Model Law.
[30] Art 21(1) and (2) UNCITRAL Rules.

The written submissions are typically submitted sequentially; the statement of claim is followed in time by the respondent's statement of defence and subsequent responses to counter-claims are followed by joinders and rejoinders. This process is natural given that the claimant has initiated arbitral proceedings and hence the respondent will generally be unable to present its case and evidence at the same time as the claimant. Exceptionally, the tribunal may direct the parties to submit their written pleadings simultaneously, especially in situations where it is disputed which of the two parties is the claimant.

We have already alluded to the importance of time limits in the production and submission of written pleadings. While some procedural rules may set out time limits for the production of written pleadings, including documentary evidence,[31] others may leave the determination of deadlines to the tribunal as part of its broader competence. In fact, the practice of international arbitration suggests that tribunals will listen to the parties in advance and after assessing the complexity of the dispute at hand will set out realistic deadlines. An experienced panel of arbitrators will instinctively realise when the parties are abusing its power to extend time limits and will dismiss frivolous requests.

6.6 Evidence: the general rule

It is natural that litigators instinctively rely on their experience derived from common law or civil law jurisdictions in order to deal with evidence before international arbitral tribunals. Two important considerations should, however, be emphasised. Firstly, the *lex arbitri* does not impose mandatory evidence rules, nor do any pertinent treaties. Secondly, one of the reasons why the parties choose arbitration in the first place is precisely in order to dispose of the strict and technical evidence rules found in national laws.[32] Even so, some degree of regulation is desirable so as to avoid conferring upon arbitrators extensive discretion. While institutional rules, as well as the UNCITRAL rules, have gone some way to introducing a

---

[31] Art 25 of the UNCITRAL Rules, for example, stipulates that relevant deadlines should not exceed forty-five days.

[32] However, it should be pointed out that Art 1(1) of the UNCITRAL Rules allows parties to agree in advance for a particular national law to govern evidentiary matters.

rudimentary set of non-technical evidence rules, these have been further developed and shaped by international practice. In addition, the IBA has produced a very significant (soft law) instrument, namely, the Rules on Taking of Evidence in International Arbitration (2010). The use of the IBA Rules has been extensive and many national courts often refer to the Rules as reflecting customary practice in international arbitration.

There are three broad categories of evidence, namely: documents (including e-documents) and physical objects; witnesses of fact; and evidence derived from expert testimony. Each party produces the evidence it relies upon and has the burden of proof. This obligation, which is central to arbitral proceedings, is clearly spelt out in all pertinent instruments. Article 27(1) of the UNCITRAL Rules provides that: 'Each party shall have the burden of proving the facts relied on to support its claim or defence.'

The following subsections will discuss the implications of this rule, namely, the admissibility of evidence, its particular weight (including applicable standards of proof), the tribunal's power to request the production of evidence as well as any adverse inferences it may draw where the parties fail to produce the evidence ordered.

6.6.1 Admissibility, relevance and materiality

The fact that a party must prove its case does not necessarily mean that all the evidence relied upon must be deemed and declared *admissible* by the tribunal. Article 27(4) of the UNCITRAL Rules sets forth the general rule, according to which: 'The arbitral tribunal shall determine the admissibility, relevance, materiality and weight of the evidence offered.'[33] What this provision declares is merely the authority of the tribunal, but provides no guidance as to how these terms are to be construed, save from the general assumption that in doing so the tribunal is not constrained by time-consuming technical rules. Further guidance may be sought from the more detailed framework set out in Article 9(2) of the IBA Rules. According to this:

The arbitral tribunal shall, at the request of a party or on its own motion, exclude from evidence or production any document, statement, oral testimony or inspection for any of the following reasons:

---

[33] Equally, Art 9(1) IBA Rules.

(a) lack of sufficient relevance to the case or materiality to its outcome;

(b) legal impediment or privilege under the legal or ethical rules determined by the arbitral tribunal to be applicable;

(c) unreasonable burden to produce the requested evidence;

(d) loss or destruction of the document that has been shown with reasonable likelihood to have occurred;

(e) grounds of commercial or technical confidentiality that the arbitral tribunal determines to be compelling;

(f) grounds of special political or institutional sensitivity (including evidence that has been classified as secret by a government or a public international institution) that the arbitral tribunal determines to be compelling; or

(g) considerations of procedural economy, proportionality, fairness or equality of the parties that the arbitral tribunal determines to be compelling.

This guidance is particularly useful and based on common sense. *Relevance* and *materiality* will always give rise to contention, but they clearly involve a balancing test between the essence of the dispute, as identified by the tribunal, and the facts of the case at hand. Equally, parties cannot be expected to produce classified or confidential information, because even if they could the award may be set aside by the courts of the seat or later by the courts of the enforcement state; not to mention the possibility of civil and criminal suits against all concerned parties. If such determinations regarding admissibility were left to the parties the goal of efficient and swift proceedings may not always be achieved.

In the course of a sports-related arbitration, the tribunal relied on an unlawfully obtained video recording which ultimately proved to be decisive. The Swiss Federal Supreme Court held that the admission of otherwise unlawful evidence did not breach a fundamental principle of Swiss procedural law. It went on to note that tribunals, just like courts, possess the authority to undertake a case-specific assessment of whether illegally obtained evidence should be admitted or not.[34]

6.6.2 Standard of proof

There is no indication in the UNCITRAL Rules, institutional rules, or the IBA Rules what the standard of proof is for proving a given argument with a particular piece of evidence. A standard of proof encompasses a

---

[34] Joined *cases 4A_362/2013* and *4A_448/2013* judgment (28 May 2014).

quantitative dimension as well as a qualitative one. The quantitative aspect determines whether a particular matter requires a significant amount of corroborating evidence, or whether it may be satisfied by a more humble quantity. However, even where a significant amount of evidence may be required to prove a particular claim, the quantity of the evidence is meaningless absent a qualitative dimension.[35] Should the evidence be such as to leave no doubt as to the argument with which it is connected, or is it sufficient that it is merely perceived as convincing? Some commentators suggest that the general standard applied by tribunals is predicated on a balance of probability.[36] Others propose that the required standard 'is always to satisfy the tribunal that there is a preponderance of evidence in its favour'.[37] In practice, at least from the perspective of the jurisprudence of the Iran–US Claims Tribunal, which applied the UNCITRAL Rules, there is no single, uniform standard, because the complexities and requirements of each case are different. There, in cases involving serious criminal charges, such as document forgery, the Tribunal applied a high threshold standard of proof, such as 'clear and convincing' or 'beyond a reasonable doubt'. In yet other cases involving notorious facts, no proof was required by the Tribunal.[38] Valid invoices, for example, are perceived as constituting sufficient proof as to the existence of the amount at issue, in which case the burden of proof to demonstrate that said amount is in fact erroneous shifts to the other party.[39]

6.6.3 Production of evidence and document requests

The parties are naturally free to produce their own evidence, provided they satisfy the conditions of admissibility. In addition, much like litigation, they may request the production of documents allegedly in the hands of

[35] A qualitative aspect of evidence may concern its authenticity. Crucial documentary evidence that is wholly unauthenticated and is refuted as fraudulent by the other party will carry less weight with the tribunal in comparison to authenticated documents. See R. Pietrowski, Evidence in International Arbitration, (2006) 22 *Arbitration Int* 373.

[36] N. Blackaby and A. Partasides, *Redfern and Hunter on International Arbitration* (Oxford University Press, 2009), 388.

[37] C. Croft, C. Kee and J. Waincymer, *A Guide to the UNCITRAL Arbitration Rules* (Cambridge University Press, 2013), 305.

[38] D. D. Caron and L. M. Caplan, *The UNCITRAL Arbitration Rules: A Commentary* (Oxford University Press, 2nd edition, 2013), 558–9.

[39] Ibid., at 560.

their adversaries (and perhaps in the possession of third parties) if they are material to the outcome of the case. However, the requested party may refuse to comply on the basis of any of the grounds listed above.[40] It is clear that given the tribunal's key role in evidence-gathering and assessment, it would be unable to perform its duties if it were precluded to make relevant requests. Article 27(3) of the UNCITRAL Rules provides that:

> At any time during the arbitral proceedings the arbitral tribunal may require the parties to produce documents, exhibits or other evidence within such a period of time as the arbitral tribunal shall determine.

In practice, it is the parties themselves that are aware of the kind of evidence withheld by their opponents and which they feel is material to the case. Given the absence of a rule equivalent to discovery in arbitration, neither party is under a general obligation to disclose evidence detrimental to its case. It is therefore imperative that the parties' counsel identify potentially helpful evidence and make a 'request to produce' application. Such requests are, in practice, subject to sensible limitations. Article 3(3) of the IBA Rules requires that a request to produce shall contain:

(a) (i) a description of each requested document sufficient to identify it, or

 (ii) a description in sufficient detail (including subject matter) of a narrow and specific requested category of documents that are reasonably believed to exist; in the case of documents maintained in electronic form, the requesting party may, or the arbitral tribunal may order that it shall be required to, identify specific files, search terms, individuals or other means of searching for such documents in an efficient and economical manner;

(b) a statement as to how the documents requested are relevant to the case and material to its outcome; and

(c) (i) a statement that the documents requested are not in the possession, custody or control of the requesting party or a statement of the reasons why it would be unreasonably burdensome for the requesting party to produce such documents, and

 (ii) a statement of the reasons why the requesting party assumes the documents requested are in the possession, custody or control of another party.

---

[40] See chapter 5 section 5.5.2 concerning documentary disclosure in the hands of third parties, which is typically ordered by the courts of the seat following a request by the parties or the tribunal.

If the requested party has reservations about the request it may try to convince the tribunal, albeit the ultimate decision rests with the tribunal,[41] unless of course the parties have otherwise agreed. Where a requested party fails without satisfactory explanation to make available documentary or witness evidence as requested by the tribunal, the latter is free to infer that such evidence or document would be adverse to the interests of the requested party.[42] Moreover, the tribunal may take such failure into account in its assignment of costs, including costs connected with the production of evidence.[43]

The issue of request orders has surfaced more poignantly as regards the disclosure of electronic documents. The practical problem here is that the parties, particularly multinational corporations, hold large quantities of data and hence if ordered to disclose even a relatively small part this would incur significant effort and cost, as well as access to sensitive information. Some commentators refer to the Sedona Principles for Electronic Document Production (2007) for a reflection of best practice, but these principles focus on litigation and discovery and hence are not particularly useful in the context of arbitration. Guideline 3(a) of the ICDR Guidelines on Information Exchanges stipulates that the tribunal may, upon application, require one party to disclose documents in its possession, provided that they are reasonably believed to exist and are relevant and material to the outcome of the case. In respect of electronic documents Guideline 4 provides that:

the party in possession of such documents may make them available in the form (which may be paper copies) most convenient and economical for it, unless the tribunal determines, on application and for good cause, that there is a compelling need for access to the documents in a different form. Requests for documents maintained in electronic form should be narrowly focused and structured to make searching for them as economical as possible. The tribunal may direct testing or other means of focusing and limiting any search.

The CIArb Protocol for E-Disclosure in Arbitration iterates relevant principles, namely that the parties should agree in advance of documents they wish disclosed and that in case of disagreement the tribunal may order the

---

[41] Art 3(7) IBA Rules.
[42] See Arts 9(5) and (6) IBA Rules. See *INA Corp and Islamic Republic of Iran*, Award No 184–161-1, (1985-I) 8 Iran–US CTR 73, at 382.
[43] Art 9(7) IBA Rules.

production of evidence suitably identified and material to the outcome of the case, subject to reasonableness and proportionality, equal treatment, equal opportunities to present one's case and considerations of cost.[44] Rule 7 of the CIArb Protocol makes an important inroad by specifying that:

> The primary source of disclosure of electronic documents should be reasonably accessible data; namely, active data, near-line data or offline data on disks. In the absence of particular justification it will normally not be appropriate to order the restoration of back-up tapes; erased, damaged or fragmented data; archived data or data routinely deleted in the normal course of business transactions. A party requesting disclosure of such electronic documents shall be required to demonstrate that the relevance and materiality outweigh the costs and burdens of retrieving and producing the same.

This standard does not impose unreasonable obligations on the parties, particularly those holding significant quantities of data. The cost criterion introduced in the final sentence is no doubt quantifiable by the tribunal and ensures that unnecessary fishing expeditions by the requesting party will be rejected.

6.6.4 Fact witness evidence

The function of a fact witness is to supplement or corroborate other evidentiary material with a view to satisfying the tribunal's standard of proof. Although witness testimony may turn out to be of value, especially in respect of disputes where no written evidence exists (e.g. as to whether the cargo left on time), the witness will typically be connected to the pertinent party and hence he or she will derive some form of interest from the outcome of the dispute. This does not, however, diminish the value of the evidence put forward by the fact witness.[45] It is moreover open to the parties to interview or discuss with the witness, although this should not be interpreted as a licence to write or dictate the witness statement or to coach the witness to hide the truth. Article 4(3) of the IBA Rules is clear that:

---

[44] Rule 6 CIArb Protocol.
[45] See Art 4(2) IBA Rules. The same principle is reiterated, albeit slightly more convincingly, in Art 27(2) UNCITRAL Rules.

It shall not be improper for a party, its officers, employees, legal advisors or other representatives to interview its witnesses or potential witnesses and to discuss their prospective testimony with them.

The practice of international tribunals is to require that fact witness testimony be submitted in writing, usually in the form of an affidavit, in advance of the oral hearing so that each party is aware of the evidence its counterpart intends to rely upon.[46] In addition, there is no restriction as regards the parties themselves acting as fact witnesses, although their testimony will naturally carry less weight, especially if it is not corroborated with other documentary evidence.

6.6.5 Expert evidence

There are two kinds of expert evidence; that which is supplied by the parties at their own initiative (party-appointed) and that which is commissioned by the tribunal on its own motion. That the tribunal has the capacity to request independent expert evidence, unless the parties mutually decide otherwise, is an integral part of the tribunal's powers.[47] Expert evidence is not binding on the tribunal, but in the vast majority of cases, particularly where the dispute hinges on whether a particular condition exists or not (e.g. whether construction was consistent with specific standards as agreed in the parties' agreement), the tribunal would be hard pressed not to base its assessment of the case on the report of the expert. In cases where the dispute is in essence dependent on expert evidence, tribunals may converse with party-appointed experts in order to reach a common position. This assumes that while party-appointed experts may owe some allegiance to their appointees, the fact that their testimony is provided under oath (under sanction of civil and perhaps criminal penalties) entails that their evidence must be truthful. In this light, Article 5(4) of the IBA Rules provides that:

The arbitral tribunal in its discretion may order that any party-appointed experts who will submit or who have submitted expert reports on the same or related issues meet and confer on such issues. At such meeting, the party-appointed experts shall attempt to reach agreement on the issues within the scope of their expert reports, and they shall record in writing any such issues on which they reach agreement, any remaining areas of disagreement and the reasons therefore.

---

[46] Art 4(4) IBA Rules; Art 27(2) UNCITRAL Rules; Art 28(2) SCC Arbitration Rules.
[47] Art 26(1) UNCITRAL Model Law; Art 2(4) ICC Rules.

6.6.6 Inspection of the subject matter of the dispute

Inspections are common in construction and engineering disputes, among others, and so it makes sense to appoint arbitrators that are knowledgeable in the particular subject matter of the dispute so as to avoid the need for external experts, which add both cost and delay to the proceedings. Tribunals are typically empowered to appoint experts if the interests of the case so demands. The general rule with respect to tribunal-appointed experts is that they must act impartially and independently and that the parties, or their representatives, are entitled to attend any such inspection.[48] If the tribunal fails to invite one of the parties the award will be set aside as a matter of failing to observe mandatory *lex arbitri* rules.[49] The tribunal will typically draw up terms of reference and the expert will be required to produce a reasoned report subject to certain formalities. The parties may well have their reasons in disputes involving a substantial element of inspection to choose arbitral resolution rather than expert determination.[50]

6.7 Oral hearings

Just like written pleadings institutional rules do not contain detailed regulation of oral hearings. In fact, the parties may just as well dispense with oral hearings if they are content that a documents-only process suffices to present their evidence. The Swiss Federal Supreme Court in *Re TA G v H Company* held that the right of the parties to be heard does not include a right to be heard orally, so long as this rule is consistently applied and is not fundamentally opposed to the wishes of the parties.[51] The same Court has held, however, that the right to be heard includes a minimum duty to examine all issues material to the outcome of the case, as counterbalanced with the freedom of the tribunal to afford the weight it chooses to the available evidence.[52] This necessarily means that the tribunal is under

---

[48] Art 7 IBA Rules.
[49] See *Hebei Import & Export Co v Polytek Engineering Co Ltd*, (1999) 2 HKC 205.
[50] For a brief overview of expert determination, see chapter 1 section 1.4.1.
[51] *Re TA G v H Company*, (1997) ASA Bull 316.
[52] *Case 4A_669/2012* Swiss Federal Supreme Court judgment (17 April 2012).

no obligation to address all arguments raised by the parties, particularly if an argument is objectively irrelevant.[53]

The parties' demand for flexibility, cost-efficiency and speed entails that the hearing process should not conform to the hearing rules of either civil law or common law jurisdictions. In practice, the duration of oral proceedings is short and arbitrators have a duty to ensure that the parties' counsel do not unnecessarily prolong the process, whether by examining immaterial or already discussed evidence, or simply by taking their time with witnesses.[54] Irrespective of the manner in which the tribunal chooses to implement this duty it must not discriminate between the parties. If the tribunal is able to dispense only a limited number of days to the oral proceedings it will naturally devise a case management strategy to ensure effective and timely completion. It will, in all likelihood, convene a pre-hearing conference with the parties for this purpose where, after hearing their views, it will make an order as to the sequence of actions and the procedures to be followed. Some of the issues will have already been submitted to the tribunal through the parties' memorials and this may be true of witness and expert statements (under oath), in which case the tribunal may decide that there is no compelling reason why they should be presented again. Exceptionally, where the parties question the truth or integrity of these statements or the people who made them, the tribunal shall permit a degree of cross-examination, but will set the boundaries concerning the conduct of counsel in this respect. Equally, in its case management function, the tribunal will probably also demand pre-hearing briefs by the parties with a view to summarising and exposing the oral evidence which the parties seek to rely upon. The sequence of presentations and the responses or objections by one party against the claims of the other usually follow the procedures adopted in adversarial civil litigation proceedings. Article 8(3) of the IBA Rules on the Taking of Evidence provides that the sequence may be as follows:

(a) the claimant shall ordinarily first present the testimony of its witnesses, followed by the respondent presenting the testimony of its witnesses;
(b) following direct testimony, any other party may question such witness, in an order to be determined by the arbitral tribunal. The party who initially

---

[53] *Case 4A_564/2013*, Swiss Federal Supreme Court judgment (14 May 2014).
[54] Art 8(2) IBA Rules.

presented the witness shall subsequently have the opportunity to ask additional questions on the matters raised in the other parties' questioning;

(c) thereafter, the claimant shall ordinarily first present the testimony of its party-appointed experts, followed by the respondent presenting the testimony of its party-appointed experts. The party who initially presented the party-appointed expert shall subsequently have the opportunity to ask additional questions on the matters raised in the other parties' questioning;

   . . .

(e) if the arbitration is organised into separate issues or phases (such as jurisdiction, preliminary determinations, liability and damages), the parties may agree or the arbitral tribunal may order the scheduling of testimony separately for each issue or phase;

(f) the arbitral tribunal, upon request of a party or on its own motion, may vary this order of proceeding, including the arrangement of testimony by particular issues or in such a manner that witnesses be questioned at the same time and in confrontation with each other (witness conferencing);

(g) the arbitral tribunal may ask questions to a witness at any time.

Given that arbitral proceedings are legal proceedings in the sense that they culminate in a binding award, the witnesses are under a duty to tell the truth.[55] In most jurisdictions, there is no legal impediment against sworn testimonies in arbitral proceedings, in which case an untruthful witness may be sanctioned under the civil and criminal laws of the seat. Moreover, since it is the tribunal that ultimately needs to be convinced of the claims and counter-claims, it may request any person to give oral evidence if material to the outcome of the dispute. In this case, however, both parties may also question the witness called by the tribunal.[56]

6.8 Representation in arbitral proceedings

In the vast majority of nations there is no requirement that the parties be represented by legal counsel in international arbitral proceedings, let alone by local counsel. This is the direct result of the international nature of arbitration as well as party autonomy. In practice, it is unlikely that any party to a business dispute will not avail itself of legal representation, although it is common for the parties to enjoin technical experts in their

---

[55] Art 8(4) IBA Rules.   [56] Art 8(5) IBA Rules.

legal teams, albeit they may be better placed as expert witnesses. Unlike litigation where the parties' representatives are members of the local bar and subject to the ethical and disciplinary standards thereof, in international arbitration there is generally no requirement that the representative be a lawyer or possess any other professional capacity. As a result, there is no general standard applicable to counsel. There exists no formal qualification for appointment as arbitrator or as counsel to arbitration. Even so, given the judicial nature of arbitral proceedings – although confidentiality may be an issue here – and the fact that the parties are usually represented by lawyers, it is natural to assume that the ordinary ethical rules apply *mutatis mutandis* to arbitration. This solution is not free from problems because counsel in a particular case may come from a variety of jurisdictions and hence in theory each one must be assessed on the basis of his or her national standard; one may certainly be weaker than the other. Even so, several empirical studies have shown a consistency among counsel as to the acute ethical issues in international arbitration, such as delay and guerrilla tactics.[57]

Unlike ethical codes for arbitrators there is no equivalent for counsel, although in 2011 the IBA adopted a set of Principles on Conduct for the Legal Profession. However, this applies to all types of legal proceedings and has not yet received universal approval. Some arbitral institutions have drafted relevant guidelines, such as the LCIA's General Guidelines for the Parties' Legal Representatives, which are binding on the parties – and by implication their legal representatives – because they are an integral part of their arbitration rules, which are binding on the parties, but not their legal representatives. The parties are obliged to ensure that their representatives have agreed to comply as a condition of representation.[58]

Advanced jurisdictions, such as New York, have begun a trend whereby counsel are sanctioned in respect of frivolous applications to set aside awards.[59] Ethical issues are no less important in the context of investment arbitration. In at least two ICSID cases tribunals were faced with claims that counsel practised in the same chambers (essentially a law firm for barristers in England) as those of one arbitrator and that therefore counsel should be removed. The tribunal entertained the claim in one

---

[57] E. Sussman and S. Ebere, All's Fair in Love and War (2011) 22 *Am Rev Int Arb* 611.
[58] Art 18.5 LCIA Rules.
[59] *DigiTelCom Ltd v Tele2 Sverige AB,* 12 Civ 3082 (SDNY, 2012).

case[60] but not in another,[61] naturally noting the absence of a hard rule in this respect. Although in practice tribunals are reluctant to remove counsel for improper behaviour, they possess an inherent right to both rebuke and remove in situations where they threaten the integrity and operation of proceedings.[62]

In closing, it should be noted that the use of registered legal counsel is warranted (by law) where the parties make representations to the local courts. By way of illustration, where the parties seek interim measures or apply for set aside proceedings before the courts of the seat they must naturally do so through local counsel at the seat of the arbitration.

---

[60] *Hrvatska Elektroprivreda v Slovenia*, ICSID case ARB/05/24, ruling regarding the participation of David Mildon QC in further stages of the proceedings (6 May 2008).
[61] *Rompetrol Group NV v Romania*, ICSID case ARB/06/3, decision of the tribunal on the participation of a counsel (14 January 2010).
[62] See Art 18.6 LCIA Rules.

Arbitral awards and challenges against awards

7.1 Introduction

This chapter aims to introduce the reader to the variety of arbitral awards and the reasons for choosing one form over another. It will go on to demonstrate the differences between an order and an award and the consequences arising from this distinction. Moreover, an analysis of the binding nature of awards and their subsequent production of *res judicata* will help the reader understand under what circumstances a party may be estopped from further pursuing claims and issues already decided by an existing arbitral award. In addition, the chapter will discuss the preconditions for valid awards, as well as the remedies which the parties can seek from the tribunal. These range from simple monetary compensation to restitution and gap-filling in the parties' contract. Once we have explained the nature of arbitral awards we shall go on to explore the possible challenges against them. We identify three grounds for challenges, namely jurisdictional, procedural and challenges on points of law. A large part of this chapter is predicated on an analysis of pertinent domestic laws and practice and although an effort is made to discern general principles, the reader should view references to domestic law as merely an illustration of practice and not as hard law that applies uniformly throughout the world.

7.2 Legal nature of awards and *res judicata*

7.2.1 The legal nature of awards

The purpose of arbitration is to resolve disputes by arriving at an award that is in conformity with the law of the seat. These two qualities of the award, namely its dispositive dimension and legality (or validity), *can* be guaranteed by the tribunal because they lie within its power. This suggests that there are qualities or dimensions to an award which lie beyond the authority of arbitrators. By way of illustration, although arbitrators must 'make every effort to ensure that the award is enforceable'[1] they cannot foresee the peculiarities (especially the minute ones) of every legal system and the requirements they impose for the enforcement of foreign awards. It is, of course, a wholly different matter if the parties have notified the

---

[1] Art 41 ICC Rules; equally, Art 32.2 LCIA Rules.

tribunal as to where they intend to seek enforcement of the award and the tribunal subsequently fails to address the requirements of the enforcement state even though it could easily have done so. The two qualities of the award culminate in rendering the award binding between the parties; that is, the award becomes final, or binding, between the parties in respect of the issues decided and there is no further recourse to appeal,[2] save for applicable set aside (and other exceptional) proceedings under the law of the seat.[3] In civil litigation, in contrast, the losing party may appeal on the ground that the judgment erred in its legal and factual determination; on the flip side, a civil judgment need not be subjected to further challenges in the country where enforcement is sought, assuming that a pertinent international agreement exists. Moreover, the award produces *res judicata*, that is, it constitutes a form of estoppel against future claims between the same parties under the same cause of action.

A further practical dimension serves to distinguish civil judgments from awards. The courts are permanent institutions which can re-examine a case long after its commencement, irrespective of the person of the judge that issued the original judgment. Tribunals, however, even if forming part of an arbitral institution, are personal in nature and once their mandate has been fulfilled their office and authority come to an end (*functus officio*). Of course, the tribunal may be requested to clarify or revise an award, but there are precise time limits within which such requests may be made.[4]

The crucial question is what ultimately distinguishes an award from other orders or pronouncements (e.g. injunctions) of arbitral tribunals. Given that only awards dispose of the parties' dispute and are enforceable under the terms of Article I(2) of the 1958 New York Convention, anything less than an award will lack these two qualities. Neither the 1958 New York Convention nor other international instruments, such as the UNCITRAL Model Law, provide a definition of 'awards', chiefly (but not exclusively) because a number of states are not hostile to tribunals cladding in the form of 'award', determinations that do not finally settle the issues set forth by the disputing parties. Under German law, for example, the form of award is reserved for final awards on the merits, decisions on costs (which may be

---

[2] See Art 32(2) UNCITRAL Rules and Art 34(6) ICC Rules.
[3] See below section 7.5ff for a discussion of applicable challenges against arbitral awards.
[4] Art 33(1) and (2) UNCITRAL Model Law; see also below section 7.7.

rendered through a separate award),[5] or additional awards.[6] Exceptionally, some jurisdictions allow tribunals to decide the precise form of their decision regarding challenges to arbitral jurisdiction. Under Article 18(8) of the Portuguese Arbitration Law (PAL), for example, the tribunal possesses discretion in rendering a decision on jurisdiction in the form of an order or an award. This is a significant power, the effect of which is that if the decision is issued as an award it is final, whereas if it is issued as a mere order it is subject to a challenge before the local courts.[7] This power under the PAL also extends to the tribunal's authority to issue interim measures.[8] This is contrary to the position in most states, as is the case with France, whereby decisions on mere interlocutory issues, such as those relating to the tribunal's finding of jurisdiction and generally all those that do not terminate the procedure are not afforded the status of awards.[9] Even so, under French law arbitral decisions on provisional measures that settle all or part of the parties' dispute are considered as either final, partial or interim awards.[10] Several courts in other nations have equally dismissed labels and have gone on to enforce orders granted by tribunals, particularly if the order in question constituted a final disposition of the issues at hand.[11]

We have yet to tackle the question whether in situations where a tribunal is allowed to decide an issue in the form of an award or an order this determination is objective or subjective. Put simply, is this a matter for the tribunal to decide unilaterally or is the scope of the decision (essentially, the range of issues it resolves) that which determines whether it should be classified as an award (and thus subject to set aside and/or enforcement proceedings) rather than a mere order? In practice, states typically opt for an objective test which is now reflected in the leading case of *Brasoil*.[12]

---

[5] s 1057 ZPO.   [6] s 1058 ZPO.   [7] Art 18(9) PAL.   [8] Art 20(2) PAL.

[9] *Société Crédirente v Compagnie Générale de Garantie*, Paris Court of Appeals judgment (29 November 2007), [2009] *Rev Arb* 741.

[10] *SA Otor Participations v SARL Carlyle*, Paris Court of Appeals judgment (7 October 2004) [2005] *Rev Arb* 982.

[11] *Publicis Communication v True North Communications Inc*, 3 F 3d 725 (2nd Cir. 2000); but see the opposite view in *Resort Condominiums International Inc (USA) v Ray Bolwell and Resort Condominiums (Australasia) Pty Ltd (Australia)*, (Queensland Supreme Court,1993), 118 ALR 644.

[12] *Braspetro Oil [Brasoil] Services Co v The Management & Implementation Authority of the Great Man-Made River Project (Libya)*, Paris Appeals Court judgment (1 July 1999), [1999] *Rev Arb* 834.

> **Case Study**
>
> Brasoil was engaged by the Libyan Authority (for the management
> and implementation of the Great Man-Made River Project) for
> the drilling of wells in the Libyan desert. Following disagreement
> over the quality of the works the parties commenced arbitral proceed-
> ings in France. A partial award[13] on liability was initially issued by
> the tribunal against Brasoil, but when at the damages phase the
> Authority submitted documents which Brasoil claimed had been
> fraudulently withheld, Brasoil requested the tribunal to review its
> partial award in light of these circumstances. The tribunal denied
> the request on the ground that it was an order, not an award, but
> this did not stop Brasoil from initiating set aside proceedings against
> the 'order' before French courts. The Paris Appeals Court upheld
> Brasoil's request on the ground that the qualification of a decision
> as an award or order does not depend on the tribunal's classification.
> In the case at hand, the order (partial award) in fact settled one of the
> parties' chief disputes, namely Brasoil's liability in respect of the
> quality of the works undertaken.

7.2.2 *Res Judicata*

The principle of *res judicata* provides that a fact or right (entitlement)
already determined by a competent court or tribunal cannot subsequently
become the subject of litigation or arbitration as between the same parties.
It should be noted from the outset that the principle of *res judicata* comes
into operation only when the award has become final, namely after the
time limits for bringing challenges have elapsed. Finality is therefore a
precondition for *res judicata*. The effects of *res judicata* should be further
distinguished from the principle of *stare decisis*, which is essentially
equivalent to the doctrine of precedent. Precedent, both domestic and
international,[14] presupposes a structured and hierarchical legal system
(e.g. the Swiss legal system or the EU law system) where the decisions of

---

[13] Partial and interim awards are explained in section 7.3.2 of this chapter.

[14] By way of illustration, the Estonian Court of Appeals, in its interpretation of the 1958 New
York Convention takes into consideration the authority and practice of other nations. *Case
no 2–05–23561*, Court of Appeals judgment (9 March 2007).

a higher court exert authority on lower courts, in the sense that the legal principles enunciated must be adhered to, unless a departure is warranted by the operation of a subsequent law. In the common law world courts will generally adhere to precedent[15] and this is increasingly the case in civil law jurisdictions despite the absence of compulsion.[16] The body of international arbitration, despite the existence of several international treaties such as the 1958 New York Convention, does not constitute a structured hierarchical legal system and hence arbitral awards do not give rise to precedent. The situation is further exacerbated by the fact that most arbitral awards remain confidential. In investment arbitration, on the other hand, awards create significant authority, largely because the applicable law is international law, which is well codified and from which departures are exceptional, if at all. Questions of *res judicata* many times interface with determinations of *lis pendens*, which concern conflicts of jurisdiction over the same cause of action. This matter is dealt with in some detail in chapter 5.[17]

Res judicata assumes the existence of an award between the same parties (encompassing both privity and mutuality), the same subject matter and the same claim of relief; the so-called triple identity test. This test is grounded in Article 1351 of the French Civil Code, but is by no means exclusive to France as it applies universally, albeit under distinct legal categorisations. In the common law, the principle of *res judicata* is a form of estoppel, which in turn is a rule of evidence.[18] More specifically, it constitutes both a cause of action estoppel as well as an issue estoppel.[19] As a cause of action estoppel the emphasis is procedural, namely the action for arbitral resolution, which is naturally precluded. Issue estoppel, on the other hand, concerns the issue or right that has already been the subject of an award, and which may not be arbitrated anew.[20] It is generally agreed that issue estoppel is not restricted to the dispositive part of the award, but

---

[15] See *Planned Parenthood of Southeastern Pennsylvania v Casey*, 505 US 833 (1992).

[16] Several civil law jurisdictions in Europe, particularly those with a communist past, do not recognise that judgments issued even by their supreme courts are binding on lower courts, albeit they are certainly of persuasive value.

[17] See chapter 5 section 5.3.2.

[18] *Carl-Zeiss Stiftung v Rayner & Keeler Ltd (No 2)* [1966] 2 All ER 536 at 564, per Lord Guest.

[19] In US law one speaks of claim preclusion and issue preclusion (or collateral estoppel) which is roughly equivalent to the two forms of estoppel under English law.

[20] See International Law Association (ILA), Final Report on *Res Judicata* and Arbitration (Toronto, 2006), Part II, paras 4 and 5.

also extends to its reasoning as well as any available counter-claims.[21] However, subsidiary or collateral matters, as well as orders on procedural issues are not covered by issue estoppel. Cause of action estoppel, on the other hand, prevents a party asserting or denying a particular cause of action that has already been entertained by a tribunal between the same parties. All claims arising from a single event and relying on the same evidence qualify as constituting the same cause of action. A third category is also recognised, namely abuse of process, whereby a party is precluded in subsequent litigation from raising a claim or an issue which could have been brought in earlier proceedings had the party exercised due diligence.[22] Civil law jurisdictions differ in their approach as compared to their common law counterparts. They take the view that *res judicata* gives rise to a cause of action estoppel that is limited to the dispositive part of the award.

So far we have restricted our analysis to an examination of the effects of *res judicata* to existing disputes. Although, as we have already emphasised, arbitral awards do not create precedent in respect of future disputes, there are circumstances whereby an issue of fact or the legal consequences of a fact that is already the subject of an award may have some degree of precedential value. In *Associated Electric and Gas Insurance Services Ltd v European Reinsurance Co of Zurich*, the parties to re-insurance arbitration had concluded a confidentiality agreement which prevented them from disclosing material to third parties. An arbitral award was issued but one of the parties commenced subsequent arbitral proceedings under the same re-insurance contract as the first arbitration. The question was whether the issues determined in the first award could be taken as *res judicata* in the course of the subsequent arbitral proceedings, despite the existence of the confidentiality agreement. The Privy Council, acting as a final appellate court, accepted that a tribunal was able to rely on an issue finally determined by an arbitral award, this being 'a species of the enforcement of the rights given by the [prior] award', adding further that this did

---

[21] Ibid., Part I, paras 52–3; in *Apotex Holdings Inc and Apotex Inc v USA [Apotex III]*, ICSID Award (25 August 2014), para 7.42, it was held that under the *res judicata* doctrine 'operative part[s] as a "*dispositive*" can and should be read with the relevant "*motifs*" or reasons for that operative part'. In the case at hand the ICSID tribunal referred to the determination of an activity as an investment by means of a prior award under the UNCITRAL Rules.

[22] *Henderson v Henderson* (1844) 6 QB 288; see ILA Final Report, Part I, para 2.11.

not constitute a breach of the parties' confidentiality agreement.[23] This is a significant development, which has not, however, been universally tested. Undoubtedly, some arbitrators may be apprehensive, fearing set aside or enforcement challenges on due process grounds, particularly that the tribunal failed to hear the parties equally on the issue that was determined by a prior award. Needless to say, some degree of uniformity, perhaps through a treaty mechanism, needs to be established at global or regional level with a view to sustaining the *res judicata* effect of issues already determined by lawfully constituted tribunals.

7.3 Types of awards

Having examined the legal nature of awards (and their qualities), we shall now proceed to identify and analyse the variety of available awards on the basis of the quantity of substantive issues they purport to dispose of, as well as the manner (essentially the procedure) by which a tribunal reaches its award.

7.3.1 Final awards

A final award is that which disposes all the issues submitted to the tribunal by the parties' submission agreement. When the tribunal disposes of *all* the pertinent issues two particular implications arise: firstly, the award is final in respect of these issues and secondly any subsequent recognition and enforcement of the award abroad encompasses these very issues. As a result, if the award does not go on to resolve all the issues submitted to it (i.e. it is an *infra petita* award), the parties may request the tribunal either to revise the award with a view to addressing the omitted issues or to issue an additional award in which it determines solely the omitted issues.[24] Conversely, if the tribunal has passed judgment on more issues than were submitted to it by the parties (*ultra petita* award) any of the parties may have recourse to set aside proceedings on the ground that the tribunal exceeded its authority under the arbitration

---

[23] *Associated Electric and Gas Insurance Services Ltd v European Reinsurance Co of Zurich* [2003] 1 WLR 1041.

[24] Art 33(3) UNCITRAL Model Law; see below section 7.5.

agreement.[25] It is therefore possible that at the end of the proceedings the tribunal may have issued several awards on the merits of the dispute, particularly where several interim awards have been granted. It is of no legal significance whether one of these may be classified as final (on the ground perhaps that it disposes of the majority of issues) given that all *awards*, whether final or otherwise, produce *res judicata*[26] and are enforceable under the 1958 New York Convention. The tribunal may just as well, assuming it is expedient, dispose of preliminary (e.g. jurisdictional) and substantive claims in a single (final) award, but this has no greater legal value than a series of discrete awards disposing the same set of issues.

Commentators note the tradition in Denmark whereby arbitrators ask the parties whether instead of a final award they would rather have a simplified ruling, often confined to legal reasoning and conclusion (*tilkendegivelse*). This is not, however, an award and the benefits include less drafting for arbitrators and hence it reduces their fees, which may serve as an attraction for some parties.[27] Obviously, such a document provides no *res judicata* and no guarantee of compliance and it is not surprising that it has been criticised by the Danish Supreme Court.[28]

7.3.2 Interim and partial awards

Whereas the judicial economy of rendering a single final award at the end of arbitral proceedings may make sense in most cases, there may well arise circumstances where the tribunal must decide a particular issue before it reaches a final award on the merits.[29] For example, if one of the parties raises serious jurisdictional claims it would be wrong for the tribunal not to dispose of this issue first in the form of an order or interim (preliminary)

---

[25] Under Art 34(2)(a)(iii) of the UNCITRAL Model Law *ultra petita* awards may be set aside as a whole, unless 'decisions on matters submitted to arbitration can be separated from those not submitted'.

[26] See s 47(3) English AA.

[27] O. Spiermann, National Report for Denmark (2009), in J. Paulsson (ed.), *International Handbook on Commercial Arbitration* (Kluwer, 2004, Supp no 57, 2009), 21.

[28] *H. J. Nielsen, Oscar Nordland and Henning Remmen v Copenhagen Admiral Hotel I/S*, Danish Supreme Court judgment (17 March 1994).

[29] The Svea [Sweden] Court of Appeal has held that an interim award on the advance of costs is not only enforceable but may also form the basis for an application for bankruptcy. *Consafe IT AB v Auto Connect Sweden AB*, judgment (11 March 2009).

award. The same is true of preliminary disputes regarding the applicable law. Equally, as in the *Brasoil* case, the tribunal may deem it expedient to first resolve the issue of liability, especially in complex cases that have the potential to drag on for considerable time, before delivering a judgment on damages and costs. The parties may have a direct interest in obtaining such a partial award. By way of illustration, there may well be other contractual or business relationships between the parties elsewhere and the winning party may wish to demonstrate to other courts and arbitral tribunals that its counterpart habitually violates its contractual obligations. It is also common for tribunals to offer partial awards in order to address complex issues of liability first, before using the award on liability as a platform for assessing quantum, i.e. the range, scale and quality of applicable damages. On the other hand, however, claims for interim awards may be the cause of delay and ultimately protract proceedings to the detriment of the parties. As a result, the tribunal must assess whether the granting of partial awards in a particular case is in the parties' best interests.

In practice, tribunals routinely grant partial awards, their authority stemming from the *lex arbitri*, which is generally permissive,[30] as well as institutional rules,[31] subject to any contrary agreement by the parties.

7.3.3 Consent awards

Where the parties succeed in reaching agreement while arbitral proceedings are ongoing and before the tribunal has issued a final award they may notify the tribunal and request that their agreement or settlement be recorded by the tribunal in the form of an award. The authority of the tribunal to record a consent award is recognised in Article 30 of the UNCITRAL Model Law as well as national legal systems.[32] If tribunals did not possess such authority they could either do so on an unofficial basis – with a view to assisting the parties, although such an option would lack legality and may later raise grounds for challenging the award – or alternatively the parties could record their settlement in the form of a contract. Given that contractual freedom naturally allows the parties to a dispute to reach a mutual settlement, it would be absurd if they could not request an existing tribunal to record their settlement in the form of an award.

---

[30] s 47(3) English AA.   [31] Art 32(1) UNCITRAL Rules; Art 26.1 LCIA Rules.
[32] See s 47 English AA.

Article 30 of the UNCITRAL Model Law, however, imposes an important qualification to consent awards, particularly that the terms of the settlement must be accepted by the tribunal, which means that where the parties reach settlement the tribunal is not a mere notary which records their settlement in the form of an award but continues to exercise its judicial function. Arbitrators will not bear liability for choosing not to record the settlement in the form of an award, but if they record it as an award they must ensure that the form satisfies the relevant criteria under the *lex arbitri* and the intended countries of enforcement (e.g. reasoned and signed by the arbitrators).

An increasing number of anecdotal cases are surfacing where the parties trigger arbitral proceedings and then suddenly reach a settlement which conceals elements of money laundering (e.g. by agreeing to excessive compensation in order to launder illicit proceeds) and other illicit activity with the objective of getting an arbitral award which they can enforce elsewhere. Besides settlement agreements concealing illegal activity, which tribunals are under a duty to reject, it is unclear whether tribunals may accept an agreement that is blatantly unjust. The UNCITRAL Model Law does not specifically address this issue but it is assumed that if an agreement of this nature is not valid under the law applicable to the dispute or the *lex arbitri*, the tribunal should not record it as an award. The tribunal's decision to accept or reject a settlement has implications on costs. If the length of the proceedings were short, the institutional rules will generally demand that the parties' costs and fees are lower than if the case had been heard in full.

7.3.4 Default awards

It is not unusual for the respondent in arbitral proceedings to reject the applicant's claim and refuse to participate. State instrumentalities, in particular, may even suggest that the tribunal lacks jurisdiction, despite an arbitration agreement to the contrary, on the ground of immunity. A respondent may otherwise choose to default (i.e. not participate in proceedings) because he realises that the claim against him will ultimately succeed and hopes to minimise his losses by not incurring legal fees.

Where the claimant fails to communicate his statement of claim the proceedings naturally come to a close as there is no longer a dispute to speak of.[33] In the event that the respondent fails to communicate his

---

[33] Art 25(a) UNCITRAL Model Law.

statement of defence or at a later stage abandons the proceedings the tribunal shall continue 'without treating such failure in itself as an admission of the claimant's allegations'.[34] As a result, the tribunal may well decide that despite the respondent failing to provide any counter-arguments on the basis of the evidence furnished by the claimant, the latter's claim was not sufficiently proven. It is also clear that the tribunal must examine the merits of every argument[35] and conduct the proceedings as though the respondent was present at every stage thereof. This authority of tribunals to grant default awards is important because otherwise the defaulting party could later claim (e.g. at the phase of enforcement) that his or her due process rights were violated. Default awards, just like other types of awards, have the legal value of final awards.

7.4 Validity of awards

Awards must be valid otherwise they will be set aside at the seat of the arbitration or later at the phase of enforcement. Validity concerns the form of the award as well as the substantive and procedural grounds for setting awards aside. For the purpose of clarity the following sections will focus on the form or formalities associated with arbitral awards and at the end of the chapter we shall discuss in length the (substantive and procedural) grounds upon which an award may be set aside. There are several criteria to rendering a valid award under the law of the seat. The first concerns its form and content, followed by the observation of applicable time limits, notification to the other party and finally registration (or deposit), if and where necessary.

7.4.1 Form of award

The form of the award is generally dictated by the applicable institutional rules and the law of the seat, although the parties' agreement may play some role especially where it modifies non-mandatory rules. It is not sufficient that the tribunal discharge the proceedings fairly and consistently in

---

[34] Art 25(b) UNCITRAL Model Law; see equally, s 41(4) English AA.

[35] This is true to the extent that an argument is material to the outcome of the case. See chapter 6 sections 6.6.1. and 6.7.

accordance with the parties' agreement and the *lex arbitri*. The award itself must satisfy several formalities in respect of its content, lest it be set aside.[36] The UNCITRAL Model Law and the UNCITRAL Rules make it clear that:

- the award shall be in writing;
- the award shall be signed by the arbitrators, or at least the majority thereof, stating reasons where an arbitrator has failed to sign;
- the award shall state the reasons upon which the tribunal's conclusions are based;
- the award shall state its date and place of arbitration.[37]

These basic requirements are imposed by the majority of legal systems,[38] with some flexibility and variation as will be discussed later. Whereas the requirement for a written and dated award is straightforward, the others are not. We have already discussed the complex legal situation associated with truncated tribunals, particularly the validity of awards following the substitution or replacement of an original arbitrator.[39] Where all arbitrators are present at the award stage but one or more refuse to sign the award they are no doubt aware that the award may be considered invalid. The key motivating factor underlying such a stance is disagreement on the application of law or the construction of facts, resulting in the arbitrator being disinclined to identify himself with the particular award. Such a disagreement could just as well be alleviated by a dissenting opinion,[40] where this is permitted, but given that awards are valid where the majority appends their signature – as opposed to all arbitrators – this issue need not create insurmountable problems to the parties.

The requirement for a reasoned award constitutes the norm in the practice of international commercial arbitration and is prescribed in all institutional rules.[41] Although the UNCITRAL Model Law and Rules thereof suggest that awards may not be reasoned if the parties so wish, caution should be exercised where the intended country of enforcement (or even

---

[36] That is why Art 33 of the ICC Rules requires that 'no award shall be rendered by the arbitral tribunal until it has been approved by the Court as to its form'.

[37] Art 32 UNCITRAL Rules; Art 31(1)–(3) UNCITRAL Model Law.

[38] See s 52 English AA; Art 823 Italian CCP.   [39] See chapter 4 section 4.11

[40] Few, if any, institutional rules expressly refer to dissenting opinions, but in principle there is no rule forbidding them, except where the deliberations between a panel of arbitrators are presumed to be confidential. Only r 47(3) of the ICSID Arbitration Rules explicitly caters for dissenting opinions.

[41] Art 31(2) ICC Rules; Art 48(3) ICSID Convention.

the seat) demand reasoned awards irrespective of the parties' agreement. Of course, the depth of the tribunal's reasoning must be consistent with the dispute at hand. Disputes concerning whether goods have actually been supplied do not require lengthy analyses; they either occurred or not, but even so the tribunal must record the evidence for its 'yes' or 'no' answer. Typical reasoning records the facts and then relates these to the applicable law in order to reach a sensible conclusion. Exceptionally, the US Supreme Court, in contrast to European arbitration statutes, has held that arbitrators have no obligation to the court to provide reasons for an award.[42] The Swedish Supreme Court has held that although awards must be reasoned, an award will only be set aside if it lacks reasoning *in toto* (completely).[43]

One should be mindful of the distinction between non-reasoned awards and awards that wrongly applied the law to the facts. The absence of reasons renders the award defective, but this is not the case where the arbitrators got the law wrong.

7.4.2 Time limits

Time limits for rendering an award may be set by the parties' agreement, the law of the seat as well by institutional rules.[44] The objective of such time limits is to make arbitration speedy and deter the parties from delaying the process. If the tribunal fails to observe a time limit set by the parties or by law (mandatory limits) the award is considered null and the arbitration agreement no longer effective.[45] Although the threat of such an outcome is an incentive for speedier proceedings – not to mention a potential source of liability for the arbitrators[46] – it may also culminate in hastiness and poor proceedings, especially if the case is more complex than originally anticipated. It is common, therefore, in institutional rules and arbitral statutes for the tribunal or the courts to possess the authority to extend the relevant time limits in the interests of justice. Article 24(2) of

---

[42] *United Steelworkers of America v Enterprise Wheel Car Corp*, 363 US 593 (1960), at 598.

[43] *Soyak International Construction and Investment Inc v Hochtief AG*, [2009] NJA 128. It went on to say, however, that providing reasons is a guarantee of due process, which has to be balanced against the interest in the finality of awards.

[44] Art 30(1) ICC Rules provides a six-month time limit within which the tribunal must render its award, which starts from the date of the last signature by the tribunal, or by the parties of the terms of reference.

[45] Luxembourg District Court *judgment, no 11376* (15 January 2009).

[46] Art 37(2) Spanish AA; but see chapter 4 section 4.7.

the ICC Rules stipulates that: 'The Court may extend this [six-month] time limit pursuant to a reasoned request from the arbitral tribunal or on its own initiative if it decides it is necessary to do so.'

Most nations do not impose a mandatory time limit and in any event the courts of arbitration-friendly countries have demonstrated an inclination to preserve awards that have failed (not grossly or substantially) to meet the time limits set upon them. In Germany, the OLG Koblenz has held that this is not a valid ground for non-enforcement of a foreign award, especially if the challenging party failed to object when the time limit had expired.[47]

7.4.3 Notification and registration of awards

Once an award is issued the arbitral institution, usually through its secretariat, must communicate the award to the parties through a formal process of notification.[48] Lack of notification does not render an award defective as such, but given that in most legal systems the time limits for recourse against awards commence from the day this is communicated to the parties,[49] it is clear that a non-communicated award is not yet final.

Some legal systems may provide for the registration of awards, whether in mandatory or optional terms. In accordance with Article 37(8) of the Spanish Arbitration Act the award may be formalised before a notary public. Any of the parties, at their own expense, may require the arbitrators, before notification, to formalise the award before a notary public. Quite clearly, this is not a requirement that renders awards enforceable. The advantages of registration and notarisation are the existence of an official record which may be useful for subsequent usages, including enforcement abroad. This is indeed the rationale underlying Article 193(2) of the Swiss PILA, whereby the parties may request the court, and at their own expense, to certify the enforceability of awards rendered in Switzerland. Where the registration of awards is compulsory for rendering the award final the winning party must be vigilant in satisfying this requirement.[50]

---

[47] OLG Koblenz, judgment (27 November 2012).
[48] Art 34(1) ICC Rules; Art 32(6) UNCITRAL Rules.   [49] See s 55(2) English AA.
[50] Under Art 825(1) of the Italian CCP arbitral (*rituale*) awards produce *res judicata* upon deposit with the registry of the tribunal of the district in which the arbitration has its seat. The court, after ascertaining that the award meets all formal requirements, shall declare the same enforceable by decree.

Elsewhere, the process is more formal and requires an additional level of hearing. In accordance with Article 43 of the Finnish Arbitration Act final or partial awards require writ (or exequatur) from the local courts for their enforcement. The party against whom it is sought may be given an opportunity to be heard, although this does not amount to an appeal on the facts or merits of the dispute.

7.5 Remedies

The ultimate purpose of arbitration is to satisfy particular claims arising from a dispute. The claimant in its statement of claim and the respondent in its statement of defence do not request the tribunal to resolve their dispute in the abstract, but after deciding on liability to provide one or more remedies to the winning party. Of course, the tribunal is not obliged to grant every remedy sought by the winning party because some of these may be contrary to public policy (or the law of the seat more generally) or beyond the scope of the parties' agreement. By way of illustration, an award rendered by a tribunal seated in Europe which imposes punitive (triple) damages on the basis that the governing law of the contract was US law – where punitive damages are recognised in cases such as anti-trust – would be challenged as an excess of power under the law of the seat because European laws do not recognise triple damages.[51] However, if the parties' agreement is broad enough to clearly encompass a remedy of punitive damages the courts of the seat would be hard pressed to set that remedy aside. No doubt, enforcement problems may arise in third nations on the ground of public policy concerns.

It is not a straightforward assumption that a tribunal can order *any* appropriate or just remedy. The range of remedies available to the courts is prescribed in legislation, as is the case with the remedies for breach of contract. Arbitral statutes, on the other hand, cannot impose remedies on arbitral tribunals, especially in international arbitration, because of the risk that these may clash with the parties' agreement, the remedies under their chosen conflict of laws or the law of the country of enforcement. If the

---

[51] The sole arbitrator in *Caldera Resources Inc v Global Gold Mining LLC and Global Gold Corp*, ICDR case no 50 (2010) 00674, Award (10 November 2014) awarded punitive damages against Caldera for the defamatory publications made by its principal against Global Gold.

arbitral statute of country X obliged the tribunal to impose interest, such an award could not be enforced in a Muslim country prohibiting all types of interest. In order to avoid, as much as possible, these aforementioned clashes, institutional rules are now open to the same kind of remedies as those available to the courts and at the same time modern arbitral statutes, such as the English Arbitration Act, provide ample juridical space to tribunals in accordance with the wishes of the parties.[52]

The most commonly sought remedy is monetary compensation, which in many cases is quantifiable, for example, by a simple calculation of direct and indirect losses or earnings. Even so, disputes may arise as to the appropriate currency, despite the existence of an explicit agreement. Section 48 of the English Arbitration Act allows tribunals to order payment of an award in any currency, unless the parties have agreed otherwise. Quite clearly, the authority of the tribunal is conditional upon the arbitration agreement. This was emphatically recognised by the House of Lords in the *Lesotho Highlands* case. Lord Steyn pointed out that although the tribunal erred in its exercise of power under section 48 (i.e. by ordering payment in a currency not contemplated in the parties' agreement on the ground that the local Lesotho currency had been hugely depreciated since the agreement had been entered) it had not exceeded its power as such.[53] As a result, that part of the award was sustained because an error in law – as opposed to an excess of power – is not a ground for vacating arbitral awards.

Requests for monetary compensation almost always seek the payment of simple and/or compound interest. Although the authority to award interest is founded on the parties' agreement, its extent, calculation and legal nature, unless otherwise agreed, is dependent on the applicable law. By way of illustration, Saudi law prohibits all types of interest, whereas English and Australian law empower tribunals to decide the time from which interest is due as well as its amount on the basis of equitable principles.[54]

In most cases the arbitration agreement will dictate the range of remedies desired by the parties and this will also be reflected in their chosen institutional rules. If in doubt as to whether a particular power is conferred under the parties' agreement the tribunal will have to examine whether

---

[52] s 48 English AA. The only restriction relates to a performance order relating to land under s 48(5)(b).

[53] *Lesotho Highlands Development Authority v Impregilo SpA and Others* [2005] 3 All ER 789.

[54] See s 49(3) English AA; ss 25(1) and 26 Australian International Arbitration Act 1989.

such a power exists under the law of the seat. The filling of gaps and adaptation of contracts are remedies that are not uncommonly sought in international arbitration. The former aims to fill an obvious gap in a contract, the gap itself being the very object of the parties' dispute – is the gap intentional or simply an omission? Contract adaptation typically involves some kind of impossibility of performance by reason of hardship which itself arises from a fundamental change of circumstances (*rebus sic stantibus*). An unfortunate application of this remedy was examined earlier in the *Lesotho Highlands* judgment. In both gap-filling and contract adaptation, where the parties' agreement and their chosen law is silent, it is not at all obvious, or indeed just, for the tribunal to adapt the contract even in respect of fundamentally changed circumstances. Surely, the parties are responsible for drawing up an agreement that caters for all foreseeable circumstances and even unforeseeable ones. In the absence of such clauses why should the tribunal presume that said actions were implicitly intended by the parties in the first place? Such a presumption constitutes a direct attack against party autonomy and threatens the parties' legitimate expectations. Hence, in the absence of express authority stemming from the arbitration agreement or by the operation of law the tribunal must not assume the authority of adapting the parties' contractual obligations.

Some remedies available under statute in international arbitration raise questions of appropriateness, rather than legality. The English Arbitration Act, for example, envisages both specific performance[55] and restitution.[56] Specific performance arises from a breach of contract whereby the claimant requests its counterpart to perform an action that was promised to the claimant and in respect of which there is an expectation of performance. Equally, restitution entails a particular manifestation of specific performance, whereby the aggrieved party seeks to be reinstated in the same position it would have occupied had the breach or other unlawful act not taken place. Although in actions between private actors such remedies may be appropriate, where one of the parties is a state entity, as in the case of expropriation, restitution would be meaningless because of the underlying hostility between the home state and the foreign investor and their mutual

---

[55] See s 48(5)(b) English AA.
[56] See s 48(5)(a) English AA, which confers on tribunals the authority to order any remedies available to the courts.

disinclination for furtherance of their investment or commercial relationship. Moreover, it is impractical for a tribunal to demand that a state act in one or other way in respect of its natural resources or other assets situated on its territory and this is exactly why the standard remedy for expropriation under international law is fair, prompt and adequate compensation. As a result, monetary compensation is preferred over and above restitution and specific performance.[57]

A particular type of remedy that seeks to highlight a breach but not necessarily hamper or jeopardise the parties' existing relationship is that of declaratory relief.[58] A request for declaratory relief seeks an acknowledgment of a breach of contract or recognition of the parties' existing rights and obligations. In the *Aramco* case the tribunal found no issue with a request for declaratory relief as to whether one of the parties (the Saudi government) had entered into a subsequent contract with a competitor by which it had breached its obligation to grant Aramco exclusive rights to transport oil.[59] Of course, an award granting declaratory relief, although recognisable, is not capable of enforcement, but this is not the purpose for which it is sought, as the *Aramco* case amply illustrates. Recently, English courts have confirmed that a declaratory arbitral award which simply states that a party is not liable can be enforced like a judgment.[60] The aim here is not to compel the losing party to comply with the award, as the award does not impose any particular behaviour, but rather serves the purpose of avoiding recognition and enforcement of a conflicting foreign judgment on the same subject matter.

7.6 Challenges against awards

The general rule is that once an award becomes final it produces *res judicata*. This means that if the losing party seeks further recourse to litigation or arbitration on the resolved issues it will be refused. It may seem unfair that there are no further layers of appeals against arbitral awards as this gives rise to a disincentive for the production of good awards and in addition it ignores the likelihood of unjust outcomes. Even so, the

---

[57] See Art 1135 NAFTA.   [58] See s 48(3) English AA.

[59] *Saudi Arabia v Arabian American Oil Company (Aramco)*, (1963) 27 ILR 117.

[60] *West Tankers Inc v Allianz SpA and Generali Assicurazione Generali SpA*, [2011] 2 All ER (Comm) 1, paras 28–30.

parties to an arbitration agreement are well aware of the absence of an appeals procedure which they may well view as an advantage, particularly if they desire a speedy and confidential process away from the tardiness of the courts. However, a sensible line should be drawn between the absence of an appeals procedure (on the merits of the award) and some kind of recourse against such conduct and omissions by the tribunal that infringe fundamental tenets of the legal system (e.g. party equality) or violate the very essence of arbitration, as is the case with a tribunal ignoring the parties' agreement. In the latter category of cases, annulment or set aside proceedings have been instituted at domestic level with a view either to setting aside the arbitral award as a whole or in order to salvage, where possible, parts of the award.

One may identify three types of challenges against awards, on the basis of the pertinent grounds (for the challenge). At a first level one encounters jurisdictional challenges. Secondly, a party may claim violation of procedural rules, which is broadly equivalent to set aside proceedings. Finally, there could well be challenges against the substance of the award where the claimant alleges the existence of an error in law or fact. Depending on the entity entertaining the challenge a further distinction may be identified, namely internal (submitted to the tribunal itself) and external (submitted to the courts) challenges.

7.6.1 Internal challenges

Before proceeding to examine the three types of challenges it is important to recall and expand on the range of challenges available to the parties against an award by recourse to the tribunal itself or, exceptionally, the arbitral institution. We have already discussed the possibility of challenges against the tribunal's jurisdiction (e.g. non-arbitrability or lack of arbitration agreement) with the tribunal employing its competence-competence powers to resolve such challenges,[61] although ultimately the parties may have recourse to the courts.[62] In equal measure, where the award is unclear, contains (typographical or technical) errors or fails to resolve all the issues submitted by the parties (*infra petita* awards), any of the parties may seek a clarification (or interpretation) of the parts that are unclear and, in the case

---

[61] See Art 16(1) UNCITRAL Model Law; see chapter 4 section 4.3.2.
[62] For example, s 1040(3) ZPO.

of *infra petita* awards, the tribunal may be requested to decide the missing issues.[63] Moreover, a request for the correction of minor errors may be made.[64] In every case, the correction, interpretation or additional award is part of the main award and produces *res judicata*.

There may well exist situations whereby the parties prefer arbitration to litigation but nonetheless desire some sort of appeal against the award, whether in respect of factual or legal mistakes. In many legal systems, appeals against factual or legal mistakes are prohibited under all circumstances.[65] In others, however, if the parties express their mutual consent to an appeal the courts may validly assume jurisdiction.[66] Even so, the parties may have yet another option under their chosen institutional rules, which may provide that if they so agree the award may be subjected to an internal (institutional) appeal procedure.[67] Such an appeal may be heard by another panel of arbitrators or exceptionally by an executive organ of the arbitral institution.

In all other cases, challenges against awards are heard by the courts and hence are of an external nature. We shall now turn to the various types of challenges, although it should be noted that the remedies available under domestic law do not always follow this neat categorisation.[68]

7.6.2 Jurisdictional challenges

We have already discussed the competence-competence power of arbitral tribunals in respect of assessing the reach of their jurisdiction.[69] If the

---

[63] Art 36 Swedish AA.   [64] Art 33 UNCITRAL Model Law.

[65] In the USA, for example, see *Hall Street Associates LLC v Mattel Inc*, (2008) 552 US 576.

[66] Art 35(1) of the Greek LICA and Art 895 CCP; Article 1205(2) of the Polish CCP; in Portugal this is only possible in respect of international awards and only if the parties so mutually consent, in accordance with Art 53 of the Portuguese Arbitration Law.

[67] Spanish Court of Arbitration Rules (2011). See R. Platt, The Appeal of Appeal Mechanisms in International Arbitration: Fairness over Finality? (2013) 30 *JOIA* 531.

[68] Under Art 339 of the Swiss CCP, two possible challenges against awards rendered in domestic arbitration in Switzerland exist, namely objection [which is equivalent to setting aside] and review. A third one, namely revision, also exists in order to challenge arbitral awards. It has been held by the courts to be an extraordinary appeal and arises where the applicant discovers afterwards relevant facts or conclusive evidence on which it could not rely in the previous proceedings. Cases *4A_688/2012* and *4A-126/2013*, Federal Supreme Court judgment (9 October 2013). Article 396(2) CCP contains an additional ground for review, namely on the grounds of a violation of the ECHR. Swiss commentators generally regard this provision as redundant because in their opinion the ECHR is not directly applicable to arbitral proceedings. See below note 85.

[69] See chapter 4 section 4.3.2.

decision is issued in the form of an order and any of the parties disagrees, further recourse may be had to the courts, whose judgment is final. If the decision is issued in the form of a preliminary award it may be subject to annulment/set aside proceedings before the tribunal reaches a final award on the merits. Alternatively, jurisdictional matters may be dealt with in the body of the final award. Jurisdictional challenges generally seek to dissolve the authority of the tribunal, whether because the subject matter of the dispute is not arbitrable,[70] there is an absence of arbitration agreement, or other.

Although judicial attitudes vary from country to country, it is generally accepted that a refusal by a tribunal to sustain its jurisdiction will only be upheld by the courts if the fault is significant. In a Scottish case, a party challenged a preliminary award refusing arbitral jurisdiction, which led the arbitrator to declare that notice given to one party was improper. When set aside proceedings were heard against the preliminary award the Outer House of the Court of Session ultimately remitted the case to the arbitrator to consider the merits of the dispute, arguing that the arbitrator had focused on technicalities and not on the original intention of the parties and the factual background of the case.[71]

7.6.3 Set aside proceedings (annulment)

In accordance with Article 34(2) of the UNCITRAL Model Law, an arbitral award may be set aside if:

(a) the party making the application furnishes proof that:
- (i) a party to the arbitration agreement referred to in Article 7 was under some incapacity; or the said agreement is not valid under the law to which the parties have subjected it or, failing any indication thereon, under the law of this state; or
- (ii) the party making the application was not given proper notice of the appointment of an arbitrator or of the arbitral proceedings or was otherwise unable to present his case; or
- (iii) the award deals with a dispute not contemplated by or not falling within the terms of the submission to arbitration, or contains decisions on matters

---

[70] Although this is also a reason for setting an award aside. See Art 34(2)(b)(i) UNCITRAL Model Law.

[71] *G1 Venues Ltd v Glenerrol Ltd*, Opinion of Lord Malcolm, [2013] CSOH 202, decision (21 December 2013).

beyond the scope of the submission to arbitration, provided that, if the decisions on matters submitted to arbitration can be separated from those not so submitted, only that part of the award which contains decisions on matters not submitted to arbitration may be set aside; or

(iv) the composition of the arbitral tribunal or the arbitral procedure was not in accordance with the agreement of the parties, unless such agreement was in conflict with a provision of this Law from which the parties cannot derogate, or, failing such agreement, was not in accordance with this Law; or

(b) the court finds that:

(i) the subject-matter of the dispute is not capable of settlement by arbitration under the law of this state; or

(ii) the award is in conflict with the public policy of this state.

Where any of these grounds is established by the claimant the court will set aside (annul) the award, in which case not only is there no *res judicata* but, more significantly, the arbitration agreement ceases to have any legal effect because its subject matter has effectively been dissolved. However, in situations where the court believes that the infringement is not serious enough to annul an otherwise good award it will either dismiss the challenge as a whole, suspend set aside proceedings in order to allow the tribunal to rectify the alleged defect, or remit the award to the tribunal for rectification.[72] By way of illustration, Article 46(8) of the PAL stipulates that: 'the competent state court, when asked to set aside an arbitral award, may, where appropriate, and if it is so requested by one of the parties, suspend the setting aside proceedings for a period of time determined by it, in order to give the arbitral tribunal the opportunity to resume the arbitral proceedings or to take such other action as the arbitral tribunal deems likely to eliminate the grounds for setting aside'. Equally, Belgian law makes it clear that the courts should not set aside awards lightly but should remand these to the arbitral tribunals for further remedy in order to salvage them.[73]

National arbitral statutes vary as to the number of grounds for challenging awards. Some require more than the UNCITRAL Model Law whereas others demand less. Besides the reasons offered by the Model Law,[74] Belgian law offers three additional grounds for setting aside awards. These are: a) absence of reasoning (essentially lack of justification);[75] b) excess of

---

[72] Art 34(4) UNCITRAL Model Law.   [73] Art 1715(7) JC.   [74] Art 1717(3) JC.
[75] Art 1717(3)(a)(iv) JC. In *C v S*, the Brussels Court of First Instance, judgment (18 August 2011), held that contradiction in the reasoning of an award constitutes a ground for setting

powers on the part of the tribunal;[76] and c) the award was obtained by fraud (this ground may be raised *ex officio* by the court seized of an annulment request, like the grounds based on a breach of public policy or inarbitrability).[77] A breach of due process may only be invoked if it was not known and therefore could not be raised during the arbitration process and will justify annulment only if it cannot be proven that the irregularity did not have consequences on the award (burden of proof rests on the defendant to the annulment proceedings).[78]

The effect of annulling an award by the courts of the seat necessarily means that the award lacks *res judicata* and therefore cannot be enforced. Article V(1)(e) of the 1958 New York Convention stipulates that the country where enforcement is sought may refuse to do so where the award has been set aside in the seat.[79] Exceptionally, under French legal doctrine, awards set aside at the seat of the arbitration may still be recognised and enforced in France.[80] This outcome is based on the rationale that the validity of an international award must be assessed by the rules of the country where recognition and enforcement is sought. As a result, the suspension of a foreign award by the courts of the seat does not bind French courts when assessing the recognition and enforcement of said award.[81]

In the following sections we shall undertake a brief analysis of all the grounds for challenge encompassed under Article 34(2) of the UNCITRAL

---

it aside when it has 'an impact on the result of the award'. A misunderstanding by the tribunal in its explanation or reasoning of the award does not constitute lack of reasoning that could culminate in setting the award aside. See *Africa Industrial Services v Polycra*, case No C 04.0452N, judgment (10 November 2005).

[76] This is not only where it has bypassed its powers under the submission agreement. In *A v B*, case No 2010/RG/927, judgment (28 April 2010), the Liege Court of Appeal held that failure to honour the time-limit set out in the submission agreement is considered an excess of power.

[77] Art 1717(3)(b) JC.

[78] See Arts 1717(3)(a)(ii) and (v) of the JC.

[79] See *International Standard Electric Corp (ISEC) v Bridas Sociedad Anonima Petrolera Industrial y Comercial*, 745 F Supp 172 (SDNY, 1990), at 178, which noted that the setting aside process relates to procedural law (the law and authority of the courts of the seat) and is wholly unrelated to the governing law of the contract (which represents substantive law).

[80] *Société Hilmarton Ltd v Société OTV*, French Court of Cassation judgment (23 March 1994), [1995] 10 Yb Com Arb 663.

[81] *Société Polish Ocean Line v Société Jolasry*, French Court of Cassation judgment (10 March 1993), [1993] *Rev Arb* 255. See chapter 8 section 8.4.2.5.

Model Law, despite the fact that several aspects of these have already been discussed in other chapters.

7.6.3.1 Incapacity and invalidity of arbitration agreement

This is a conflation of two distinct grounds. Incapacity[82] concerns the ability of the person (physical or legal, i.e. a corporation) to enter into an arbitration agreement in the first place. Capacity is determined by one's personal law, which usually coincides with the place of residence or nationality. Capacity does not therefore follow the governing law of the parties' agreement. In the case of corporations or entities with complex multinational structures, the law of the country of incorporation or effective seat is assumed to be pertinent to ascertaining capacity. While a legal person might have general capacity to enter into an arbitration agreement, the person officially representing the legal person may not possess authority under its internal by-laws. In such cases, unless the absence and nature of authority is serious and foreseeable, it is assumed that the lack of formal authority is not an impediment to capacity as such. Where a party claims that it lacked capacity to enter into an arbitration agreement it is also asserting that the arbitration agreement itself is invalid. Even so, capacity and invalidity may in other circumstances be viewed as independent issues because the UNCITRAL Model Law subjects the validity of the arbitration agreement to the governing law of the contract (failing which to the law of the seat),[83] not the parties' personal law, as is the case with capacity.

7.6.3.2 Lack of notice and inability to present one's case

Both of these strands pertain to the parties' due process rights. Given that arbitration constitutes an exception to the general rule whereby ordinary (state) courts possess authority to settle private disputes, it may be queried whether arbitral tribunals satisfy all the criteria pertinent to the right to fair trial and access to justice. The ECtHR has confirmed that arbitration is consistent with the right to judicial remedies,[84] in the sense that the organisation of arbitration and its supervision by the local courts satisfies

---

[82] See chapter 3 section 3.5.
[83] For an extensive discussion of the agreement to arbitrate and the conditions for its validity, see chapter 3.
[84] The relevant case law is consistent. In *Sumukan Limited v Commonwealth Secretariat* [2007] EWCA Civ 243, the English Court of Appeal held that an agreement in an arbitration clause to exclude an appeal to a court on a point of law under s 69 of the English AA (the exclusion

fair trial guarantees.[85] Party autonomy alone cannot substitute these guarantees and as the Paris Court of Appeal has emphasised, arbitral tribunals are not exempt from applying fair trial guarantees in their proceedings.[86] The UNCITRAL Model Law (Article 18) has also long sub-scribed to the fair trial principle in arbitral proceedings. Readers should consult the relevant discussion in chapter 6 section 6.2.1.

Due process challenges are a common feature of set aside proceedings. Although in theory due process violations constitute human rights breaches (right to fair trial), in practice, the courts, particularly those of the seat, perceive them as civil procedure infractions. In Greece, a violation of the parties' right to equal treatment by the tribunal is sufficient reason to set the award aside.[87] The same is true where the arbitrator failed to hold oral hearings.[88] Obviously, if the parties had agreed that no oral hearings should take place then the tribunal would be exceeding its power if it were to conduct an oral hearing. Similarly, the Swiss Federal Supreme Court has held that the right of the parties to be heard does not include a right to be heard orally (as long as this is consistently applied or is against the wishes of both parties).[89] The same Court has emphasised, however, that the right to be heard includes a minimum duty to examine all relevant issues, as counter-balanced with the freedom of the tribunal to afford the weight it chooses to the available evidence.[90]

7.6.3.3 Excess of arbitral power and *ultra petita* awards

The tribunal's powers are derived directly from the parties' submission agreement.[91] With the exception of gap-filling or revising some of the terms of the contract, where this is permissible,[92] the tribunal may not

---

agreement) did not breach the right to a fair trial as provided by Art 6 of the ECHR. See chapter 6 section 6.2.1.

[85] This notwithstanding, the Swiss Federal Supreme Court has held that because arbitral tribunals are not 'established by law' as dictated by Art 6 of the ECHR (right to fair trial) they are not encompassed within the juridical space of the ECHR. See *Abel Xavier v UEFA*, [2001] Bull ASA 566. The Court, nonetheless, stressed that tribunals are bound to respect fundamental rights of due process.

[86] *Société Licensing Projects and Others v Société Pirreli & C SPA and Others*, Paris Appeals Court judgment (17 November 2011); see also *Mousaka v Golden Seagull Maritime* [2001] 2 Lloyd's Rep 657.

[87] Areios Pagos judgment 511/2007.   [88] Areios Pagos judgment 112/1982.

[89] *Re TA G v H Company*, (1997) ASA Bull 316.

[90] *X Ltd v Y Ltd*, case 4A_669/2012 judgment (17 April 2013).

[91] For an extensive discussion, see chapter 4 section 4.3.1.

[92] See section 7.5 of this chapter.

modify its terms of reference unilaterally. This is true even where the award deals with an issue that is central to the parties' dispute but which the parties did not incorporate in the submission agreement. In the eventuality that the tribunal decides matters that are beyond the scope of the parties' agreement the award may be set aside by the courts of the seat. As is discussed elsewhere in this chapter the court may, if it deems that the excess issues may be severed from the body of the award, remit the award back to the tribunal. Article 39(1) of the Spanish Arbitration Act provides for the possibility of the parties applying to the tribunal for removing those parts of the award that constitute excess of power. However, especially in complex cases, this is not always feasible.

7.6.3.4 Unlawful composition and procedure

The composition of tribunals has already been discussed in detail elsewhere.[93] It has also been explained that the parties may challenge arbitrators in the course of arbitral proceedings, but only on the basis of their impartiality and lack of independence.[94] Once again, it is the parties' submission agreement that will dictate the person or persons appointed as arbitrators. A party will, however, be estopped from challenging the presiding arbitrator appointed in accordance with the parties' chosen institutional rules, even if it opposed that particular arbitrator.

The procedure which a tribunal is obliged to follow equally stems from the parties' agreement, which in turn refers to particular institutional rules (unless the arbitration is of an ad hoc nature). However, few institutional rules are overly elaborate, in order to allow flexibility for proceedings taking place across the globe.[95] In practice, the parties, after consulting with the tribunal, fill or modify the 'gaps' of institutional rules, unless mandatory provisions in the *lex arbitri* leave no room for manoeuvre. Hence, it is not always easy to discern a violation of the procedures agreed to by the parties.

7.6.3.5 Arbitrability and public policy

Both arbitrability[96] and public policy[97] have been analysed in detail elsewhere. Two issues are important for the purposes of set aside proceedings.

---

[93] See chapter 4 sections 4.5–4.6.   [94] See chapter 4 sections 4.9–4.10.
[95] See, for example, Art 19 ICC Rules.   [96] See chapter 1 section 1.8.2.
[97] See chapter 8 section 8.4.2.7.

Firstly, awards will be annulled only if they violate the arbitrability and public policy rules of the seat of arbitration. Secondly, when a question of arbitrability arises this is usually the result of a public policy restriction. Most national laws distinguish between international and domestic arbitral proceedings in their application of arbitrability restrictions. They take the view that since the subject matter of the dispute is unconnected with the legal order of the seat there is no compelling reason to apply domestic arbitrability rules. Nations which make this distinction in respect of arbitrability usually take the same approach with public policy.

In France, under Article 1514 of the CCP an award will not be recognised or enforced there if it is in conflict with international public policy. Domestic French public policy (which applies to domestic arbitration) is significantly broader as compared to international public policy. As a result, a violation of domestic public policy does not necessarily entail a violation of international public policy.[98] In *Planor Afrique SA v Société Emirates Télécommunications corporation 'Etisalat'*, the Paris Appeals Court set aside an arbitral award that disregarded an earlier judgment issued by a foreign court and recognised in France under an international convention.[99] In general, French international public policy is defined as the body of rules and values which the French legal order regards as fundamental in disputes of an international character.[100] French case law distinguishes between substantive and procedural international public policy, as grounds for setting awards aside. A substantive public policy violation arises where the act or omission in question is actual, blatant and concrete.[101] In respect of procedural public policy claims, the claimant must demonstrate that the breach actually caused it harm.[102]

---

[98] *Intrafor Cofor v Gagnant*, Court of Appeals judgment (12 March 1985), [1985] *Rev Arb* 299; *Laboratoires Eurosilicone v Bess Medisintechnik*, Paris Court of Appeals judgment (27 May 2003).

[99] *Planor Afrique SA v Société Emirates Télécommunications Corp 'Etisalat'*, [2012] *Rev Arb* 569.

[100] *LTDC v Société Reynolds*, Paris Court of Appeals judgment (27 October 1994), [1994] *Rev Arb* 709.

[101] *Verhoeft v Moreau*, Court of Cassation judgment (21 March 2000), [2001] *Rev Arb* 807; *Société SNF SAS v Société Cytec Industries B V SNF*, Paris Court of Appeals judgment (23 March 2006), [2006] *Rev Arb* 483.

[102] *Nu Swift PLC v White Knight*, Paris Court of Appeals judgment (21 January 1997), [1997] *Rev Arb* 583.

Other legal systems may suggest a generic form of public policy irrespective of the international or domestic nature of the arbitration. Pursuant to section 751(2) of the Estonian CCP, the country's courts shall annul the award based on the request of a party or at the court's initiative if the court establishes that the award is contrary to Estonian public order or good morals.[103] Awards may be annulled when they violate 'good morals'. The Estonian Court of Appeals has interpreted the term 'against good morals' as being concerned with rights and morals, including activities that are generally condemned.[104]

7.6.4 Appeals on points of law

Two qualifications are necessary before the more detailed analysis that follows. Firstly, challenges on points of law are exceptional and, secondly, two types of challenges exist, namely those that seek a clarification of an important – and far-reaching – legal issue and those that seek the correction of a legal mistake made by the tribunal. Applications for the clarification of important legal issues are not challenges per se, but are encompassed here for the purpose of coherency.

Under section 69 of the English Arbitration Act any of the parties may appeal on a point of law, which requires the consent of both parties, assuming the court provides appropriate leave. Such leave may be granted where, in accordance with section 69(3), the court is satisfied:

a. that the determination of the question will substantially affect the rights of one or more of the parties;
b. that the question is one which the tribunal was asked to determine;
c. that, on the basis of the findings of fact in the award–
   i) the decision of the tribunal on the question is obviously wrong, or
   ii) the question is one of general public importance and the decision of the tribunal is at least open to serious doubt; and
d. that despite the agreement of the parties to resolve the matter by arbitration, it is just and proper in all the circumstances for the court to determine the question.

The scope of the right to appeal on points of law against arbitral awards under the English Arbitration Act was confirmed in *Cottonex Anstalt v Patriot*

---

[103] *Case no 3-4-1-1-08*, Supreme Court order (5 February 2008).
[104] *Case no 2-07-14594*, Court of Appeals judgment (29 June 2007).

Spinning Mills.[105] The court acknowledged that when the right to appeal under section 69 of the Act is invoked by a party, the appeal must concern the issues already under dispute in arbitral proceedings. This does not, however, entail an obligation or authority on the respondent to raise additional issues in its appeal. The court emphasised that an appeal under section 69 involves only those points of law determined by an arbitral tribunal. The respondent, on the other hand, may raise further issues of law if found to be connected with the facts established by the arbitral tribunal.

A similar remedy is also available under German law. Section 1065(1) of the German ZPO recognises challenges on points of law as a unique remedy. This provision stipulates that:

A complaint on a point of law to the Federal Court of Justice (*Bundesgerichtshof*) is available against the decisions mentioned under section 1062 (1)(2) and (4) [i.e. appointment of arbitrator; admissibility of arbitration agreement; and setting aside or decision on enforceability] if an appeal on points of law would have been available against them, had they been delivered as a final judgment. No recourse against other decisions in the proceedings specified in section 1062(1) may be made.

In accordance with paragraph 2 of section 1065 ZPO, the Federal Court of Justice may only examine whether the order is based on a violation of a treaty or of another statute. In Belgium, although there is no possibility of appeal against the decisions of the court,[106] exceptionally recourse to the Supreme Court on points of law remains available. In Scotland, there exists a non-mandatory right of challenge on a point of Scots law.[107] In an interesting appeal against a (domestic) award for failure to apply the law correctly, it was held that an arbitrator had erred in law with his approach to determining the minimum and maximum rents due by a tenant by taking into account the terms of the market rather than the terms of the lease, which stated that the basis ought to be 7 per cent of the tenant's gross turnover. The award was thus found to be inconsistent with the parties'

---

[105] *Cottonex Anstalt v Patriot Spinning Mills* [2013] EWHC 236 (Comm).

[106] Art 1680(5) JC. However, only the parties to arbitral proceedings may raise an appeal by way of third party opposition against the order of exequatur issued by the court of first instance. See *International Hotels Worldwide Inc v Etat Belge and Banca Monte Paschi Belgio*, Court of Cassation judgment (4 October 2013).

[107] Rule 69, Scottish Arbitration Rules (SAR); see also *X v Y*, Court of Session, judgment (27 January 2011), [2011] CSOH 164, per Glennie L, who held that an appeal against an award as regards the onus of proof 'must be on the party seeking to persuade the arbitrator to depart from the assessment [as designated by the terms of the contract]'.

intention and did less than justice to the full terms of the rental provisions in the lease.[108] In Greece, the Areios Pagos has held that a mistaken assessment of the evidence by the arbitrators is not a valid ground for setting an award aside.[109]

Some legal systems make even further distinctions as regards remedies against arbitral awards. Under the Swedish Arbitration Act, awards may be challenged on two grounds, namely invalidity (section 33) and set aside proceedings (section 34). An award (or part thereof) is *invalid*:

a) if it includes determination of an issue which, in accordance with Swedish law, may not be decided by arbitrators;
b) if the award, or the manner in which the award arose, is clearly incompatible with the basic principles of the Swedish legal system; or
c) if the award does not fulfil the requirements with regard to the written form and signature in accordance with section 31(1).

In respect of both challenges, the petition shall be brought before the Court of Appeals. The determination of the Court of Appeals is not subject to further appeal. Exceptionally, however, it may grant leave to appeal the determination where it is of importance as a matter of precedent that the appeal be considered by the Supreme Court.[110]

7.7 Waivers from challenges against awards

Two types of waivers are generally available in international arbitration in respect of remedies otherwise offered by domestic law. The first is implicit and concerns one's failure to bring a challenge within a specified time despite being aware of the defect.[111] This amounts to a waiver by reason of conduct-based estoppel. The second type is by express agreement, either in the form of a declaration before the tribunal or as a clause in the arbitration agreement. However, arbitral statutes, with a view to ensuring equality of arms and due process rights, generally forbid express waivers the effect of which is to jeopardise such fundamental guarantees. In practice, therefore,

---

[108] *Manchester Associated Mills Ltd v Mitchells and Butler Retail Ltd*, Court of Session (Outer House), case P1013/12, judgment (10 January 2013).
[109] Areios Pagos judgment 1273/2003.   [110] s 43(2) Swedish AA.
[111] Art 4 UNCITRAL Model Law; Art 817(3) Italian CCP.

waivers from challenges against domestic awards are rarely permitted, whereas the situation is different with respect to international awards.

Article 192 of the Swiss PILA sets out the possibility of waiver or exclusion of set aside proceedings in respect of arbitrations where 'none of the parties has its domicile, its habitual residence or a business establishment in Switzerland'. Such parties may by 'an express statement in the arbitration agreement or by a subsequent agreement in writing, exclude all set aside proceedings or they may limit such proceedings to one or several of the grounds listed in Article 190(2) of the PILA'. Where the parties have excluded set aside proceedings the provisions of the 1958 New York Convention apply by analogy in accordance with Article 192(2) of the PILA. Equally, in Sweden, where none of the parties is domiciled or has its place of business in Sweden, they may exclude or limit the application of the grounds for setting aside an award as set forth in section 34 of the Swedish Arbitration Act through an express agreement. In this case, the recognition and enforcement of such award, even if the tribunal was seated in Sweden, shall be subject to the regime of foreign awards.[112]

7.8 Time limits for making a challenge

There are definite time limits within which the parties wishing to challenge an award must lodge their claim. Article 33(3) of the UNCITRAL Model Law suggests that in respect of challenges for an additional award as to claims presented in the proceedings but omitted in the award, the parties must present their claims to the tribunal within thirty days from the receipt of the award. As regards set aside proceedings, applications are inadmissible after three months have elapsed from the date on which the party making the application had received the award.[113] Many countries, even non-Model Law ones such as Sweden, have taken great care to conform to such time limits. There, the three-month time limit for setting awards aside begins when the party in question received the award in its entirety.[114] In addition, the challenging party must satisfy the pertinent legal grounds.[115] In

---

[112] s 51 Swedish AA.   [113] Art 34(3) UNCITRAL Model Law.
[114] *AB Akron-Maskiner v N-GG*, (2002) NJA 377.
[115] *Bostadsrättsforeningen Korpen v Byggnads AB Ake Sundvall*, Svea Court of Appeal, judgment (16 February 2007).

Fastigheten Preppen v Carlsberg the challenging party submitted its challenge within the three-month period but its application did not include any grounds. The court granted an extension to satisfy this omission, but Carlsberg argued that because the grounds had not been identified until well after the three-month deadline the application should be dismissed. The court agreed with this argument, noting that Carlsberg had noted its objection in time, and went on to dismiss the challenge in its entirety.[116]

---

[116] See, for example, *Fastigheten Preppen v Carlsberg*, (2009) RH 91; K. Hobér, *International Commercial Arbitration in Sweden* (Oxford University Press, 2011), 310.

8 Recognition and enforcement of Arbitral awards

8.1 Introduction

This chapter concerns the final phase of international arbitration. Many (or most) international awards ultimately need to be recognised and enforced in jurisdictions other than the seat in order for the winning party to satisfy its award. The process is not straightforward as the chapter demonstrates. We shall begin by distinguishing between pre-finality challenges, such as set aside remedies from challenges against a final award in a jurisdiction other than the seat, which constitutes the subject matter of this chapter. From there we shall discuss the differences between enforcement as such and recognition of a foreign award. Given that the most eminent and near-universally ratified treaty in the field of enforcement is the 1958 New York Convention, our discussion of formalities and applicable grounds of challenge against foreign awards at the forum (country of enforcement) will be predicated on the provisions of this instrument. The grounds for challenging foreign awards under the Convention are almost identical to set aside challenges and hence the pertinent discussion will only focus on their application to enforcement proceedings.

The chapter concludes with three complex issues peculiar to enforcement. Firstly, it is not entirely clear whether the forum may recognise and enforce an award that was set aside at the seat of the arbitration. The relevant discussion demonstrates that such an eventuality is legitimate and finds ample support from state practice. Secondly, it is equally unclear from the text of the 1958 New York Convention whether failure to raise objections or challenges against the award or the arbitral procedure prior to the award's finality at the seat precludes a subsequent challenge before the courts of the forum. As will be explained, national courts are fairly consistent in their preclusion of enforcement challenges raised for the first time by the claimant, particularly where the possibility of making these at earlier stages of arbitral proceedings existed. Finally, we look at the implications of the international law of sovereign immunity to enforcement proceedings against state property following the issuance of an arbitral award against a state. It should be stated from the outset that this chapter relates exclusively to international commercial – not investment – arbitration.

8.2 Pre-finality challenges and enforcement of awards

In the previous chapter we examined the process of issuing an award and the formal requirements mandated under international law and the law of the seat. It will have become obvious that when an award is issued by the tribunal it is not immediately final between the parties. Rather, the law of the seat will set a deadline during which any of the parties may challenge the validity of the award, whether through set aside proceedings or challenges against points of law (where applicable). Where the deadlines for making such challenges expire or alternatively the courts of the seat pass judgment in set aside or other proceedings the award becomes final and produces *res judicata* between the parties (and potentially against other third parties). Even so, certain states may further require that the final award be registered with the courts, a notary or an arbitral institution, but this is usually a formality that has no legal consequence on the finality of the award. With few exceptions, this process towards finality applies to both domestic and international awards rendered in the seat.

In most cases, the losing party will honour its obligation[1] and perform the dispositive part of the award, whether by paying compensation, restitution or other remedy. Where, however, the losing party refuses to comply there is a need to enforce the award against the losing party. If the assets of the losing party are not situated in the territory of the seat, then by means of the 1958 New York Convention or other regional conventions (relating to the enforcement of foreign arbitral awards) the winning party may present its final award to the judicial authorities of the intended country of enforcement and seek recognition or enforcement of the award there. This chapter will focus on the recognition and enforcement of foreign arbitral awards, but some reference should be made to enforcement of awards in the seat, irrespective of whether the arbitration was domestic or international. Several options are generally available to the parties. Firstly, where an award has been deposited with a local court[2] it may be enforced under the same procedure as if it were a judgment of the court. Secondly, where no deposit or registration is required the winning party may apply to the local courts for leave to enforce. Thirdly, the law of the seat may require some form of recognition procedure (or exequatur) before granting leave for enforcement; understandably, this process adds further cost and delay to the enforcement of the award.[3] Finally, in situations where the law and courts of the seat are hostile to arbitration and awards are not easily enforced, the winning party may sue on the award in order to achieve a court judgment as to the debt, in which case the award is merely evidence of the debt. This is not only cumbersome and expensive but, moreover, exposes the award to challenges against the merits, which

---

[1] This obligation is expressly prescribed in all institutional rules and arbitral statutes and even if it is not it is certainly implicit. Art 32(2) of the UNCITRAL Rules stipulates that 'the parties undertake to carry out the award without delay'.

[2] See chapter 7 section 7.4.3.

[3] The Singapore High Court, as a paradigm of arbitration-friendliness, has emphasised that it is inappropriate to conduct a detailed examination of the documents filed in support of an application to enforce a foreign award. *Strandore Invest A/S and Others v Soh Kim Vat*, [2010] SGHR 174.

have already been finally determined by the tribunal.[4] So, clearly, this is very much a desperate option.

So far, we have distinguished between challenges against an award that has not yet become final (i.e. set aside and challenges on points of law) from the procedure which the winning party must follow after the award has become final, namely recognition and enforcement. Besides enforcement of the award at the seat, when the arbitration is international the winning party will in all likelihood seek to enforce the award in jurisdictions other than the seat. The choice of recognition and enforcement will be determined very simply by reference to the country where the losing party has sufficient assets. Assets may be spread across several jurisdictions, in which case there is no reason why enforcement proceedings may not be commenced in all of them. Practical concerns may dictate against such an eventuality, however. Enforcement proceedings may be costly and the advice of local counsel will certainly be required. Moreover, certain jurisdictions place unnecessary limitations (as well as obstacles) on the enforcement of foreign awards, especially if against local parties, and hence the winning party will have to consider lengthy litigation and the prospect of unsuccessful enforcement in these jurisdictions. Hence, unless absolutely necessary, they are best avoided. The winning party should focus on enforcing its award in countries where its losing counterpart has sufficient assets to meet the award and in addition ensure that these countries are enforcement-friendly.

It is evident that recognition and enforcement of foreign arbitral awards is not a process than begins once the award is issued. The losing party, especially if it realises that its case is weak, will attempt to dissipate its assets in such a way that they are not traceable. It is, therefore, imperative that the claimant make every possible effort, even before initiating arbitral proceedings, to investigate and identify the assets of the respondent. Once proceedings are commenced and even prior to the tribunal's constitution, the claimant may apply for emergency relief to the courts or its chosen arbitral institution (through an emergency arbitrator)[5] with a view to getting worldwide freezing or similar injunctions, the aim of which is to prevent the respondent from dissipating its assets. The same process may

---

[4] N. Blackaby and C. Partasides, *Redfern and Hunter on International Arbitration* (Oxford University Press, 5th edition, 2009), 626.

[5] Such as that established under Art 29 ICC Rules.

be undertaken once arbitral proceedings have commenced, although the risk that some assets may be lost by that time will no doubt be apparent to the claimant.

Ideally, when an award is final under the law of the seat and the winning party is fully aware of one or more jurisdictions where the losing party has sufficient assets to meet the award, enforcement of the award may be sought there. The process usually involves an application to the designated courts of the country of enforcement, which may require some formalities, such as a translated (in the local language) and certified copy of the award and of the arbitration agreement[6] and perhaps some (other) proof that it is final. In less than ideal circumstances, however, the losing party may challenge the validity of the award on several grounds. This challenge concerns recognition and enforcement of the award and should be distinguished from the challenges analysed in chapter 7, which pertain to awards not yet final under conditions laid down by the law of the seat. The grounds for challenging final awards before the courts of the country where enforcement is sought (the forum) are laid out in Article V of the 1958 New York Convention. These grounds will be explored in depth in a subsequent section.

8.3 The difference between recognition and enforcement

Where the winning party seeks to *enforce* its award in a third jurisdiction (other than the seat) it is implicitly also seeking *recognition* of the award in that country. Hence, enforcement necessarily encompasses recognition,[7] whereas a request for recognition does not entail or imply that the award will be enforced. A request for recognition is meant to ensure that the foreign award is recognised as valid in a country other than the seat. Although winning parties typically apply for enforcement with a view to satisfying the dispositive part of the award, there are circumstances where a request for mere recognition suffices. This may be because the winning party is confident that its counterpart will ultimately satisfy the award and as a result finds no compelling reason to pursue enforcement proceedings. Equally, although the winning party may be in some doubt as to whether the award will be voluntarily satisfied, it may nonetheless feel that the process of enforcement will alienate and frustrate the losing party,

---

[6] Art IV 1958 New York Convention.   [7] See Art I(1) 1958 New York Convention.

particularly where there is some likelihood of reconciliation.[8] In both situations the cost or (potential) length of enforcement proceedings may also constitute prohibitive factors. Recognition, as opposed to enforcement, may also be sought in order to definitively identify the issues that have been resolved by the award, in which case they constitute *res judicata* with respect to new court proceedings commenced by the losing party. Furthermore, the winning party may wish to recognise the issues already resolved by the award in order to invoke them by way of defence or set-off in other proceedings instituted by the losing party.[9]

Other than the aforementioned circumstances, particularly where the losing party is recalcitrant about satisfying the award, enforcement is strongly advised. Before an award is enforced by the courts of the forum, the claimant cannot satisfy the award in that country, despite the fact that it is final in the seat and enforceable there. It is only after the award receives a certificate of enforcement in the forum that the award can be satisfied in the same manner as a court judgment. Enforcement entails a series of legal actions which are intended to compel the recalcitrant party to execute the award. These may include seizure, attachment or other measures as provided for in the forum's civil procedure rules. Before the award is enforced no such measures are possible, or indeed available to the winning party.

8.4 Enforcement under the 1958 New York Convention

If there was no truly global multilateral agreement whereby arbitral awards rendered in one country could be recognised and enforced in other countries, the very rationale of international arbitration would be seriously undermined. Awards would be redundant and meaningless if winning parties could not recognise and enforce them elsewhere with a high degree of legal certainty. Mere reliance on comity or bilateral agreements would not only limit the parties' options but would critically constrict any sense of predictability. It is for this reason that several regional and global

---

[8] We have already referred to circumstances where the parties may not necessarily desire an enforceable award, as is the case with expert determinations and the practice of *irrituale* awards in the Italian legal system. See chapter 1 section 1.4.

[9] See, e.g., s 101(1) English AA.

multilateral agreements have appeared at the international scene with a view to establishing a uniform, predictable and binding regime for the enforcement of foreign arbitral awards. A brief exposition of these regional treaties has already been offered in chapter 2.[10] The key instrument, however, is the 1958 New York Convention on the Recognition and Enforcement of Foreign Arbitral Awards, which has been ratified by more than 140 countries, thus rendering it truly global.[11] This replaces (as between parties to the 1958 New York Convention) the 1923 Geneva Protocol on Arbitration Clauses as well as the 1927 Geneva Convention on the Execution of Foreign Arbitral Awards. The New York Convention constitutes a significant improvement to the 1927 Convention, which only applied to awards rendered in one of the contracting states and between parties subject to the jurisdiction of the contracting states.[12] More importantly, Article I(1)(d) of the Geneva Convention required that as a precondition to enforcement the award must have become final at the seat, which was interpreted as requiring leave of enforcement (exequatur) from both the courts of the seat as well as from those of the intended country of enforcement. This requirement of so-called double exequatur rendered the process of enforcement cumbersome and somewhat inefficient.[13] These restrictions have been eliminated by the 1958 New York Convention.

In fact, one of the key advantages of arbitration over litigation, in terms of transnational enforcement, is that whereas arbitral awards may be recognised and enforced in the more than 140 countries that are signatories to the 1958 New York Convention, the enforcement of civil and commercial judgments across jurisdictions is severely limited due to the absence of an equivalent global convention for the enforcement of civil

---

[10] See chapter 2 sections 2.2.5 and 2.3. Enforcement under the ICSID Convention is discussed in chapter 10. The 1961 European Convention on International Commercial Arbitration and its 1972 Moscow counterpart are wholly overshadowed by the 1958 New York Convention and deserve no special merit. On the contrary, the 1975 Inter-American Convention on International Commercial Arbitration (Panama Convention) is the most significant regional instrument, but is largely influenced by the New York Convention.

[11] Other global, as opposed to regional, instruments also refer to enforcement, such as the UNCITRAL Model Law, but unlike the 1958 New York Convention the UNCITRAL Model Law is not a treaty. See chapter 2 section 2.5. The 1967 Washington (ICSID) Convention is both global and a treaty, but it concerns only investment awards, not international commercial awards.

[12] Art I(1) 1927 Geneva Convention.

[13] R. Wolff (ed.), *New York Convention Commentary* (CH Beck, 2012), 11.

and commercial judgments. As a result, each state develops rules, reinforced sometimes by bilateral agreements, through which it regulates enforcement of foreign judgments.[14] In chapter 2 we examined one of the few instruments in this regard, namely Council Regulation 44/2001 of 22 December 2000 on jurisdiction and the recognition and enforcement of judgments in civil and commercial matters. Nonetheless, its application only extends to the relations between EU member states.[15] The only equivalent global instrument, although remotely, is the 2005 Hague Convention on Choice of Court Agreements, which is, however, limited to judgments rendered pursuant to exclusive choice of court agreements between the parties, thus excluding judgments rendered according to the ordinary jurisdiction of national courts (including through the operation of conflict of laws).[16]

Let us now turn to the scope of application of the 1958 New York Convention, although this will have become evident by our discussion thus far. Article I(1) emphasises that:

This Convention shall apply to the recognition and enforcement of arbitral awards made in the territory of a state other than the state where the recognition and enforcement of such awards are sought, and arising out of differences between persons, whether physical or legal. It shall also apply to arbitral awards not considered as domestic awards in the state where their recognition and enforcement are sought.

The 1958 New York Convention applies to two types of awards, namely: a) domestic awards rendered in a country other than that of enforcement, which are naturally foreign to the country of enforcement; and b) all international awards,[17] as long as the country of enforcement does not

---

[14] In England, for example, this is achieved through the Foreign Judgments (Reciprocal Enforcement) Act 1933, which codifies existing common law regarding the enforcement of civil judgments from the Commonwealth as well as some non-Commonwealth nations. The following conditions are required: a) the foreign judgment be issued by a competent court; b) be final and conclusive and; c) must concern a fixed sum of money. See C. M. V. Clarkson and J Hill, *The Conflict of Laws* (Oxford University Press, 4th edition, 2011), 164ff.

[15] See chapter 2 section 2.2.1. The Recast Brussels I Regulation which came into effect in 2015 makes it clear in recital 12(3) and Art 73(2) that the 1958 New York Convention takes precedence over the competence of EU national courts to issue judgments on the merits of an arbitral dispute. See chapter 5 section 5.3.2.2.

[16] Even so, by late 2014 the only party was Mexico, with the USA and EU having merely signed the text of the convention, with the latter preparing to ratify.

[17] For an analysis of the international character of arbitral awards on the basis of domestic law, see chapter 1 section 1.7.1.

coincide with the country of the seat of the arbitration. Where the two countries do coincide, although the 1958 New York Convention is inapplicable, the award will be enforceable at the seat on the basis of its legislation regarding final awards. In practice, enforcement-friendly jurisdictions, such as the USA, tend to expand the boundaries of domestic awards. In fact, section 202 of the FAA, which concerns enforcement of Convention awards, has been construed as encompassing awards issued in the USA and between US parties, whether because performance is envisaged abroad,[18] or because the governing law was foreign and the procedure subject to foreign institutional rules.[19] In China, the nationality of an award is not determined by reference to the seat, the nationality of the parties, their residence (or incorporation in respect of legal persons) or by the international or domestic nature of the dispute. Rather, the nationality of an award is based on the seat of the arbitral institution.[20]

In previous chapters we examined issues that are pertinent to the enforcement of foreign awards. Chief among these is the very existence of a *final award*.[21] It will be recalled that both the UNCITRAL Model Law as well as many legal systems allow tribunals to issue awards not only in situations where the tribunal disposes of all the issues submitted to it by the parties. Rather, tribunals may, where applicable, issue interim awards and even injunctions (although admittedly this is rare) in the form of awards, among others.[22] The question that arises, therefore, is whether such (non-final) awards may be subject to the regime of the 1958 New York Convention and if so whether the determination of a Convention award is to be made in accordance with the law of the seat or the law of the country of enforcement. The answer to this question possesses several dimensions. At the first level, being a treaty, the 1958 New York Convention must be construed in accordance with pertinent rules of treaty interpretation. In the case at hand, given the absence of any express exclusion or distinction between final and non-final awards,

---

[18] *Millmaker v Bruso and Sovereign Oil and Gas Co*, WL 4560624 (SD Tex, 2008).

[19] *RZS Holdings AVV v PDVSA Petroleos SA*, 598 F Supp 2d 762 (ED Va, 2009).

[20] Wolff, above note 13, at 67.

[21] Quite clearly, non-arbitral awards, such as expert determinations, mediated settlements and other similar deliberations are not encompassed under the 1958 New York Convention.

[22] See chapter 7 section 7.2.1.

member states must not frustrate the Convention's object and purpose. As a result, the preferred interpretation is not a narrow domestic one (as understood by each state) but one that coincides with the international character of arbitration and the Convention's very rationale. Not surprisingly, all enforcement-friendly jurisdictions have held that the 1958 New York Convention must be interpreted in accordance with international law as opposed to the law of the country of enforcement.[23] This objective international law approach must be juxtaposed (or cushioned) against the application of reciprocity between member states, which will be examined in the next section. It suffices at this junction to note by way of illustration that if country A is generally receptive to the enforcement of injunctions clad as awards issued by tribunals in country B, it will expect country B to do likewise with respect to injunction-awards rendered by tribunals in country A. If B fails to observe reciprocity in this regard, then A is equally entitled to observe its own practice in relation to awards from country B. In practice, such a reciprocity reservation (i.e. in relation to injunctions-would-be-awards) does not exist within the legal framework of the 1958 New York Convention.

By way of conclusion, therefore, the Convention does not apply solely to final awards.[24] Nonetheless, a certain degree of caution should be exercised as there is no general international standard and the courts of each state may differ as per their individual perspectives on this matter. In *Publicis v True North Communications*, a US Court of Appeals enforced a foreign disclosure order made by a tribunal even though the order had not resolved the main issue between the parties.[25] Conversely, the Supreme Court of Queensland refused to enforce an 'interim order and award' until the tribunal issued a final award on the merits of the dispute. Its underlying rationale was that a decision that could be modified at any time did not qualify as an arbitral award.[26]

---

[23] See, for example, *Hebei Import and Export Corp v Polytek Engineering Co Ltd* [1999] 2 HKC 205. Such an interpretation is consistent with Art 31(1) of the 1969 VCLT, according to which a treaty shall be interpreted in good faith and in accordance with the ordinary meaning of its terms 'in their context and in light of its object and purpose'.

[24] See also Wolff, above note 13, at 34ff, equally endorsing this view.

[25] *Publicis v True North Communications*, 206 F 3d 725 (7th Cir. 2000).

[26] *Resort Condominiums International Inc v Bolwell and Resort Condominiums Pty Ltd* (1993) 118 ALR 655.

8.4.1 Formalities and limitations under the 1958 New York Convention

It is natural that some degree of formality will be required to enforce a foreign award in the legal system of each forum. The reception of a foreign award is to be undertaken in accordance with the civil procedure rules of the enforcing (forum) state in accordance with Article III of the 1958 New York Convention. However, as this provision points out:

> There shall not be imposed substantially more onerous conditions or higher fees or charges on the recognition or enforcement of arbitral awards to which this Convention applies than are imposed on the recognition or enforcement of domestic arbitral awards.

This provision unequivocally confers national treatment status to foreign awards, which means that in case an award is discriminated in relation to the formalities expected from other domestic awards in the forum, the latter will (in theory at least) incur state responsibility by reason of having committed an internationally unlawful act.[27] National treatment must be distinguished from other types of treatment, particularly most favoured nation, whose application is not stipulated, nor is it in any other way implicit in the text of the 1958 New York Convention.[28]

In terms of actual formalities, Article IV(1) of the Convention requires merely two, in addition to those possibly mandated under the *lex forum*, namely: the duly authenticated original award or a duly certified copy thereof, as well as the original arbitration agreement or a certified copy thereof. In the event that these documents are in a language that is different to that of the country of enforcement, a certified translation is required. Enforcement-friendly jurisdictions require no further formalities, as is the case with section 102 of the English Arbitration Act, which reproduces verbatim Article IV(1) of the 1958 New York Convention.

Besides the formalities associated with the country of enforcement, there are two limitations built into the 1958 New York Convention, both of which have, however, lost much of their initial significance. These two limitations entail that the Convention may apply only in respect of

---

[27] See Arts 2–4, ILC Articles on State Responsibility (2001), UNGA Res 56/83 (12 December 2001).

[28] For an analysis of most favoured nation (MFN) treatment, see chapter 10 section 10.7.4.

commercial awards, subject furthermore to *reciprocity*. Article I(3) of the Convention provides that:

When signing, ratifying or acceding to this Convention, or notifying extension under Article X hereof, any state may on the basis of reciprocity declare that it will apply the Convention to the recognition and enforcement of awards made only in the territory of another contracting state. It may also declare that it will apply the Convention only to differences arising out of legal relationships, whether contractual or not, which are considered as commercial under the national law of the state making such declaration.

Given that reciprocity and the commercial nature of the award are optional and, therefore, not binding limitations upon members states (... 'any state *may*'), it follows that they may only be applied as (permissible) reservations to the 1958 New York Convention, further transposed into the forum's domestic arbitral law. The reason for both limitations/reservations is purely historical and their importance has diminished significantly in practice.[29] The courts of arbitration-friendly nations typically do not investigate reciprocity, even if their governments have entered a reservation to that effect. As a prominent commentary to the Convention points out:

National courts should not be expected to conduct a 'reciprocity due diligence' in relation to the recognition and enforcement of each foreign arbitral award as this would conflict with the purpose of the Convention to promote and facilitate the recognition and enforcement of foreign awards. Moreover, the enforcement courts would be faced with the practical difficulty of verifying if reciprocity is actually granted ... It has been questioned whether declaring such a reservation is appropriate in the context of the Convention, as this may go against the interest of a contracting state's own citizens. When the parties have chosen a 'neutral' state as the seat of their arbitration, which is oftentimes the case, the arbitral awards rendered in that neutral state may lack enforceability in the winning party's home state where the losing party has assets.[30]

In terms of the *commercial* reservation, it is suggested that a broad interpretation of 'commercial' should be applied, for no other reason than that it conforms to legal developments[31] and trade usages. This notwithstanding,

---

[29] Art 35(1) of the UNCITRAL Model Law, for example, has removed the reciprocity option altogether.
[30] Wolff, above note 13, at 79–80.
[31] See, for example, footnote 2 to Art 1(1) of the UNCITRAL Model Law, which provides a definition of the term 'commercial'.

certain categories of awards are excluded from the scope of the Convention, particularly those that are not encompassed even under this broad 'commercial' interpretation, such as (business to) consumer awards.[32] Given the requirement for an agreement to arbitrate, as a precondition for valid awards, awards issued by means of mandatory arbitration do not readily satisfy the 1958 New York Convention.[33] Online awards, on the other hand, provided that they concern a commercial dispute and offer due process guarantees to the parties, are no different to regular awards.

8.4.2 Challenges against enforcement

Where the winning party seeks to enforce its award in a country other than the seat, the legal process associated with enforcement should be dispensed with by a mere application. Even so, such an application constitutes a *new* judicial process which may be concluded speedily by the courts if both the arbitration agreement and the award suffer from no serious defects, or if they go unchallenged. In the eventuality that the losing party wishes to challenge the award, there is a risk of protracted proceedings. The list of grounds upon which an award may be refused recognition or enforcement are not unlimited and they are common to both the 1958 New York Convention and the UNCITRAL Model Law and by extension to the majority of nations. Article V of the Convention stipulates that a foreign award 'may be refused' recognition and enforcement in the forum only if the party challenging the award furnishes proof that:

(1) (a) The parties to the [arbitration] agreement were, under the law applicable to them, under some incapacity, or the said agreement is not valid under the law to which the parties have subjected it or, failing any indication thereon, under the law of the country where the award was made; or

   (b) The party against whom the award is invoked was not given proper notice of the appointment of the arbitrator or of the arbitration proceedings or was otherwise unable to present his case; or

   (c) The award deals with a difference not contemplated by or not falling within the terms of the submission to arbitration, or it contains decisions on matters beyond the scope of the submission to arbitration, provided that, if the decisions on matters submitted to arbitration can be separated from

---

[32] See chapter 9 for an extensive discussion of consumer arbitration.
[33] See chapter 1 section 1.3 for a discussion of compulsory forms of arbitration.

those not submitted, that part of the award which contains decisions on matters submitted to arbitration may be recognized and enforced; or

(d) The composition of the arbitral authority or the arbitral procedure was not in accordance with the agreement of the parties, or failing such agreement, was not in accordance with the law of the country where the arbitration took place; or

(e) The award has not yet become binding on the parties, or has been set aside or suspended by a competent authority of the country in which, or under the law of which, that award was made.

(2) Recognition and enforcement of an arbitral award may also be refused if the competent authority in the country where recognition and enforcement is sought finds that:

(a) The subject matter of the difference is not capable of settlement by arbitration under the law of that country; or

(b) The recognition or enforcement of the award would be contrary to the public policy of that country.

The reader will no doubt notice significant similarities between the grounds for setting aside awards at the seat with the grounds for refusal of recognition or enforcement under the 1958 New York Convention. This is precisely why arbitration-friendly courts refuse to be drawn into protracted enforcement challenges against awards that have already undergone set aside challenges at the seat. This stance is further justified by the fact that to a large degree these grounds are uniform and consistent across jurisdictions and hence possess an international dimension rather than a narrow domestic meaning.[34] Conversely, challenges based on arbitrability and public policy claims are meant to be informed by domestic considerations, but even so, as will be demonstrated shortly, enforcement-friendly nations place fewer obstacles to the enforcement of foreign as opposed to domestic awards in terms of public policy limitations.

Case study: The rights of parties pending challenges against a foreign award

When leave for enforcement in respect of a foreign award has been submitted to the forum and the respondent is challenging enforcement, this may be a pretext for the respondent to dissipate its assets

---

[34] The grounds for challenge under Art V of the New York Convention are virtually the same as those listed in Art 36 of the UNCITRAL Model Law.

while the proceedings are ongoing. It is, therefore, crucial for the claimant to possess the right to pray to the courts of the forum for injunctive relief. Following a final award from the Moscow Court of Arbitration the winning party sought enforcement in Turkey, which was granted, but before the enforcement judgment became final it was appealed by the respondent. While the challenge (appeal) proceedings were ongoing the claimant applied for an injunction because the respondent was in the process of concealing and selling its assets. The court of first instance rejected the injunction on the basis that the effect of the appeal was to suspend pertinent proceedings. The Istanbul Court of Appeals reversed the ruling of the lower court relying on several legal grounds, among which that since an injunction is a temporary legal measure there is no need that the award (in respect of which an injunction is sought) be finally enforced in the forum.[35]

8.4.2.1 Incapacity and invalidity of arbitration agreement

The first ground for refusal to recognise and enforce under the 1958 New York Convention concerns incapacity and invalidity of the parties' arbitration agreement. The issue of incapacity has already been discussed in chapter 3.[36] Unlike the bulk of international arbitration whereby party autonomy overrides the application of conflict of laws rules, Article V(1)(a) of the 1958 New York Convention clearly provides that the determination of capacity is predicated on the 'law applicable to the parties', from which there is no derogation. As has already been explained elsewhere, this coincides with one's law of nationality or residence and in the case of legal persons the law of their seat or that of their incorporation. Which of these laws is applicable is further determined by the conflict of laws rules of the forum (country of enforcement).

The situation is different as concerns government entities, whose capacity is complex. On the one hand, the country creating them subjects them to a regime of public law, but in their commercial relations with foreign private entities they enter into agreements regulated by private law. Countries adhering to a strict public law regime stipulate that state entities, even those with a commercial dimension, have no independent authority

---

[35] Cases *E 2014/3906* and *K 2014/4941*, Court of Appeals judgment (14 March 2014).
[36] See chapter 3 section 3.5.

(essentially capacity) to enter into arbitration agreements with foreign entities or that if they do possess capacity this does not extend to matters for which arbitration is not permitted.[37] From an international law point of view this situation is unsatisfactory because it overrides the principle of good faith in the parties' contractual relations. As a result, such domestic laws which preclude enforcement of awards rendered against state entities lacking 'capacity' are invalid under customary international law, because Article 46 of the VCLT prevents states from invoking their national law to avoid fulfilling an international obligation. In fact, several national arbitral statutes expressly stipulate that such a defence of incapacity will not be entertained there.[38]

As regards the invalidity of the arbitration agreement, this is the subject matter of chapter 3. It suffices to note here that unlike the issue of capacity, Article V(1)(a) allows the forum to consider the validity of the arbitration agreement only in accordance with the law to which the parties have subjected it, or failing the insertion of an explicit choice of law clause 'the law of the country where the award was made'. As a result, the courts of the forum have no authority to apply their conflict of laws rules in order to determine the law applicable to the arbitration agreement. In the absence of a choice of law clause, the 'country where the award was made' will coincide with the juridical seat of the tribunal. It is evident that there are few grounds on the basis of which the forum can declare an arbitration agreement invalid, save where it links the agreement with arbitrability and public policy restrictions.

8.4.2.2 Proper notice and due process irregularities

Proper notice and due process irregularities as grounds for setting aside arbitral awards at the seat have already been discussed in chapter 7[39] as well as chapter 6 more generally. Given that challenges against recognition and enforcement constitute a new judicial procedure, it is queried what is the appropriate due process standard under the 1958 New York Convention and whether this is necessarily different from set aside or other

---

[37] See, for example, *Major Repairs and Construction Agency at the Health Dept of Moscow v Arbat Stroy*, Russian Supreme Arbitrazh Court Resolution 11535/13 (28 January 2014) in cases A40-148581/12 and A40-160147/12, which held that public procurement disputes (in the case at hand, carrying out certain works in Moscow hospitals) are not arbitrable under Russian law.

[38] Art 2(2) Spanish AA; Art 177(2) Swiss PILA.   [39] See chapter 7 section 7.6.3.2.

proceedings. Three general approaches have been endorsed by national courts and commentators.[40] The first, which is not supported by the *travaux* of the Convention, suggests that the *lex arbitri* or the law of the arbitration agreement should determine the appropriate due process standard under Article V(1)(b) of the Convention. No doubt, due process standards under the *lex arbitri* are pertinent in order for the award to be declared valid by the courts of the seat, but they are of little relevance to enforcement proceedings in a third nation.

The second approach is based on the notion that the appropriate standard of procedural fairness must be assessed by reference to the law of the forum (the enforcement state). An underlying rationale to this approach is that it would be absurd to expect the forum to recognise and enforce a foreign award that was in violation of its due process guarantees, even if the award was otherwise in conformity with the *lex arbitri*. However, countries adhering to this approach do not solely apply their own domestic standards but take into consideration the international character of the arbitral process. US courts, for example, apply a so-called 'minimal requirements of fairness' standard, which differs from the ordinary due process standard.[41]

The third approach is predicated on the universality and treaty character of the 1958 New York Convention. Going a step further from the previous approach, this approach seeks to establish a uniform international standard derived from an autonomous interpretation of Article V(1)(b) of the 1958 New York Convention. Although the application of an international standard would guarantee legal certainty, the complexity of due process guarantees in the context of a process that is largely permissive renders the pursuit of such a standard somewhat elusive.[42]

The 1958 New York Convention does not expressly require a causal nexus between the procedural or due process irregularity and the outcome of the award. Yet, in the practice of many national courts a foreign award will be refused recognition and enforcement on due process grounds only if

---

[40] See Wolff, above note 13, at 283–8.

[41] *Iran Aircraft Indus v Avco Corp*, 980 F 2d 141 (2nd Cir. 1992), at 146; *Karaha Bodas Co v Perusahaan Pertambangaan Minyak Dan Gas Bumi Negara*, 364 F 3d 274 (5th Cir. 2004), at 298.

[42] In the context of Europe, one may perhaps be able to extrapolate the mandatory due process rules of arbitration and juxtapose them against the fair trial guarantees of the ECHR and the established jurisprudence of the ECtHR.

it is demonstrated that had it not been for the irregularity the award would have been differently decided.[43] Even so, the standard required for such a causal nexus between the irregularity and the outcome of the arbitration is relatively low and in several cases the nexus is even presumed by the courts.[44]

The discussion on due process rights is vast and we shall not attempt to reopen it here. The guiding rule is that the parties are free to decide the conduct and method of their procedure, which national courts are obliged to respect under the 1958 New York Convention, save for circumstances where a fundamental (*jus cogens* or *peremptory*) rule overrides party autonomy.[45] By way of illustration, whereas parties have a right to be heard by the tribunal, there exists no overriding requirement to hold oral hearings where the parties have opted for a 'documents-only' process.[46] On the other hand, the right to equal treatment by the tribunal cannot be waived by the parties and despite the fact that it is not expressly written into the 1958 New York Convention it constitutes a fundamental rule under customary international law as well as a general principle of law.[47]

8.4.2.3 Excess of competence or jurisdiction

Excess of competence and jurisdiction has already been discussed as a ground for setting awards aside at the seat.[48] The tribunal's powers and competence are discussed generally in chapter 4. Challenges alleging an excess of jurisdiction necessarily require an understanding of the jurisdictional competences conferred upon the tribunal by the parties' arbitration agreement. Hence, the forum court must first determine the matters submitted for resolution, the special powers, if any, conferred on the tribunal (e.g. as *amiable compositeur*) and the governing law. The enforcement court will declare an excess only where it finds that the tribunal failed to address one or more issues submitted by the parties (or otherwise dealt with matters not so submitted). Equally, it will declare an excess where the

---

[43] *Chantiers de Atlantique SA v Gaz Transport & Technigaz SAS* [2011] EWHC 3383, at para 292; *Apex Tech Investment Ltd v Chuang's Development (China) Ltd* [1996] HKLR 155, at 157.

[44] Wolff, above note 13, at 286–7.   [45] See chapter 6 section 6.2.1.

[46] See *Generica Ltd v Pharmaceutical Basics Inc*, 125 F 3d 1123 (7th Cir. 1997), at 1130; see also Art 24(1) UNCITRAL Model Law.

[47] Art 18 UNCITRAL Model Law; Art 182(3) Swiss PILA; *Paklito Investment Ltd v Klockner East Asia Ltd* [1993] 2 HKLR 39.

[48] See chapter 7 section 7.6.3.3.

governing law was not applied or where the tribunal assumed special powers not conferred upon it by the arbitration agreement.

Certain qualifications should be made here in order to reinforce the pro-arbitration rationale of the 1958 New York Convention. The arbitration agreement may not necessarily be confined to the contract in which it is incorporated. In chapter 3 we discuss in what manner several contracts may be connected to a single arbitration clause by reason of their close connection, in which case the arbitration clause in one contract covers disputes arising in other contracts; joint ventures are typical examples, but everything depends on the parties' intent and the circumstances of each individual case.[49] Equally, the scope of the arbitration agreement will determine whether the tribunal possessed authority to examine relevant counter-claims or set-off claims.[50] In case the intent of the parties' as to the scope of the arbitration agreement is unclear the power of the tribunal to decide issues not expressly covered by the agreement is based on the governing law and the *lex arbitri*. Hence, if the tribunal decided a set-off claim not expressly or implicitly precluded by the arbitration agreement but permitted under the *lex arbitri*, the tribunal would not have exceeded its jurisdiction. Moreover, in the eventuality that the tribunal adheres to the governing law designated by the parties but in order to aid its interpretation of this law applies international legal principles (such as the UNIDROIT Principles or *lex mercatoria*) it will not be exceeding its powers, save if it was never authorised to apply these principles, even as interpretative tools.[51]

One of the fundamental principles underlying arbitration is that the parties assume the risk of an erroneous award by reason of the absence of the possibility of appeal against such award. As a result, while Article V(1)(c) of the 1958 New York Convention allows the forum to refuse enforcement of an award whereby the tribunal applied a law other than that designated by the parties, the forum is not so empowered as concerns a wrong interpretation of the governing law or the facts of the case.

---

[49] *JJ Ryan & Sons Inc v Rhône Poulenc Textile SA*, 863 F 2d 315 (4th Cir. 1988); see chapter 3 section 3.3.4.

[50] These are discussed in more detail in chapter 3 section 3.6. Although a matter of contract construction, set-off claims with no connection to the contract containing the arbitration agreement fall outside the jurisdiction of the tribunal. See *Econet Satellite Services v Vee Networks Ltd*, [2006] EWHC 1664 (Comm).

[51] *Ministry of Defence and Support for the Armed Forces of Iran v Cubic Defence Systems*, 385 F 3d 1206 (SD Cal, 1998).

The forum may not re-examine the merits of the award under any circumstances.[52]

As regards the possibility of partial recognition and enforcement in respect of those matters which clearly fell within the tribunal's jurisdiction – to the exclusion of excess matters – the forum's discretion is severely constrained. Although Article V(1)(c) stipulates that the forum court 'may' separate and enforce parts of an award, thus seemingly suggesting a broad discretionary power, partial recognition and enforcement of an award 'is mandatory where a clear separation is possible between the parts of the award that are covered by the arbitration agreement from those which are not'.[53]

8.4.2.4 Improper tribunal composition and proceedings

The proper composition of the tribunal has already been discussed in chapter 4,[54] as well as chapter 7; the latter as a ground for setting aside in addition to improper proceedings.[55] Equally, chapter 6 is devoted to the procedure of arbitral proceedings, which the reader should also consult. In order to avoid unnecessary duplication with relevant issues already covered in other chapters, it suffices here simply to emphasise a very basic rule pertinent to recognition and enforcement under the 1958 New York Convention. The forum's assessment of whether the tribunal was improperly constituted or otherwise applied a flawed procedure must be predicated solely on the parties' agreement (in the first instance). Reference to the *lex arbitri* is impermissible if the arbitration agreement is explicit. The *lex arbitri* is only relevant where the arbitration agreement is silent on these issues and the law governing them. In this connection, it may be queried whether the mandatory provisions of the seat of the arbitration override the parties' agreement, in which case the courts of the (enforcement) forum may validly take them into consideration in deciding whether or not the tribunal's composition or procedure was lawful. However, such a proposition is not only disputed but disregarded in both theory and practice. The mandatory provisions of the *lex arbitri* are no doubt binding on the parties and the tribunal, but if they are not complied with during the

---

[52] *Four Seasons Hotels and Resorts BV v Consorcio Barr SA*, 613 F Supp 2d 1362 (SD Fla, 2009); See *Lesotho Highlands Development Authority v Impregilo SpA and Others* [2005] 3 WLR 129; *Parsons & Whittemore Overseas Co Inc v Société Générale de l' Industrie du Papier (RAKTA)*, 508 F 2d 969 (2nd Cir. 1974).

[53] Wolff, above note 13, at 329.   [54] See chapter 4 section 4.5

[55] See chapter 7 section 7.6.3.4.

arbitral process any of the parties, or the courts of the seat *ex officio*, may request that the award be set aside. If the award is not set aside by the courts of the seat the mandatory provisions of the seat are no longer pertinent to the recognition and enforcement of the award in a third jurisdiction. Of course, an award that is otherwise inconsistent with the mandatory provisions of the *lex arbitri* may be refused recognition or enforcement under other grounds of Article V of the 1958 New York Convention, particularly sub-Articles (1)(a) and (e); even so, these grounds should be construed narrowly.

8.4.2.5 Awards set aside by the courts of the seat or not yet binding

When an award is set aside by the courts of the seat, the party in whose favour the award was rendered may feel aggrieved by this outcome. Despite the fact that an annulled award generally produces no *res judicata* the aggrieved party may, nonetheless, wish to pursue recognition and enforcement proceedings in a third jurisdiction under the hope that the original award may somehow be declared enforceable. How realistic is this hope?[56] The practice of international law suggests that on the basis of comity rules the courts of one state should not (without serious cause) invalidate or otherwise pass judgment on the decisions issued by the courts of other states. Article V(1)(e) of the 1958 New York Convention stipulates that the courts of the enforcement state *may* refuse to recognise and enforce foreign awards annulled (or not yet binding) at the seat.[57] Of course, this limitation (or perhaps discretion) must be construed in light of the Convention's pro-arbitration dispensation, which means that the forum is not obliged to refuse recognition or enforcement to annulled awards. Although such an outcome seemingly violates the previously mentioned principle whereby national courts should not overturn the judgments of the courts of other nations, its application to international arbitral proceedings is not convincing.

Annulment proceedings against an international award are pertinent as regards the legal effects of the award at the seat. However, such awards are distinguishable from the seat in many respects, chiefly because they are

---

[56] See generally, C. Alfons, *Recognition and Enforcement of Annulled Foreign Arbitral Awards* (Peter Lang, 2010).

[57] The discretionary character of sub-paragraph (e) through the use of the word 'may' is traced back to Art V(1), which extends to all subsequent sub-paragraphs.

circumscribed by the governing law of the contract (as well as general international law, such as the 1958 New York Convention), rather than the law of the seat. This is reflected in the practice of several nations, and the courts of states that are willing to enforce and recognise foreign awards annulled at the seat do not follow a single rationale as the following examples clearly demonstrate.

In practice, the majority of nations are inclined to adhere to the pronouncements of the courts of the seat. If an award was annulled there they will refuse recognition and enforcement. Exceptionally, several jurisdictions take a different approach. Under French law, for example, awards set aside at the seat may still be recognised and enforced in France.[58] This outcome is based on the rationale that the validity of an international award must be assessed by the rules of the country where recognition and enforcement is sought. As a result, the suspension of a foreign award by the courts of the seat does not bind French courts when assessing its recognition and enforcement.[59]

The Amsterdam Court of Appeal has held as much, albeit through an altogether different lens and rationale. It is of the view that where an award has been set aside by the courts of a country whose justice system is perceived as weak, biased or corrupt, while at the same time Dutch courts are able to closely scrutinize both the arbitral proceedings underlying the award and the merits of the award itself, they are competent to recognise and enforce an otherwise annulled award. This rationale was put in good use in *Yukos Capital v Rosneft*[60] in respect of an award set aside in Russia. The Amsterdam Court of Appeal distinguished the general obligation incumbent on Dutch courts to respect set aside judgments of foreign courts (as a matter of comity), from the authority granted to Dutch courts under private international law to refuse recognition to judgments involving a breach of due process rights. In the case at hand, the chief argument against affording credence to the judgment of the Russian court was its alleged partiality.

In Germany, the formal requirements for arbitration agreements set forth under Article II of the 1958 New York Convention are considerably

---

[58] *Hilmarton v Omnium de Traitement et de Valorisation*, French Court of Cassation judgment (23 March 1994), (1995) XX *YB Com Arb* 663.
[59] *Société Polish Ocean Lines v Société Jolasry*, French Court of Cassation judgment (10 March 1993), [1993] *Rev Arb* 255.
[60] *Yukos v Capital Rosneft*, judgment (28 April 2009), LJN BI2451; see case comment by A. J. van den Berg (2010) 27 *JOIA* 179.

narrower than those contained in section 1031 of the ZPO. In the face of uncertainty, the BGH held that as a result of the most favourable treatment rule contained in Article VII of the 1958 New York Convention, a foreign award is enforceable in Germany if the underlying arbitration clause complies with section 1031 of the ZPO, notwithstanding its non-compliance with Article II of the 1958 New York Convention or with the requirements applicable at the seat of arbitration.[61]

In respect of awards not yet binding, the reader should consult chapter 7 and the discussion there on what constitutes *res judicata*.[62] From the perspective of enforcement two issues are abundantly clear. Firstly, that the party seeking to enforce an award at the forum is not required to obtain an exequatur in the country where the award was rendered (the so-called double exequatur), which was one of the most notable impediments prior to the 1958 New York Convention and which was expressly eliminated, as is evident from the *travaux*. Secondly, an award is considered binding even though an action to set it aside is pending at the seat, given that Article V(1)(e) does not stipulate that awards subject to set aside proceedings may be refused recognition and enforcement.[63] Even so, whether or not an award is binding for the purposes of recognition and enforcement must be determined by reference to some law or legal principles, on which the 1958 New York Convention is silent. In practice, three, non-mutually exclusive, approaches have been followed. The first, which is the most prevalent, refers to the applicable arbitration law, which typically coincides with the law of the seat (the *lex arbitri*) as well as any institutional rules.[64] Under the second approach, a foreign award will be considered binding by reference to 'ordinary means of recourse' in the country where it was rendered. Thirdly, an award is not considered binding if it is susceptible to challenges before a higher (appeals) arbitral tribunal,[65] as opposed to annulment proceedings at the seat.[66]

Where the forum employs any of the aforementioned approaches and finds an award to be binding, the award may, nonetheless, turn out to

---

[61] Case no *III ZB 69/09* BGH judgment (30 September 2010), [2011] XXXVI *YB Com Arb* 273.

[62] See chapter 7 section 7.2.2. [63] See Wolff, above note 13, at 358.

[64] Although the *lex arbitri* will usually determine the formalities for a binding award, enforcement courts will also be inclined to look to the texts of well-entrenched institutional rules whose formalities are adhered to by the parties. See *Intl Trading & Industrial Investment Co v Dynocorp Aerospace Technology AS*, 763 F Supp 2d 12 (DDC, 2011).

[65] For a discussion of internal arbitral appeals, see chapter 7 section 7.6.1.

[66] See Wolff, above note 13, at 358–62.

resolve no substantive issue and hence be of no real significance to the winning party. In chapter 7 we undertook an extensive discussion of which arbitral decisions may or may not assume the status of an award. Although parties to the 1958 New York Convention are at liberty to recognise and enforce any binding 'award', it is generally accepted that an award is a decision by an arbitral tribunal that finally disposes an issue pertinent to the merits of a dispute.[67] This may be achieved by a final, interim, partial or other award, but probably not by means of a jurisdictional award because such decisions even if they are clad under the title of award do not generally deal with the merits of a dispute.

8.4.2.6 Objective arbitrability

Objective arbitrability, namely whether a particular dispute may be submitted to arbitration rather than to compulsory litigation, has already been discussed extensively in chapter 1.[68] Objective *arbitrability* should be distinguished from its *subjective* counterpart; the latter refers to the capacity of an entity or legal person to submit its dispute to arbitration. Although an assessment of arbitrability will typically be predicated on the governing law of the agreement or (secondarily) on the law of the seat, in the context of recognition and enforcement of foreign awards the forum and its courts possess authority to determine arbitrability on the basis of its own law. This is clearly emphasized in Article V(2) of the 1958 New York Convention ('in the country where recognition and enforcement is sought'). Moreover, unlike the grounds in Article V(1) of the Convention, whereby challenges against recognition and enforcement may be made only 'at the request of a party', arbitrability and public policy challenges are governed by the procedural law of the country of enforcement, whose competent authority may act on its own motion.[69]

It should be reminded that there is no single standard of arbitrability, given the variety of issues that fall under its umbrella and it would be wrong to assume the existence of general principles (of law).[70] This is because even if the vast majority of nations allow parties to submit a particular dispute to arbitration, the fact that others do not qualifies as a

---

[67] *Publicis Communication v True North Communications Inc*, 206 F 3d 725 (7th Cir. 2000).
[68] See chapter 1 section 1.8.2.
[69] *Nitron Intl Corp v Panagia Maritime Inc*, (SDNY, 1999), [2000] *YB Com Arb* 924.
[70] For a general overview, see L. A. Mistelis and S. L. Brekoulakis (eds.), *Arbitrability: International and Comparative Perspectives* (Kluwer, 2009).

form of persistent objection. There is equally no international arbitrability in commercial arbitration, as opposed to the general rule in investment arbitration whereby any dispute is arbitrable if so covered in an investment treaty (whether bilateral or multilateral), domestic law or the parties' agreement. Finally, although state parties to the 1958 New York Convention are free to set the boundaries of arbitrability in their domestic laws, they must not employ arbitrability arguments in order to restrict the enforcement of foreign awards in a manner that violates legal certainty.

8.4.2.7 Public policy

Public policy has already been discussed briefly in chapter 7 as a ground for setting aside awards at the seat.[71] Just like the treatment of arbitrability in the 1958 New York Convention, the assessment of public policy by the competent authority of the forum is based on the *lex fori* (the law of the forum). While this outcome renders the law of the forum decisive, public policy considerations should not be employed arbitrarily with a view to denying enforcement of otherwise good foreign awards.[72] We must necessarily begin with a definition of public policy, but such does not readily exist. Public policy or *ordre public* refers to a substantive or procedural standard of justice, domestic legal order[73] and, or, morality that permeates the law and institutions of a particular state at a given time.[74] Whereas for some countries public policy may be circumscribed by positive law,[75] in

---

[71] See chapter 7 section 7.6.3.4.

[72] See *International Bechtel Co Ltd v Department of Civil Aviation of the Government of Dubai*, Dubai Court of Cassation, case No 503/2003, judgment (15 May 2004). This same result was later reaffirmed by the Dubai Cassation Court in *case No 322/2004*, judgment (11 April 2005). There, it refused to enforce a foreign arbitral award rendered in favour of the claimant on the ground that the arbitrator had failed to swear witnesses in the proceedings in the manner prescribed by UAE law for court hearings.

[73] s 55(2) of the Swedish AA defines public policy as encompassing any incompatibility with the basic principles of the Swedish legal system. The *travaux* to the AA include several examples of public policy, such as threats of physical violence or bribes based upon criminal acts such as debts from unlawful gambling. See K. Hobér, *International Commercial Arbitration in Sweden* (Oxford University Press, 2011), 370-1.

[74] In *Parsons & Whittemore Overseas Co Inc v Société Générale de l'Industrie du Papier RAKTA and Bank of America*, 508 F 2d 969 (2nd Cir. 1974), it was famously held that enforcement of a foreign award should be denied 'only where enforcement would violate the forum state's most basic notions of morality and justice'.

[75] Art 3 of the UAE Civil Code defines public policy as: 'Rules relating to personal status such as marriage, inheritance, descent, and rules concerning governance, freedom of commerce, trading in wealth, rules of personal property and provisions and foundations on which

others it may be prescribed by religious rules or moral considerations at the discretion of the courts.[76] In the vast majority of cases, because public policy is in a constant state of flux it is generally not written in any particular statute, or if it is this is accomplished in rather general terms and hence it is difficult to always identify and interpret it with any degree of precision or certainty.

So-called Islamic public policy is a good illustration because it is generally perceived as fixed on account of the fact that it is situated in the Qur'an and other secondary sources that are considered as possessing an immutable character. Al-Ahdab has stated that in Islam 'the concept of public policy is based on the respect of the general spirit of the *sharia* and its sources and on the principle that individuals must respect their clauses, unless they forbid what is authorised and authorise what is forbidden'.[77] The 1983 Riyadh Convention on Judicial Cooperation between States of the Arab League reinforces the argument that Muslim public policy is distinguished from the public policy of non-Muslim nations. Article 37(e) of the Riyadh Convention stipulates that arbitral awards are not to be recognised and enforced among signatory nations where any part of the award contradicts 'the provisions of the Islamic *sharia*, the public order or the rules of conduct of the requested party'. However, even among signatories to the Riyadh Convention there are significant variations; whereas some states strictly forbid usury, others expressly allow it within their national banking systems.

Although Article V(2)(b) of the 1958 New York Convention is clear that the appropriate public policy standard is that which is prescribed under the *lex fori*, many advanced arbitral jurisdictions have attempted to set out a

---

society is based in a way that do not violate final decisions and major principles of Islamic sharia'. Art 27 of the UAE Civil Code stipulates that 'the provisions of all the laws which would be against the Islamic *sharia*, public policy or good morals of the state of the United Arab Emirates shall not be applied'. This test supplements that which is found in Art 3 of the Civil Code.

[76] In *Attorney-General of the Republic of Kenya v Bank für Arbeit und Wirtsschaft AG*, judgment on jurisdiction (28 April 1999) [2000] XXV *YB Com Arb* 692, the Cypriot Supreme Court defined public policy as: 'the fundamental principles which a society, at a given time, recognises as governing transactions, as well as other manifestations of the life of its members, on which the established legal order is based'.

[77] A. H. El-Ahdab, General Introduction on Arbitration in Arab Countries, in A. J. van den Berg (ed.), *ICCA: International Handbook* (Kluwer, 1998), Annex I, at 12; see equally A. H. El-Ahdab, Enforcement of Arbitral Awards in Arab Countries, (1995) 11 *Arbitration Int* 169.

more uniform and internationally oriented standard with a view to achieving greater legal certainty, at least in respect of international awards. As a result, two particular strands of public policy have been developed; international and transnational. Transnational public policy refers to a standard that is common among many nations (essentially giving rise to general principles of law), whereas international public policy is set out by reference to treaties and custom. Corruption, proceeds of serious crime and other matters falling within the sphere of transnational or global crime treaties may be considered part of a regime of transnational or international public policy. Countries such as France and Switzerland have shown themselves willing to substitute domestic public policy with international public policy in their assessment of foreign awards.[78] Such an approach is certainly welcome for international business people because it narrows the application of the public policy defence.

At the other extreme, several countries have no problem recognising and enforcing foreign awards that violate international treaties and which rather blatantly involve the commission of a serious offence. The Cypriot Supreme Court has gone as far as to claim that allegations (even if proven) of corruption against an award do not constitute sufficient public policy grounds for non-enforcement as the policy underlying the recognition and enforcement of awards outweighs the policy against other illicit conduct, such as bribery.[79] In equal measure, although by no means consistent, several courts in industrialised nations have assessed public policy violations from the perspective of the laws of the country where the conduct took place, finding that although the conduct would have been reprehensible in the forum it was not so under the laws and practice of that other country.[80] In *Honeywell v Meydan Group* the High Court in London upheld

---

[78] The Swiss Federal Tribunal in *W v F and V*, (1995) Bull ASA 217, specifically intimated in favour of a 'universal conception of public policy, under which an award will be incompatible with public policy if it is contrary to the fundamental moral or legal principles recognised in all civilised countries'. The Paris Court of Appeal in *European Gas Turbines SA v Westman International Ltd*, [1994] Rev Arb 359, held that bribery was not only contrary to French public policy but moreover contravened the ethics of international commerce.

[79] *Beogradska Banka DD v Westacre Developments Inc*, (2008) 1B CLR 1217, at 1222–4.

[80] In *Lemenda Trading Co Ltd v African Middle East Petroleum Co Ltd* [1988] QB 448, the parties had gone to arbitration over a contract that envisaged illicit payments to a Qatari official in exchange for business favours. An award was rendered in that case but its enforcement in England was refused on several grounds, among which was that it violated the public policy of Qatar. A different conclusion was reached in *Westacre*

a DIAC award against the owner of a racecourse in Dubai rejecting allegations that the underlying contract was procured through bribery and despite
the fact that bribery proceedings were ongoing in Dubai.[81] It is the opinion
of this author that the regime of the 1958 New York Convention (and
international commercial arbitration more generally) is not fragmented or
distinct from general international law. Hence, a construction of public
policy by the forum should not lead to the recognition and enforcement
of awards encompassing transnational and international offences. Overall,
public policy defences very rarely succeed in pro-arbitration industrialised
states. In France, in addition to the application of a narrow international
public policy, French courts further require, in respect of a substantive
public policy violation, that the act or omission in question be actual,
blatant and concrete.[82] In respect of procedural public policy claims, the
claimant must demonstrate that the breach actually caused it harm.[83]

In recent years it has been queried whether the country of enforcement
may impose conflict of laws requirements as these would ordinarily apply
to the parties' agreement, despite the fact that these are not listed in the
1958 New York Convention. The opinion of this author is that this is not
permissible. The US Court of Appeals for the Second Circuit has taken an
antithetical position, relying on *forum non conveniens* to dismiss a petition
for enforcement of a Peruvian award because of its fundamentally
Peruvian nature and public interest factors entrenched in the country's
domestic law.[84] This is in line with what commentators describe as a
deferential, albeit selective, stance to the decisions of seat courts setting
aside arbitral awards on dubious grounds.[85]

Investments Inc v Jugoimport-SPDR Holding Co Ltd and Others [1999] 3 WLR 811, whose
facts were not very different from *Lemenda*. In this case, however, the court effectively
held that fraud and bribery in a contract to be executed in Kuwait did not offend that
country's public policy and could therefore be considered arbitrable under the laws of
England.

[81] *Honeywell v Meydan Group LLC*, [2014] EWHC 1344 (TCC).

[82] *Verhoeft v Moreau*, Court of Cassation judgment (21 March 2000), [2001] *Rev Arb* 807;
Société SNF *SAS v Société Cytec Industries B V SNF*, Paris Court of Appeals judgment (23
March 2006), [2006] *Rev Arb* 483.

[83] *Nu Swift PLC v White Knight*, Paris Court of Appeals judgment (21 January 1997), [1997]
Rev Arb 583.

[84] *Figueiredo Ferraz e Engenharia de Projeto Ltda v Peru*, 635 F 3d 384 (2d Cir. 2011).

[85] See *TermoRio SA Esp & LeaseCo Group v Electranta SP et al*, 487 F 3d 928 (2007), which
again applied the *forum non conveniens* argument; see *contra*, *Corporación Mexicana de
Mantenimiento Integral v Pemex-Exploración y Producción* (SDNY 27 August 2013).

> **Case study: Refusal to enforce on constitutional grounds**
>
> States may still refuse to recognise and enforce an award against them where the tribunal dismissed claims based on fundamental incompatibility with their constitutional law. In a case decided by the Caribbean Court of Justice (CCJ) the outgoing government of Belize had granted favourable tax concessions in a confidential deed without subjecting it to parliamentary scrutiny. The successor government repudiated the concession and the concessionaire won an LCIA award for the breach and was awarded compensation which the Belize courts refused to enforce. The CCJ held that the concessions were illegitimate because they violated fundamental principles of constitutional legal order and to 'disregard these values is to attack the foundations upon which the rule of law and democracy are constructed'.[86]

8.5 Preclusion

The 1958 New York Convention is silent as to whether the party challenging an award before the courts of the country where enforcement is sought must have availed itself of pertinent remedies available at the seat of the arbitration, namely set aside proceedings. This observation is significant because set aside remedies are almost identical to challenges against awards under the 1958 New York Convention and hence failure to avail oneself of the former may be perceived as an abuse of process which serves to *preclude* later challenges at the enforcement stage. Given the absence of a direction in the Convention two considerations are relevant. On the one hand, the Convention clearly grants the right to challenge recognition and enforcement of a foreign award without subjecting it to preclusion limitations; this individual entitlement must no doubt be preserved. On the other hand, the Convention gives significant weight to the *lex fori* and it is natural that the aforementioned individual entitlement under the Convention cannot override the forum's fundamental principles of civil procedure. This argument is even more convincing where such civil procedure principles are common to several nations, thus giving rise to a general principle of law.

---

[86] *BCB Holdings Ltd and Belize Bank Ltd v Attorney-General of Belize*, [2013] CCJ 5 (AJ).

The practice of national courts demonstrates some uniformity in their approach to a party's failure to raise defences before the courts of the seat, especially if it had participated in the arbitral proceedings. As regards challenges against arbitral jurisdiction these must be raised no later than one's statement of defence. In respect of other challenges under sub-paragraph (1) of Article V of the 1958 New York Convention failure to raise a challenge in the course of arbitral proceedings generally precludes similar objections in enforcement proceedings.[87] Three legal justifications are utilized in order to preclude subsequent challenges, namely estoppel, waiver (especially by conduct) and bad faith. Estoppel precludes the invocation of an otherwise legitimate claim by reason of the fact that the claimant has consistently induced others to rely on prior contradictory conduct. The French Court of Cassation has employed estoppel to bar further challenges under Article V of the Convention if: a) there is a change in position of the concerned party; and b) its behaviour is such as to mislead the other party with a view to relying on said behaviour.[88] A waiver suggests that the claimant has implicitly waived its right to invoke a particular claim by consciously failing to exercise that claim, or by engaging in conduct that necessarily extinguishes the claim.[89] Preclusion on the basis of bad faith is similar to estoppel in that the claimant is not permitted to rely on its claim after having misled its counterpart. A party will be precluded from making fresh challenges under the 1958 New York Convention, as a matter of bad faith, where its behaviour is contradictory and at the same time said behaviour constitutes an abuse of law.[90]

Overall, despite the clear inclination in favour of precluding challenges not raised in the course of arbitral proceedings (including set aside), if the claimant was for some compelling reason prevented from exercising its right to challenge the award at the seat, the forum should not lightly preclude its claims against enforcement.

---

[87] *National Wrecking Co v International Bhd of Teamsters*, 990 F 2d 957 (7th Cir. 1993), at 960; *SOCAR v Fronter*, Svea Appeals Court judgment (4 April 2009).

[88] *Merial v Clocke Verspakung-Service Gmbh* [2010] *Rev Arb* 93; *Hebei Import & Export Corp v Polytek Engineering Ltd* [1999] 2 HKC 205. See Wolff, above note 13, at 256–7.

[89] See *International Standard Electric Corp v Bridas Sociedad Anonima Petrolera Industrial v Comercial*, 745 F Supp 172 (SDNY, 1990); Swiss Federal Supreme Court, case *no 4A_348/2009* and *4A_69/2009*; Spanish Supreme Court (TS) judgment in *Union Générale de Cinéma SA v X Y Z Desarrollos SA*, (2007) XXXII *YB Com Arb* 525.

[90] BGH judgment (17 April 2008), *SchiedsVZ* (2008), 196.

8.6 The defence of sovereign immunity in enforcement proceedings

Immunity is a procedural defence on the basis of which a state entity, or a subdivision entity thereof, is entitled not to be sued before the national courts of a third state. In this sense, the plea of immunity relates to the jurisdictional competence of the court in which the suit is pending. Despite the fact that immunity was once *absolute*, that is, it pertained to all aspects of a state's international relations, since the end of the Cold War, at least, it is *restricted* only to those aspects of state activity that are considered of a public nature (*acta jure imperii*). As a result, the commercial relations of a state (*acta jure gestionis*) are not covered by the privilege of immunity. Immunity extends to both natural as well as legal persons and persists for the entire duration that the entity in question retains its sovereign character. By way of illustration, a government agent may have his status terminated by its principal (the state) and government property may subsequently be sold to a private corporation. In both cases, the immunity of the agent and the property are dissolved and both may be the subject of civil or criminal suits in the courts of third states without the benefit of immunity.

For the purposes of this chapter, we should further distinguish between immunity from jurisdiction (explained above) and immunity from enforcement (or measures of constraint, as it is otherwise known), which is predicated on a court judgment ordering enforcement measures against the assets of a state. The general rule is that whereas states do not enjoy immunity from the jurisdiction of foreign courts in situations where the impugned conduct is of a private nature, they always enjoy immunity from jurisdiction in respect of acts of a public nature; although admittedly the distinction is not always clear-cut. Moreover, states enjoy immunity from enforcement regardless of the nature of the impugned act. The object of this section is to discern possible exceptions to this general rule as well as situate arbitral proceedings and arbitral awards within the framework of the general rule.

Given the consensual character of arbitration through the pivotal role of the arbitration agreement it is not possible for a state to become a respondent to arbitral proceedings without its consent. The state will typically have entered into an agreement with a private entity in which an arbitration clause will have been inserted to the satisfaction of both parties. Legal certainty and party equality would be non-existent had international law permitted states to enter into arbitration agreements with private actors which they had no intent of honouring by invoking their immunity as a general defence. As a result, arbitration clauses to which states are parties imply consent to the supervisory jurisdiction of a national court to implement the arbitration agreement and implicitly give rise to a waiver of immunity on the part of the state.[91] Article 17 of the UN Convention on Jurisdictional Immunities of States and their Property, which is largely reflective of customary international law, provides that:

> If a state enters into an agreement in writing with a foreign national or juridical person to submit to arbitration differences relating to a commercial transaction, that state cannot invoke immunity from jurisdiction before a court of another state which is otherwise competent in a proceeding which relates to:
>
> a) the validity, interpretation or application of the arbitration agreement;
> b) the arbitration procedure; or
> c) the confirmation or setting aside of the award, unless the arbitration agreement otherwise provides.

The application of the general rule in Article 17 of the UN Convention extends only to proceedings in the exercise of the court's supervisory jurisdiction in respect of the arbitration. Proceedings related to the recognition and enforcement of arbitral awards are excluded,[92] although this is somewhat in contrast to several important domestic immunity statutes, such as section 9 of the UK Sovereign Immunities Act or indeed section 1605(a)(6) of the FSIA, which stipulates that in certain circumstances 'an agreement to arbitrate constitutes a waiver of immunity in an action to enforce that agreement or the resultant award'.

As regards the enforcement of measures of constraint against the property of a losing state, two broad categories are generally recognised, namely pre-judgment and post-judgment (essentially pre- and post-award) immunity claims. Pre-judgment measures essentially involve interim measures (injunctions) while arbitral proceedings are pending with a view to securing assets (through freezing or similar orders) or avoiding their dissipation. In practice, the most common measure is the arrest of state ships, which although permissible in several jurisdictions is

---

[91] *Svenska Petroleum Exploration AB v Lithuania and AB Geonafta*, [2006] EWCA Civ 1529.
[92] R. O'Keefe and C. J. Tams (eds.), *The United Nations Convention on Jurisdictional Immunities of States and their Property: A Commentary* (Oxford University Press, 2013), 284.

not allowed under Article 18 of the UN Convention.[93] In accordance with Article 18 of the UN Convention, no pre-judgment measure of restraint against a state is permissible unless the state has specifically consented.[94]

Post-judgment (or post-award) measures of constraint against state property are generally impermissible. Article 19 of the UN Convention makes it clear that:

No post-judgment measures of constraint, such as attachment, arrest or execution, against property of a state may be taken in connection with a proceeding before a court of another state unless and except to the extent that:

a) the state has expressly consented to the taking of such measures as indicated:
    i) by international agreements;
    ii) by an arbitration agreement or in a written contract; or
    iii) by a declaration before the court or by a written communication after a dispute between the parties has arisen; or
b) the state has allocated or earmarked property for the satisfaction of the claim which is the object of that proceeding; or
c) it has been established that the property is specifically in use or intended for use by the state for other than government non-commercial purposes and is in the territory of the state of the forum, provided that post-judgment measures of constraint may only be taken against property that has a connection with the entity against which the proceeding was directed.

It is clear from this provision that there are very few circumstances under which state property may be constrained as a result of an award against a state entity.[95] Exceptionally, the courts of the seat may deem it appropriate to issue worldwide orders once an award has become final in order to assist the winning party's subsequent efforts to enforce the award. In *Republic of Argentina v NML Capital Ltd*, which was not, however, related to arbitral proceedings, the US Supreme Court affirmed a US District Court's worldwide post-judgment discovery order directed to two banks with presence in the US, thereby rejecting Argentina's argument that the order was barred

---

[93] Ibid., at 300–1.

[94] Few states ever expressly make such an undertaking. A rare exception is a dispute settlement provision entered into by Argentina in a fiscal agency agreement. See *NML Capital v Argentina*, [2011] UKSC 31.

[95] This general rule was confirmed by the ICJ in emphatic terms in *Germany v Italy* [Greece intervening], Jurisdictional Immunities of the State, judgment (3 February 2012), paras 113–20; see also to the same effect the judgment of the German BGH, *Sedelmayer v Russia*, (2006) 1 ASA Bull 175.

by the FSIA. It held that the FSIA focuses only on two types of immunity, namely from jurisdiction and execution and hence it is silent on discovery in aid of execution of a foreign sovereign judgment debtor's assets.[96]

Private parties to an arbitration agreement with a state, or a state entity, will do well to ensure that the state has either declared its willingness to submit to enforcement proceedings or has otherwise earmarked property for the satisfaction of an award against it. Where this is the case, national courts have been inclined to permit measures of execution. In France, if a state enters into an arbitration clause which contains an express undertaking to honour a subsequent award, French courts will consider that state to have waived its immunity from execution of the award in France.[97]

---

[96] *Republic of Argentina v NML Capital Ltd*, 695 F 3d 201 (2014) *affirmed*.

[97] *Société Creighton Ltd v Ministère des Finances et le Ministère des Affaires Municipales et de l' Agriculture du Gouvernement de l'Etat de Qatar*, [2003] *Rev Arb* 417, French Supreme Cassation Court judgment (6 July 2000); but see *contra, Joint Stock Corp v Czech Republic*, Austrian Supreme Court judgment (11 July 2012) which dismissed a claim for enforcement (following an arbitral award) against the assets of the Czech Republic on the basis of immunity.

9 Consumer and online arbitration

9.1 Introduction

The subject matter of this chapter, particularly consumer arbitration, has not traditionally been included in textbooks on international arbitration because it is perceived as being of domestic concern only and not wholly relevant to commercial law. While this is true to a large degree, the author suggests several approaches which tend to show both its commercial and international character. Given the explosion of consumerism, both offline and online it is certainly prudent for those interested in arbitration to be aware of developments in consumer arbitration and its possible linkages to commercial arbitration. Consumer arbitration is a special form of arbitration, alongside commercial and investment arbitration. The chapter will go on to show how consumer arbitration and the underlying agreement to arbitrate consumer disputes have developed differently between EU and US lawmakers and the courts. We shall then attempt briefly to sketch the perilous waters of class arbitration before finally getting to grips with the operation and regulation of online arbitration, which is a hybrid (but not distinct) between consumer and commercial arbitration.

9.2 The nature of consumer disputes

Consumer disputes should be distinguished between business-to-consumer (B2C) and business-to-business (B2B). The reason why they are of concern is because the average consumer is at a disadvantage against the majority of businesses when it comes to dispute resolution. For one thing, there exists a significant financial disparity between businesses and their consumers. Secondly, the majority of consumers do not typically find it cost effective to institute proceedings against businesses, especially with respect to products and services whose value is relatively small. Thirdly, although the purchase of a product by a consumer may give rise to consumer arbitration in the event of dispute, it is unimaginable that even the most diligent of consumers would condition their purchase on the dispute resolution clause in their contract with the business. Where, for example, a consumer purchases a product in person or online the contract between seller and consumer is often indistinguishable from the receipt, a warrantee or (in the case of online purchases) the agreement of sale – typically appearing at the very end of the process – which requires a 'tick' by the consumer. In such situations the consumer is unlikely to read a lengthy agreement wherein the arbitration clause is intertwined with other mundane provisions. In order to assist consumers, EU nations generally provide for small claims court jurisdiction, which is generally fast and effective. The EU has recently made possible the resolution of transnational small claims through a distinct and user-friendly mechanism, given that a French tourist would be dissuaded from filing a suit against an English car hire agency for a defective car during his stay there if required to file the claim in England.[1] Fourthly, when a dispute reaches the courts, there is clearly a disparity of arms between the consumer and the business. By way of illustration, the business may have access to expensive counsel or be

---

[1] Regulation (EC) No 861/2007 of the European Parliament and of the Council of 11 July 2007 establishing a European small claims procedure, OJ L 199 (2007).

disinterested in the length of proceedings,[2] both of which are prohibitive factors for the average consumer who must continue working in the interim.[3]

It is generally perceived that access to ordinary courts provides consumers with better guarantees of justice as compared to an unregulated form of arbitration that is not premised on fundamental principles of consumer law – or even human rights law.[4] The underlying rationale is that, at the very least, consumers before the regular courts may have recourse to some form of legal aid (whereas this is not available in arbitration) and that in any event the principle of equality of arms is better guaranteed by the courts on the basis that the relevant civil procedure rules are mandatory, whereas the procedural rules in arbitration may be freely decided by the parties,[5] which would place the weaker party (namely the consumer) in a disadvantageous position. Moreover, given that the parties cannot dispense the law of tort[6] or contract in the course of civil litigation – whereas they can instruct the arbitral tribunal to apply any law, or principles thereof, as they wish – the judge may likely rule in favour of the consumer in situations where the business has violated relevant rules, or where the contractual terms are grossly unfair, even if no breach has taken place. The risk that arbitrators may validly – through the parties' consent – bypass such rules raises the risk

---

[2] See, for example, *McDonald's Corp v Steel and Morris*, [1997] EWHC 366 (QB), which was not a consumer dispute as such, but a libel case against two activists claiming that McDonald's produced poor food under environmentally heinous conditions. The trial dragged on for years with arguments heard on a daily basis. The defendants were denied legal aid and argued the case themselves. The process is conveniently referred to as the *McLibel* case. Several years later the ECtHR held that the defendants had been denied a fair trial under Art 6 ECHR. See *Steel and Morris v UK* (2005) 41 EHRR 22.

[3] According to a 2009 report, out of 301 consumer cases handled by the AAA, consumers were represented by counsel in 150 cases (49.8%). See Searle Civil Justice Institute, *Consumer Arbitration before the AAA* (March, 2009), 72.

[4] There has been a movement in recent years to equate consumer rights with human rights. See I. Bantekas, Consumer Rights as Human Rights, (2012) 1 *Cyprus Human Rights Law Review* 184–97; I. Benöhr, *EU Consumer Law and Human Rights* (Oxford University Press, 2013).

[5] See chapter 6 section 6.2.

[6] Unlike arbitration whose existence in any given case is based on privity, namely the contracting parties' agreement to submit a dispute to arbitration, a consumer dispute need not only arise from contract but also a relationship premised on a tort. A good example is the relationship between the manufacturer of a defective product and the ultimate consumer; there is no contractual relation between the two. In such cases, classic arbitration would be impossible because of the absence of a relevant agreement between consumer and manufacturer, unless they subsequently entered into a post-dispute agreement.

that consumer arbitration, if applied and practised in the same way as ordinary commercial arbitration, may have an adverse effect on the rights of consumers and society as a whole.

As this chapter will go on to demonstrate, the real problem generally associated with consumer arbitration is not that arbitral tribunals are unable or unwilling to guarantee fair trial rights as compared to the courts. Rather, it is the consumer's explicit consent that raises legal and ethical issues. Standard contract forms containing an arbitration clause are not deemed (at least in the EU) as having been freely entered into by the consumer for reasons already explained. In such circumstances, it would be fair for the consumer, as the party that does not dictate the terms of the contract, if the choice of dispute settlement was agreed after the dispute arose by means of a new, post-dispute, agreement. In this manner, the choice of dispute settlement would not be dictated by a standard arbitration clause that was meaningless to the consumer prior to the dispute and the consumer could decide in his or her own time whether an arbitral tribunal was more appropriate than a court. The following sections will explain the vastly opposing rationale of US and European law on this issue.

9.3 The international dimension of consumer arbitration

While it is true that consumer arbitration is more likely than not to arise between a business and consumer situated in the same jurisdiction, there are situations where it possesses an international dimension. For one thing, cross-border consumer relationships are now very common, particularly through online transactions. This gives rise to questions about the breadth of the concept of consumer, given its centrality to consumer arbitration. The general definition is largely common to all EU member states. Under section 13 of the German Civil Code (BGB) a consumer is defined as 'a natural person who is concluding a legal transaction (*Rechtsgeschäft*) for a purpose which can be regarded as outside his trade or self-employed profession'. The BGH has taken the view that the reference to arbitration in standard terms contained in a contract between a domestic consumer and a foreign stock broker is unfair in accordance with section 1031(5) ZPO.[7] The Austrian Supreme Court has held that a

---

[7] *German consumer v US broker*, BGH judgment (25 January 2011), XI ZR 350/08.

consumer is anyone who is not an entrepreneur and therefore anyone for whom a legal transaction falls outside the scope of her or his business; this definition also encompasses legal entities. A shareholder may be considered a consumer by reference to economic criteria, particularly by reference to an alignment of shareholder and company interests. Another important criterion is the degree to which the shareholder actually dictates the management of the company. Consequently, where a shareholder is found to possess more than 50 per cent of the company's shares, his influence is considered significant and cannot therefore be considered a consumer.[8] Some sensible limits are necessary to better delineate the concept of consumer. Individual holders of government bonds, for example, cannot be classified as consumers because sovereign states cannot be assimilated to businesses and in any event in the majority of cases the bond does not specify recourse to arbitration.[9] If the dispute between bondholder and bond issuer is ultimately resolved through arbitration this will not be of a consumer nature.

A second international dimension of consumer arbitration arises from the parties' desire to recognise and enforce consumer awards abroad. While, no doubt, several states will be happy to enforce foreign consumer awards, others will refuse to do so, especially where they have reserved their right under the 1958 New York Convention to only recognise and enforce foreign commercial awards.[10]

Finally, even in the context of domestic consumer arbitration, the parties' rights, particularly those of the consumer, are governed by supranational rules, such as the EU Consumer Protection Directive, in addition to pertinent international and regional human rights norms, as is the case with Article 6 (right to fair trial) of the ECHR. Consequently, while the arbitration is domestic as such, the rules governing the arbitration are international and if a question of law, such as EU law, were to reach the courts of the seat they may request a preliminary ruling from the CJEU.

---

[8] *Case No 6 Ob 43/13m*, Austrian Supreme Court judgment (16 December 2013).

[9] It may, however, contain a collective action clause, which can lead to arbitration if the majority of bondholders so agree. See also M. Waibel, Opening Pandora's Box: Sovereign Bonds in International Arbitration, (2007) 101 *AJIL* 711.

[10] See chapter 8 section 8.4.

9.4 Pre-dispute arbitration clauses

9.4.1 Pre-dispute B2C arbitration clauses in European law

The starting point for this discussion is Directive 93/13/EEC of 5 April 1993 on unfair terms in consumer contracts, Article 3(1) of which states that:

A contractual term which has not been individually negotiated shall be regarded as unfair if, contrary to the requirement of good faith, it causes a significant imbalance in the parties' rights and obligations arising under the contract, to the detriment of the consumer.

Article 6(1) of the Directive further provides that:

Member States shall lay down that unfair terms used in a contract concluded with a consumer by a seller or supplier shall, as provided for under their national law, not be binding on the consumer and that the contract shall continue to bind the parties upon those terms if it is capable of continuing in existence without the unfair terms.

Clearly, the Directive does not suggest that consumer arbitration is unfair, but that only agreements between consumers and businesses that have not been individually negotiated are deemed unfair. Therefore, if the business demonstrates that its pre-dispute arbitration agreement with the consumer was individually negotiated – and that it was not therefore imposed under standard terms – it will be valid. In practice, such individually negotiated pre-dispute agreements are rare and businesses typically only enter into post-dispute individually negotiated agreements to arbitrate with consumers. Even so, the Directive does not impose a definition of unfairness on EU member states and does not set arbitrability limitations. In a case concerning the unfairness or not of an arbitration clause in a mortgage agreement, the CJEU held that:

Article 3(1) and (3) of Council Directive 93/13/EEC ... must be interpreted as meaning that it is for the national court concerned to determine whether a clause contained in a mortgage loan contract concluded between a bank and a consumer – vesting exclusive jurisdiction in a permanent arbitration tribunal, against whose decisions there is no judicial remedy under national law [i.e., no right of appeal], to hear all disputes arising out of that contract – must, having regard to all of the circumstances surrounding the conclusion of that contract, be regarded as unfair under those provisions. In the context of its assessment, the national court must, in particular:

– verify whether the clause at issue has the object or effect of excluding or hindering the consumer's right to take legal action or exercise any other legal remedy; and

– take account of the fact that the communication to the consumer, before the conclusion of the contract at issue, of general information on the differences between the arbitration procedure and ordinary legal proceedings cannot alone rule out the unfairness of that clause.

If the clause is held to be unfair, it is for that court to draw the appropriate conclusions under national law in order to ensure that the consumer is not bound by that clause.[11]

In line with the Directive the CJEU has naturally assumed a consumer-friendly stance to pre-dispute arbitration agreements. In *Mostaza Claro v Centro Movil Millennium SL*,[12] Mrs Claro's mobile phone standard agreement with a Spanish operator contained an arbitration clause. When she failed to comply with the minimum subscription period the mobile company initiated arbitration according to the terms of the standard agreement. She participated in the ensuing arbitral proceedings without having fully comprehended the validity of the arbitration clause. When she did realise that the arbitration clause may have been defective under the Directive she challenged the award on the ground of the invalidity of the arbitration clause. The Spanish court seized of the matter made a referral to the CJEU, which emphasised that if the arbitration clause was unfair the award should be set aside even though the consumer had not pleaded the invalidity of the arbitration clause in the course of the arbitration proceedings. According to the CJEU, a different conclusion would undermine the protection established by the Directive, namely: to protect the weaker party; to prevent individuals from being bound by an unfair term and to ensure that member states provide adequate and effective means to prevent the continued use of unfair terms in contracts. In *Asturcom* the CJEU held that claims concerning unfair arbitration agreements can be raised at any stage of a procedure even after an arbitral award has been issued, if the national law in question allows for such re-examination.[13]

---

[11] Case C-342/13, *Katalin Sebestyén v Zsolt Csaba Kővári and Others*, CJEU Order (3 April 2014), para 36.

[12] Case C-168/05, *Mostaza Claro v Centro Movil Millennium SL* [2006] All ER (D) 322.

[13] Case C-40/08 *Asturcom Telecommunicationes v Christina Rodrigues Noguera* [2009] ECR I-9579.

In practice, where the parties to consumer disputes in Europe have recourse to arbitration this is usually conducted by pertinent trade associations. Aside from the issue of the legality of pre-dispute arbitration clauses, the arbitral procedure itself has been of some concern to the EU authorities for some time. A recent Directive adopted by the Parliament and Council requires that where domestic and cross-border consumer disputes are submitted to ADR institutions – including those handled by trade associations – they should be subject to the principles of fairness, transparency, legality (procedural and substantive) and protection of fundamental rights (including privacy and data protection) and that the consumer's right to judicial remedies not be compromised.[14]

This stance towards pre-dispute arbitration agreements is to a large degree consistent and uniform throughout all EU member states. In Sweden, section 6(1) of the country's Arbitration Act stipulates that where a dispute between a business enterprise and a consumer concerns goods, services, or any other products supplied principally for private use, an arbitration agreement may not be invoked where such was entered into prior to the dispute. In Spain, arbitration agreements with consumers that are not encompassed within the mandatory consumer arbitration regime are considered abusive[15] and therefore null and void.[16] In addition, the amendment introduced by Law 3/2014 provides that pre-dispute arbitration agreements entered into by the consumer are not binding on the consumer but only for the business.[17] In Germany, section 1031(5) of the ZPO requires that the arbitration agreement be concluded after a dispute arises, either in the form of a contract containing no other issues, or through a notarised document. Failure to observe this statutory requirement invalidates the agreement and the consumer is no longer obliged to submit to arbitral proceedings, even if the party challenging the agreement is not the consumer.[18] Article 617(1) of the Austrian CCP stipulates that consumer disputes are arbitrable but an agreement to this effect can only be drawn up once the dispute between a business and a consumer arises. In addition, the arbitration agreement, whatever contractual form this takes,

---

[14] Directive 2013/11 on Consumer ADR (21 May 2013), L 165/63. Although para 29 of the Directive's Récital initially suggests that arbitration is not encompassed within the purview of ADR, Art 2(2) does not specifically exclude it.

[15] Art 90(1) of Royal Legislative Decree 1/2007, as lastly amended by Law 3/2014.

[16] Ibid., Art 83.   [17] Ibid., Art 57(4).

[18] *D v C*, BGH judgment (19 May 2011), II ZR 16/11.

must be distinct from any other terms between the parties (which must therefore be inserted in a distinct agreement).[19] The Austrian Supreme Court has held that arbitration clauses in consumer contracts do not violate Austrian public policy so long as they were individually negotiated.[20]

Even so, EU member states are disinclined from alienating businesses and consumers from arbitration. As a result, they have rightly avoided any statements to the effect that all pre-dispute arbitration agreements are unfair. In Sweden, for example, section 6(2) of the Arbitration Act dictates that pre-dispute arbitration agreements are valid where they concern disputes between an insurer and a policy-holder concerning insurance based on a collective agreement or group agreement and handled by representatives of the group. Spain, as we shall explore later, has introduced a collective consumer arbitration mechanism. Article 7(2) of the Danish Arbitration Act, while requiring post-dispute arbitration agreements, does not mandate that said agreements be individually negotiated or that they should not contain any other provisions. In France, it is suggested that individually negotiated pre-dispute B2C arbitration clauses with little, or no, bargaining disparity between the parties are not unfair.[21] It should be noted that the French Court of Cassation has been generally disinclined to nullify pre-dispute arbitration clauses in transnational consumer contracts.[22]

9.4.2 Pre-dispute B2C arbitration clauses in US law

In the USA the courts have always demonstrated their concern for the public enforcement of statutory rights, consumer rights falling within this category. The first port of call is an assessment of arbitrability. The Supreme Court's current approach is that unless Congress explicitly precludes arbitration of disputes arising from statutory rights, the dispute in

---

[19] Art 617(2) CCP.

[20] *LAS (Denmark) v Jürgen H, Judith Elizabeth H and Others*, case no 30b144/09m, judgment (22 July 2009).

[21] See P. B. Rutledge, and A. W. Howard, Arbitrating Disputes between Companies and Individuals: Lessons from Abroad (Feb 2010) *Dispute Resolution Journal* 30, at 34. This distinction is shared by almost all other EU member states. German courts accept, for example, that B2C pre-dispute arbitration clauses are fair if they are written in an 'intelligible and transparent manner' under the good faith requirement of section 307(1) of the Civil Code (BGB).

[22] See *Dame Rado v Painvewebber and Others*, French Cassation Court judgment (21 May 1997), [2005] *97 Rev Arb* 115.

question may validly be submitted to arbitration. As a result, the Court has extended arbitration to core consumer areas such as consumer lending, while at the same time removing such actions from constitutional due process guarantees.[23] Of course, if a claimant were to successfully argue that the exercise of his statutory rights was impossible because of the high costs of arbitration the dispute would be remanded to litigation.[24] In practice, this is unlikely, with the Supreme Court holding in *Green Tree v Randolph* that even claims arising from the Truth in Lending Act (TILA) may be subject to arbitration.[25] In that case the Court set a high burden for consumers to demonstrate their inability to pay prohibitive arbitral costs, such that hinder them from fully exercising their TILA claims. The Court noted that this was so because in the case at hand the arbitrators had the power to limit or excuse fees for hardship and that in any event the lender promised to cover any prohibitive costs.[26]

Having dispensed with consumer arbitrability we may now turn to the treatment of pre-dispute consumer arbitration clauses in US law and judicial practice. The general rule is that unless a statute forbids pre-dispute agreements in a particular area, such as those relating to mortgage contracts under the Dodd-Frank Act,[27] the agreement is potentially enforceable. The agreement must be conscionable, which is roughly equivalent to unfair clauses in consumer agreements in the EU context. Such conscionability will be determined both procedurally and substantively on the basis of the negotiations, disclosure of the arbitration terms, their fairness, inconvenient arbitration venue, as well as other relevant factors.[28] Where the arbitration clause is not unconscionable and the consumer is found to be fully aware of its existence and implications US courts are willing to extend arbitrability to statutory consumer protection claims and enforce the parties' agreement. In *Mintze v American General Financial Services, Inc,*[29] the Third Circuit held that although bankruptcy courts enjoy absolute authority over core bankruptcy

---

[23] See M. A. Weston, Universes Colliding: The Constitutional Implications of Arbitral Class Actions, (2006) 47 *Wm & Mary L Rev 1711*, at 1745–62.

[24] *Ball v SFX Broad Inc*, 165 F Supp 2d 230 (NDNY, 2001).

[25] *Green Tree Fin Corp Ala v Randolph*, 531 US 79 (2000), at 89–92.

[26] Ibid., at 91–2. See A. J. Schmitz, American Exceptionalism in Consumer Arbitration (2013) 10 *Loy U Chi Int'l L Rev* 81, at 86–7.

[27] Dodd-Frank Wall Street Reform and Consumer Protection Act, 124 Stat 1376 (2010).

[28] See *Arnold v United Companies Lending Corporation*, 511 SE 2d 854 (1998).

[29] *Mintze v American General Financial Services, Inc.* 434 F 3d 222 (3rd Cir. 2006).

proceedings but less so over non-core proceedings, 'the core/non-core distinction does not . . . affect whether a bankruptcy court has the discretion to deny enforcement of an arbitration agreement'. The lack of bankruptcy issues in *Mintze* meant that there was no inherent conflict between arbitration and federal consumer law.

9.5 Collective or class arbitration

Collective civil claims are hardly unknown in most jurisdictions. The underlying rationale is that a closed class of persons unified (as a class) by reason of a common injury and claim, such as several thousand purchasers of the same product from the same business, may enjoin their common claim against the business. Such a joinder has the effect of eliminating the consumers' inequality of arms (had they been acting independently), ensures judicial economy by avoiding thousands of individual hearings on the same matter and it eliminates the risk of conflicting judgments.[30] No doubt, the aforementioned benefits of class actions materialise when all the claimants seek the same remedy. Whereas the purchasers of a faulty toaster will naturally be united in their claim for a refund, the various foreign holders of government bonds of a country that intends to default on its repayments – by means of a haircut to the bonds – are usually divided as to whether they should accept a compromise deal offered by the bond issuer. Some will be driven to accept the offer, fearing that they may ultimately end up with nothing, whereas others may be determined to fight to the bitter end, whether through litigation, arbitration or some form (usually coercive) of diplomatic protection.[31] In such situations there will usually be a single class action, followed by several individual actions. A class action, however, need not only concern litigation but may take the form of class arbitration.

---

[30] Because this discussion of class arbitration is situated in the consumer arbitration chapter our emphasis is on the consumer dimension. However, class arbitration may equally apply to other categories of persons, such as shareholders, bondholders and others, although this is not generally described as 'class arbitration' in the sphere of investment arbitration. See chapter 10 section 10.4.2.

[31] Where the bonds contain collective action clauses the bondholders have a variety of options, but the majority may join together and accept an offer from the state. See D. Billington, European Collective Action Clauses, in R. M. Lastra and L. Buchheit (eds.), *Sovereign Debt Management* (Oxford University Press, 2014).

The *Abaclat* case before an ICSID tribunal, although not a consumer case, demonstrates that mass claims may fall within the purview of investment arbitration. In the case at hand, 60,000 Italian bondholders of Argentine bonds refused to accept an offer by Argentina for a significant haircut to the value of their bonds. They initiated investment arbitration and succeeded in establishing jurisdiction on the ground that the Italy–Argentina BIT designated the purchase of bonds as an investment and that therefore it would be absurd not to allow mass investment claims when a similar claim by a single investment would have been clearly admissible.[32]

In the USA, civil class actions have a long history and relatively recently consumers were given the option of transforming such actions into class arbitration, subject to conscionability limitations as discussed above. The central issue is whether the parties' agreement provides for class arbitration in the first place. In order for class arbitration to be valid, consumers must first waive their statutory right to a civil class action and this is typically achieved in the pre-dispute agreement between consumers and businesses in the form of a standard clause. There is one significant limitation, however. Given that the right of *locus standi* before the courts has a constitutional basis it may not be waived without express and unambiguous agreement, thus necessitating that the consumer is fully aware of the implications of the waiver.[33] This task, and the onus to prove as much, befalls the seller.[34]

In the absence of an explicit reference to class arbitration in the pre-dispute agreement, the Supreme Court in *Green Tree v Bazzle* held that such a determination fell within the authority of the tribunal.[35] In *Stolt-Nielsen*, however, the Court went on to say that in the absence of an express class arbitration clause it could not be assumed that the parties,

---

[32] *Abaclat (formerly Beccara) v Argentina*, Decision on Jurisdiction and Admissibility (4 August 2011).

[33] In *Discover Bank v Superior Court*, 36 Cal. 4th 148 (2005), a putative class action against a credit card issuer was made for improper charges relating to late fees. The credit card issuer argued that the class action was impermissible on account of the arbitration clause, which barred customers from proceeding with their claims on a class action basis. The California Supreme Court held that it is unconscionable under California law for a corporation, by way of a contract of adhesion, to bar customers with small individual claims from bringing or participating in a class action. On remand, however, the California Court of Appeals upheld the Delaware choice of law clause in the credit card contract and found that Delaware law would allow the contractual ban on class actions.

[34] See, for example, *Nelson v Cyprus Baghdad Copper Corp.*, 119 F 3d 756 (9th Cir. 1997).

[35] *Green Tree Fin Corp v Bazzle*, 539 US 444 (2004), at 451–3.

all of which were experienced business people, intended by their silence to allow for class arbitration.[36] In *AT&T v Concepcion* the Supreme Court limited the courts' authority to imply class arbitration in the absence of explicit consent in the parties' agreement.[37]

Class arbitration and the AT&T v Concepcion case

Vincent and Liza Concepcion were promised a 'free' mobile telephone by their mobile phone operator, AT&T, but later discovered that they had to pay sales tax. Hence, the phone was not really 'free'. Their agreement with AT&T provided for arbitration, but precluded the tribunal from ordering class arbitration; that is, it included a class action waiver. The couple filed a suit which was turned into a class action with the participation of other disgruntled customers. AT&T moved for a court order compelling the parties to (bilateral) arbitration as per their contract. The Concepcions argued that the arbitration clause with its waiver of class arbitration was unconscionable. Although the California district court agreed that the waiver was express (and thus *prima facie* valid), it went on to emphasise that because the bilateral arbitration would not provide the same degree of deterrence and protection to consumers as would a class action, it should as a result be considered unconscionable. This application of conscionability was predicated on a California contract law construction to the arbitration agreement (and the class waiver thereof)[38] despite the fact that the US FAA takes precedence over state law which prevents contracts disallowing class actions. The US Supreme Court, with a narrow majority, reversed the judgment of the Californian district court. It emphasised that it was unacceptable for state courts to employ contract law in order to compel class arbitration where the parties had explicitly provided for a waiver in their agreement.

In Europe, class arbitration is relatively unknown and it was only recently that a limited number of jurisdictions even started to think

---

[36] *Stolt-Nielsen SA v AnimalFeeds Int'l Corp*, 130 S Ct 1758 (2010), at 1769.
[37] *AT&T Mobility LLC v Concepcion*, 131 S Ct 1740 (2011).
[38] Relying also on the precedent established by the California Supreme Court in *Discover Bank v Superior Court*, above note 33.

about its potential benefits for consumers.[39] The most impressive model is that established by the *lex specialis* regime of the Spanish Royal Decree 231/2008, which sets up class consumer arbitration administered by consumer arbitration boards. Submission to class arbitration is optional and is effected through a post-dispute agreement whereby the cause must arise out of a common factual basis and affect the interests of a determinable number of consumers. The innovative feature of the process is that arbitral proceedings are not initiated by the parties, but by the president of the relevant consumer arbitration board. In every case, the parties must ultimately consent to class arbitration, although it is not required that all affected consumers subscribe to this process. Disputes under this process are resolved on equitable grounds,[40] unless the parties decide otherwise.[41]

9.6 Online arbitration

The remainder of this chapter will discuss the operation and regulation of online arbitration. Much of the analysis related to the right to fair trial in this and other chapters, is relevant also here and naturally many consumer disputes are dealt online and hence the reader should also consult the previous sections as consumer law and arbitration is very much relevant to the bulk of online arbitration.

9.6.1 How online dispute resolution works in practice

There are two distinct dimensions to online dispute resolution, of which arbitration is part, which also encompasses mediation, negotiation and others. As to the first dimension, whereas traditional dispute resolution takes place when the parties and the arbitrator/mediator are present at the same location and time (synchronous), online arbitration may be asynchronous, in the sense that all three actors need not participate in the

---

[39] France introduced Law No 2014-1081 (1 October 2014) on consumer class actions (not by means of arbitration) and then only through the medium of a limited number of consumer groups filing class actions on behalf of consumers.

[40] For an analysis of equity-based arbitration, see chapter 2 section 2.2.2.2.

[41] See generally, S. I. Strong, *Class, Mass and Collective Arbitration in National and International Law* (Oxford University Press, 2013).

relevant process (e.g. document exchange, hearings) at the same time. The obvious benefit is cost, because the parties and the arbitrator need not travel to a single location and spend time without earning profit from their ordinary work. Equally, they can focus on their case during times of the day that would ordinarily be considered out-of-office hours. In this manner, online arbitration significantly decreases the parties' expenses. This represents the first dimension of online arbitration, namely that the parties and the arbitrator may undertake the process while situated in distinct locations and under asynchronous time schedules.

The second dimension relates to the actual use of information and communication technology (ICT) as a facilitator of the proceedings or even as a substitute, in limited cases, for the judicial function typically assumed by arbitrators. As to the first of these, ICT systems have been developed which allow the parties to file documents online (and sort these on the basis of relevance, theme, or other), highlight pertinent points, bring up relevant forms as well as perform other functions the objective of which is to save the parties' time. However, there are situations where ICT is much more than a tool or a resource for the parties conducting arbitral proceedings online. In so-called automated negotiation, especially that which is known as double-blind bidding, the parties are not disputing liability but are otherwise focused on achieving an economic settlement in respect of an outstanding claim. They, therefore, feed the relevant software with up to three offers (the parties' bids are hidden), which then proceeds to settle the dispute either when the offers come within a predetermined range or a midpoint. The parties will have agreed from the outset the binding nature of the settlement produced by the software.[42]

It is obvious that online dispute resolution is particularly relevant to consumer disputes, particularly those concerning small claims.[43] The procedure may be operated by a platform (linked to a trade association or an arbitral institution) where the parties initially fill in a standard web-based claim form that directs them to appropriate processes and available remedies, followed by assisted negotiation and finally online arbitration.

---

[42] See generally, E. Katsh, Bringing Online Dispute Resolution to Virtual Worlds: Creating Processes through Code (2004) 49 *New York Law School Law Review* 271.

[43] See generally, P. Cortes, *Online Dispute Resolution for Consumers in the European Union* (Routledge, 2010).

9.6.2 The regulation of online arbitration

It should be stated from the outset that there exist no distinct instruments regulating online arbitration as distinct from offline arbitration. This is true even in respect of the recent Regulation on Online Dispute Resolution (ODR) for Consumer Disputes,[44] which is explained further below. It is assumed *a priori* that online arbitration is subject to the same legal principles as its offline counterpart. It differs from the latter because both the consent to arbitration and the proceedings themselves are conducted online (or a combination of both offline and online). Although online arbitration is increasingly being used between traders and other commercial actors, as has already been stated, it is also employed in B2C relationships and as a result the aforementioned principles of consumer law and consumer arbitration apply *mutatis mutandis*. There is an absence of a regulatory regime, at least in the sense of affirming that online arbitration produces the same legal effects as its offline counterpart, in the text of the 2013 Consumer ADR Directive.[45] What the Directive does, however, is to insist that relevant ADR institutions be transparent, fair, effective and independent and provide ample information to their end users, whether proceedings are conducted off or online. As will be explained in a subsequent section, such a requirement suggests that if online arbitration satisfies the due process rights of the parties, particularly the (weaker) consumer, there is no reason why the award cannot be assimilated for legal purposes with any other arbitral award.

In practice, there seem to be minor divergences from the traditional arbitration paradigm which give rise to a need for some uniformity, clarity and ultimately sensible regulation. First of all, unlike traditional arbitration where the true consent of the parties is of paramount importance – see the discussion above regarding the unfair nature of pre-dispute arbitration clauses in B2C contracts in Europe – where the arbitration agreement (or the arbitration clause) is entered online in the form of a standard document there may well be instances precluding free and true consent. Compulsion (to enter into an arbitration agreement) may be indirect in this context where the clause is an intrinsic part of the purchase or other online agreement and the parties cannot waive or exclude it, lest they are forced

---

[44] Regulation 524/2013/EU of the European Parliament and of the Council of 21 May 2013 on alternative dispute resolution for consumer disputes and amending Regulation (EC) No 2006/2004 and Directive 2009/22/EC (Directive on Consumer ADR) OJ L 165.

[45] Directive 2013/11 on Consumer ADR (21 May 2013), L 165/63.

to abandon the purchase or other activity altogether. By way of illustration, the Internet Corporation for Assigned Names and Numbers possesses a monopoly on the regulation and registration of domain names. Each domain name registrar is required to insert a particular ADR clause in its contract with customers (the so-called Uniform Domain Name Dispute Resolution Policy (UDPR), which is a quasi-arbitration procedure designed to resolve disputes between trademark owners and registrants). As a result, the entire industry is necessarily subject to this particular form of arbitration. If the matter were to be resolved according to the relevant consumer protection directives, such an ADR clause would be deemed well and truly unfair. Nonetheless, commentators suggest that in such cases consent may be viewed as having been (adequately) replaced by fairness.[46]

9.6.3 The seat in online arbitration

If online arbitration is, as is generally the case, conceived as falling within the regulatory remit of traditional arbitration, then the determination of the appropriate *lex arbitri* would pose no serious problems. Nonetheless, unlike offline arbitration where the seat coincides with the location the actual proceedings (in which all parties are present) are taking place, in the case of online arbitration the location of the parties may not necessarily coincide. The arbitration may be conducted in country X because that is the place where the arbitrator resides, whereas the parties may be situated in countries B and A. Traditional arbitration has always taken it for granted that the proceedings and the parties (including the arbitrator) are always together in the same location, or at least most of the time and that in any event the majority of their schedules coincide or that they have, at the very least, agreed on a juridical seat. The *process* has therefore always determined the seat of the arbitration and by extension the applicable *lex arbitri*.

With this in mind, it is not entirely clear which aspect of the process – if taken apart or deconstructed – overshadows the others.[47] Why, for example,

---

[46] G. Kaufmann-Kohler and T. Schultz, *Online Dispute Resolution: Challenges for Contemporary Justice* (Kluwer, 2004), 169.

[47] This has led several commentators to wonder whether online arbitration comes close to the (largely theoretical) model of so-called delocalised arbitration which is conducted in no particular geographical location and hence not subject to any particular *lex arbitri*. See Y. Hong-Lin and N. Motassem, Can Online Arbitration Exist within the Traditional Arbitration Framework? (2003) 20 *JOIA* 471.

should the seat be determined by reference to the arbitrator's residence (who may handle parts or all of it while in transit from one country to another) and not the residence of the parties, especially if this is the same? Given the absence of a predetermined solution to this conundrum, it is wise to follow the general rule laid out under Article 18(1) of the UNCITRAL Arbitration Rules, according to which:

If the parties have not previously agreed on the place of arbitration, the place of arbitration shall be determined by the arbitral tribunal having regard to the circumstances of the case. The award shall be deemed to have been made at the place of arbitration.

Of course, there are no guarantees that an award produced through an arbitral process which the parties or arbitrator agree as being seated in country X will be recognised by that country as a valid award, particularly if it is argued that only a minor part of the process was associated with country X. Equally, even if country X does give credence to such an award, there is no assurance that the courts of the countries where enforcement is sought will afford it recognition, either on the ground that it offends their public policy[48] or that it is not in accordance with the law of the seat (including the argument that country X is not the proper seat).[49] These are no doubt theoretical possibilities, yet it would make little sense for a court to set aside a transnational online award solely because the tribunal made use of the general rule enshrined in the UNCITRAL Rules.

9.6.4 Due process rights

Another problematic feature of online arbitration relates to the parties' due process rights. In traditional arbitration, the process must resemble in every respect its equivalent in judicial proceedings, unless of course the parties freely choose to exclude certain non-mandatory procedures for purposes of expediency (e.g. the parties may agree on a fast-track discovery process to save time). Given that the primary purpose of online arbitration is to speed up proceedings and at the same time reduce costs and overheads, some ADR institutions or arbitrators conducting online arbitrations may be inclined towards limiting due process guarantees. Although such an

---

[48] Art V(2)(b) 1958 New York Convention.   [49] Ibid., Art V(1)(d).

outcome would generally lead to the award's nullity, especially in B2C cases involving significant negotiating disparity between the parties, it may be remedied in situations of relevant parity where it is demonstrated that the parties truly and freely consented to the curtailment of one or more procedural (but not fundamental) guarantees with a view to achieving speed and affordability. By way of illustration, the parties may question witnesses by audio or remote technologies, but this must not be done in such a way as to deprive the parties of their equal rights or the ability to conduct a fair trial.

Fairness in online platform dispute resolution in B2C disputes

In *Alassini and others v Telecom Italia SpA*[50] the CJEU was faced with a question of whether Italian law, which required the parties to rely on a mandatory out-of-court dispute resolution procedure prior to initiating court proceedings, would affect the exercise of rights conferred on individuals under the Universal Service Directive.[51] The CJEU did not find that the mandatory settlement procedure at hand affected individual rights of the parties subject to such procedure. First, the CJEU held that the outcome of the online conciliation was not binding upon the parties and therefore it did not prejudice the parties' right to bring legal proceedings. Second, the CJEU stated that the use of mandatory conciliation did not contribute to a significant delay for initiating court proceedings by the parties. Third, the CJEU noted that since the online conciliation procedure was free of charge the parties were not exposed to any significant costs that such procedure could entail. Finally, the CJEU held that the consumers could not be obliged to participate in online-proceedings if their access to technology was limited. The general rule is therefore that the use of mandatory online out-of-court settlement procedures should not hinder the parties' right of access to justice should such procedures be accessible only by electronic means.

---

[50] *Alassini and others v Telecom Italia SpA*, Joined Cases C-317/08 to C-320/08, [2010] ECR I-2213.

[51] Directive 2002/22/EC of the European Parliament and of the Council of 7 March 2002 on universal service and users' rights relating to electronic communications networks and services (Universal Service Directive), OJ L 108 [2002].

9.6.5 The nature of online arbitration awards and problems with enforcement

In addition to other recognition and enforcement issues noted above, a distinctive feature of many disputes settled by online arbitration is that the award is not intended to be binding or final. The parties may choose that the award is only conditionally binding or that it is unilaterally binding,[52] or that it is not final or even binding upon them. Many legal systems, such as Article 58(1) of the English Arbitration Act, leave it to the discretion of the parties to decide whether an award should be considered (in their mutual relations) as final or binding. Nonetheless, if the parties decide that a particular award is not final, or indeed binding, this will not be enforceable under the terms of the 1958 New York Convention. One should note at this juncture that it is not only final judgments and arbitral awards that are executable. The outcome of mediation is equally binding and subject to execution under the terms of the EU Mediation Directive,[53] having thereafter the force of a court judgment.[54] However, unlike an award, a mediation outcome is not enforceable under the 1958 New York Convention, but is otherwise susceptible to recognition and enforcement under relevant treaties (or directives in the case of EU member states[55]) dealing with court judgments. In any event, we have already made reference several times in this book to 'awards' which the parties have no desire to enforce under the New York Convention despite, on many occasions, the large monetary sums involved. Excellent illustrations include the outcome of expert determination as well as *irrituale* awards under Italian law.

---

[52] Unilaterally binding online arbitration entails situations whereby only one party to arbitration proceedings is legally bound with either the arbitration agreement or the outcome of the proceedings. The non-binding and unilaterally binding forms of online arbitration are not considered as 'true' arbitration processes. This is partially so because the decisions issued in the course of non-binding or unilaterally binding arbitration proceedings are subject to *de novo* review by the courts upon a relevant application made by a party. In practice, however, the parties rarely challenge these somewhat informal decisions in courts.

[53] Directive 2008/52/EC of 21 May 2008 on certain aspects of mediation in civil and commercial matters, OJ L 136 (2008).

[54] Ibid., Art 6. Art 8(1) states that mediation procedures have no effect on applicable limitation and prescription periods and thus parties are not in danger of being subsequently denied access to judicial and arbitral determination. See also chapter 1 section 1.4.

[55] Council Regulation 44/2001 of 22 December 2000 on jurisdiction and the recognition and enforcement of judgments in civil and commercial matters [2001] OJ L 12. This Regulation is conveniently known as Brussels I and is examined in detail in chapter 2 section 2.2.1.

One recent international treaty, the 2005 UN Convention on the Use of Electronic Communications in International Contracts (ECC), facilitates the enforcement of arbitral awards rendered as a result of binding online arbitration processes. The ECC applies to cross-border electronic communications in business-to-business (B2B) contracts, where at least one party has its place of business in a contracting state.[56] The ECC is based on the principle of *functional equivalence* and recognises electronic communications as an equivalent of paper-based communications, as well as electronic authentication methods as an equivalent of handwritten signatures.[57] As such, the ECC eliminates many of the formal obstacles associated with the 1958 New York Convention, thus facilitating the use of electronic communications in arbitration. This means that arbitral awards issued in the course of a binding online arbitration can be enforced in courts either in the form of printed online awards that are hand-signed by the arbitrators and notified to the parties, or in the form of electronic documents signed and notified to the parties electronically.

Overall, it is not suggested that online arbitration is subject to, or otherwise regulated, by a regime that is distinct, wholly or partially, from traditional arbitration. In fact, commentators generally agree that online arbitration satisfies all the requirements that underpin traditional arbitration.[58] Even the ODR Consumer Regulation, which concerns the purchase of products and services offered online, does not depart from traditional arbitration. In order to facilitate the processing of disputes, the Regulation envisages an ODR platform, which is meant to filter complaints and suits to appropriate ADR fora. There is no question that such ADR, including arbitration, should in any way deviate from established procedures.

---

[56] Art 1 ECC.   [57] Art 9 ECC.

[58] E. Katsh and J. Rifkin, *Online Dispute Resolution: Resolving Conflicts in Cyberspace* (Jossey-Bass, 2001), 138; R. Morek, The Regulatory Framework for Online Dispute Resolution: A Critical View (2006) 38 *Toledo LR* 165.

Investment arbitration 10

10.1 Introduction

Investment arbitration is an altogether different beast from commercial arbitration and that is why it was left to the very end. In order to understand the mechanics of investment arbitration, which unlike its commercial counterpart is quintessentially a field of public international law, one must be familiar with substantive international investment law. At the end of the chapter we offer a brief analysis of the fundamental guarantees affordable to foreign investors with the aim of linking the discussion on investment arbitration with substantive investment law. Given the complexity of the subject matter, an effort has been made, first of all, to demonstrate in what sense investment arbitration proper is different from other forms of arbitration with an investment dimension.

We begin by identifying inter-state, investment-related, disputes which although peripheral to investor-state disputes allow us to comprehend the operation of diplomatic protection, which was the predecessor to investor-state arbitration. From there we turn to the nature and function of investor-state disputes and their particular sources and we explain in what manner investment arbitration is different from its commercial counterpart. Given that the focus of this chapter – and a book on arbitration more generally – is on the procedure of investment arbitration, we then examine particular jurisdictional aspects, namely: cause of action, the existence of an investment dispute and the meaning of the term 'investment'. Equally, we discuss the meaning of nationality of natural and legal persons and the place of such persons in BITs and other IIAs. Key to the understanding of the uniqueness of investment arbitration is its particular requirement of consent. Unlike commercial arbitration, where consent must be expressed unequivocally by all parties, investment arbitration does not always require the express simultaneous consent of the investor, particularly where consent to arbitration is achieved by a treaty (to which the investor is not a party) or by the host state's legislation.

At the close of the chapter we examine the nature of applicable law in investor-state arbitration. By this stage the reader will be familiar with the various requirements for investment arbitration and hence the discussion on investor guarantees will make ample sense. The chapter concludes with an analysis of discrete procedural matters that pertain to investment arbitration, such as the absence of a *lex arbitri* or indeed enforcement of awards under the 1958 New York Convention or other similar regional instruments.

10.2 The range of investment disputes

10.2.1 State versus state investment disputes

While states may *invest* in other states through commercial entities or mixed joint ventures incorporated in the host state, such forms of investment do not ordinarily fall within the existing international regime of foreign investment if the entities in question retain their sovereign character.[1] This international regime of foreign investment encompasses the relationship between a foreign investor and a (host) state other than the state of nationality of the investor. Investments undertaken by a state (retaining its sovereign character) in the territory of another state will be governed by general international law and the terms of the agreement (treaty or contract) between the two states. However, there are, at least, three alternative ways for states to be embroiled in an investment-related dispute with one another without any of them having entered into an investment as such.

The first involves the exercise of diplomatic protection by a state in favour of one of its nationals, whether a natural or legal person, that

---

[1] R. Dolzer and C. Schreuer, *Principles of International Investment Law* (Oxford University Press, 2nd edition, 2012), 250. In *CSOB v Slovakia*, Decision on Jurisdiction (24 May 1999), paras 15–27, although the claimant was a state bank, its activities were found to be of a commercial nature. This functional test brought CSOB's claim within the ICSID Convention on the ground that it was acting as a commercial actor; several BITs specifically provide that they apply also to government-controlled entities without any further qualifications. See Art I(1)(b) of the 1993 Moldova–USA BIT.

happens to be an investor in a third state. Traditionally, before the advent of independent *locus standi* before international tribunals, the plight of foreign investors against acts amounting to mistreatment (which also includes expropriation) by the host state could only be assumed by the investor's country of nationality. Unlike investment arbitration, which gives rise to an entitlement (for the investor) in addition to providing a forum (in the sense that the aggrieved party may pursue remedies before a structured system of investment tribunals), under international law diplomatic protection is neither an entitlement for investors nor a guarantee that the grievance will be hosted in a judicial or other forum. Rather, its exercise is discretional[2] by the state and, where the investor's claim is indeed pursued, the first step is usually negotiation and only rarely some form of inter-state litigation or arbitration. Even so, there is no doubt that states are fully entitled to assume claims pertaining to their nationals against other states[3] and that once assumed such claims pertain to the state which lawfully exercises them on behalf of its nationals.[4] Diplomatic protection is predicated on the bond of nationality between the investor and his home state,[5] but is subject to several practical and legal limitations. Since the codification of the Calvo doctrine (of non-intervention and prohibition of force to satisfy a private debt against sovereign states) in the 1907 Hague Convention respecting the Limitation of the Employment of Force for the Recovery of Contract Debts, the use of force to collect private debts is impermissible.[6] Moreover, given that diplomatic protection is discretionary, a state may not find it politically (or even financially) expedient to entertain the claim of one of its nationals,[7] in which case the investor (in the absence of a commercial arbitration clause) can only pursue

---

[2] *Barcelona Traction, Light and Power Co Ltd (Belgium v Spain)*, judgment (5 February 1970), [1970] ICJ Rep 44, para 79.

[3] *Mavrommatis Palestine Concessions (Greece v UK)*, [1924] PCIJ Rep, Ser A, No 2, at 12.

[4] In practice, this means that if the negotiation or litigation of the claim is successful the losing state must satisfy the winning state, which in turn will subsequently satisfy the investor.

[5] *Panevezys-Saldutiskis Railway (Estonia v Lithuania)* [1939] PCIJ Rep, Ser A/B, No 76, at 16.

[6] Art 1(1) of the Hague Convention. Funnily enough, para 2 of Art 1 provides that: 'This undertaking [not to use force] is not applicable when the debtor state refuses or neglects to reply to an offer of arbitration ... or fails to submit to the award.' See M. Waibel, *Sovereign Defaults before International Courts and Tribunals* (Cambridge University Press, 2011), 29–37.

[7] As a supplement to the 1907 Hague Contractual Debts Convention, among others, the 1907 Hague Peace Conference adopted the Convention for the Pacific Settlement of Disputes, chapter IV of which (Arts 37ff) sets out a comprehensive system of inter-state arbitration.

litigation in the courts of the host state, or perhaps before other national courts. These limitations are now self-evident but not so during the turn of the twentieth century. With the advent of investment arbitration in international affairs much of the utility of diplomatic protection has lost its appeal. Even so, there might well be a conflict between parallel diplomatic protection efforts and investment arbitration. In such eventuality, diplomatic protection may be curtailed by the operation of an applicable treaty, such as Article 27(1) of the 1965 Washington Convention on the Settlement of Investment Disputes between States and Nationals of Other States (ICSID Convention), which provides that the triggering of investment arbitration terminates diplomatic protection.[8]

The second situation of an inter-state investment-related dispute may arise from a difference regarding the interpretation or application of an investment treaty. In such a case, although the contention may be traced directly to an aggrieved investor the dispute ultimately impacts on broader vital investment interests of the plaintiff state (and perhaps other states). Article 64 of the ICSID Convention provides that where there is a dispute regarding interpretation or application this is to be submitted to the ICJ, which is competent to deal with legal disputes arising between states.[9] BITs also contain inter-state dispute settlement clauses to which the (state) parties may have recourse in the eventuality of interpretative or other disagreements.[10] Naturally, states routinely engage in inter-state arbitration before the ICJ or the PCA,[11] but such disputes typically concern sovereign differences that are unrelated to investment and hence are not discussed in this section.

The third type of inter-state investor-related disputes concern matters of a global public interest – beyond the contractual ambit of the parties – which require legislative and policy reform at international and state level. This is the case with the World Trade Organization (WTO) dispute resolution mechanism, which possesses a significant, yet indirect, investment

---

[8] Obviously, if the host state fails to satisfy the award, the investor's state of nationality may re-assume diplomatic protection in its favour.

[9] Such inter-state proceedings in the ICSID context are extremely rare and in any event they may not be used – or cannot have the effect – of suspending the parallel investor-state proceedings. See *Luchetti v Peru*, Award on Jurisdiction (7 February 2005), paras 7, 9.

[10] Art 37 US Model BIT (2012).

[11] See, for example, *Malaysia v Singapore*, PCA Award in the Matter of the Railway Land Arbitration (30 October 2014). The PCA's jurisdiction was established through a submission agreement adopted by the parties in 2012.

dimension. It is indirect in the sense that a state may have violated an obligation under a WTO agreement, by, for example, providing state aid or similar privileges to local and other select businesses but not all pertinent businesses, in which case foreign investors will have suffered a degree of discrimination. Three procedures exist, namely: a) arbitration under Article 25 of the Dispute Settlement Understanding (which is rarely applied); b) arbitration under Article 21 of Dispute Settlement Understanding, which concerns determinations by arbitrators as to whether a 'reasonable period of time' has passed within which states must comply with the rulings and recommendations of a WTO Dispute Settlement Body, which may lead to a binding decision; and finally c) the adjudication of complaints by WTO panels and the WTO Appellate Body. The procedures share many commonalities with classical arbitration and option (c) involves an inter-state complaint alleging a breach of an obligation under any of the WTO agreements. If the parties fail to resolve the dispute by consultation, a three-person panel is constituted, whose decision is subject to two forms of review: a) an appeal to the WTO Appellate Body, whose review power concerns law not facts; and b) panel and Appellate Body reports which are only binding when they are formally adopted by the Dispute Settlement Body.[12]

10.2.2 State versus international organisation investment disputes

Recently, investment-related disputes between states and particular inter-governmental organisations have surfaced at the international scene. The most obvious battleground is the EU contention that all investment-related matters of member states, including investment arbitration (and of course BITs) fall within the exclusive competence of the EU in accordance with Article 207 TFEU, which states that foreign direct investment is part of the EU's Common Commercial Policy, which, pursuant to Article 3(1)(e) TFEU, falls within the exclusive competence of the Union. This state of affairs has caused problems for countries that had concluded BITs prior to their accession to the EU. Proceedings against Austria, Sweden and Finland by the EU Commission concerned provisions in pre-accession BITs which afforded foreign investors the right to a free transfer of the capital

---

[12] See M. O. Matsushita, T. Schoenbaum, P. C. Mavroidis, and M. Hann *The World Trade Organization: Law, Practice and Policy* (Oxford University Press, 3rd edition, 2015), ch 4.

connected with their investment, without any restriction. The CJEU, following the Commission's recommendation, held that the unrestricted free transfer clauses contained in the pertinent BITs constituted a breach of EU law and thus ordered the three states to remove the incompatibility between their duties under EU law and their international obligations under the respective BITs.[13] Following the adoption of Regulation 1219/2012 (commonly referred to as 'Grandfathering Regulation') existing BITs remain binding on EU member states under public international law but will progressively be replaced by agreements adopted directly by the EU.[14]

A specific manifestation of this alleged incompatibility between international investment law and EU law in the field of arbitration has arisen by the EU Commission's contention that some awards in favour of investors are akin to unlawful state aid. Following an ICSID award in the *Micula* case in 2013, which is explained in another section, the Commission issued a suspension injunction to Romania (the losing party) pursuant to Article 11(1) of Council Regulation 659/1999, which requires member state to suspend any unlawful aid (essentially payment of the award) until the Commission has taken a decision on the compatibility of the aid with the common market.[15] Such an outcome is clearly in conflict with the customary obligation of states to adhere to their international obligations irrespective of their internal law, in accordance with Articles 27 and 46 of the VCLT.

10.2.3 Investor-state disputes

A dispute between a foreign investor and the host state involves either a breach of the parties' contractual obligations or a violation of a guarantee affordable to investors under international law. Although the two may well overlap (e.g. the breached contractual obligation concerns the availability of national treatment), violations of investment guarantees are always assessed under international law, whereas contractual obligations (other than investment guarantees) can be assessed also by reference to domestic

---

[13] Case 205/06 EU *Commission v Austria* [2009] ECR I-1301; Case C-249/06 EU *Commission v Sweden* [2009] ECR I-1335; Case C-118/07 EU *Commission v Finland* [2009] ECR I-10889.
[14] Regulation (EU) No 1219/2012 of the European Parliament and of the Council of 12 December 2012 establishing transitional arrangements for bilateral investment agreements between member states and third countries, OJ L 351.
[15] See also Case C-369/07, *EU Commission v Greece*, [2009] ECR I-5703.

law, if the parties' agreement so provides. If the *lex specialis* regime of investment arbitration did not exist, the investor would always be in a disadvantageous position against the host state and in case of violations by the latter the investor would be forced to submit to the jurisdiction of local courts (or exceptionally to the courts of third states),[16] commercial arbitration (assuming the host state would have consented to an arbitration agreement), other means of ADR, or diplomatic protection. Depending on the negotiating parity of the parties, the host state would no doubt endeavour that the investor agree to submit future disputes to the exclusive jurisdiction of the courts of the forum.

In most arbitration-hostile nations local courts are predictably biased in favour of government entities and hence the likelihood of a fair trial and a just outcome for investors is futile. In such situations, local courts are also more likely to accept immunity pleas by the state. The institution of international commercial arbitration proceedings is no doubt far more desirable, especially if the seat is in a third state. The host state's jurisdictional immunity plea would fail as would any defence arising from an impossibility to perform that is grounded in a conflicting obligation under domestic law.[17] Ultimately, the investor would have to recognise and enforce the award in more than one jurisdiction; perhaps (or almost certainly) also at the host state under the regime of the 1958 New York Convention. Nonetheless, it is doubtful that the host state will succumb to arbitrate future disputes with investors by means of arbitration if it can avoid such an obligation.

As a direct result of the vulnerability of foreign investors and at the same time based on the desire to eliminate diplomatic protection as the principal method for resolving investor-state disputes, the ICSID Convention was adopted. Prior to the ICSID Convention treaties of friendship, commerce and navigation were routinely adopted at bilateral level, an aim of which was to provide guarantees to investors, albeit

---

[16] In the absence of a BIT or IIA with explicit dispute resolution procedures, the DC District Court ruled that ordinarily the nationalisation of a foreign enterprise by the territorial state would not give rise to a civil suit before the courts of the investor because of the operation of act of state defence. This defence was, however, held to be inapplicable where the nationalisation was undertaken without a law or governmental action for the benefit of the local population. In the case at hand the local government abused its position as majority shareholder, thus depriving its actions of a public character. *McKesson v Iran*, 672 F 3d 1066 (DC Cir. 2012).

[17] See chapter 7 section 7.6.

friendship, commerce and navigation treaties did not confer an independent right (*locus standi*) on investors to pursue international proceedings against the host state. The ICSID Convention established an institutional forum (just like ordinary arbitral institutions such as the ICC and the LCIA) whereby investors may potentially acquire sufficient *locus standi* to initiate arbitral proceedings against host states. We use the phrase 'potentially', because the ICSID Convention itself provides a rather small margin of independent *locus standi* whereby investors can initiate claims against foreign states. More specifically, under Article 25 states may register their consent upon or after ratification regarding the list of government entities which they wish to be subjected to investment proceedings and/or the class or classes of disputes. Such declarations of consent by ICSID member states are rare and hence the utility of the Convention as an expression of consent to arbitration by host states is limited. However, the Convention establishes an institutional forum for resolution of investor-state disputes and encourages states to agree on other avenues for expressing their consent, whether at unilateral, bilateral, multilateral, or contractual level.

Motivated by the 1959 Abs-Shawcross Draft Convention on Investments Abroad and a little later the ICSID Convention, industrialised states began a process of entering into bilateral treaties for the promotion and protection of investments.[18] The drafters of BITs capitalised on the existence of the ICSID mechanism by inserting a clause whereby the host state agrees to resolve disputes with investors on the basis of ICSID-administered arbitration. By way of illustration, Article 10(4) of the 1993 Greece–China BIT provides that:

In the case both contracting parties have become members [to the ICSID Convention], disputes between either contracting party and the investor of the other contracting party under the first paragraph of this Article may by mutual consent be submitted for settlement by conciliation or arbitration to the International Centre for Settlement of Investment Disputes.

BITs are considered not only a landmark for the protection of investor guarantees, but more importantly also for the promotion of investor-state arbitration. The very existence of a BIT with a dispute resolution provision

---

[18] See C. Brown, *Commentaries on Selected Model Investment Treaties* (Oxford University Press, 2013), 7ff.

requiring arbitration (the majority of BITs have such a provision)[19] entails consent to arbitration between a host state and an investor even if the two have never agreed to submit their disputes to arbitration by means of a contract. This unique feature of BITs, namely the absence of express and contemporaneous consent by both host state and investor which is otherwise the hallmark of arbitration, has been described as arbitration without privity.[20] By late 2014, the United Nations Conference on Trade and Development (UNCTAD) had catalogued 2,805 BITs in its database, of which 2,103 were in force.[21]

The proliferation of BITs further led to the adoption of arbitration provisions (granting *locus standi* to investors) in the investment chapters of multilateral economic cooperation treaties and FTAs. By late 2014, UNCTAD had catalogued 345 IIAs in its database, of which 271 were in force. Of these, one may mention Chapter 11 of NAFTA, Part 3 and Article 26 of the 1994 ECT and Chapter 11 of the 2014 Australia–Korea FTA.

One of the unique features of the ICSID mechanism lies in the fact that consent to arbitration (irrespective of the manner by which consent is provided), unless otherwise stated, entails the exclusion of all other remedies.[22] Crucially, although one of the key aims of the Convention was to facilitate the inclusion of arbitration clauses in state contracts with investors, the *travaux* clearly intimate that consent to arbitration could be derived equally from domestic foreign investment laws that provided for such an eventuality. Consent by unilateral acts and private contract between host states and investors will be explored in subsequent sections.

10.3 Jurisdiction in investment arbitration

In order to conveniently map the various phases of investment arbitration the following subsections will proceed by examining the pertinent jurisdictional issues inherent in the process. The concept of jurisdiction

---

[19] Australia's Productivity Commission, in a report entitled *Bilateral and Regional Trade Agreements* (2010), Recommendation 4c, at xxxviii, suggested to the government that it should no longer insert investor-state dispute settlement clauses in BITs and IIAs by reference to the principles of 'no greater rights' for foreign investors and the government's 'right to regulate' to protect the public interest.

[20] J. Paulsson, Arbitration without Privity, (1995) 10 *ICSID Rev-FILJ* 232.

[21] See http://investmentpolicyhub.unctad.org/IIA   [22] Art 26 ICSID Convention.

encompasses the existence of a cause of action under an investment agreement, in addition to a valid legal dispute (*ratione materiae*); an examination as to whether the agreement covers the parties at hand (*ratione personae*); the existence of consent; as well as any preconditions that may need to be satisfied before submitting a dispute to arbitration, such as the exhaustion of local remedies.

10.3.1 Cause of action under an applicable agreement

Although consent to investment arbitration will be examined in a later subsection, it suffices here to point out that recourse to such arbitration is possible in three alternative ways, namely: a) by express stipulation in the contract between investor and host state; b) by express reference in a BIT or IIA; or c) by express reference in a law of the host state. As already explained, it was precisely because of the scarcity of investment arbitration provisions in host states' contractual arrangements with foreign investors that BITs have mushroomed.

The first port of call, therefore, is an assessment as to the existence of a BIT or IIA, in force[23] between the investor's country of nationality and the host state. Most recent BITs extend investor guarantees to investments in existence prior to their entry into force. By way of illustration, Article 8 of the Model German BIT (2008) provides that:

This treaty shall also apply to investments made prior to its entry into force by investors of either contracting state in the territory of the other contracting state consistent with the latter's legislation.

Even so, a distinction may have been stipulated in the pertinent provision between the application of a BIT to investments made prior to its entry into force from the extension of the BIT to breaches committed before this period. Although such a distinction is rare, it was duly noted by the tribunal in *Tecnicas Medioambientales Tecmed SA v Mexico*[24] because it was

---

[23] A treaty produces legal effects only upon ratification, not upon signature. The UNCTAD database contains many BITs and IIAs which have been signed by the parties but not yet ratified by national parliaments. Depending on the constitutional arrangements of each state, treaties must either be *transformed* (through implementing domestic legislation) or directly *incorporated* (without further action) into their domestic legal systems, save if they are not deemed self-executing.

[24] *Tecnicas Medioambientales Tecmed SA v Mexico*, Award (29 May 2003), paras 48, 53, 67.

expressly provided in the BIT. The investor must also ensure that despite the BIT's ratification by both states the BIT has not subsequently been denounced by any of them, as well as that its expiration period (if any) covers the particular investment.

While general international law allows states freely to denounce their treaty obligations, such a unilateral act only releases the state from its subsequent obligations, not from those it had assumed while it was still a party.[25] Several Latin American nations have entered into unilateral denunciations of BITs[26] as well as IIAs in recent years, as was the case with the denunciation of the ICSID Convention by Bolivia, Venezuela, Nicaragua and Ecuador (also known as *Alternativa Bolivariana*) through a series of successive denunciations from 2007 to 2012. Article 71 of the ICSID Convention, just like all treaties, establishes a six-month period starting from the date of denunciation during which the Convention is binding on the denouncing party. It is natural that during this period several investors fearing hostile actions by the host state, or those that had considered initiating arbitral proceedings, will rush to submit a notice of arbitration. Bolivia officially denounced the ICSID Convention on 31 October 2007. In *Euro Telecom International (ETI) v Bolivia*, which was submitted to ICSID arbitration but subsequently withdrawn, the question was whether the six-month period in Article 71 commenced from the date of the actual denunciation or whether it required an acceptance (additional to Bolivia's offer) by ICSID.[27] In the opinion of this author, unless otherwise stated in the treaty, a denunciation is effective from the moment it is communicated to the depository authority (in the case of multilateral treaties) or the other contracting state (as regards bilateral treaties).

10.3.2 The existence of an investment dispute

Investment arbitration under Article 25(1) of the ICSID Convention requires the existence of a 'legal dispute arising directly out of an investment'. Three issues are crucial in this regard, namely, whether a particular

---

[25] See Art 72 ICSID Convention.

[26] Venezuela, for example, denounced its BIT with the Netherlands in 2008.

[27] Two cases were submitted against Venezuela during the six-month period but in respect of breaches committed prior to its denunciation. See *Saint-Gobain Performance Plastics Europe v Venezuela*, and *Valle Verde Sociedad Financiera SL v Venezuela*, which were pending before ICSID tribunals by end of 2014.

undertaking constitutes an investment, if it qualifies as a dispute and if so whether the dispute in question is of a legal nature. The first issue is explored in the following section.

Both domestic and international courts and tribunals possess competence to determine legal disputes, as opposed to political and other disputes lacking a legal dimension. The existence or not of a legal dispute in investment arbitration, a sub-species of international law because of its grounding in treaties and customary law, is determined by rules of general international law. A dispute has long been defined by the Permanent Court of International Justice (PCIJ), the predecessor of the ICJ, as a 'disagreement on a point of law or fact, a conflict of legal views or interests' by the parties to a particular relationship.[28] Scholars often distinguish between a dispute and a *situation*, by noting that a situation involves a complex chain of events giving rise to several inter-linked disputes within a single context.[29] A dispute is of a legal nature, and hence within the jurisdiction of an investment or other tribunal, if it concerns a right or obligation as this arises from a valid source of law, whether domestic or international.[30] Sometimes appearances are deceptive. A national decentralisation policy is a seemingly political act, but where it culminates in the physical displacement of an investment from its original location and as a result causes financial and reputational damage it may be deemed as constituting a breach of the host state's obligations to the investor under a pertinent BIT or IIA, among others.

A particularity arises in the sphere of investment arbitration as will be demonstrated in more detail in a subsequent section. The dispute must not only be of a legal nature but it must moreover be directly linked to the investment in question.

10.3.3 Protected investment

One of the key features distinguishing commercial from investment arbitration is the precise nature of the activity under consideration. The

---

[28] *Mavrommatis Palestine Concessions* judgment, above note 3; equally, in *ATA v Jordan*, Award (18 May 2010), paras 98–120 and *Burlington Resources v Ecuador*, Decision on Jurisdiction (2 June 2010), paras 254ff.

[29] A Abass, *International Law* (Oxford University Press, 2012), 434.

[30] See *Suez, Sociedad General de Aguas de Barcelona SA and Interaguas Servicios Integrales del Agua SA v Argentina*, Decision on Jurisdiction (16 May 2006), para 37.

protections and guarantees contained in BITs and IIAs are only affordable to 'investments'.[31] Given that the contract between the investor and the host state will not specify whether the undertaking, or parts thereof, qualify as investments, this has to be assessed by reference to an applicable international agreement or the host state's domestic laws, if any. While foreign investment scholarship and case law suggest that the concept of 'investment' requires: a) some degree of permanence; b) assumption of risk; c) contribution to the host state's development; as well as d) substantial commitment, particularly through the infusion of capital and other assets[32] – thus excluding so-called portfolio investment (*Salini* criteria) – contemporary BITs no longer place such limitations to the characterisation of a particular activity as an investment. By way of illustration, Article 1(a) of the 2013 Netherlands–UAE BIT provides that the term investment means 'every kind of asset and more particularly, although not exclusively:'

i) movable and immovable property as well as any other rights *in rem* in respect of every kind of asset, such as mortgages, usufructs, liens and pledges;

ii) rights derived from shares, bonds, securities, placements, debentures, loans and other kinds of interests in companies and joint ventures;

iii) claims to money, to other assets or to any performance having an economic value;

iv) rights in the field of intellectual property, such as copyrights, trademarks, patents, industrial designs and other industrial property rights; technical processes, goodwill and know-how;

v) rights granted under public law or under contract and permit pursuant to law, excluding natural resources for the part of the UAE.

Any change in the form of an investment will not affect its qualification as an investment.[33]

---

[31] The term is not elaborated in the text of Art 25 of the ICSID Convention and this has given rise to the debate concerning the potentiality of conflict between party autonomy under BITs to define 'investments' from the underlying (historical) understanding of the same concept under the ICSID Convention.

[32] See, for example, *Salini Construttori SpA Italstrade SpA v Morocco*, Decision on Jurisdiction (23 July 2001), paras 52–3, which set out the four general criteria for assessing whether a particular undertaking qualifies as an investment; *Société Générale de Surveillance (SGS) v Pakistan*, Decision on Jurisdiction (6 August 2003), para 133; *Saipem v Bangladesh*, Decision on Jurisdiction (21 March 2007), paras 99–111; *Malaysian Historical Salvors v Malaysia*, Decision on Annulment (16 April 2009), paras 57–81.

[33] For other IIA definitions of a similar nature, see Art 1139 NAFTA and Art 1(6) ECT; but there are, of course, treaties that exclude portfolio investment, such as Art 45 of the 2000 European Free Trade Association (EFTA)–Mexico FTA.

The question that arises, therefore, is whether the four criteria identified in the *Salini* decision, and which are considered reflective of the ICSID Convention *travaux*, can at any time supersede party autonomy. This question would be irrelevant if arbitration was conducted outside the ICSID framework (solely on the basis of the BIT), i.e. ad hoc by reference to the UNCITRAL Arbitration Rules, under the PCA or under the Rules of the SCC. However, the situation is different where the regime of a BIT and that of ICSID intersect. The answer to the original question is a vexed one. The ICSID Convention places few limitations on the party autonomy of contracting states and in any event BITs and IIAs are *lex specialis*, which always supersedes the ICSID Convention's 'definition' of investment which is *lex generalis*.[34]

However, this conclusion has been qualified by the pronouncements of arbitral tribunals which have generally held that BITs may certainly define what constitutes an investment, but at the same time the scope of the same term in the ICSID Convention retains its autonomous character. In practice, investment tribunals first examine the parties' intention in the relevant BITs, thereafter considering the application of all or some of the *Salini* criteria where such intention was not clear or where there was a serious inconsistency or departure from the ICSID rationale. In *Fakes v Turkey*, the requirement that the investor contribute to the economic development of the host state was dismissed as being allegedly encompassed under Article 25 of the ICSID Convention.[35] In *Alpha v Ukraine* the investment concerned the renovation and operation of a hotel for which the investor secured a loan. The tribunal was content that a loan qualifies as an investment, finding that under the pertinent BIT an investment amounted to an asset 'for which an investor of one of the parties caused money or effort to

---

[34] On the interplay between *lex specialis* and *lex generalis* treaty regimes the ICJ has offered persuasive arguments. See *Legality of the Threat or Use of Nuclear Weapons*, Advisory Opinion, (1996) ICJ Rep 226, para 25. From a different perspective, ICSID and BITs may be viewed as constituting distinct legal regimes, the first establishing an arbitral forum whereas BITs are agreements to arbitrate. As a result the *lex specialis* versus *lex generalis* rule is not applicable between the two.

[35] *Fakes v Turkey*, Award (10 July 2010), para 111. Even so, the tribunal admitted that investments always encompass three objective criteria, namely contribution, duration and risk. See also *Phoenix v Czech Republic*, Award (15 April 2009), paras 85 and 114, where it was held that rather than contribution to the host state's financial development (which could not be objectively assessed) the investor was required to demonstrate a contribution to the local economy, where the investment is made in accordance with the laws of the host state.

be expended and from which a return or profit is expected in the territory of the other party'.[36] This should not always be stretched too far, particularly if the relevant BIT does not favour a broad understanding of investment. In *Joy Mining v Egypt*, the tribunal ruled that although bank guarantees could constitute an investment, this was not so where they were meant to serve solely as contingent liabilities in support of a sales contract.[37]

While no tribunal has ever intimated that the *Salini* criteria have no role to play in establishing whether a particular undertaking constitutes an investment (quite the contrary), the tribunal in *Abaclat v Argentina* emphasised the complementary nature of investment definitions in BITs and the (presumably customary) requirements of investments as reflected under the spirit of the ICSID Convention:

> Thus ... as it arises further from the wording of Article 1(1) and the aim of the BIT, the definition of investment provided in the BIT focuses on what is to be protected, i.e. the fruits and value generated by the investment, whilst the general definitions developed with regard to Article 25 ICSID Convention focus on the contributions, which constitute the investment and create the fruits and value. In summary, a certain value may only be protected if generated by a specific contribution, and vice versa contributions may only be protected to the extent they generate a certain value, which the investor may be deprived of.
>
> In other words, if it is to be applied, the 'double barreled' test does not mean that one definition, namely the definition provided by the two contracting parties in the BIT, has to fit into the other definition, namely the one deriving from the spirit of the ICSID Convention. Rather, it is the investment at stake that has to fit into both of these concepts, knowing that each of them focuses on another part of the investment.[38]

10.3.4 The directness of the dispute to the investment

An investment may turn out to be a complex operation. The establishment and operation of a power plant is simply the end product of an investment effort. Its formative stages may include securing necessary loans, processing

---

[36] *Alpha v Ukraine*, Award (8 November 2010), paras 273, 308. In *American Manufacturing Trading (AMT) Inc v Zaire*, Award (21 February 1997), para 24, it was held that the pertinent BIT encompassed a broad definition of portfolio investment, including participation in the share capital of a locally incorporated company.

[37] *Joy Mining Machinery Ltd v Egypt*, Award on Jurisdiction (6 August 2004), paras 44–7.

[38] *Abaclat and Others v Argentina*, Decision on Jurisdiction (4 August 2011), paras 350–1.

the relevant patents, negotiating permits and licences, buying equipment, hiring personnel and many others. If the concept of investment does not encompass activities undertaken prior to the time the investment becomes fully operational, or activities linked to the investment but not investments in themselves, the implication is that they will not be protected by the terms of the applicable investment treaties. No doubt, investors will find such an arrangement unappealing, particularly where the duration of the preparatory investment phases is substantial, or where the investment requires other independent, but inter-linked, action. The general rule was succinctly expressed in *CSOB v Slovakia*, which formulated the principle of the 'unity of an investment' as follows:

An investment is frequently a rather complex operation, composed of various interrelated transactions, each element of which, standing alone, might not in all cases qualify as an investment. Hence, a dispute that is brought before [ICSID] must be deemed to arise directly out of an investment even when it is based on a transaction which, standing alone, would not qualify as an investment under the Convention, provided that the particular transaction forms an integral part of an overall operation that qualifies as an investment.[39]

Of course, it goes without saying that each activity undertaken by the investor will have to be assessed on its own merits as to whether it is linked in any meaningful way to the principal investment. In *Mihaly v Sri Lanka*, the investor claimed that the expenses incurred during his ultimately unsuccessful negotiations with the host state amounted to an investment. The tribunal rejected the contention that each and every expense sustained in preparation for an investment qualifies as an investment as such.[40]

It is not only the inter-linked acts of the investor that may raise questions concerning their qualification as investments, but also those of the host state in relation to their impact on the investment as a whole. The general rule is that where a unilateral measure by the host state, whether in the form of a general or specialised policy or financial measure has a direct impact (e.g. produces financial or reputational harm) on a foreign investment on its territory in a manner that violates its obligations under an applicable treaty (a contract, or under its laws) such a measure engages the jurisdiction of an arbitral tribunal. The direct effect of the

---

[39] *CSOB v Slovakia*, Decision on Jurisdiction (24 May 1999), para 72.
[40] *Mihaly International Corp v Sri Lanka*, Award (15 March 2002), para 61.

act is crucial to triggering the jurisdiction of the tribunal. In *CMS v Argentina*, the tribunal, while noting that it possessed no authority to pass judgment over Argentina's general economic policy measures, upheld its jurisdiction to:

examine whether specific measures affecting the claimant's investment or measures of general economic policy having a direct bearing on such investment have been adopted in violation of legally binding commitments made to the investor in treaties, legislation or contracts.[41]

10.3.5 The parties to investment disputes

So far we have examined several aspects of jurisdiction, such as the existence of a legal dispute, the qualification of the undertaking as an investment and a legal cause of action. In the following subsections we shall discuss the jurisdiction *ratione personae* of investment tribunals. The fact that a tribunal possesses subject matter jurisdiction does not automatically entail jurisdiction over the parties at hand. No doubt, the competence of each arbitral tribunal differs depending on its statute and the agreement of the parties. Ad hoc investment arbitration under the UNCITRAL Arbitration Rules or the SCC is free from the jurisdictional limitations contained in the ICSID Convention, which require that the claimant's country of nationality and the respondent state be contracting parties. Our analysis will be predicated on the ICSID Convention as this constitutes the dominant forum for resolving investment disputes under applicable BITs and IIAs.

10.3.5.1 The host state as a party

It should be recalled that ICSID is a forum for the settlement of investment disputes, as well as a platform for the expression of state consent to investor-state arbitration. Investment disputes may be entertained by ICSID tribunals only if both the claimant's country of nationality and the respondent state are contracting parties to the ICSID Convention. Where any of the two is not a party to the ICSID Convention this does not mean that investment arbitration is not available to the investor. The BIT between one's country of nationality and the host state, if any, as well as

---

[41] *CMS v Argentina*, Decision on Jurisdiction (17 July 2003), para 33.

the parties' agreement, may well provide for investment arbitration in an arbitral forum other than ICSID. Moreover, the BIT or other agreement may envisage access to the ICSID Additional Facility, which is available to disputes where one of the parties (or its country of nationality) is not a party to the ICSID Convention.[42]

Article 25(1) of the ICSID Convention seems to rely on general international law in its Spartan qualification of the state as a party to investment proceedings. It simply provides for a 'contracting state (or any constituent subdivision or agency of a contracting state designated to the Centre by that state)'. States may act in their foreign relations in several ways: a) in their federal governmental capacity; b) through constituent states or municipalities (subdivisions); or c) by means of discrete physical or legal persons, such as corporations, irrespective of whether they are incorporated on its territory or possess its nationality (agents).[43] In the case of ICSID, whereas a contracting state is deemed to have given its consent to arbitration upon becoming a party in respect of disputes relating to acts attributed to the federal government, paragraph 3 of Article 25 requires that consent by a constituent subdivision and an agent be specifically approved by the federal state. Such designations have been sparse in ICSID practice, but where they have been provided and the state invoked their absence, ICSID tribunals have declined jurisdiction.[44]

Although the mechanics of state consent to the specific regime of ICSID arbitration will be investigated in a subsequent section, it suffices to note

---

[42] See ICSID Additional Facility Rules, particularly Arts 2(b) and 4(3) which determine jurisdiction. The Additional Facility mechanism has proven significant for NAFTA-related disputes because Mexico and Canada are not parties to the ICSID Convention. Art 1122(2) of NAFTA, as well as Arts 17–18 of the 1994 Mexico–Colombia–Venezuela FTA, among many other IIAs, provides for access to Additional Facility Arbitration. Given that this process is outside the ICSID Convention, awards can only be enforced under the 1958 New York Convention or other regional treaties.

[43] A typical example concerns so-called state unitary enterprises, a corporate model prevalent during Soviet rule and currently in existence in all post-Soviet republics. The fundamental characteristic of a state unitary enterprise is that it is under so-called 'operative management'. This effectively means that the assets which make up its capital are not under the ownership of the legal person of the state unitary enterprise, but are instead owned by the state in one form or another. See I. Bantekas, The Legal Nature of State Unitary Enterprises under Uzbek Corporate Law, (2013) 27 *AJCL* 346.

[44] *Cable Television v St Kitts and Nevis*, Award (13 January 1997).

here that as a matter of general international law the incorporation of an arbitration clause in an agreement between a foreign investor and an agent or subdivision of a state is binding, even if the federal government had not provided its consent. That such consent was required under the domestic law of the state is irrelevant,[45] unless the investor was acting in bad faith. As the ICJ emphasised in the *LaGrand* case, although the separation of powers and competences between federal and state courts and authorities is a matter of domestic law, the effect of said separation on a country's international obligations is solely a matter of international law.[46] An important point should be highlighted at this juncture, although it may already be clear. If an agreement between a state entity and an investor envisages arbitration (and the dispute concerns an investment) but the state in question, although a party to the ICSID Convention, has not provided its consent by a declaration to ICSID or is not party to an applicable BIT, ICSID tribunals cannot assume jurisdiction. In such a case, however, the investor may validly submit the dispute to other institutional fora, particularly institutions ordinarily dealing with commercial disputes such as the ICC, assuming the arbitration clause is not inoperable or ineffective.

10.3.5.2 The foreign investor as a party

In order for an ICSID tribunal to assume jurisdiction over an investment dispute under Article 25(1)(a) of the ICSID Convention, the investor must: a) be a national of a state other than the host state; b) be a national of a state that is a party to the ICSID Convention and the same is true of course for the host state; and c) the investor must retain the nationality of an ICSID state party at the time both state parties consent to ICSID arbitration as well as the date when the request for arbitration is registered. The investor's nationality is therefore of immense importance and is not simply discharged by a mere certificate of nationality, given that a natural person may have more than one nationality. Equally, the 'nationality' of a legal person may vary depending on where and how it was incorporated, the place of its effective seat and the makeup of its shareholders. In the case of multinational corporations such questions are even more complicated.

---

[45] Art 4(1) ILC Articles on State Responsibility.
[46] *LaGrand (Germany v USA)*, [2001] ICJ Rep 466, para 139.

10.4 Nationality of claims and claimant

10.4.1 Nationality of natural persons

Although investment arbitration usually involves legal persons, several cases have concerned claims brought by physical persons. In many of these cases the respondent state argued that the claimant's alleged nationality was ineffective, or otherwise lacked a genuine link, and that therefore the claimant was not covered by a particular BIT or the ICSID Convention to which his alleged country of nationality was a party. This reference to an effective nationality traces its roots from the *Nottebohm* case decided by the ICJ in the 1950s, at a time when the politics of nationality were highly contentious in international affairs. The ICJ had ruled in the *Nottebohm* case that although states are free to confer their nationality on any person, the legal effects of such conferral were to be assessed only by reference to international law.[47]

Investment tribunals have shown a reluctance to apply the *Nottebohm* test (albeit intimating that such a test may be relevant in exceptional circumstances) involving a genuine link for two reasons; firstly because it was originally adopted to deal with diplomatic protection and secondly because it is not required in the ICSID Convention, nor indeed in most BITs.[48] In *Champion Trading v Egypt*, three of the claimants possessed dual Egyptian and US citizenship. The tribunal was disinclined to be drawn into a discussion as to the effectiveness of the claimants' US nationality, emphasising that such a criterion was not required under the ICSID framework.[49] In general, investment tribunals faced with investors enjoying dual nationality have not resorted to prioritising one over the other on the basis of an effective nationality or dominance test, as did the ICJ in the *Nottebohm* case. Rather, they are content to accept both nationalities as effective and apply the one encompassed under the BIT invoked by the claimant.[50] Such a stance has been followed by tribunals even in situations where the claimant does not reside (habitually or

---

[47] *Nottebohm* (*Liechtenstein v Guatemala*), [1955] ICJ Rep 4.

[48] In US BIT practice, as is the case with Art I(c) of the US–Bolivia BIT, the determination of nationality is based on the law of each state. In the Letter of Submittal to Congress it was further explained that 'under US law the term national is broader than the term citizen. For example, a native of American Samoa is a national but not a citizen.'

[49] *Champion Trading v Egypt*, Decision on Jurisdiction (21 October 2003), 16–17.

[50] *Olguin v Paraguay*, Award (26 July 2001), paras 60–2.

ordinarily) in its country of nationality.[51] These decisions demonstrate a clear deference to the sovereign power of states to confer nationality.

10.4.2 Nationality of corporations

The nationality of legal persons[52] or corporations is an altogether more complex affair as compared to the nationality of natural persons. Investment tribunals have been guided in this respect not so much from general international law, which lacks detail any way,[53] but from the scope of pertinent provisions in BITs and IIAs. One of the two following options is generally posited by these treaties, namely: the country under whose laws the legal person was incorporated or the country in whose seat, which may differ from the country of incorporation, it is effectively managed. The incorporation option is usually addressed in language that allows each state to prescribe the pertinent formalities under its laws. Article I(b) of the US–Bolivia BIT provides that: "'company of a party' means a company constituted or organized under the laws of that party'.[54]

The incorporation option in a BIT overrides other irregularities associated with the legal person, such as the subsequent acquisition of its majority shares by nationals of other states. This arrangement protects the investment and the underlying legal person from subsequent changes to its future status, particularly its shareholding. In *Tokios Tokeles v Ukraine*, the claimant company was incorporated in Lithuania, albeit its shareholders

---

[51] *Feldman v Mexico*, NAFTA Tribunal Decision on Jurisdiction (6 December 2000), para 30; *Micula and Others v Romania*, Decision on Jurisdiction and Admissibility (24 September 2008), para 103. It should be noted that habitual residence as opposed to nationality is the sole jurisdictional requirement in other conflict of laws instruments, such as Council Regulation (EC) 2201/2003 of 27 November 2003, [2003] OJ L 338/1, concerning jurisdiction and the recognition and enforcement of judgments in matrimonial matters and matters of parental responsibility, repealing Regulation 1347/2000 [Brussels II].

[52] Several BITs, particularly those entered into by the USA in the 1990s encompass entities that are not legal persons. Art I(a) of the US–Bolivia BIT covers entities 'whether or not for profit ... [including] a corporation, trust, partnership, sole partnership, branch, joint venture, association, or other organization'.

[53] The ICJ has made this clear in the *Diallo* case (*Guinea v Democratic Republic of Congo*), Judgment (Preliminary Objections) (24 May 2007) [2007] ICJ Rep 582, paras 61 and 87ff, where it held that under general international law, at least, a shareholder's country of nationality cannot exercise diplomatic protection on his behalf in respect of a company incorporated in a different country. The ICJ noted, however, that the *lex specialis* regime of BITs and IIAs provided more concrete solutions in favour of such shareholders.

[54] See equally Art 1(7)(a)(ii) ECT.

were 99 per cent Ukrainian nationals. Although Ukraine argued that the composition of the shareholders necessitated a finding that the company was effectively Ukrainian, the Ukraine–Lithuania BIT clearly provided that a Lithuanian investor included any entity established in Lithuania under that country's laws. The majority of the tribunal had no hesitation to enforce the BIT, declaring itself incompetent to pierce the company's corporate veil.[55]

The seat option effectively relates to the legal person's principal place of business or management. The 2009 Germany–Pakistan BIT provides in Article I(2)(a) that in respect of Germany an investor comprises:

any juridical person as well as any commercial or other company or association with or without legal personality having its seat in the territory of the Federal Republic of Germany, irrespective of whether or not its activities are directed at profit.

BIT practice also reveals a combination of the two options. This is achieved in two ways. Firstly, as is the case with Article I(2)(b) of the 2009 Germany–Pakistan BIT, the nationality of Pakistani legal persons is determined by reference to their place of incorporation, whereas that of German companies is assessed on the basis of their seat. The second practice involves a combination of both incorporation and effective seat, both of which are posited as simultaneous requirements. Article I(2) of the 1987 ASEAN Agreement for the Promotion and Protection of Investments provides that:

The term 'company' of a contracting party shall mean a corporation, partnership or business association, incorporated or constituted under the laws in force in the territory of any contracting party wherein the place of effective management is situated.

Some treaties go beyond effective management and require a *controlling interest* in the company in order to avoid the pitfalls inherent in the incorporation option. Article I(1)(a) of the Moldova–USA BIT emphasises that an 'investment' means every kind of investment in the territory of each party that is moreover 'owned or controlled directly or indirectly by nationals or companies of the other party'.[56] An assessment as to the existence of a controlling interest raises questions of fact. In *Mobil v Venezuela*, the

---

[55] *Tokios Tokeles v Ukraine*, Decision on Jurisdiction (29 April 2004), paras 21ff. See also *Saluka v Czech Republic*, Partial Award (17 March 2006), para 241.

[56] See references to this provision in *Link Trading v Moldova*, Award (18 April 2002), para 54.

pertinent investment had been made in Venezuela by the Dutch company Mobil through two of its subsidiaries in the USA and the Bahamas. Mobil possessed a controlling interest in both subsidiaries by reason of the fact that it owned them fully. The issue was crucial because Article 1(b) of the Netherlands–Venezuela BIT requires a controlling interest. The tribunal had no problem conceding that the investment was wholly controlled by Mobil.[57] In the case at hand, the tribunal relied on a Protocol appended to the BIT which quantified control on the basis of capital ownership percentages.

A variant to the controlling interest criterion which certainly satisfies the customary demands of duration and risk in the undertaking of an investment concerns the requirement of a *predominant or substantial interest* on the part of the investor. Where this applies it is not sufficient that the investor simply (and actually) control the investment, but that real economic activities in the host state are taking place. This ensures, among others, that the investment provides meaningful employment to the local workforce, import of know-how and enhances the secondary economy, among others. Article I(b) of the Egypt–USA BIT expressly requires such a 'substantial interest'.

In addition to a predominant or substantial interest clause the contracting parties to a BIT or IIA may insert a so-called *denial of benefits* clause, the purpose of which is to deny some or all of the benefits of the treaty to a company incorporated in one of the contracting states but with no economic connection to the country of incorporation. Article I(2) of the 1993 Moldova–USA BIT stipulates that:

Each party reserves the right to deny to any company the advantages of this treaty if nationals of any third country control such company and, in the case of a company of the other party, that company has no substantial business activities in the territory of the other party or is controlled by nationals of a third country with which the denying party does not maintain normal economic relations.[58]

As the ECT tribunal in *AMTO v Ukraine* succinctly pointed out, the purpose of benefits denial clauses is to exclude from the protection of BITs and IIAs (in this case the ECT) investors that have adopted a nationality of convenience. The word 'substantial' was construed by the same tribunal as referring to substance and not merely to form or quantity.[59]

---

[57] *Mobil v Venezuela*, Decision on Jurisdiction (10 June 2010), para 160.
[58] See also Art 17(1) ECT.   [59] *AMTO v Ukraine*, Award (26 March 2008), para 69.

Several states dismiss the above corporate models for the purposes of some or all types of foreign investment undertaken in their territory. As a result, they may require that all or some investments be locally incorporated and managed by a company seated there. This may be out of fear that the investor will dissipate its revenues in foreign subsidiaries and thus avoid paying appropriate taxes; of course, there are other reasons. Locally incorporated companies are common in large and long-term infrastructure projects, including oil and gas extraction and distribution. This model naturally raises doubts about the protection of the foreign investors participating in the investment and whether the 'forced' nationality of the company prevents them from enjoying the protection of a BIT or IIA to which they would ordinarily have recourse. Article 25(2)(b) of the ICSID Convention resolves this matter by providing that the term 'national of another contracting state' *also* means:

> any juridical person which had the nationality of the contracting state party to the dispute on that date and which, because of foreign control, the parties have agreed should be treated as a national of another contracting state for the purposes of this Convention.

Hence, locally incorporated companies subject to (actual) foreign control[60] will be treated as companies of another state party under the ICSID Convention. Article 25(2)(b), however, requires some form of prior agreement so as to leave no room for doubt that such companies can be treated as foreign as regards the host state. In practice, this is usually achieved through explicit or implicit provisions in BITs and IIAs, the ratification of which by both parties operates as both an offer and acceptance, or even as a form of estoppel, thereby satisfying the requirement as to the existence of a prior agreement.[61]

10.4.3 Nationality of shareholders

It is no wonder that the aforementioned carve outs have given rise to questions about the nationality of an investment on the basis solely of the citizenship of its shareholders.[62] As already mentioned, the ICJ made it

---

[60] *Millicom v Senegal*, Decision on Jurisdiction (16 July 2010), para 109.
[61] See *Micula and Others v Romania*, Decision on Jurisdiction and Admissibility (24 September 2008), paras 107–16.
[62] See B. Juratowitch, Diplomatic Protection of Shareholders, (2010) 81 *BYIL* 281.

clear in the *Diallo* case that general international law provides no right of diplomatic protection to a country's externally-based shareholders. This limitation does not exist in international investment law, however, on account of the mechanism of 'foreign control' as identified in Article 25(2)(b) of ICSID Convention and also because many BITs and IIAs explicitly provide for an independent right of action on the part of shareholders, both majority and minority.

In such situations, as Dolzer and Schreuer point out, it is not the locally incorporated company that is treated as an investor but the actual participation in the company under consideration.[63] Most contemporary BITs define investments broadly as also encompassing shares or stocks or other interests in a company.[64] As a result, it was not a far leap for the tribunal in *CMS v Argentina* to dismiss the respondent's claim that CMS as a minority shareholder to an investment in Argentina did not possess *locus standi* under the US–Argentina BIT.[65] This principle has also been extended to cases of indirect shareholding through intermediary companies.[66]

10.5 Consent to investment arbitration

Consent to investment arbitration may be exhibited in three independent ways, namely: a) by express stipulation in a contract between the host state and the foreign investor; b) by reference to a provision in the law (usually a foreign investment-related law) of the host state; and c) by express or implicit stipulation in a BIT or IIA, provided that the nationality (and nature of the undertaking as an investment) requirements, as explained above, are met.

10.5.1 Consent by contract

Just like commercial arbitration, the parties, that is, the investor and the host state, may insert an (investment) arbitration clause in their main contract in respect of future disputes, or alternatively, although rare, they

---

[63] Dolzer and Schreuer, above note 1, at 57.
[64] See, for example, the definition of 'investment' in Art 1 of the 2012 US Model BIT.
[65] *CMS v Argentina*, Decision on Jurisdiction (17 July 2003), para 48.
[66] See *Enron v Argentina*, Decision on Jurisdiction (11 January 2004), paras 41ff; *Cemex v Venezuela*, Decision on Jurisdiction (30 December 2010), paras 141ff.

can draft a *compromis* in order to submit to arbitration an existing dispute. In practice, few investors enter into a direct agreement with the host state, unless the latter is also a contracting party to the intended investment, as is typically the case with concessions or joint ventures involving public works. An agreement between a foreign investor and a state should be understood in the broad contractual sense, as involving an offer and a subsequent consideration (or acceptance).[67] In this sense, an application made by the investor, which also contains an agreement to arbitrate that is approved by the host state suffices as evidence of consent by both parties.[68]

The similarities with contract-based commercial arbitration are many, but we shall limit ourselves here to one of significance. In chapter 3 we discussed consent to arbitration on the basis of so-called *incorporation by reference*, whereby the absence of consent to arbitrate in an agreement may be remedied by the existence of such consent in other agreements between the same parties and concerning the same subject matter, especially where all the agreements are intra-referential.[69] Although the context is certainly different in investment arbitration, the rationale of the concept has been accepted by investment tribunals and in *CSOB v Slovakia*, as we have already explained, the principle of the 'unity of an investment' was highlighted.[70] As a result, incorporation by reference, as a form of consent, has been accepted by investment tribunals, provided that the scope of the arbitration clause is such that it encompasses other related agreements between the investor and the host state.[71]

A particularly thorny issue arises in situations where the parties' concession or other contract provides for recourse to local courts or local commercial arbitration but the pertinent BIT or IIA envisages access to investment arbitration. Investment tribunals have tackled this matter through pragmatism and without classifying investment treaties as hierarchically superior

---

[67] Such agreements must be construed in accordance with their applicable domestic laws, unless the parties' choice of law clause provides for a supra-national governing law, such as *lex mercatoria* or international law.

[68] *Amco v Indonesia*, Decision on Jurisdiction (25 September 1983), para 10.

[69] See chapter 3 section 3.3.4. From a comparative perspective it is interesting to note that French courts, as a particular species of conduct-based estoppel assume a 'common intent to arbitrate' where one of the parties has by its silence accepted arbitration, particularly where there is a history of consistent and repeated practice by the parties to arbitrate in successive contracts, even if the disputed contract in question contains no arbitration clause.

[70] *CSOB v Slovakia*, Decision on Jurisdiction (24 May 1999), para 72.

[71] See *Duke Energy v Peru*, Decision on Jurisdiction (1 February 2006), paras 119ff.

to private contracts, as the two constitute clearly distinguishable legal regimes. Their approach has focused on discerning between claims arising from the treaty and those arising from the parties' contract.[72] Treaty-based claims (e.g. expropriation) may be submitted to arbitration, whereas other claims arising from contract can only be submitted to local courts or local commercial arbitration. An exception to this dichotomy concerns so-called umbrella clauses, which although casually phrased as an obligation in BITs for host states to observe and respect all their obligations related to investments, have in fact been construed by some tribunals as elevating a contract breach to a treaty breach.[73]

10.5.2 Consent through the host state's legislation

Host states may express their consent to investment arbitration in respect of future disputes with foreign investors on the basis of national legislation. The pertinent law may limit arbitration to a particular class of investors or require the exhaustion of other remedies. It goes without saying that one should construe such laws carefully if one aims to rely on them as an expression of the host country's consent to investment arbitration. The promulgation of domestic laws constitutes unilateral acts that may bind the state in its international relations. Article 1 of the International Law Commission's (ILC's) Guiding Principles applicable to Unilateral Declarations of States iterates the customary rule whereby:

Declarations publicly made and manifesting the will to be bound may have the effect of creating legal obligations. When the conditions for this are met, the binding character of such declarations is based on good faith; states concerned

---

[72] See, for example, *CMS v Argentina*, Decision on Jurisdiction (17 July 2003), paras 70–6; *Frapport v Philippines*, Award (16 August 2007), paras 388–91; *Société Générale de Surveillance (SGS) v Paraguay*, Award (10 February 2012), paras 96–109.

[73] In *SGS v Pakistan*, Decision on Jurisdiction (6 August 2003), paras 166–7, a narrow interpretation was adopted, whereas in *SGS v Philippines*, Decision on Jurisdiction (29 January 2004), para 119, the tribunal upheld a broad interpretation of umbrella clauses. Since then, pertinent awards have largely endorsed the broad interpretation subject to several variations. In *EDF International SA, SAUR International SA and Leon Participaciones Argentinas SA v Argentina*, Award (11 June 2012), for example, a breach of contract between an Argentine province and an investor was found to be a breach of the umbrella clause in the BIT. In *Bureau Veritas, Inspection, Valuation, Assessment and Control, BIVAC BV v Republic of Paraguay*, Decision on Jurisdiction (9 October 2012), para 290, the tribunal held that if Paraguay did not comply with the decision of its courts, the umbrella clause claim 'might then become admissible'.

may then take them into consideration and rely on them; such states are entitled to require that such obligations be respected.

Naturally, a unilateral declaration creates an obligation on the state – in this case, to submit to investment arbitration – if it gives rise to a legitimate expectation on the part of the investor. Such a legitimate expectation must be clearly established and this is principally achieved by a firm acceptance of the state's standing offer by the investor. An acceptance is valid only so long as the offer is made available.[74] An investor may demonstrate acceptance by initiating arbitral proceedings or by simply making a formal declaration of acceptance, subject to any sensible formalities in the host state, which will usually be specified in the pertinent legislation.[75] Once an offer is accepted, the state cannot unilaterally revoke it. In *Telsim and Rumeli*, Kazakhstan had repealed its 1994 investment law in 2003, but Article 6(1) of the law provided a stabilisation clause for a period of ten years from the commencement of an investment; for the claimants at hand this was 1999. Article 27 of the law expressly permitted ICSID arbitration and by filing their request for arbitration within the aforementioned ten-year period the claimants were validly exercising their entitlement under the unilateral offer made by the Kazakh foreign investment law.[76] In a subsequent case concerning the same foreign investment law the tribunal reached a diametrically different conclusion. It held that:

The arbitration clause in the [investment law] calls for the right to arbitration to be perfected by the investor's written consent, not by an investment or by a claim arising. In other words, the claimant had no 'accrued right' to arbitration until it accepted in writing the offer of arbitration set forth in the [investment law].[77]

While in many cases the host state's standing offer will be explicit, or at best implicit, in others the alleged provision may be confusing or conditional upon other measures which the parties must satisfy. Article 22 of the 1999 Venezuelan Law for the Promotion and Protection of Investments, which was relied on by the claimant in *Mobil v Venezuela*, provided that:

---

[74] States may validly rescind their laws, in which case the unilateral offer ceases to produce any effects from the date rescinded.

[75] Alternatively, the acceptance of the host state's standing offer by the investor may be viewed as an agreement (a contract under domestic law) in its own right.

[76] *Rumeli Telekom AS and Telsim Mobil Telekomikasyon Hizmetleri AS v Kazakhstan*, Award (29 July 2008), paras 333–6.

[77] *Ruby Roz Agricol LLP v Kazakhstan*, (UNCITRAL Rules) Award on Jurisdiction (1 August 2013), para 156.

Disputes arising between an international investor whose country of origin has in effect with Venezuela a treaty or agreement on the promotion and protection of investments, or disputes to which the provisions of the Convention establishing the Multilateral Investment Guarantee Agency (MIGA) or [ICSID] are applicable, shall be submitted to international arbitration according to the terms of the respective treaty or agreement, if it so provides, without prejudice to the possibility of making use, when appropriate, of the dispute resolution means provided for under the Venezuelan legislation in effect.

Although this provision does seemingly make an offer to investors, the final part of the sentence introduces two qualifications, namely, 'without prejudice' to other means of dispute resolution under local law and the affirmation of investment arbitration in pertinent agreements to which Venezuela is a party. Where no conflict arises between the 1999 Law's standing offer and the aforementioned qualifications, there can be no dispute as to the clarity of the standing offer in Article 22. ICSID tribunals assessing this clause, however, found a divergence between Venezuela's BIT practice and its offer of consent in Article 22 and hence declined to uphold jurisdiction on this basis.[78] The tribunal in *Cemex v Venezuela* emphasised that:

if it had been the intention of Venezuela to give its advance consent to ICSID arbitration in general, it would have been easy for the drafters of Article 22 to express that intention clearly [and] that such an intention hav[ing] not been established ... it cannot conclude from the obscure and ambiguous text of Article 22 that Venezuela, in adopting the 1999 Investment Law, consented unilaterally to ICSID arbitration for all disputes covered by the ICSID Convention in a general manner.[79]

10.5.3 Consent through BITs and IIAs: exhaustion of local remedies and fork-in-the-road issues

The most prevalent form of consent in international investment arbitration is predicated on BITs and IIAs. As we have already explained the fundamental drive underlying the proliferation of BITs was precisely this, given

---

[78] *Mobil v Venezuela*, Decision on Jurisdiction (10 June 2010), paras 67–140; *Cemex v Venezuela*, Decision on Jurisdiction (30 December 2010), paras 63–139; and *Brandes v Venezuela*, Award (2 August 2011), paras 79–118.

[79] *Cemex v Venezuela*, Decision on Jurisdiction (30 December 2010), paras 138–9.

the general reluctance of host states to consent on the basis of contract or national legislation. Unlike inter-state dispute resolution clauses in BITs and IIAs, which are of a contractual nature, the dispute resolution clauses relating to the relations of the host state and the investor constitute a unilateral act just like the standing offer in domestic legislation. The same principles therefore apply *mutatis mutandis*. Despite the fact that the investor is not a party to the BIT or IIA, the unilateral act contained in the dispute resolution clause creates legal effects in favour of the investor. The investor must accept the offer of the host state. This may be achieved either by an explicit acceptance addressed to the host state in respect of future disputes or simply through the initiation of arbitral proceedings.

It is not the case that each and every dispute resolution clause invites investors to arbitration. Some may be clear on this option, whereas others may require the exhaustion of other remedies or render arbitration a supplementary, but not the first, alternative available to investors. Article 13 of the 1995 Australia–Argentina BIT states that:

1. Any dispute which arises between a Contracting Party and an investor of the other Contracting Party relating to an investment shall, if possible, be settled amicably. If the dispute cannot so be settled, it may be submitted, upon request of the investor, either to:
   (a) the competent tribunal of the contracting party which has admitted the investment; or
   (b) international arbitration in accordance with paragraph 3 of this Article.
2. Where an investor has submitted a dispute to the aforementioned competent tribunal of the contracting party which has admitted the investment or to international arbitration in accordance with paragraph 3 of this Article, this choice shall be final.
3. In the case of international arbitration, the dispute shall be submitted, at the investor's choice, either:
   (a) to [ICSID], provided that the contracting parties are both parties to the [ICSID] Convention; or
   (b) to an arbitration tribunal set up from case to case in accordance with the Arbitration Rules of [UNCITRAL]; or
   (c) to any other arbitration institution, or in accordance with any other arbitration rules, as may be mutually agreed between the parties to the dispute.

Two issues are of significance here; firstly, whether the parties are required to first settle their difference amicably – or persist through a prescribed lengthy cooling off or negotiating period before initiating arbitral proceedings – or whether alternatively they can dispense with such waiting periods if they are wholly unlikely to provide any resolution to the dispute. While the Australia–Argentina BIT does not impose (but rather suggests) amicable settlement through ADR processes, other treaties may impose an altogether different rule. The investor has no other choice but to adhere to the terms of the treaty. The only option is to invoke the MFN clause in the BIT, if any, thereby demanding that the exhaustion of ADR processes be dismissed, if such a waiver exists in other BITs to which the host state is a party. However, as will be explained subsequently, such an application of the MFN principle has come under fierce attack.[80]

The other issue of significance is whether the investor is obliged to first exhaust local remedies and in case the BIT provides for both arbitration and local remedies as potential (but equal) alternatives whether there are any implications in the investor's choice. As to the first, Article 26 of the ICSID Convention is clear that local remedies need not be exhausted 'unless otherwise stated'.[81] BITs and IIAs may, of course, provide otherwise, in which case the investor will have to endure an expensive and time-consuming process, usually without success. In *BG v Argentina*, the tribunal rejected the argument that the otherwise customary rule which did not require exhaustion of local remedies applied to investment relations, particularly where these were specifically regulated by treaty and/or contract. Hence, the investor was under an obligation to exhaust the envisaged 18-month period stipulated in the BIT. However, the tribunal went on to note that such a provision in a BIT is not an absolute impediment to arbitration:

Where recourse to the domestic judiciary is unilaterally prevented or hindered by the host state [the absurd outcome would be to] allow the [host] state to unilaterally elude arbitration.[82]

Just like the imposition of ADR mechanisms, as noted in a previous paragraph, the investor may invoke the MFN clause, if any, in the pertinent BIT in order to dismiss the local remedies requirements imposed upon him.[83]

---

[80] See *Maffezini v Spain*, Decision on Jurisdiction (25 January 2000), paras 54–64, albeit, see below the criticisms against this aspect of the *Maffezini* decision in section 10.7.4 *Vivendi Universal SA v Argentina*, Decision on Jurisdiction (3 August 2006), paras 52–68.

[81] See *Generation Ukraine Inc v Ukraine*, Award (30 April 2004), para 13.4.

[82] *BG Group PLC v Argentina*, (UNCITRAL Rules) Award (24 December 2007), para 147.

[83] MFN claims are not meant as conferring forum shopping entitlements to investors and are not susceptible to cherry-picking, in the sense that investors cannot choose one benefit but deny another because it does not suit their needs. As the tribunal in *Hochtief*

Where the BIT, or IIA, provides the investor with a choice of dispute resolution, namely recourse to the courts of the host state or investment arbitration, this is known as a 'fork-in-the-road'. The basic rule inherent in this choice, as reflected in the pertinent part of the aforementioned Australia–Argentina BIT, is that in case the investor initiates court proceedings he or she is prevented from subsequent recourse to arbitration. This rule requires some qualification. It only applies where the investor (rather than the host state) initiates court proceedings and then only insofar as the claim is not merely procedural but relates to the subject matter of the parties' dispute. By way of illustration, an application for interim relief before the local courts does not prevent the investor from initiating subsequent arbitral proceedings.[84]

Where the dispute resolution clause provides for arbitration, one should next examine and assess the precise ambit of its scope. Just like the scope of some arbitral clauses in the context of commercial arbitration (especially institutional model clauses),[85] similar provisions in BITs may be all-encompassing, in which case the implication is that the tribunal possesses competence to decide not merely BIT-based violations but also violations arising from the parties' private (investment) contract,[86] which is not automatically covered under BITs or IIAs without express stipulation. This distinction is crucial and it is certainly counter-productive for BITs and IIAs to address this issue in a confusing manner. A clause that is often encountered in BITs stipulates that the host state consents to arbitrate 'disputes with respect to investments'. Although such wording seemingly provides broad terms of reference, it was construed by one tribunal as excluding contractual differences[87] while another reached a different conclusion altogether.[88] The vast majority of contemporary BITs and IIAs specifically exclude domestic taxation measures from the scope of arbitration[89] – unless

---

v Argentina, Decision on Jurisdiction (24 October 2011), para 98, pointed out: 'The MFN provision does not permit the selective picking of components from each set of conditions, so as to manufacture a synthetic set of conditions to which no state's nationals would be entitled'.

[84] See generally, *CMS v Argentina*, Decision on Jurisdiction (17 July 2003), paras 77–82.

[85] See chapter 3 section 3.6.

[86] For example, *Salini* Decision on Jurisdiction, above note 32, para 61.

[87] *SGS v Pakistan*, Decision on Jurisdiction (6 August 2003), para 161.

[88] *SGS v Philippines*, Decision on Jurisdiction (29 January 2004), paras 131–5.

[89] See UNCTAD, *Expropriation* (UNCTAD Series on Issues in International Investment Agreements II, (2011), Doc. UNCTAD/DIAE/IA/2011/7), 133; See *El Paso Energy International Company v Argentine Republic*, Award (31 October 2011), para 290.

they are clearly expropriatory in nature – and provide for a mandatory process of negotiation between state parties known as joint tax vetoes.[90]

10.6 Applicable law

We have already noted the three sources of consent to investment arbitration, namely, contract, treaties and domestic legislation. Each of these will specify, although perhaps not, the applicable governing law. Host states will naturally make every effort to put forward their domestic law, whereas investors will strive to be bound by a neutral law, such as *lex mercatoria* or general international law, or if the host's domestic law is unavoidable (presumably under pressure) they will endeavour to insert suitable stabilisation clauses. Stabilisation clauses effectively freeze the ability of the host state to undertake any legislative changes that produce legal effects on the terms of an agreement with an investor.[91] Where the three aforementioned sources prescribe a consistent governing law, the parties' legal teams will face no difficulties. However, where there are notable differences among these or the pertinent provisions are conflicting or imprecise, the tribunal will have to make a sound determination. Unlike transnational private law relationships which are subject to a conflict of laws regime, such a regime is very rarely applicable in the context of international commercial arbitration[92] and is unfounded in

---

[90] Tax vetoes, such as Art 2103(6) of NAFTA, permit the arbitration of alleged tax expropriations, subject to prior negotiations between the pertinent states. See generally, A. Lazem and I. Bantekas, The Treatment of Taxation as Expropriatory in Investor-State Arbitration (2015) 31 *Arbitration Int* 1–46.

[91] See T. E. Waelde and G Ndi, Stabilising International Investment Commitments: International Law versus Contract Interpretation (1996) 31 *Texas Int'l LJ* 215. Despite their obvious rationale, stabilisation clauses are clearly inconsistent with the doctrine of executive necessity developed in liberal democracies, according to which contracts or promises made by the government are unenforceable in the public interest if they fetter the future competence and powers of the executive. See *Watson's Bay and South Shore Ferry Co Ltd v Whitfield* [1919] 27 CLR 268, 277; *Redericktiebolaget Amphitrite v King* [1921] 2 KB 500, 503. Ironically, the same privilege has been denied to developing states, as was the case in *Copper Revere and Brass Inc v OPIC*, (1978) 17 ILM 1343, para 44. In fairness, the tribunal in *Micula and Others v Romania*, Award (11 December 2013), paras 527–9, held that in the context of fair and equitable treatment, absent a stabilisation clause, investors must expect legislation to change.

[92] See chapter 2 sections 2.2.1. and 2.2.2.

investment arbitration.[93] Where the confusion lies in the treaty, the tribunal will resort to regular treaty interpretation in accordance with the VCLT and customary international law. If the conflict is between a treaty and the parties' contract, the tribunal will distinguish between disputes/violations arising from the treaty (and accordingly apply the governing law prescribed in the treaty) from disputes/violations arising from the contract and accordingly apply the governing law prescribed there. In *Wena Hotels v Egypt*, the ICSID Annulment Committee rejected the contention that Egyptian law, which was designated as the governing law in the commercial lease agreements between the parties, applied to claims under the BIT.

The leases deal with questions that are by definition of a commercial nature. The [BIT] deals with questions that are essentially of a governmental nature, namely the standards of treatment accorded by the state to foreign investors. It is therefore apparent that Wena and [Egypt] agreed to a particular contract, the applicable law and the dispute settlement arrangements in respect of one kind of subject, that relating to commercial problems under the leases. It is also apparent that Wena as a national of a contracting state could invoke the [BIT] for the purpose of a different kind of dispute, that concerning the treatment of foreign investors by Egypt. This other mechanism has a different and separate dispute settlement arrangement and might include a different choice of law provision or make no choice at all.[94]

Most contemporary BITs recognise both the need for clarity and the pitfalls inherent in the possible application of the host state's law. Article 18(8) of the 2013 Japan–Myanmar BIT aptly provides that:

An arbitral tribunal [whether under the ICSID Convention, the UNCITRAL Rules or other] shall decide the issues in dispute in accordance with this Agreement and applicable rules of international law.

This wording is equally reflected in Article 1131 of NAFTA, as well as Article 26 of the ECT. The default position in the ICSID Convention is set out in Article 42(1) as follows:

The tribunal shall decide a dispute in accordance with such rules of law as may be agreed by the parties. In the absence of such agreement, the tribunal shall apply the

---

[93] Although, in fairness, Art 42 of the ICSID Convention sets out a self-contained, albeit imprecise, conflict of laws rule.

[94] *Wena Hotels Ltd v Egypt*, Decision on Annulment (5 February 2002), para 36.

law of the contracting state party to the dispute (including its rules on the conflict of laws) and such rules of international law as may be applicable.

Other than the situations described above, interpretative difficulties usually arise where there is an overlap between domestic and international law, in situations where both are applicable without a clear hierarchy. Scholars usually suggest that in such situations the tribunal is competent to dispel the conflict on the basis of its competence-competence and in the majority of cases general international law is preferred.[95] In practice, tribunals have noted the synergy between domestic and international law[96] (where both are designated in the BIT) and have accordingly emphasised the applicability of the host state's domestic law to relationships which arise from that law, provided they are not in conflict with international law, while at the same time applying international law to relationships which are prescribed under this legal regime, such as the interpretation of fair and equitable treatment or attribution for the purposes of state responsibility.[97]

10.7 Standards of treatment and guarantees afforded to investors under international law

Substantive investment guarantees under BITs, IIAs and customary international law fall within the realm of substantive international investment law. It is a subject far too detailed to be dealt with adequately in a chapter dealing with procedure.[98] Even so, a very brief account of the principal investment guarantees will be provided so that the reader can link the discussion on investment arbitration to the types of breaches usually committed by host states. Besides the fundamental guarantees discussed in the following subsections there are potentially many others, such as

---

[95] H. E. Kjos, *Applicable Law in Investor-State Arbitration: The Interplay between National and International Law* (Oxford University Press, 2013), 213ff; see, for example, *Compânia del Desarrollo de Santa Elena SA v Costa Rica*, Award (17 February 2000), para 64; *Enron Corp and Ponderosa Assets LP v Argentina*, Decision on Jurisdiction (14 January 2004), paras 206–9.

[96] *CMS v Argentina*, Decision on Jurisdiction (17 July 2003), paras 115–16.

[97] *MTD Equity Sdn Bhd & MTD Chile v Chile*, Decision on Annulment (21 March 2007), para 72.

[98] See generally Dolzer and Schreuer, above note 1; M. Sornarajah, *The International Law on Foreign Investment* (Cambridge University Press, 3rd edition, 2010) and S. P. Subedi, *International Investment Law: Reconciling Policy and Principle* (Hart, 2012).

free transfer of capital and profits, freedom from performance requirements and others.

10.7.1 Fair and equitable treatment and the international minimum standard

This principle has long been recognised under international law but was
not defined in early BITs and IIAs. Contemporary BITs offer a greater
degree of elaboration, principally as a result of the growing case law.
Article 5(2) of the 2012 US Model BIT stipulates that fair and equitable
treatment encompasses:

the customary international law minimum standard of treatment of aliens as the
minimum standard of treatment to be afforded to covered investments. The concepts of 'fair and equitable treatment' and 'full protection and security' do not
require treatment in addition to or beyond that which is required by that standard,
and do not create additional substantive rights. The obligation . . . to provide:

a) 'fair and equitable treatment' includes the obligation not to deny justice in criminal, civil, or administrative adjudicatory proceedings in accordance with the
principle of due process embodied in the principal legal systems of the world; and
b) 'full protection and security' requires each party to provide the level of police
protection required under customary international law.

Article 5(2) gives weight to the requirement of a stable and predictable
investment environment.[99] Save for the existence of a stabilisation clause,
a state is prohibited from acting 'unfairly, unreasonably or inequitably in
the exercise of its legislative power'.[100] One of the key ingredients inherent
in this principle is the protection of the investor's legitimate expectations.[101] Good faith suggests that an investor would not invest in a country
had he or she known that the foundations (both legal and substantive)
relied upon for choosing that state as its preferred place of investment
would subsequently be removed, whether directly or indirectly.[102]

---

[99] *LG & E International Inc v Argentina*, Decision on Liability (3 October 2006), para 12.
[100] *Parkerings-Compagniet v Lithuania*, Award (11 September 2007), para 332.
[101] *Saluka Investments BG v Czech Republic*, (UNCITRAL Rules) Partial Award (17 March
2006), para 302; *Técnicas Medioambientales TECMED SA v Mexico*, Award (29 May
2003), para 154.
[102] In fact, stabilisation clauses aside, a shift in the tax regime applicable to investments
can result in a violation of fair and equitable treatment (FET) if the investments were
made on the basis of receiving tax incentives (and others) under a legislative regime for

In the context of NAFTA, there has been some debate as to whether the so-called 'minimum standard of treatment' is synonymous with fair and equitable treatment (as explained above) as this is set out in Article 1105(1) of NAFTA. In *Waste Management v Mexico*, the tribunal held that:

> the minimum standard of treatment of fair and equitable treatment is infringed by conduct attributable to the state and harmful to the claimant if the conduct is arbitrary, grossly unfair, unjust or idiosyncratic, is discriminatory or exposes the claimant to sectional or racial prejudice, or involves a lack of due process leading to an outcome which offends judicial propriety.[103]

In *Apotex III*, the claimant, a Canadian pharmaceutical company operating in the US, was prevented from further distributing its products through an import alert without prior notice. The claimant argued a breach of Article 1105(1) because it was given no time to prepare a defence or an opportunity to present its position before an impartial administrative authority. The tribunal rejected the claim and concluded that administrative remedies were in fact available to the claimant and that no 'exceptional circumstances' justified the decision by the claimants not to pursue those remedies.[104] After an exhaustive survey of state practices, the tribunal expressed the view that there was no discernible customary law regarding the procedures states should take for the inspection and approval of drug manufacturing facilities, or processes they need to follow in excluding from their markets drugs from facilities that do not meet those standards.

10.7.2 Full protection and security

Customary international law has long required that host states protect the life, integrity and property of aliens on their territory, even in situations of turmoil where the integrity of their own nationals is jeopardised. This rule has long been maintained and in fact several mixed commissions have been set up in the nineteenth and early twentieth century to deal with situations of uprising in which foreign investors and foreign nationals

---

a specific period of time. See *Micula and Others v Romania*, Award (11 December 2013), paras 677–86.

[103] *Waste Management Inc v Mexico*, Award (30 April 2004), para 98.

[104] *Apotex Holdings Inc and Apotex Inc v USA* [*Apotex III*], Award (25 August 2014), para 9.58.

were forced to abandon their investments and properties.[105] In the
majority of such cases the host state will attempt to circumvent its liability
by arguing that it had no control of the 'crowds' or, if it was in opposition at
the crucial time, that it had no control over the organs of government.
Article 10(1) of the ILC Articles on State Responsibility dismisses such
arguments, providing that: '[t]he conduct of an insurrectional movement
which becomes the new government of a state shall be considered an act of
that state under international law'. In all other cases, the state will be
absolved from its liability under international law unless it acknowledged
the illegal conduct as its own,[106] or if it can be proved that the perpetrators
were effectively *de facto* agents of the state. A state discharges its positive
obligation to an investor under this principle by means of due diligence
and to a very large degree this obligation is breached where it fails to
prevent the physical destruction of property, whether because it failed to
take ordinary police measures or because it did not have an appropriate
policy in place.[107]

10.7.3 National treatment

A common guarantee often offered to foreign investors is that they will
be treated no less favourably than the nationals and companies of the host
state. Unlike fair and equitable treatment, which is quantifiable from the
outset (at least in terms of its fundamental principles), the national treatment standard is clearly relative and can only be assessed by reference to
the treatment offered to the host state's nationals in one of several fields,
such as preferential corporate taxation. It is understood as encompassing
matters concerning regulation, such as the application of anti-trust laws, in
addition to treatment afforded by means of contract.[108] Given the relative
nature of this treatment, it is to be afforded to an investor in 'like circumstances'. In some instances this has been construed as referring to the

---

[105] A prominent example is the US–Mexico General Claims Commission (1924–37), which
was based on a bilateral treaty, the 1923 General Claims Convention. See *Youmans v
Mexico*, (1925–26) AD 223, which allowed a claim arising from the failure of Mexican
authorities to prevent or punish a mob from attacking and killing US nationals in Mexico.

[106] Art 11, ILC State Responsibility Articles; *United States Diplomatic and Consular Staff in
Tehran (USA v Iran)*, [1980] ICJ Rep 3, paras 69–79.

[107] *Rumeli Telekom AS and Teslim Mobil Telekommunikasyon Hizmetleri AS v Kazakhstan*,
Award (29 July 2008).

[108] Dolzer and Schreuer, above note 1, at 199.

same business activity,[109] whereas elsewhere the comparison took into consideration businesses operating under similar financial and other circumstances.[110] The first of these seems to conform more closely to the jurisprudence of investment tribunals. Article 3(1) of the 2012 US Model BIT provides that:

Each party shall accord to investors of the other party treatment no less favorable than that it accords, in like circumstances, to its own investors with respect to the establishment, acquisition, expansion, management, conduct, operation, and sale or other disposition of investments in its territory.

The term 'no less favourable' has generally been construed as referring to equivalence, rather than a qualitative comparison (better or worse) to the treatment accorded to the comparator.[111] Dolzer and Schreuer suggest that tribunals have generally taken care not to interpret 'the basis of comparison for the applicability of the national treatment standard too narrowly'.[112]

10.7.4 Most favoured nation (MFN) treatment

MFN is yet another relative standard that traces its roots in the customary law of diplomatic protection.[113] The essential characteristic of MFN treatment, contrary to what its name suggests, is that if an MFN clause exists in a treaty covering the investor he is entitled to be treated no less favourably than companies and nationals of any other state.[114] In *MTD v Chile*, for example, a Malaysian investor relied on an MFN clause in the Malaysia–Chile BIT in order to ensure application of the Croatian and Danish BITs with Chile, which, among others, obliged the host state to grant necessary permits.[115] Most of the contemporary BITs specify the areas in which MFN

---

[109] *Feldman v Mexico*, Award (16 December 2002), para 171.
[110] *Occidental v Ecuador*, Award (1 July 2004), para 173.
[111] *Pope and Talbot Inc v Canada*, Award on the Merits of Phase II (10 March 2001), para 111.
[112] Dolzer and Schreuer, above note 1, at 200.
[113] See specifically for its application in the *Anglo-Iranian Oil case* (*UK v Iran*), Decision on Jurisdiction [1952] ICJ Rep 93, where the MFN principle was clearly excluded in respect of dispute settlement; equally, *Case Concerning Rights of Nationals of the USA in Morocco* (*France v USA*) [1952] ICJ Rep 176.
[114] Art 4, US Model BIT (2012).
[115] *MTD Equity Sdn Bhd & MTD Chile v Chile*, Award (25 May 2004), paras 100ff.

applies, but even so it is still not entirely clear whether in the absence of an elaboration its application extends to both procedural and substantive rights and whether the investor may cherry-pick some rights or forms of treatment at the exclusion of others.

In *Maffezini v Spain*, the Argentine–Spain BIT included a dispute resolution clause which required submission to local courts first and if no decision was rendered within eighteen months the parties could submit to investment arbitration. In order to bypass this burdensome requirement, the claimant relied on the Chile–Spain BIT which merely contained a six-month cooling off period and no recourse to local courts. The tribunal, relying on *Ambatielos*,[116] held that the protection of the rights of investors by means of dispute resolution clauses fell within the ambit of MFN treatment and hence the investors at hand could rely on more favourable dispute settlement provisions in a treaty between third parties.[117]

The reasoning in *Maffezini* has been effectively overturned in *Plama v Bulgaria*.[118] There, the dispute settlement clause in the Cyprus–Bulgaria BIT was restricted to determining the amount of compensation in the event of expropriation. The claimant sought to rely on ICSID arbitration by virtue of the more generous dispute settlement provisions in other BITs to which Bulgaria was a party, particularly the one with Finland. According to the *Maffezini* decision such a claim would have succeeded. The tribunal in *Plama*, however, rejected this argument. It held that the treaty provisions relied upon by the parties to initiate international arbitration must be clear and unambiguous, even if they involve some form of incorporation by reference, which is the case with MFN clauses. As a result, there is an assumption that unless the MFN clause also extends to jurisdictional matters (i.e. the dispute resolution clause), it covers only substantive rights.[119] Any other outcome, emphasised the tribunal, would produce a 'chaotic situation'.[120]

---

[116] *Ambatielos* case (*Greece v UK*), Judgment [1953] ICJ Rep 10.

[117] *Maffezini v Spain*, Decision on Jurisdiction (25 January 2000), paras 43–50 and 59ff.

[118] *Plama Consortium Ltd v Bulgaria*, Decision on Jurisdiction (8 February 2005).

[119] This was despite the fact that the pertinent MFN clause expressly applied in 'respect of all matters'.

[120] *Plama v Bulgaria*, above note 118, para 219; this position was also adopted in *Inspection and Control Services Ltd v Argentina*, (UNCITRAL Rules) Decision on Jurisdiction (10 February 2012).

10.7.5 Protection against expropriation

Expropriation entails the taking of property, assets and control of an investment by the host state. Whereas international law recognises the right of states to expropriate foreign assets on their territory under particular circumstances, it circumscribes the legality of the taking and provides that in any event the host state is always liable to prompt, adequate and effective compensation. This rule is clearly established in all BITs and IIAs, which, however, generally require host states to refrain from adopting measures tantamount to expropriation, whether direct or indirect, including measures equivalent to expropriation, save if such measures are necessary, as provided in Article 6(1) of the 2012 US Model BIT:

a) for a public purpose;
b) in a non-discriminatory manner;
c) on payment of prompt, adequate and effective compensation; and
d) in accordance with due process of law and [the application of the minimum standard of treatment rule].

The majority of investment treaties do not define the scope and content of 'measures' that may give rise to an expropriation but the few that do encompass a broad understanding through the use of expressions such as 'any law, regulation, procedure, requirement, or practice'[121] of the host state. This broadness encompasses 'driven actions' of the state[122] that result in expropriation as well as 'inactions' (i.e. the refusal of the state to take action) with the inaction also capable of causing an expropriation.[123]

The taking need not only be direct, which is the most obvious manifestation of expropriation. It may also come about indirectly (otherwise known as 'creeping'), or through 'equivalent measures' in circumstances where only particular rights or benefits of the investment are expropriated while keeping intact the control, use and enjoyment of the investment as a whole. In such situations the investment ultimately incurs losses rather than profits and the investor is forced to abandon it.[124] Under international

---

[121] 1998 Canada–Costa Rica BIT.
[122] *Olguin v Republic of Paraguay*, Award (26 July 2001), para 84.
[123] *CME Czech Republic BV (The Netherlands) v Czech Republic*, (UNCITRAL Rules), Partial Award (13 September 2001), para 607.
[124] Dolzer and Schreuer, above note 1, at 119; see also *Middle East Cement Shipping and Handling Co SA v Egypt*, Award (12 April 2002), in which the tribunal accepted that a licence granted to the investor for the bulk importation and storage of cement was an

law an indirect taking amounts to expropriation only if it amounts to a *substantial deprivation* of the investment as a whole. The applicable threshold is therefore rather high. In order to assess the existence of indirect expropriation (including creeping and equivalent measures) one needs to ascertain and distinguish between: a) the content of a measure versus its impact; b) the intent belying the measure versus its effect; c) the extent of deprivation, namely, whether this is substantial or otherwise; and d) the existence of legitimate and reasonable investment-backed expectations of the investor.

It should have become clear from the outset that a mere breach of contract by the host state does not amount to expropriation.[125] Of course, if a state acting in its sovereign capacity nullifies the legal effect of a right conferred to the investor by contract, such as the abrogation of a concession by a subsequent decree, the breach will give rise to a valid claim for expropriation.[126] A concession, whether conferred by contract or by decree on a particular investor constitutes an undertaking and an assurance on the part of the state, which in turn creates legitimate expectations.

The most difficult issue in expropriation claims is ascertaining whether the fine line between a state's sovereign authority to regulate in a particular case is such as to go far beyond the satisfaction of a concrete public aim. In certain fields, such as tax, there is in practice an assumption in favour of states.[127] In the *Methanex* case, the tribunal held that the banning of a harmful gasoline additive was legitimate because it was not discriminatory and was undertaken within the scope of the host state's *bona fide* police powers.[128] The tribunal in *Saluka* fleshed out the competing tensions as follows:

It is now established in international law that states are not liable to pay compensation to a foreign investor when, in the normal exercise of their regulatory powers, they adopt in a non-discriminatory manner *bona fide* regulations that are aimed

---

investment (para 101) under the Egypt–Greece BIT and that the revocation of the licence amounted to an expropriation of the licence as an investment (para 107).

[125] *Waste Management Inc v Mexico*, Award (30 April 2004), para 175.

[126] *Compãnia de Aguas del Aconquija SA and Vivendi Universal SA v Argentina*, Award (21 November 2000), para 7.5.22.

[127] The tribunal in *El Paso Energy International Company v Argentine Republic*, Award (31 October 2011), at para 297, considered the export withholding taxes imposed on the investor to be 'reasonable governmental regulation within the context of the [Argentinian] crisis'.

[128] *Methanex Corp v USA*, (UNCITRAL Rules), Award (3 August 2005), para 7 of part IV.

at the general welfare. [Given the absence of an appropriate international definition] it thus inevitably falls to the adjudicator to determine whether particular conduct by a state crosses the line that separates valid regulatory activity from expropriation.[129]

The fact that host states possess authority to undertake regulatory actions in the pursuit of general welfare (i.e. for a public purpose) does not mean that they can directly or indirectly substantially deprive the enjoyment of the investment. Rather, if a pressing public purpose does in fact exist, a taking will be considered legitimate, but the investor will have to be compensated. This situation reflects the fragmentation between international investment law and general international law (despite their otherwise convergence), particularly in public interest spheres, such as human rights and environmental protection.[130] This dichotomy between intent versus effect was eloquently iterated in the *Santa Elena* case as follows:

While an expropriation or taking for environmental reasons may be classified as a taking for a public purpose, and thus may be legitimate, the fact that the property was taken for this reason does not affect either the nature or the measure of the compensation to be paid for the taking. That is, the purpose of protecting the environment for which the property was taken does not alter the legal character of the taking for which adequate compensation must be paid. The international source of the obligation to protect the environment makes no difference.[131]

The *Metalclad* definition of expropriation is by now paradigmatic and sums up perfectly why the effect is viewed by tribunals as always trumping the state's intent. As a result, expropriation 'includes not only *open*, *deliberate* and *acknowledged* takings of property, such as outright seizure or formal or obligatory transfer of title in favor of the host state, but also covert or incidental interference with the use of property which has the *effect* of depriving the owner, in whole or in significant part, of the use or

---

[129] *Saluka Investments BV v Czech Republic*, Partial Award (17 March 2006), paras 262, 264.

[130] In *Achmea BV v Slovak Republic*, PCA (UNCITRAL Rules) Award on Jurisdiction (20 May 2014), para 251, the tribunal held that it is not empowered to interfere in the democratic processes of a state, as is the case with its design of a public healthcare policy. It went on to emphasise that the design and implementation of such a policy 'is for the state alone to assess and the state must balance the different and sometimes competing interests, such as its duty to ensure appropriate healthcare to its population and its duty to honor its international investment protection commitments'.

[131] *Compañia del Desarrollo de Santa Elena SA v Costa Rica*, Award (17 February 2000), para 71.

reasonably-to-be-expected economic benefit of property even if *not necessarily to the obvious benefit* of the host state'.[132]

10.8 Some procedural aspects of investor-state arbitration

10.8.1 No *lex arbitri* in investment proceedings

Space constraints prevent us from offering a lengthy exposition of procedural issues, so we shall confine ourselves only to those areas that differ markedly from international commercial arbitration. The parties may, depending on the source of their consent, opt for administered arbitration, such as ICSID or PCA, or alternatively have recourse to ad hoc arbitration, most commonly through the use of the UNCITRAL Arbitration Rules. Additionally, they may choose common institutional arbitration, particularly ICC, LCIA and SCC, in which case they may apply that institution's procedural rules or other (e.g. those of UNCITRAL). Unlike commercial arbitration, where there are relatively few major differences among institutions (and their rules), in the context of investment arbitration its differences with commercial arbitration are significant.

Arbitration under ICSID, as well as under other internationalised investment tribunals such as the Iran–US claims tribunal, entails that the process is de-nationalised and, unlike commercial arbitration, is devoid of a national *lex arbitri* (effectively delocalised).[133] This means that the seat of the tribunal does not and cannot impose any mandatory civil procedure rules on the arbitral process. As a result, the tribunal itself has competence through the applicable treaty to request interim or other similar measures, which the parties to the treaty are obliged to adhere to.[134] Equally, in the absence of a traditional *lex arbitri*, the treaty will set

---

[132] *Metalclad Corporation v Mexico*, Award (30 August 2000), para 103 (emphasis added).

[133] For a recollection of the nature and function of *lex arbitri* in international commercial arbitration, see chapter 2 section 2.2.3.

[134] Although such a conclusion is not *prima facie* supported by Art 47 ICSID Convention, which renders interim measures akin to recommendations ('may recommend'), several tribunals have held that these are binding on their addressees. See *Maffezini v Spain*, Procedural Order No 2 (28 October 1999), para 9; *Occidental v Ecuador*, Decision on Provisional Measures (17 August 2007), para 58; see Rule 39 ICSID Arbitration Rules.

out all other matters pertinent to the arbitral procedure, such as challenges against arbitrators,[135] the production and presentation of evidence[136] and others. Finally, and this is perhaps a major advantage of administered arbitration by an institution such as ICSID, once the award becomes final there is no need to make use of the 1958 New York Convention in order to recognise and enforce it in third nations.[137] Parties to the ICSID Convention, as well as parties to other internationalised (investment or claims) tribunals, are obliged to recognise and enforce all awards issued under these tribunals' founding treaty.[138] Conversely, investment arbitrations administered by the ICC or LCIA (known also as territorialised investment tribunals) are subjected to the mandatory law of their seat (*lex arbitri*) and awards issued therefrom may only be recognised and enforced abroad through the 1958 New York Convention or equivalent regional treaties.[139] The same considerations are relevant in respect of ad hoc investment arbitrations under UNCITRAL or other arbitration rules, unless a bilateral treaty exceptionally provides otherwise.

10.8.2 Procedural rules in investment proceedings

The parties to ICSID arbitration will typically rely on the ICSID Convention, as well as ICSID's Arbitration Rules. Article 44 of the ICSID Convention allows parties, if they so agree, to choose other procedural rules. The internationalised nature of investment tribunals, such as ICSID, means that they are not bound by the judgment or decision of a national court pertinent to the arbitral proceedings under consideration and under the same cause of action. As a result, ICSID tribunals possess competence-competence jurisdiction to decide all matters falling within the sphere of the case at their disposal, constrained no doubt by the ICSID Convention and the terms of the parties' agreements (BIT, contract and, or, national legislation).

---

[135] Arts 56–58 ICSID Convention; Rule 9 ICSID Arbitration Rules.
[136] Arts 43–46 ICSID Convention.   [137] Arts 53 and 54 ICSID Convention.
[138] See, e.g., *Dallal v Bank Mellat* [1986] QB 441, where it was held that an award issued by the US–Iran Claims Tribunal was not enforceable in the UK under the 1958 New York Convention.
[139] See footnote 42 of this chapter for an assessment of enforcement of awards issued under the ICSID Additional Facility Rules.

10.8.3 Public interest and transparency in investment proceedings

A significant departure from the traditional confidential nature of commercial arbitration was introduced in ICSID arbitration through the 2006 revision of the ICSID Arbitration Rules. Article 37(2) of the Rules enhanced the public interest dimension of investment arbitration by permitting the presence of third parties as *amici* to the tribunal.[140] Article 37(2) stipulates that:

After consulting both parties, the Tribunal may allow a person or entity that is not a party to the dispute (in this Rule called the 'non-disputing party') to file a written submission with the Tribunal regarding a matter within the scope of the dispute. In determining whether to allow such a filing, the Tribunal shall consider, among other things, the extent to which:

a) the non-disputing party submission would assist the Tribunal in the determination of a factual or legal issue related to the proceeding by bringing a perspective, particular knowledge or insight that is different from that of the disputing parties;

b) the non-disputing party submission would address a matter within the scope of the dispute;

c) the non-disputing party has a significant interest in the proceeding.

This is potentially a significant tool for public interest groups to influence arbitral proceedings, albeit under the fragmented nature of investment arbitration, as discussed above, their impact is unlikely.[141] However, it is the erosion of the private nature of proceedings by express stipulation in many contemporary BITs, through arbitral transparency clauses, that constitutes a radical departure.[142]

Despite the similarities between commercial and investment arbitral procedure and the absence of an intervening *lex arbitri*, it may surprise

---

[140] Unlike the string of cases such as *Piero Foresti, Laura de Carli and others v South Africa*, Letter regarding non-disputing parties (5 October 2009) where NGOs were allowed to present an independent view and illuminate the tribunal, a similar request was turned down for alleged want of independence of the requesting NGO in *Bernard von Pezold and Ors v Zimbabwe and Border Timbers Ltd v Zimbabwe*, Procedural Order No 2 (26 June 2012).

[141] This procedure has also been applied in non-ICSID proceedings. See *United Parcel Services v Canada*, (UNCITRAL Rules), Decision on Petitions for Intervention and Participation as *Amici Curiae* (17 October 2001).

[142] See Art 29 US Model BIT (2012). See generally, A. Kulick, *Global Public Interest in International Investment Law* (Cambridge University Press, 2012).

the reader to learn that investment proceedings are in practice far more cumbersome and final awards take, in most cases, several years to be issued. In addition, the costs are staggering and although they are afford-able to large multinational corporations, they are prohibitive to developing countries, which ultimately have to reduce their development budgets (e.g. in education or healthcare) in order to meet such costs.[143]

10.8.4 Remedies against awards

Given the denationalised character of administered internationalised investment arbitration, there is naturally no appeal to local courts (on points of law), nor set aside proceedings, as is otherwise the case with commercial arbitration. The ICSID Convention provides for two chal-lenges against awards, in addition to the remedy of interpretation as to the meaning and scope of an award.[144] These two challenges concern: (a) the *revision* of awards on the ground 'of discovery of some fact of such a nature as decisively to affect the award, provided that when the award was rendered that fact was unknown to the tribunal [and the parties without negligence on their part]';[145] (b) annulment of an award, the grounds for which are similar in some respects to set aside proceedings in commercial arbitration. Article 52(1) of the ICSID Convention invites annulment requests on any of the following grounds:

a) that the tribunal was not properly constituted;
b) that the tribunal has manifestly exceeded its powers;
c) that there was corruption on the part of a member of the tribunal;
d) that there has been a serious departure from a fundamental rule of procedure; or
e) that the award has failed to state the reasons on which it is based.

---

[143] See N. Horn (ed.), *Arbitrating Foreign Investment Disputes* (Kluwer, 2004), at 106. It is no wonder that third party funding has become exceedingly popular (also) in investment arbitration, although the sole end-users are investors, rather than states. See I. Bantekas and L. Oette, *International Human Rights Law and Practice* (Cambridge University Press, 2013), chapters 12 and 17 for a critique as to why the current regimes of foreign investment and international trade contribute to under-development and poverty; see footnote 91 of this chapter for a brief reference to the doctrine of executive necessity.

[144] Art 50 ICSID Convention.   [145] Art 51 ICSID Convention.

Index